straplez.com

COLLECTED AND EDITED BY ROSE EDEN

EDITION Skylight

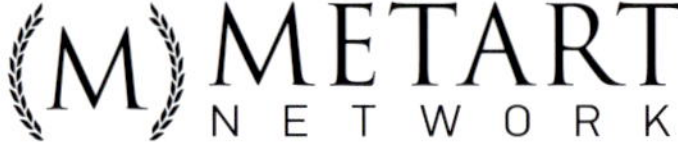

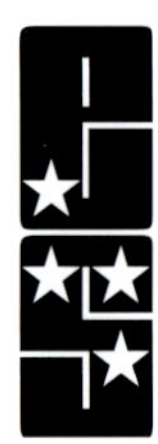

First edition 2024
Copyright © 2024 by Edition Skylight

EDITION SKYLIGHT
Rosengartenstr. 13B
CH-8608 Bubikon/Zürich
Switzerland
info@edition-skylight.com
www.edition-skylight.com

ISBN 978-3-03766-702-6

Bibliographic information published by Die Deutsche Bibliothek
Die Deutsche Bibliothek lists this publication in the
Deutsche Nationalbibliografie; detailed bibliographic data
are available in the Internet at http://dnb.ddb.de.

Printed in the Czech Republic

straplez.com is pure and genuine girl-on-girl pleasure and a real experience to enjoy!

This photo book about www.straplez.com presents the hottest collection of lesbian beauties enjoying sizzling strap-on sex! See these gorgeous girls rock each other's world with passionate pussy licking and intense dildo riding, all captured in stunning pictures. Lovers of glamorous models in pantyhose/nylons and high heels will go wild for the explicit action as these uninhibited sapphic sweethearts use their fingers, tongues and strap-on dildos to give each other real orgasms.

Launched over a decade ago, Straplez is synonymous with high-quality lesbian erotica. It's now a part of the multi-award-winning MetArt Network, elevating it to new heights of technical excellence and creative vision. Enjoy the action of georgeous Euro models like **Bonnie Dolce, Stacy Cruz, Oxana Chic, Lil Karla, Mia, Jenny Wild, Tiffany Tatum, Barbie Brill, Marina Gold, Candee Licious** and many more ...

About the author

Of course, with a name like *Rose Eden* any connoisseur thinks it must be a pseudonym. And they would be right, because it is. There is an actual *Rose Eden*, of course, but she's not known under that name. So, her fictional biography we present as follows: born yes, location unknown, age unknown. What is her task? *Rose Eden* lives and works in Europe and Los Angeles and she loves to explore erotic photography, especially around everything concerning the Metart universe. So, if you want to have more detailed information on this secret star, I'm afraid we're sworn to secrecy! Just enjoy these hot selections of our «under cover» top editor!

straplez.com ist reiner, heisser Girl-on-Girl-Genuss und ein echtes Erlebnis!

Dieses Fotobuch über www.straplez.com präsentiert einige der besten Bilderfolgen lesbischer Schönheiten, die intensiven Strap-on-Sex genießen! Sehen Sie, wie diese wunderschönen Mädchen sich gegenseitig mit leidenschaftlichem Lecken und Dildo-Reiten in feucht-fröhliche Orgasmen treiben. Liebhaber glamouröser Modelle in Strumpfhosen/Nylons und High Heels werden von der expliziten Action begeistert sein, während diese sapphischen Schönheiten ihre Finger, Zungen und Strap-on-Dildos benutzen, um miteinander ihre Lust bis zur Erschöpfung auszukosten.

Vor über einem Jahrzehnt ins Leben gerufen, ist Straplez ein Synonym für hochwertige lesbische Erotik. Straplez.com ist jetzt Teil des mehrfach preisgekrönten MetArt-Netzwerks und liefert niveauvolle, exzellente Qualität und kreative Visionen. Genießen Sie die hemmungslosen erotischen Spiele von Lieblingsmodellen wie **Bonnie Dolce, Stacy Cruz, Oxana Chic, Lil Karla, Mia, Jenny Wild, Tiffany Tatum, Barbie Brill, Marina Gold, Candee Licious** und vielen mehr ... Straplez.com ist reiner, heisser Girl-on-Girl-Genuss und ein echtes Erlebnis.

Über die Autorin

Na klar, denkt der Connaisseur, ein Name wie *Rose Eden*, der kann doch nicht wirklich stimmen? Und da liegen Sie richtig, denn es handelt sich um ein Pseudonym, die *Rose Eden* gibt es in der Realität schon, aber eben nicht unter diesem Namen. Also, die fiktive Biographie präsentieren wir wie folgt: Geboren ja, Ort unbekannt, Alter unbekannt, immer auf der Suche nach aussergewöhnlicher erotischer Fotografie, speziell Metart betreffend. *Rose Eden* ist eine Agentin «under cover» und lebt und arbeitet in Europa und Los Angeles.

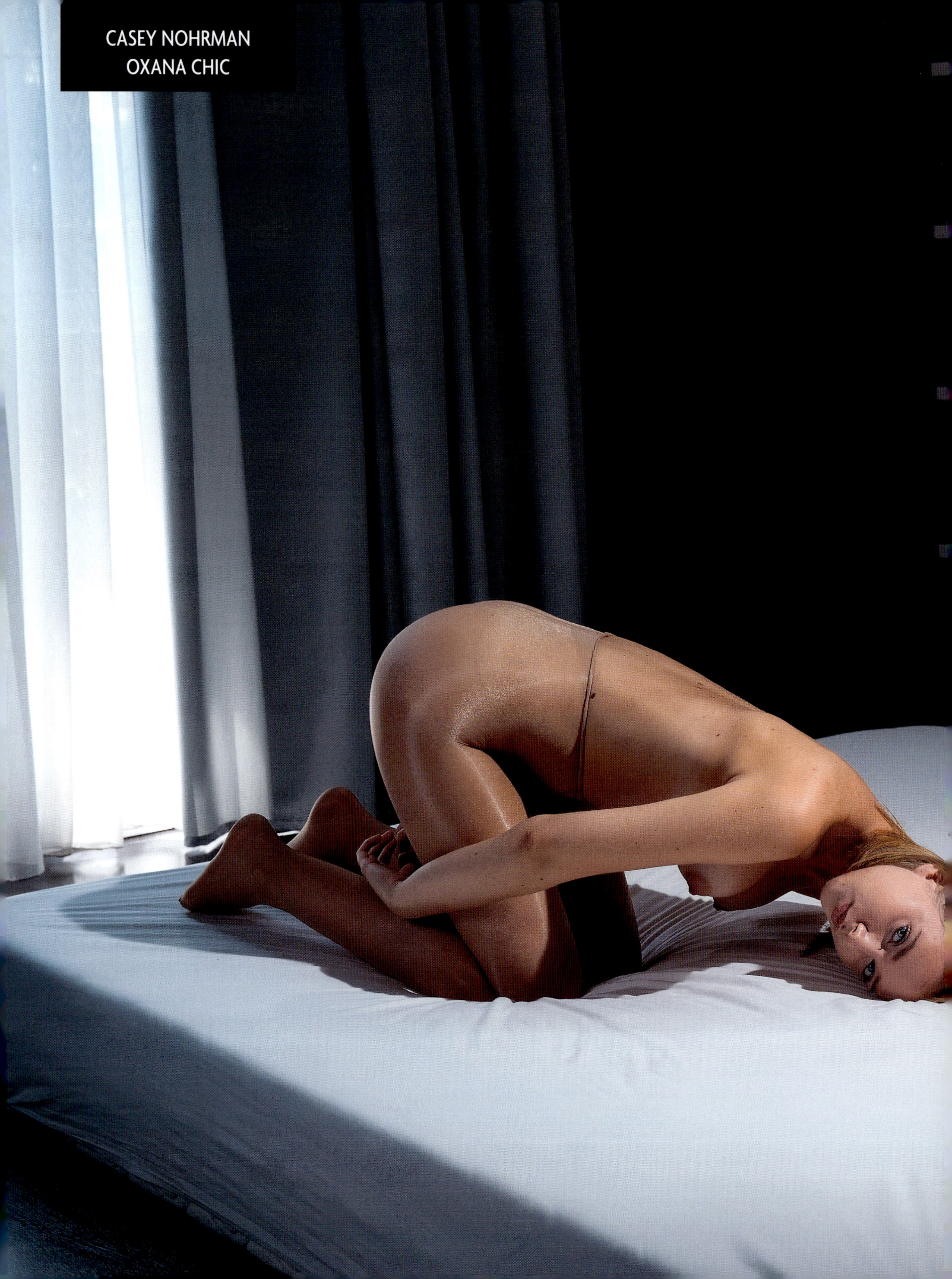
CASEY NOHRMAN
OXANA CHIC

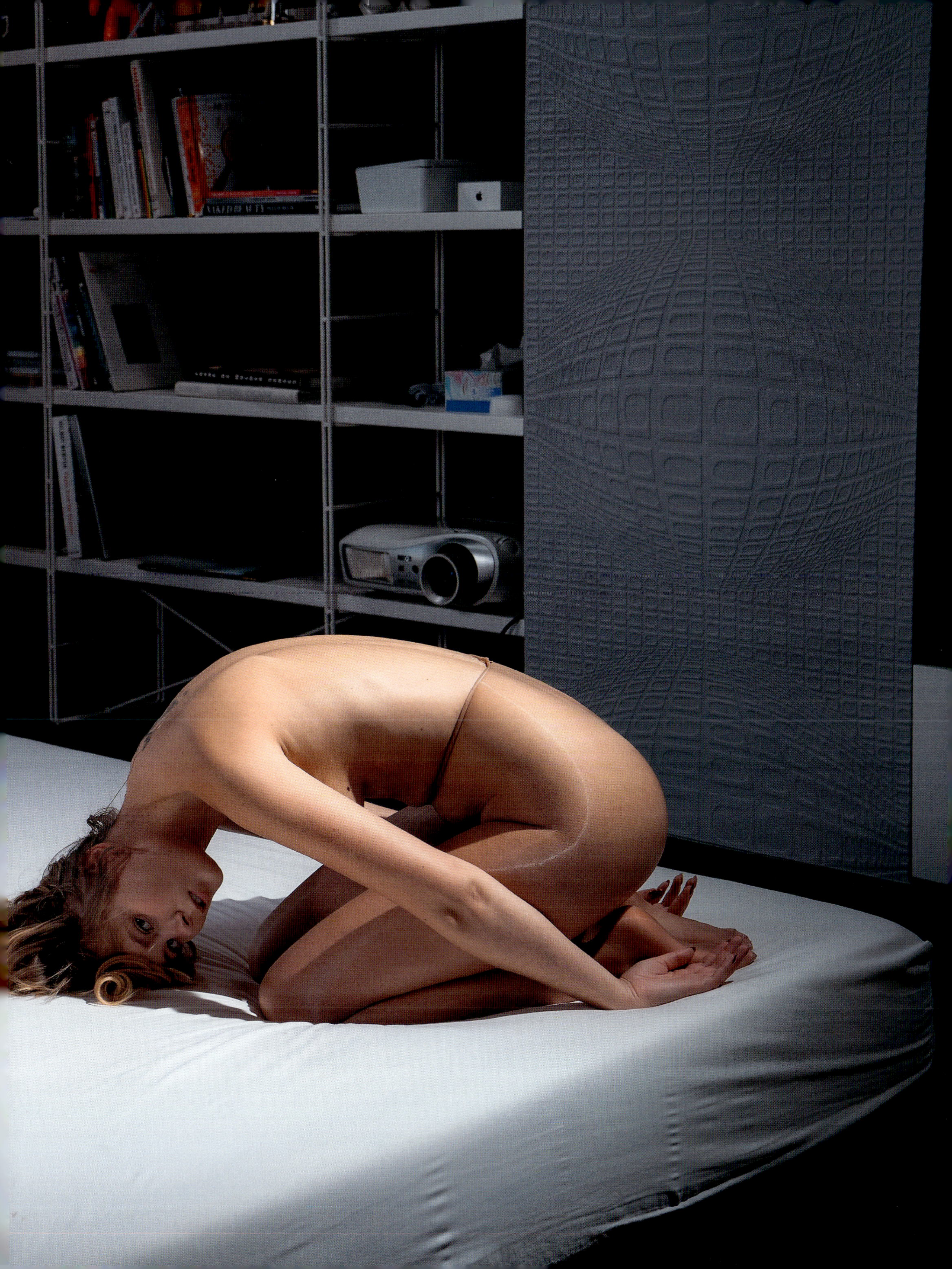

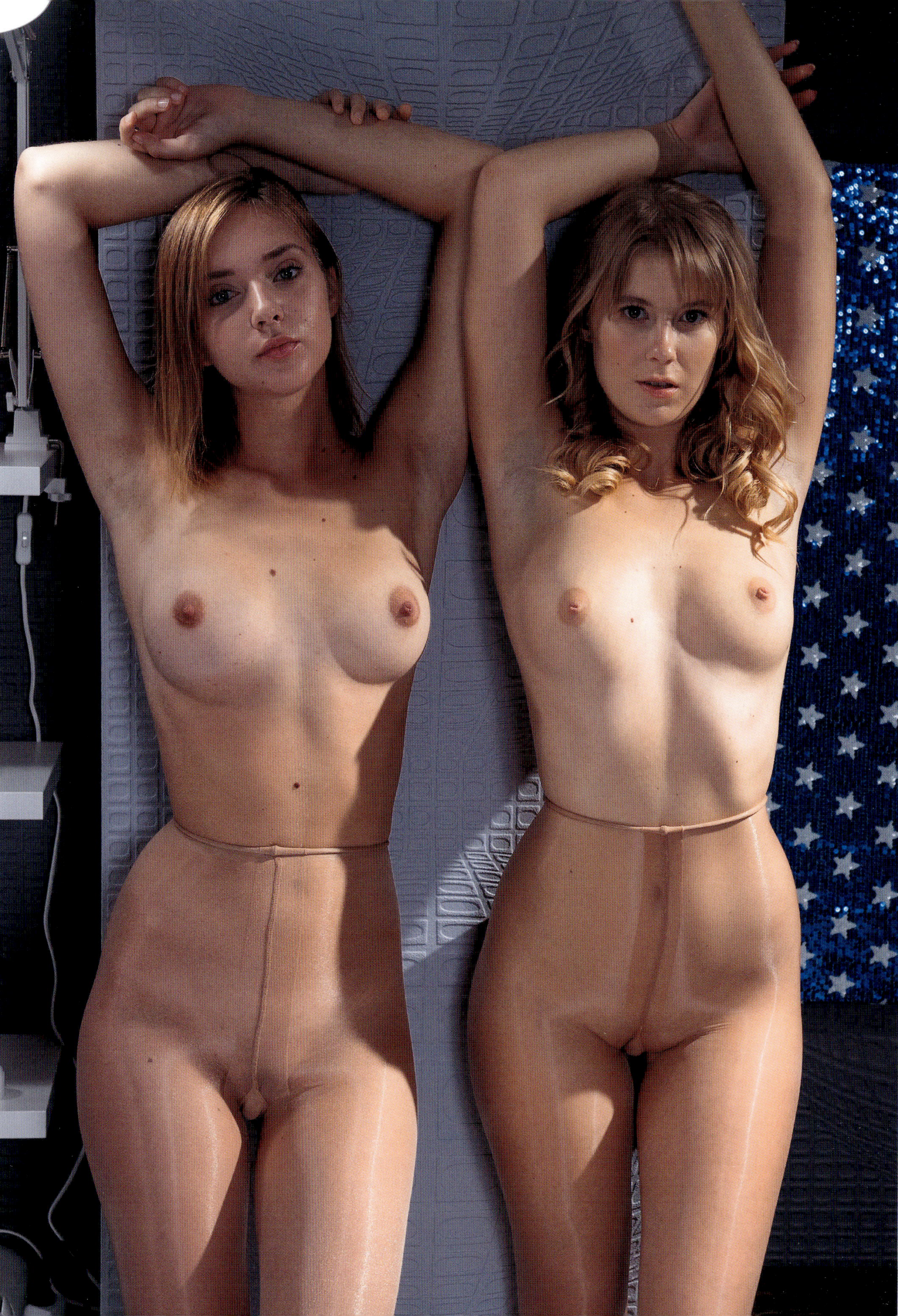

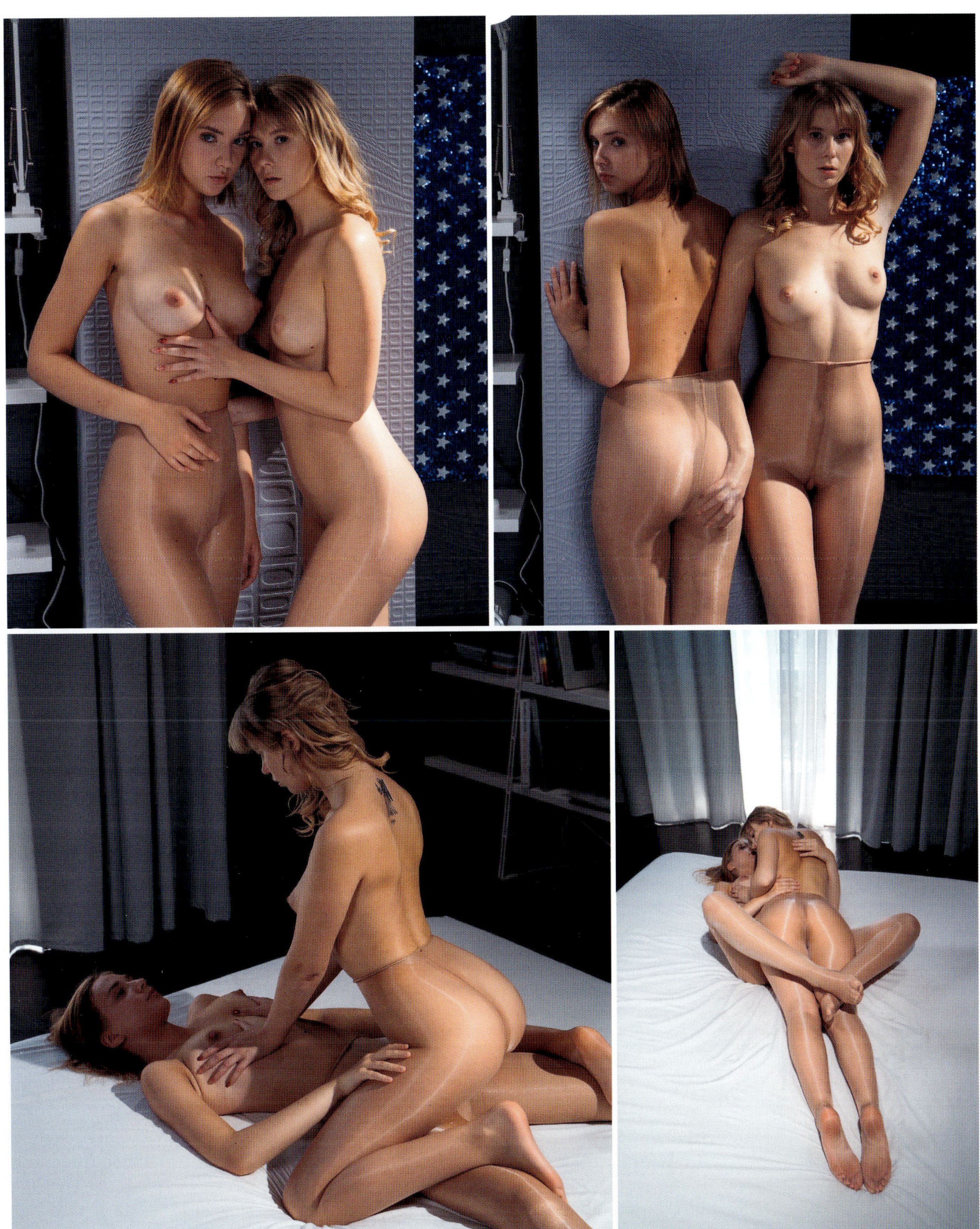

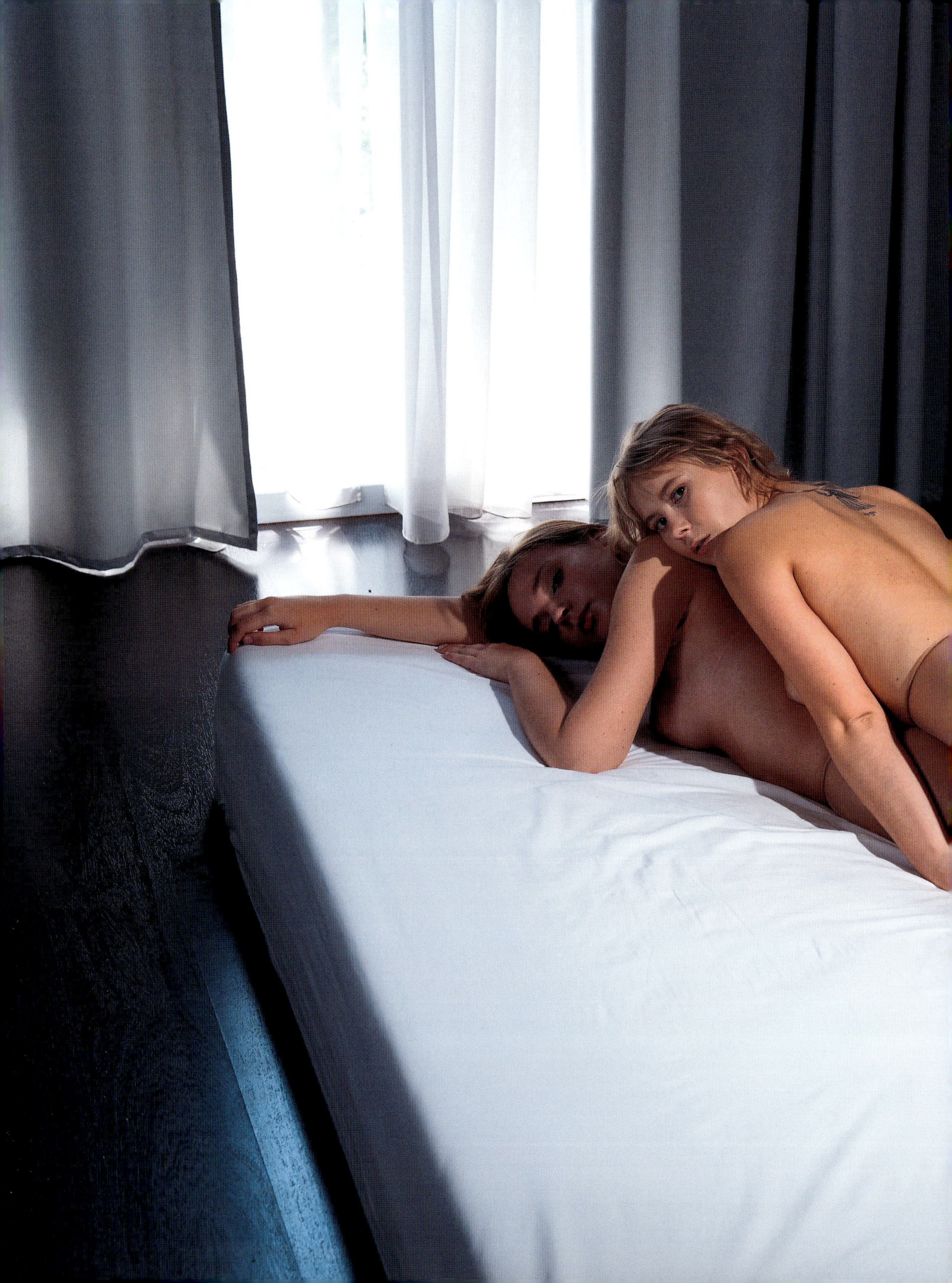

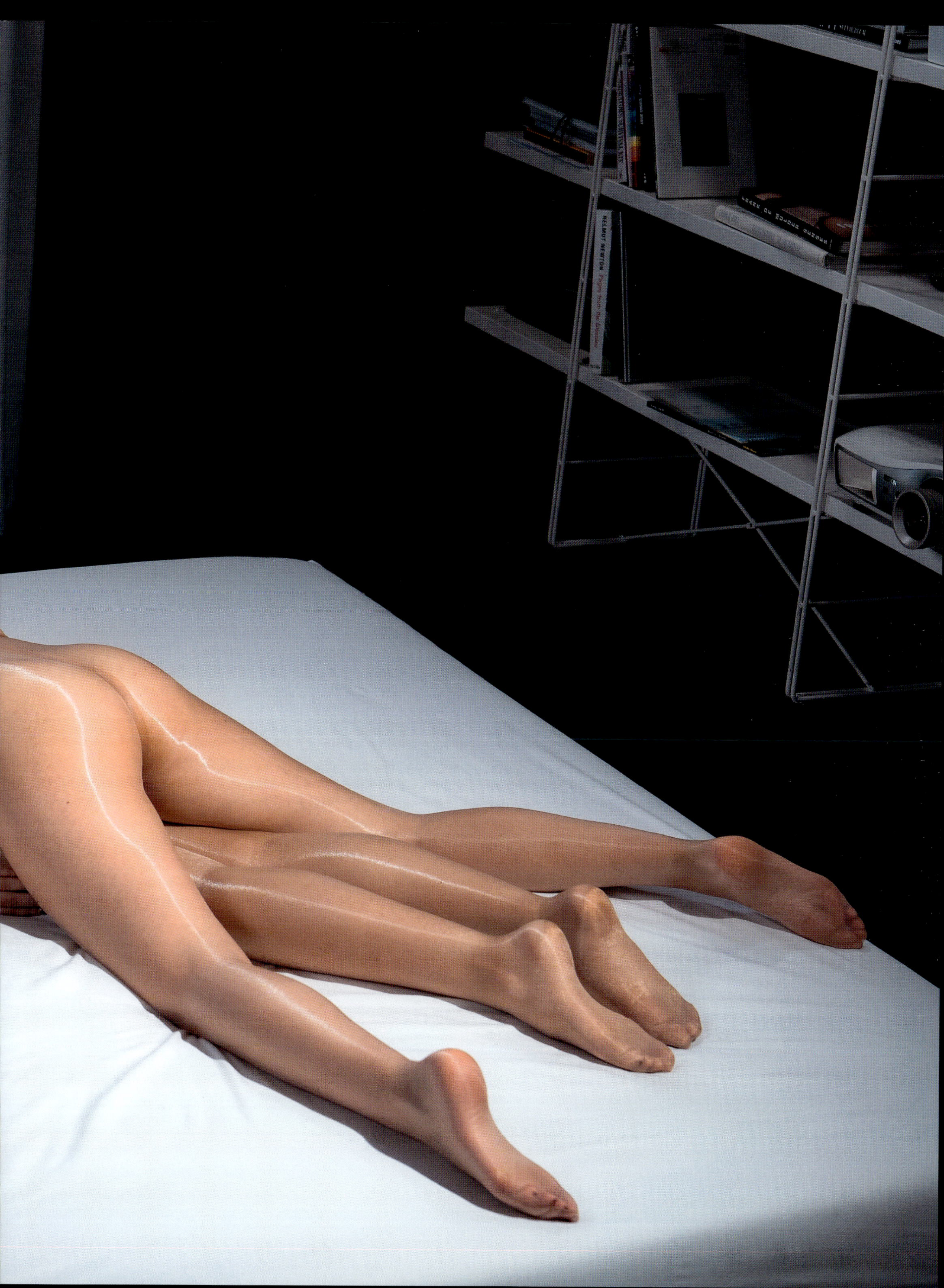

HELMUT NEWTON

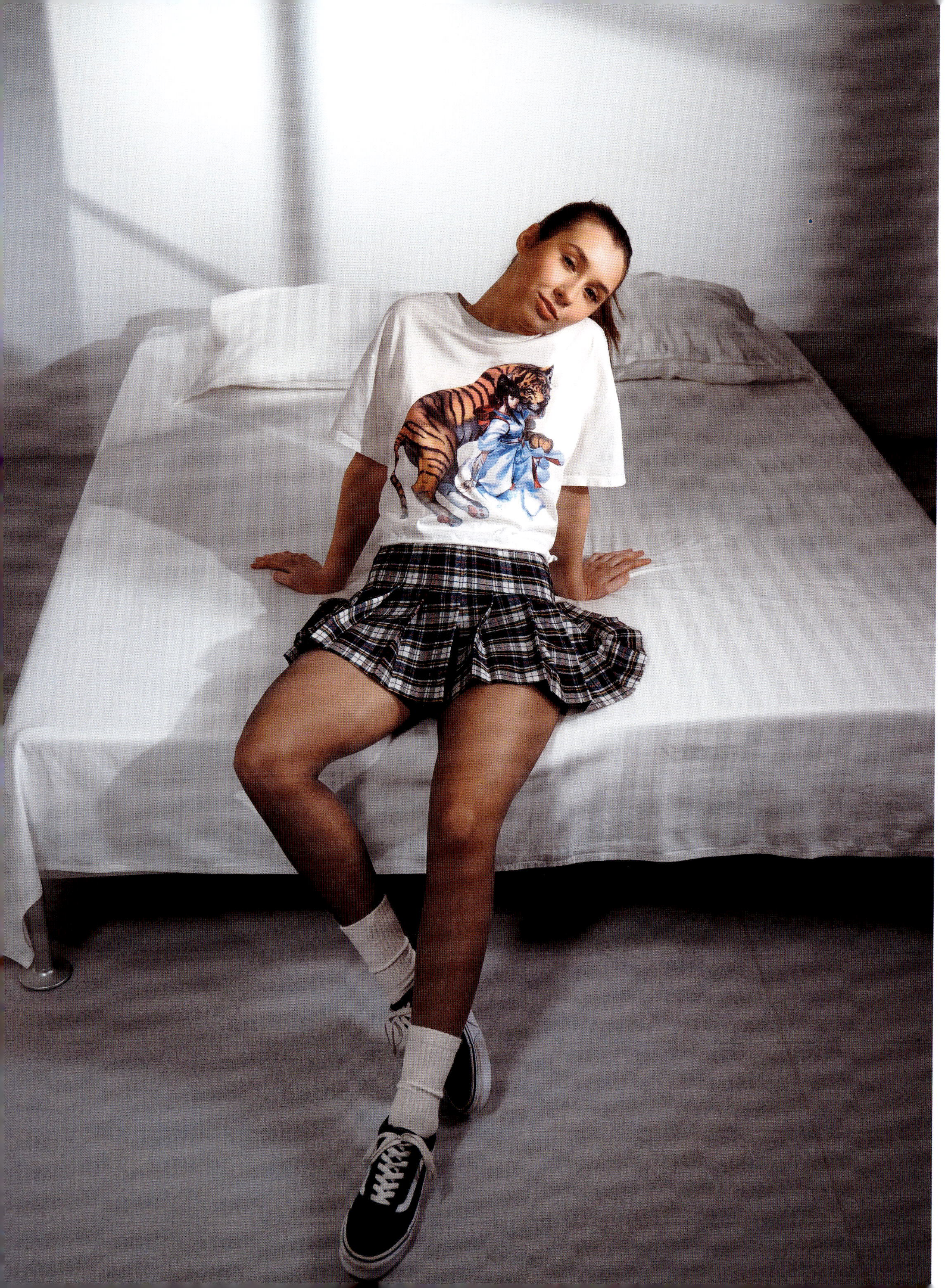

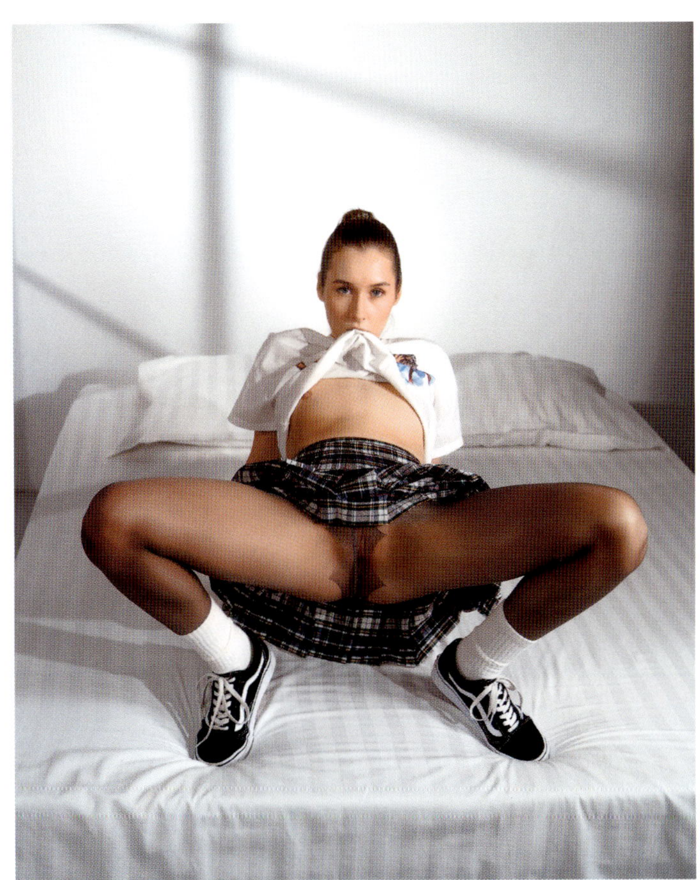
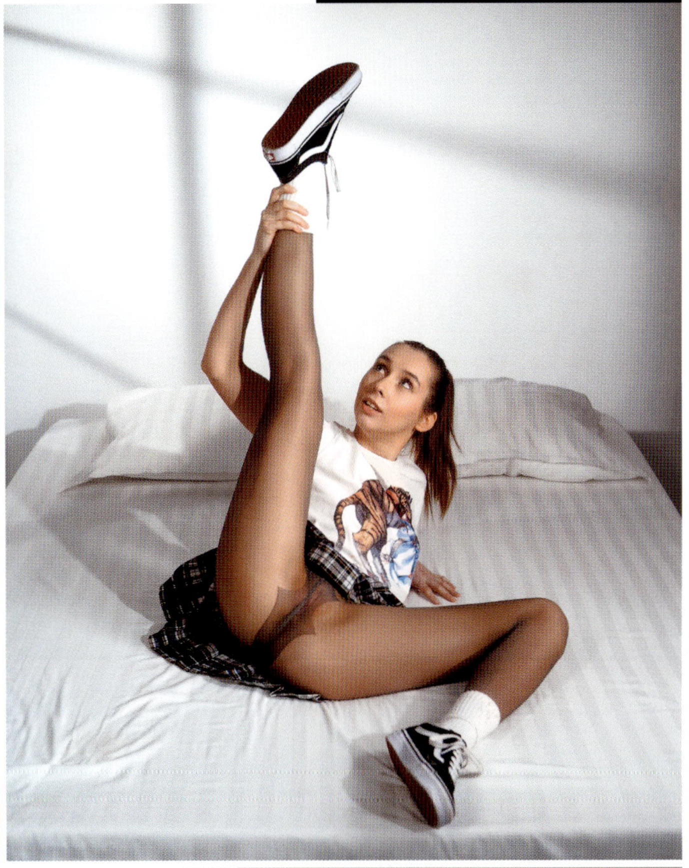
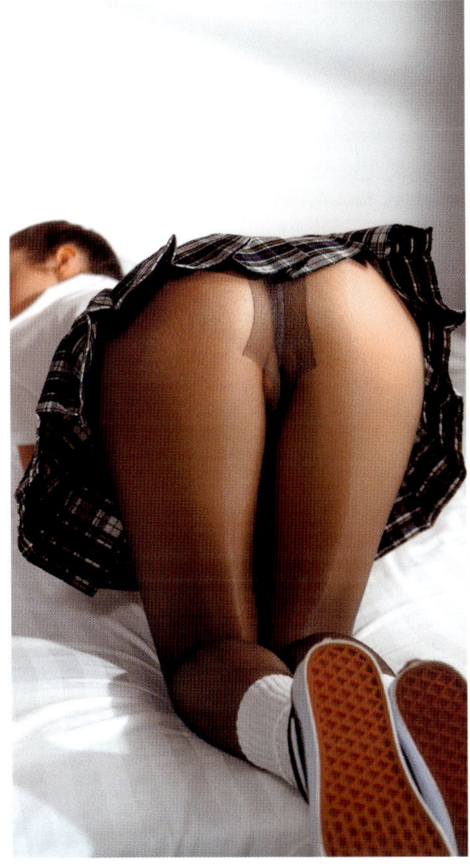
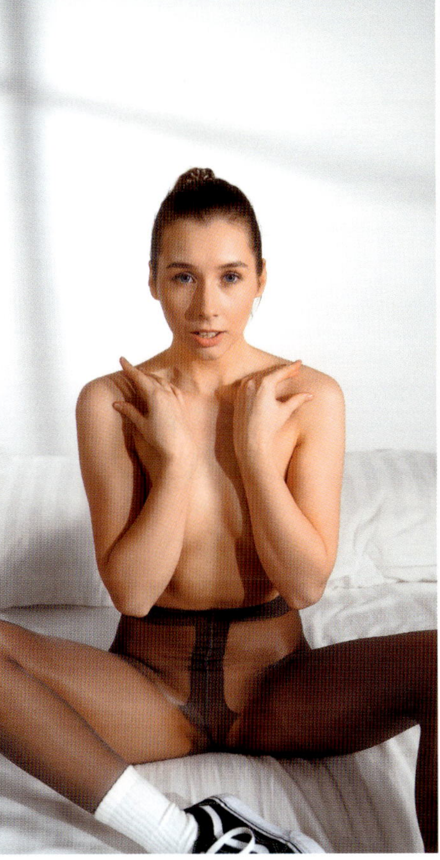
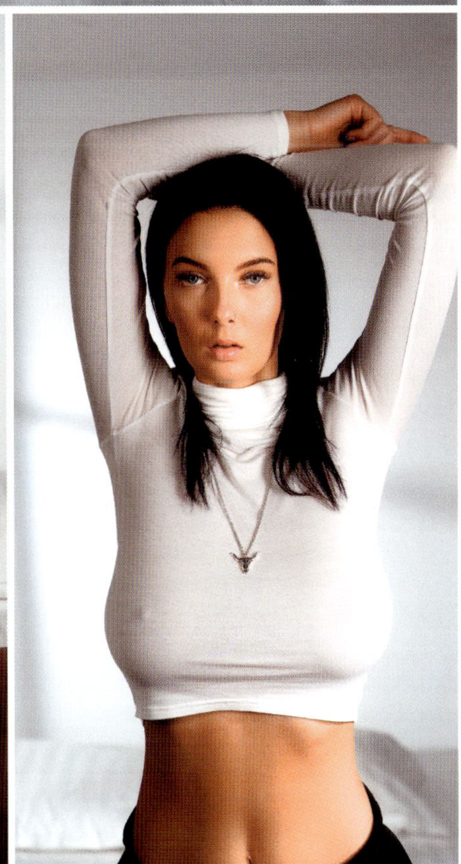

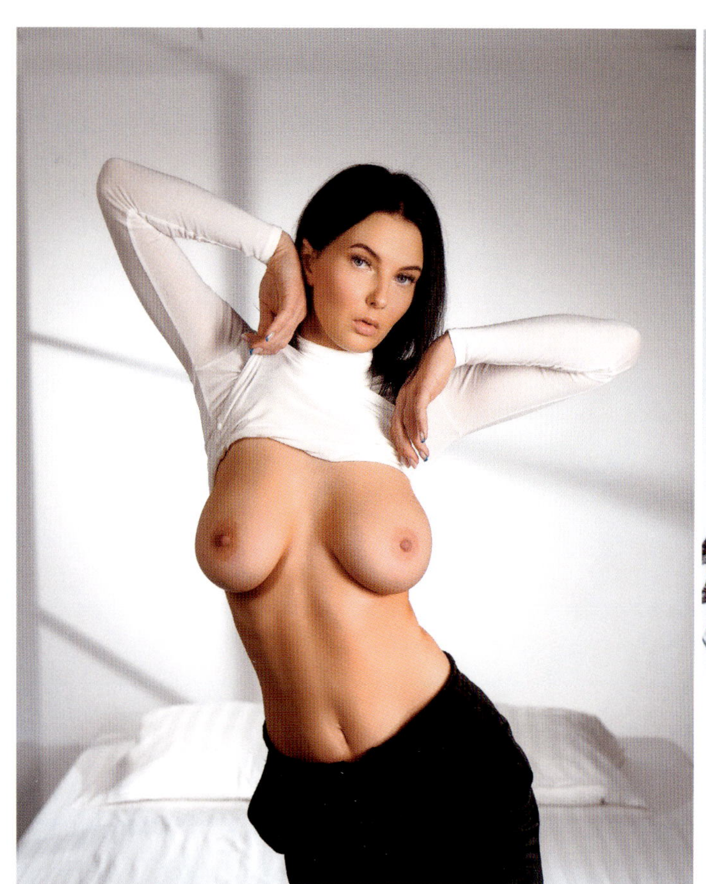
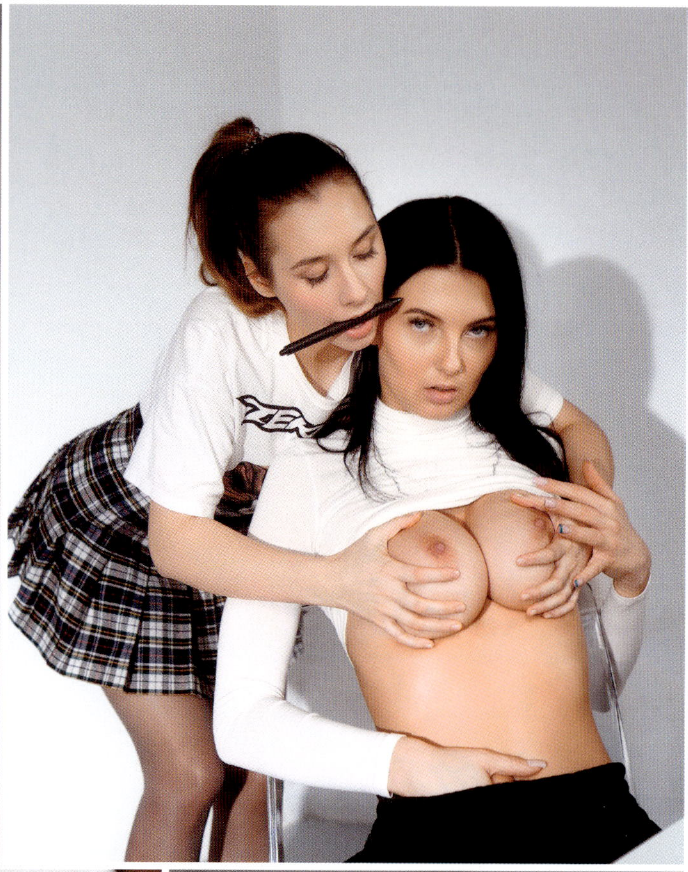
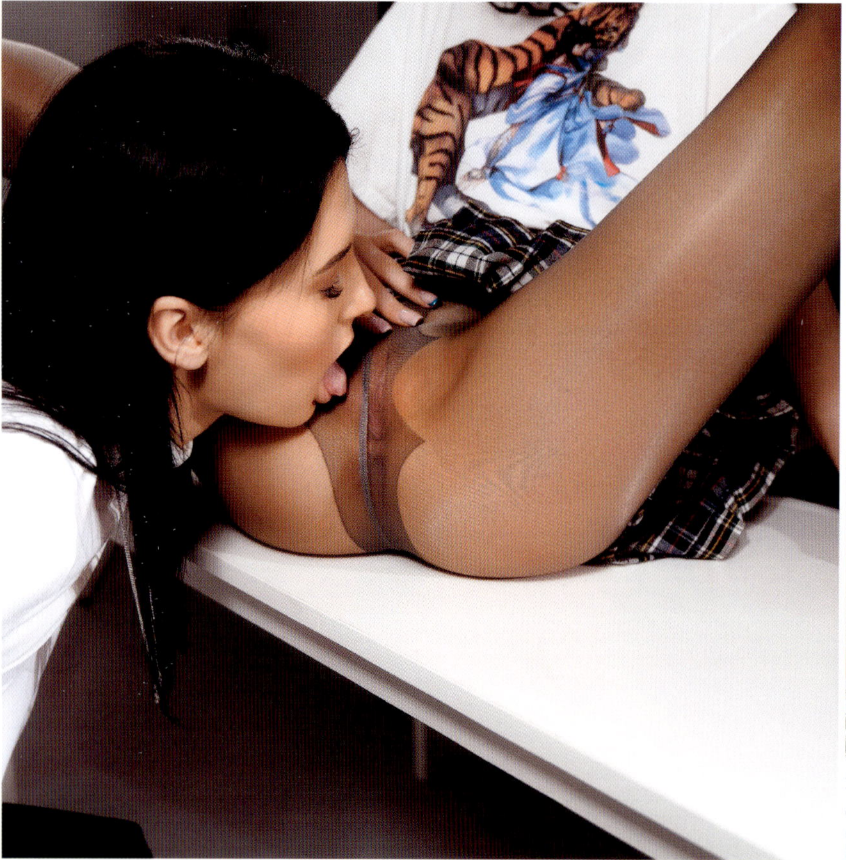
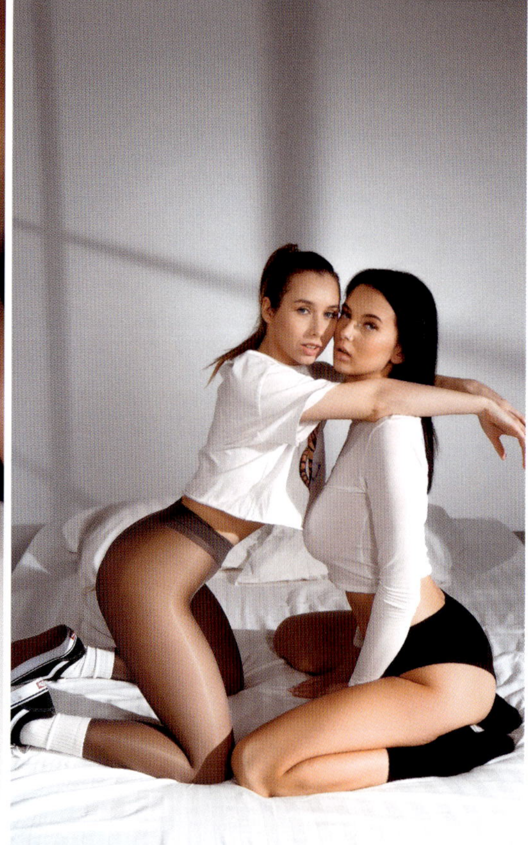

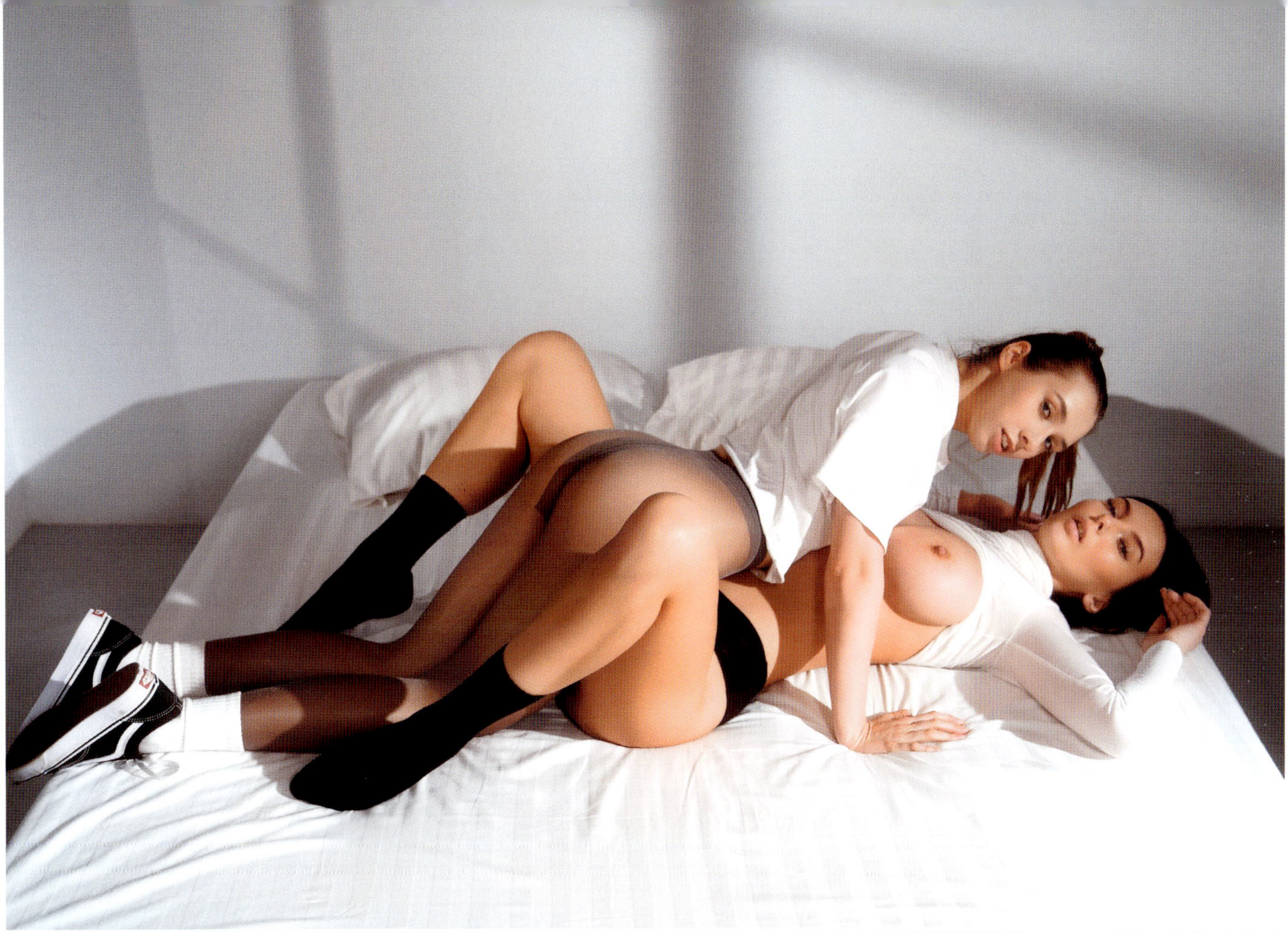

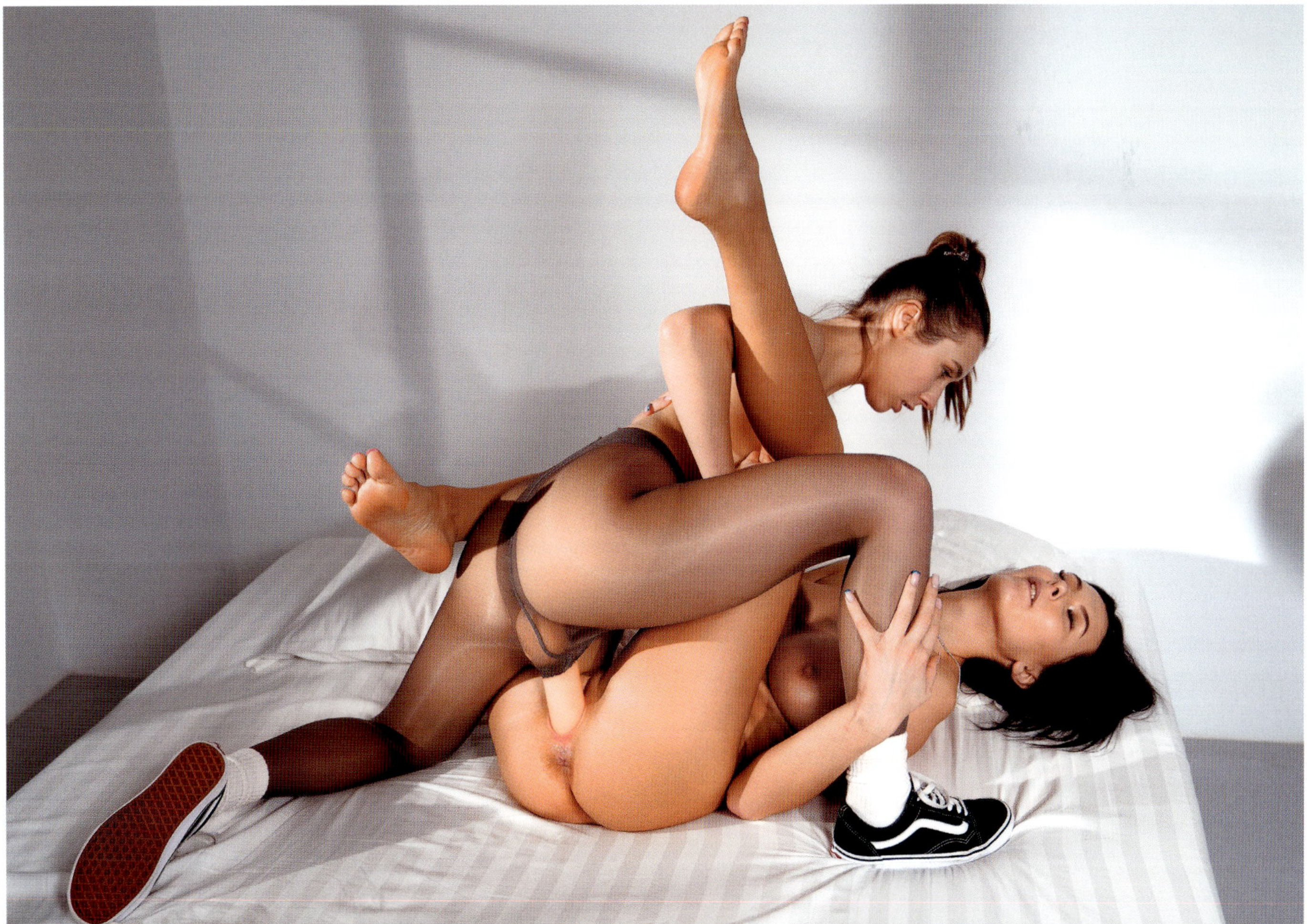

SIMON
MIA

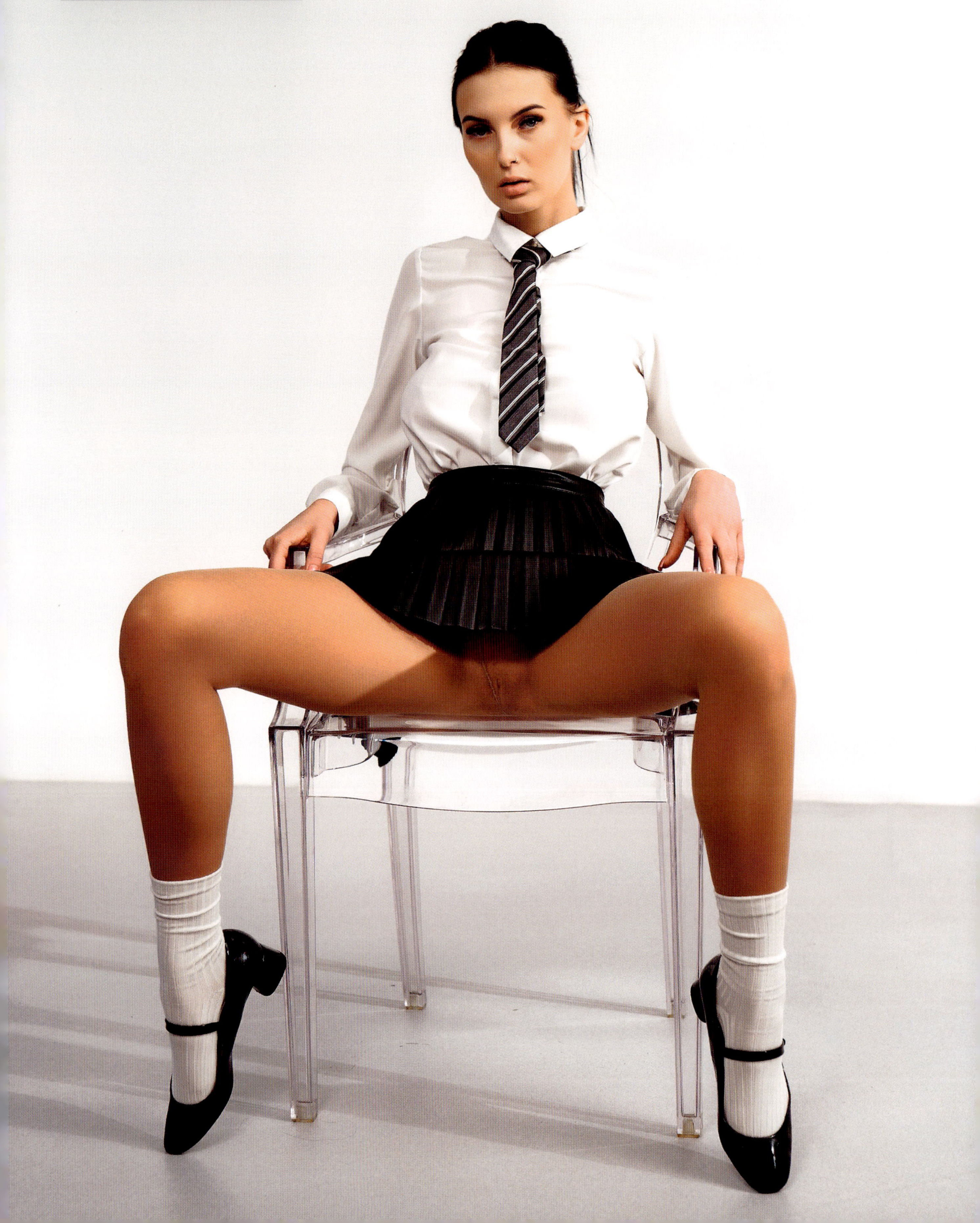

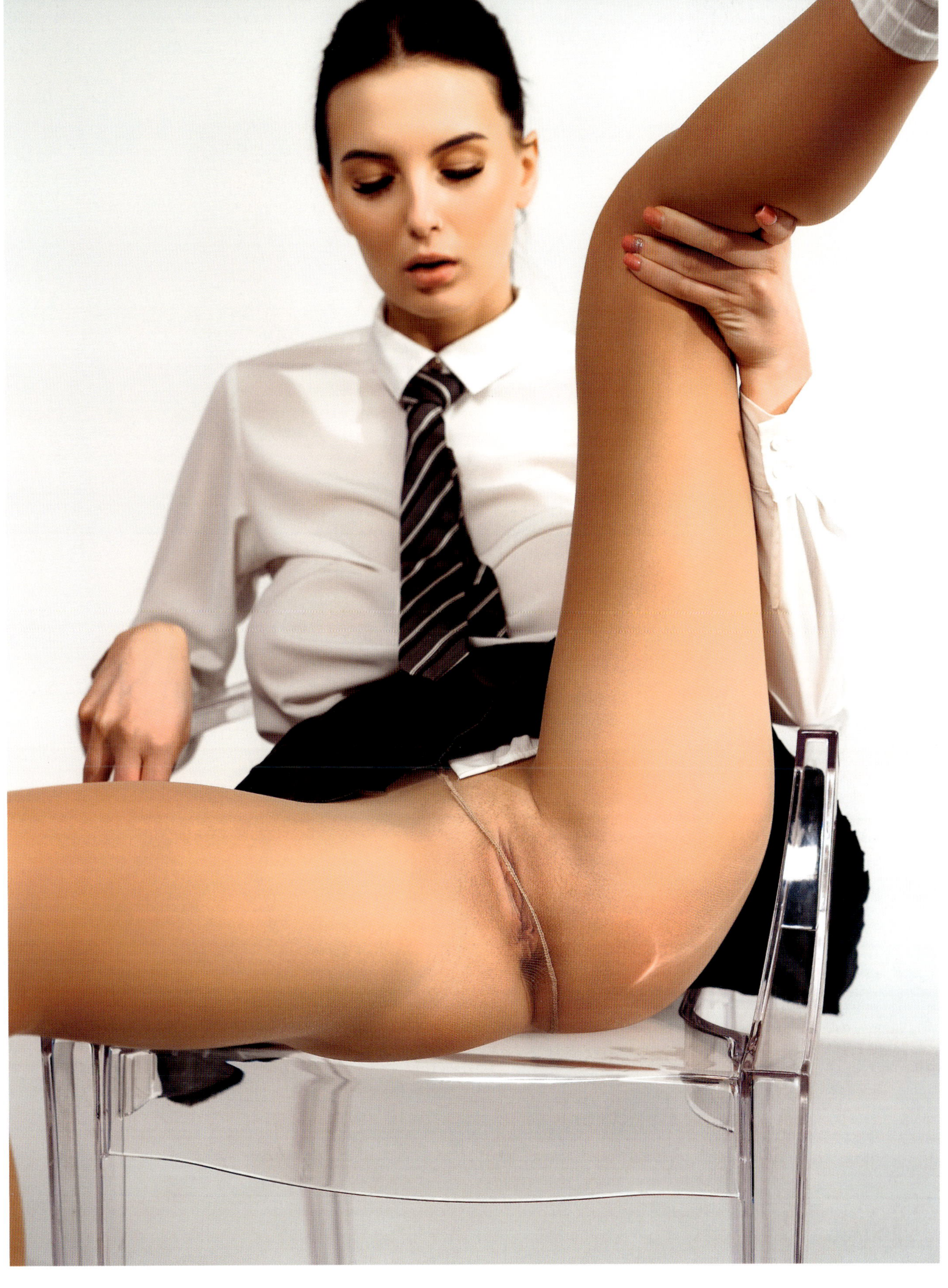

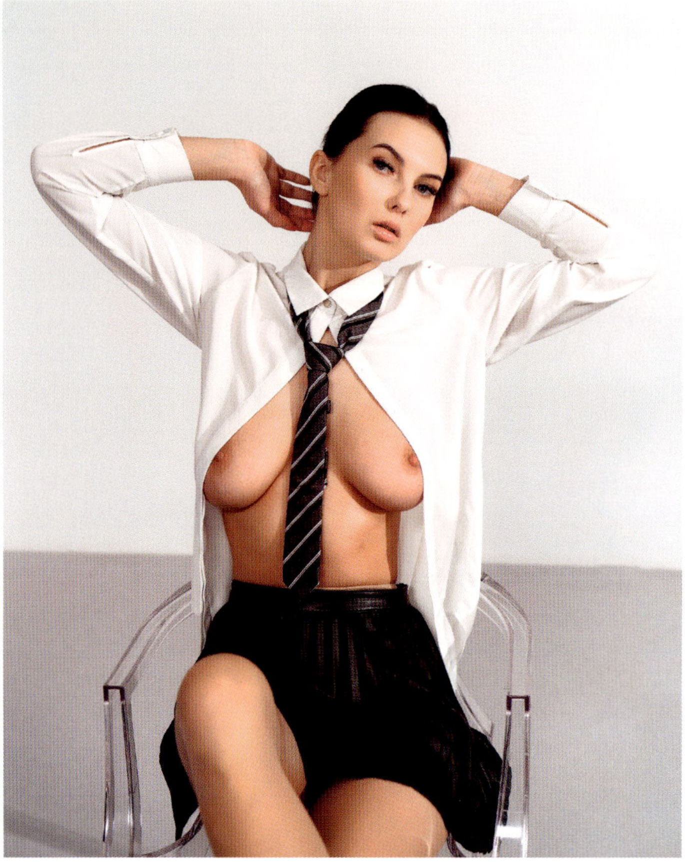

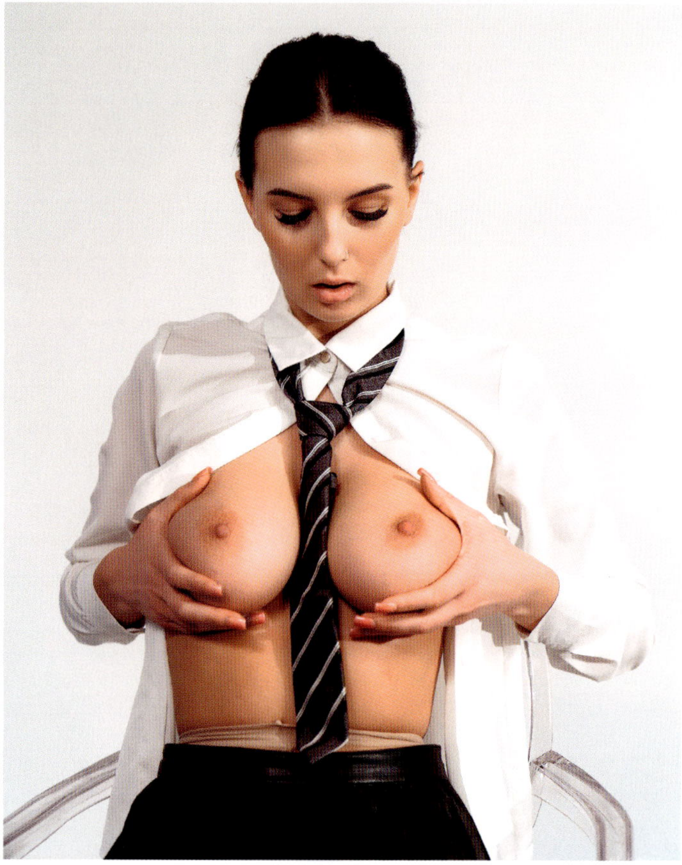

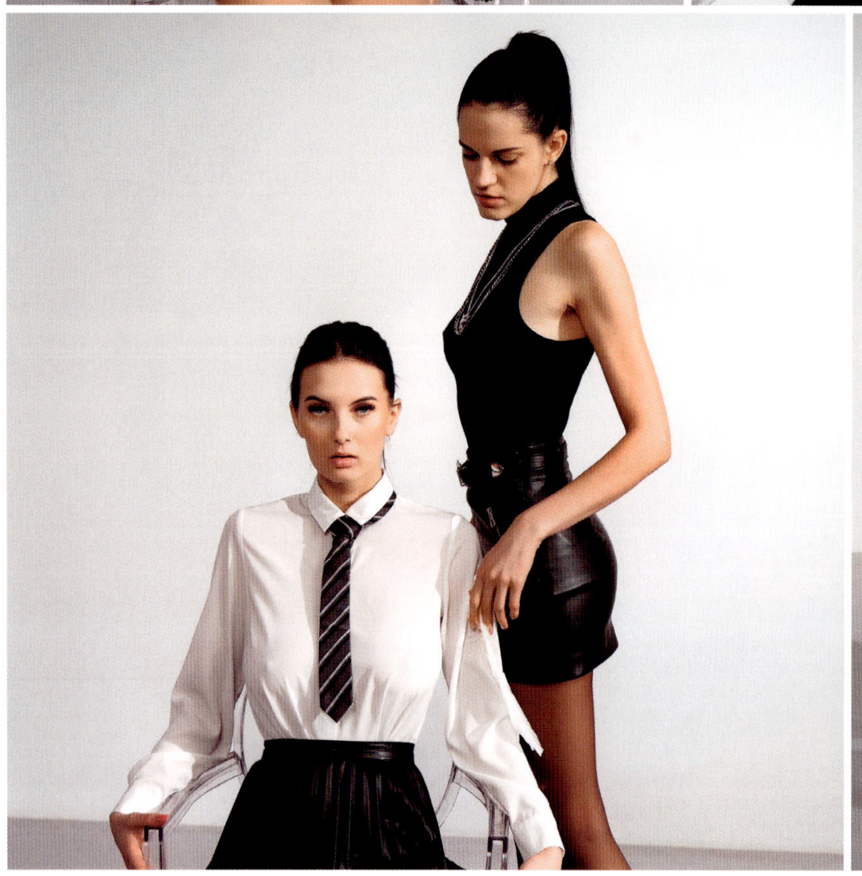
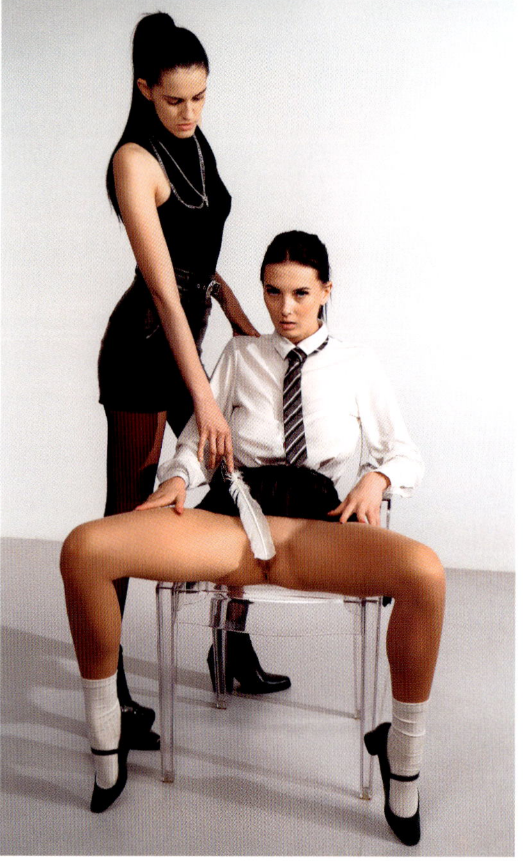

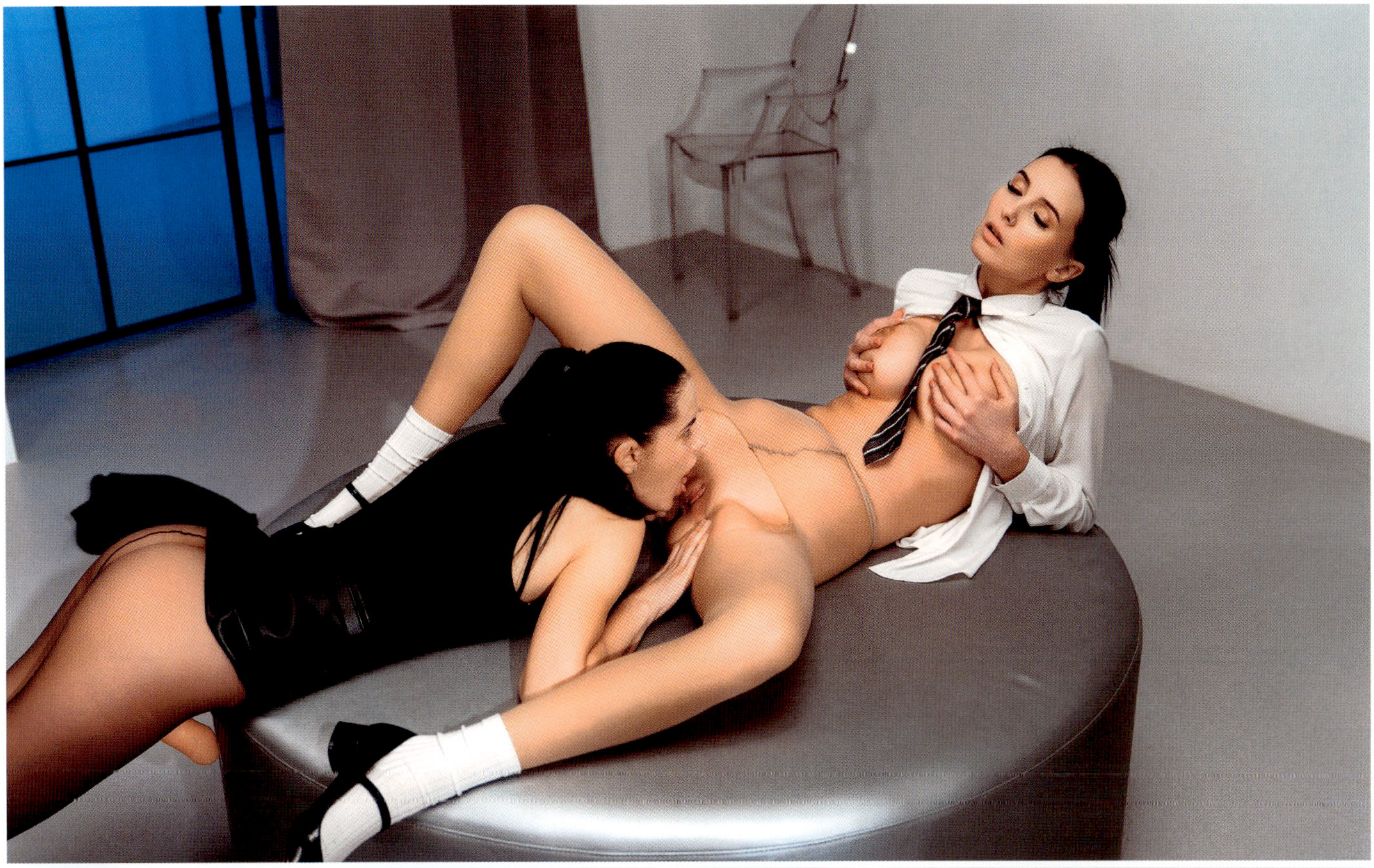

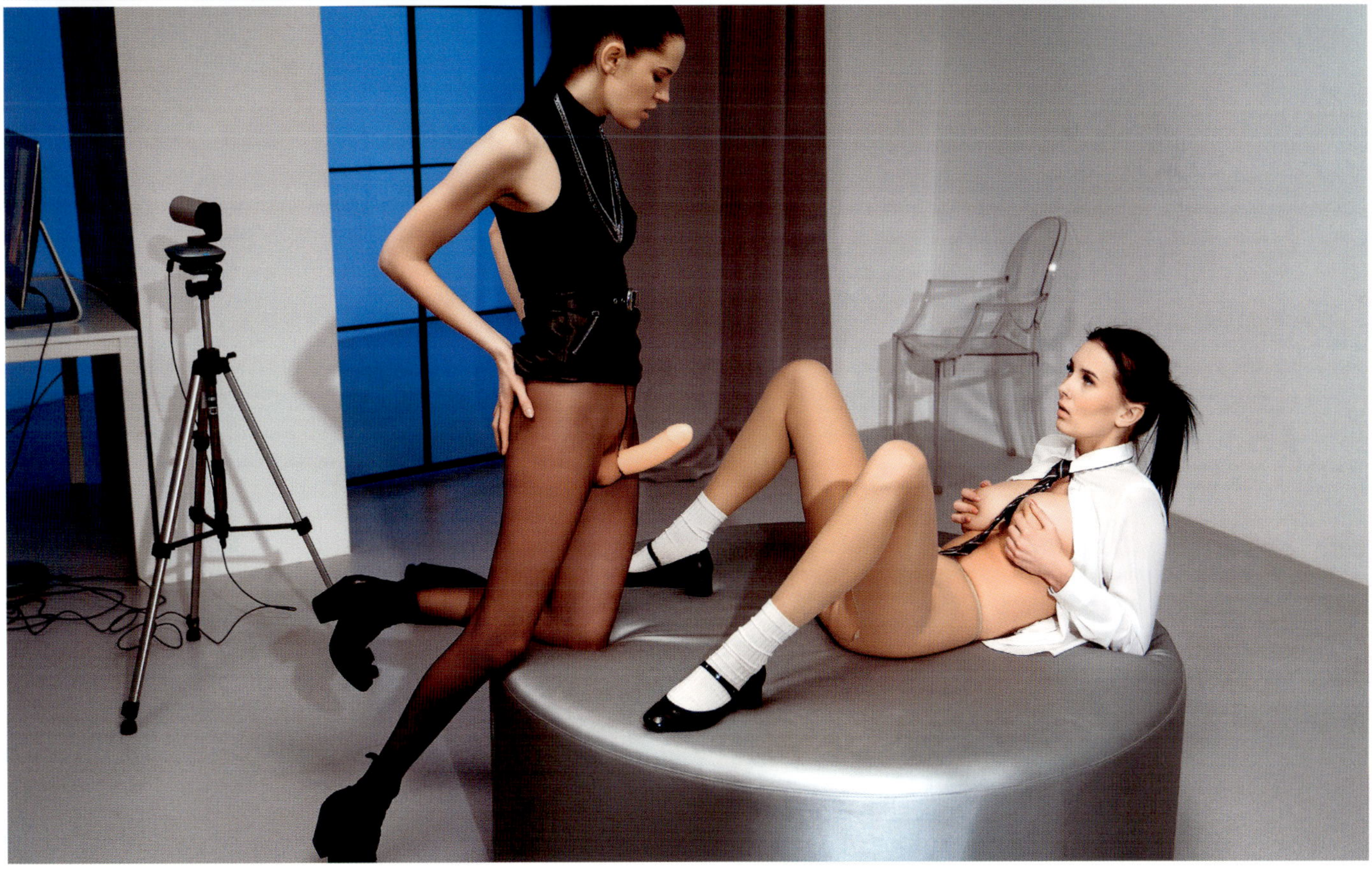

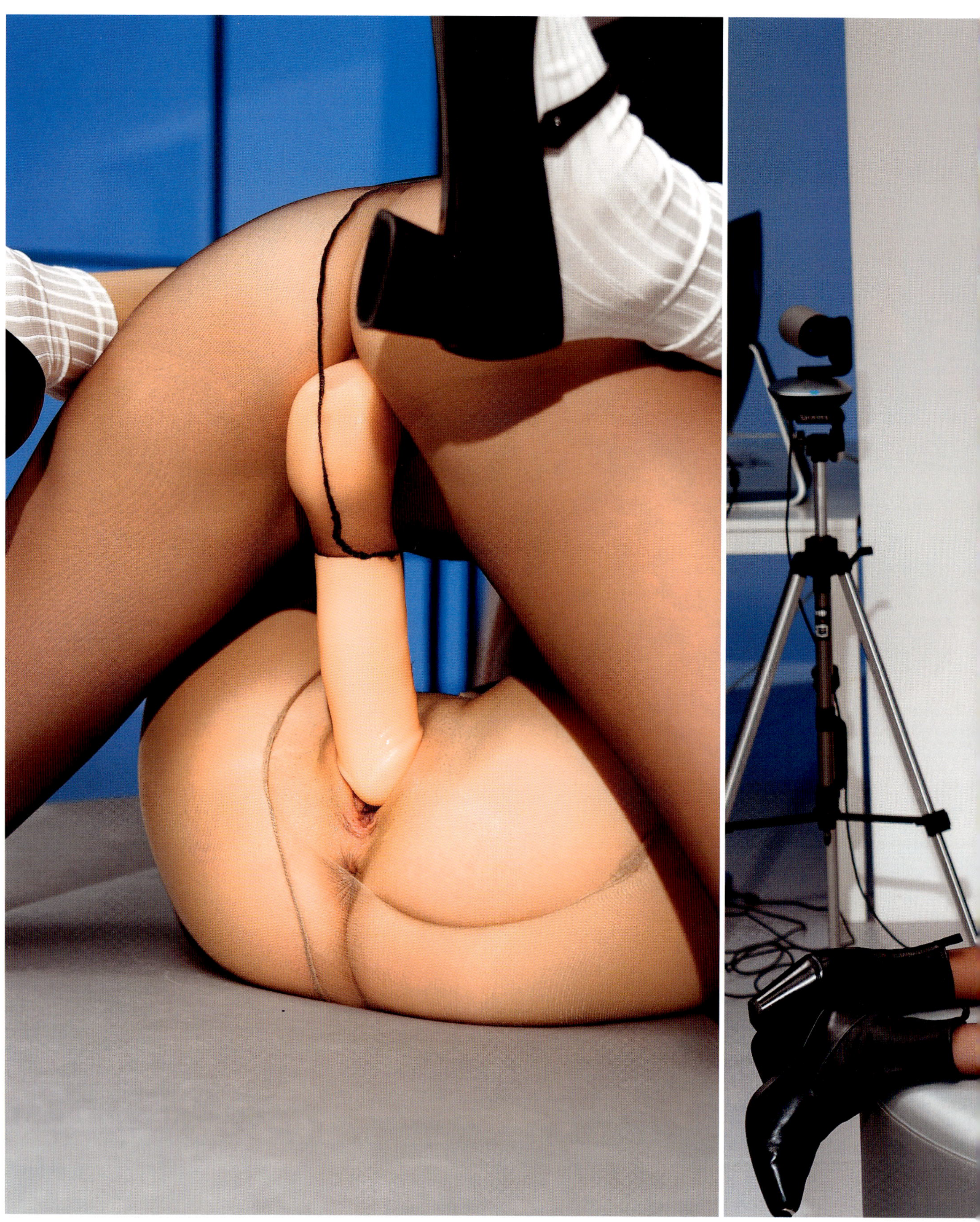

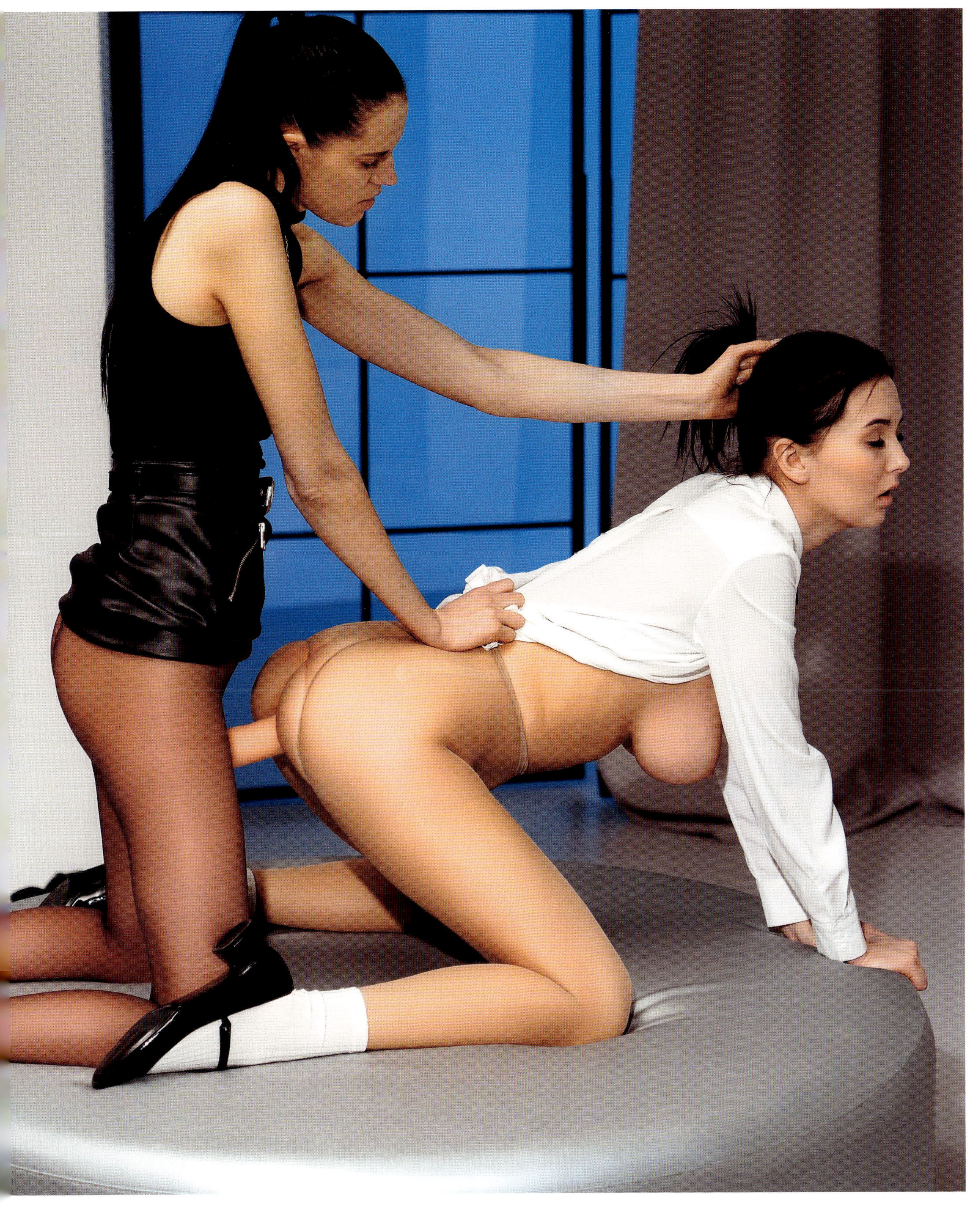

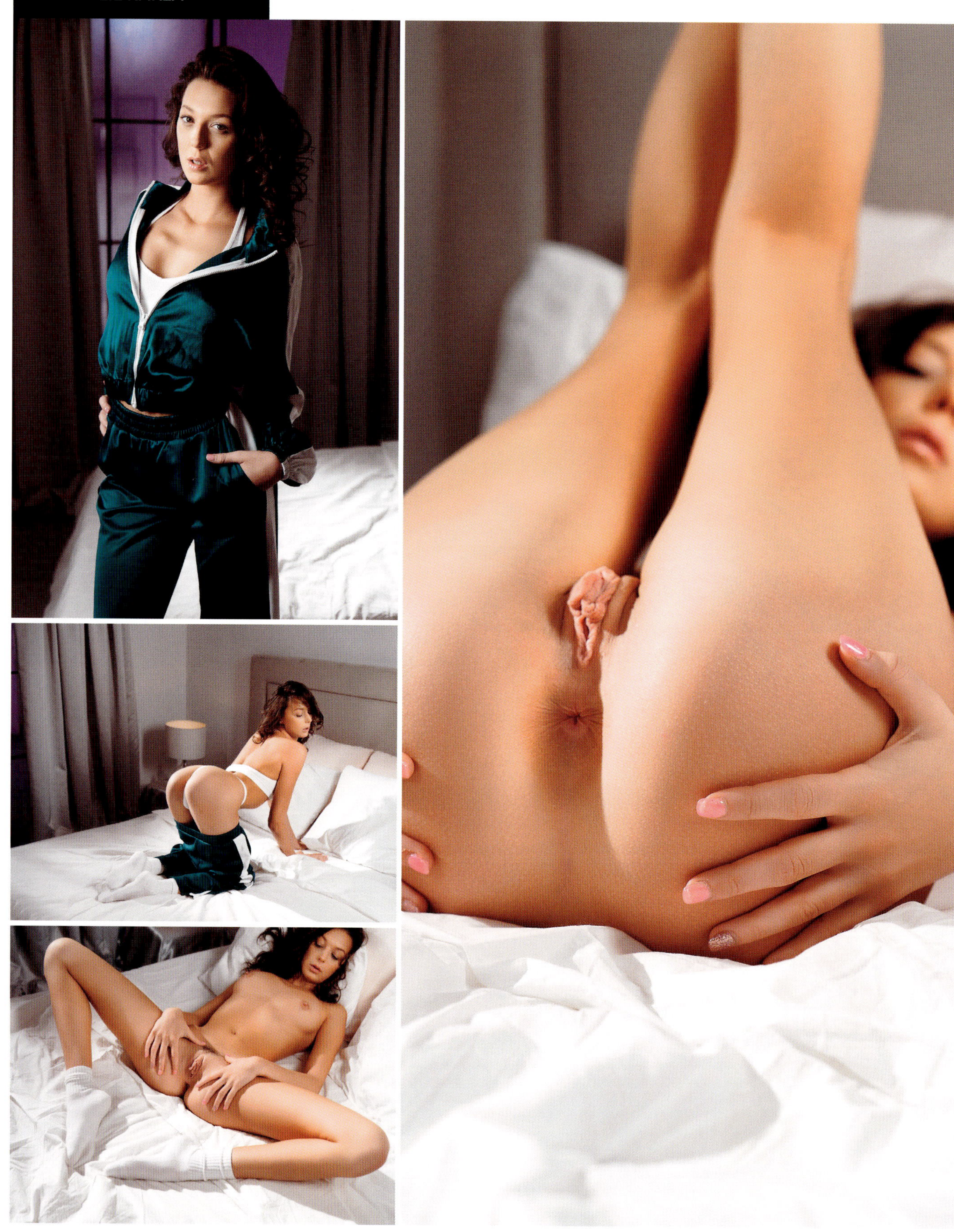

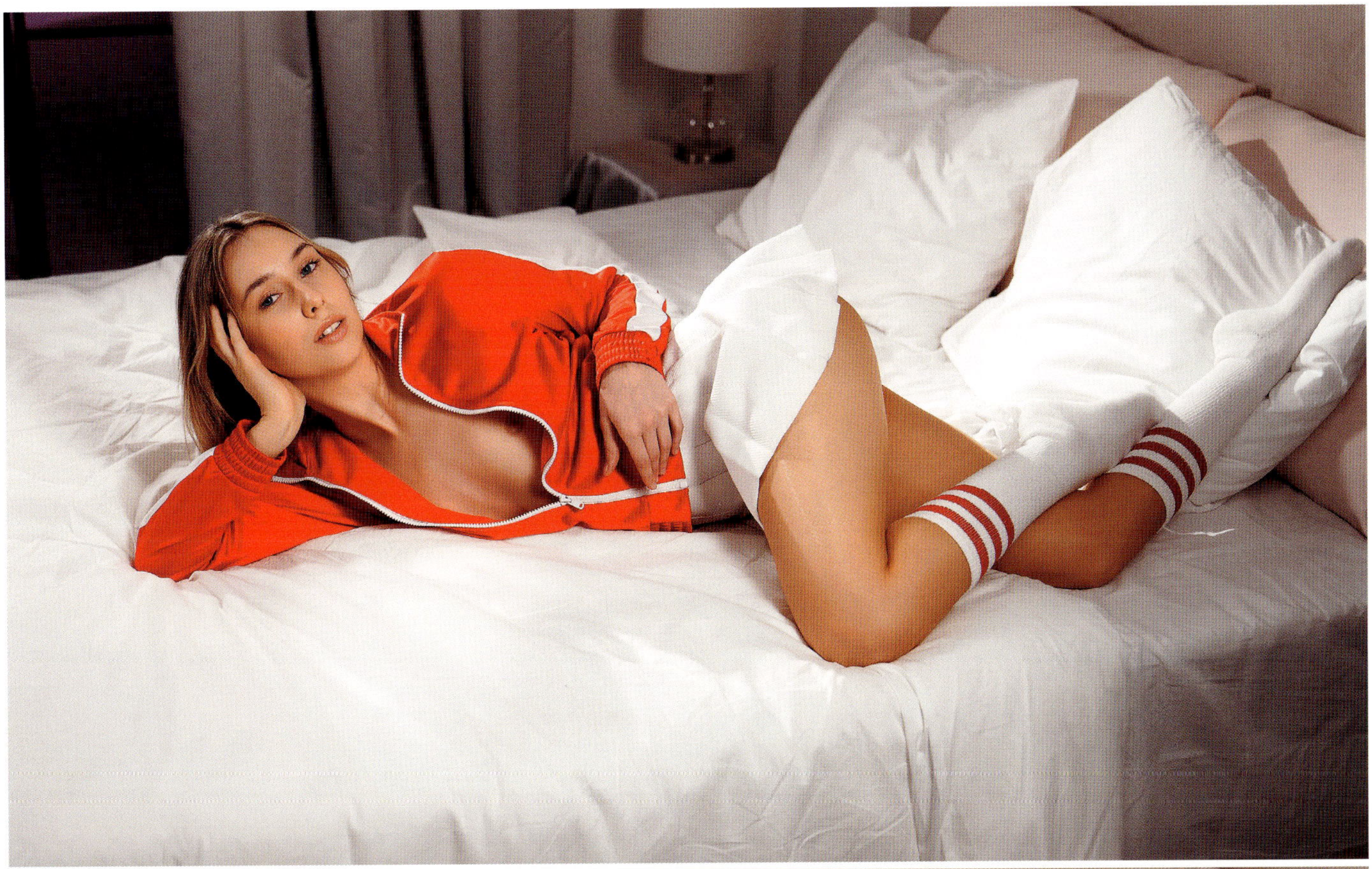

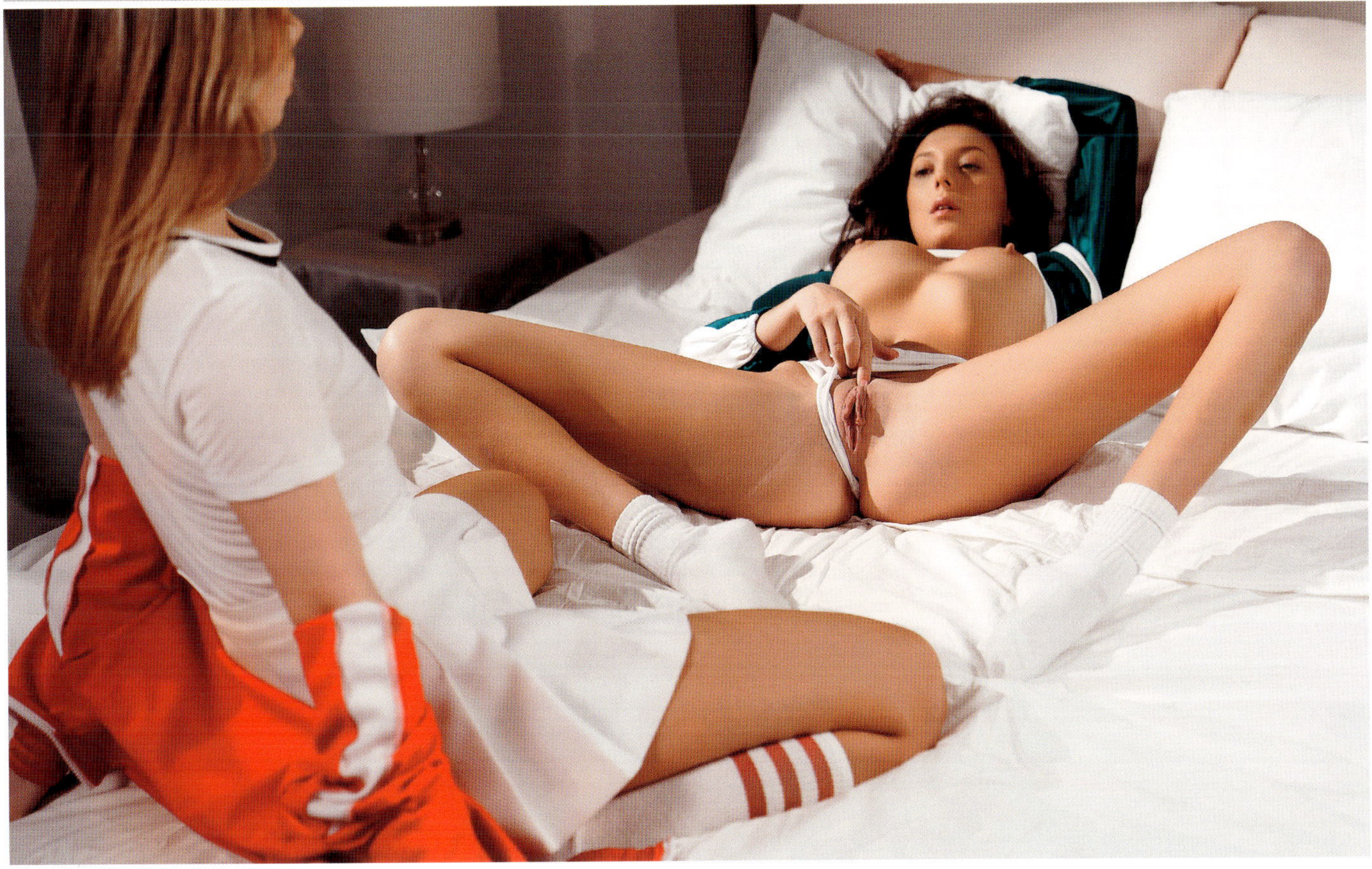

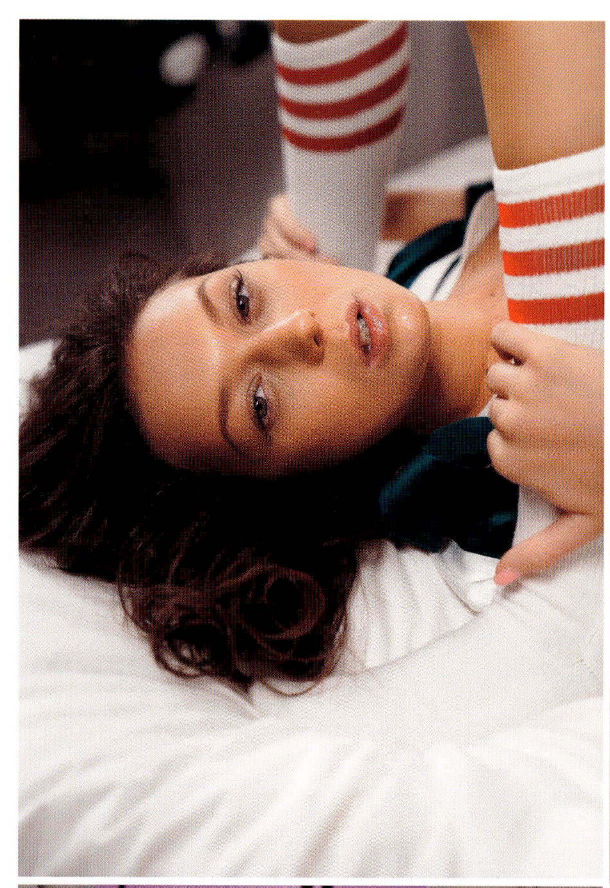
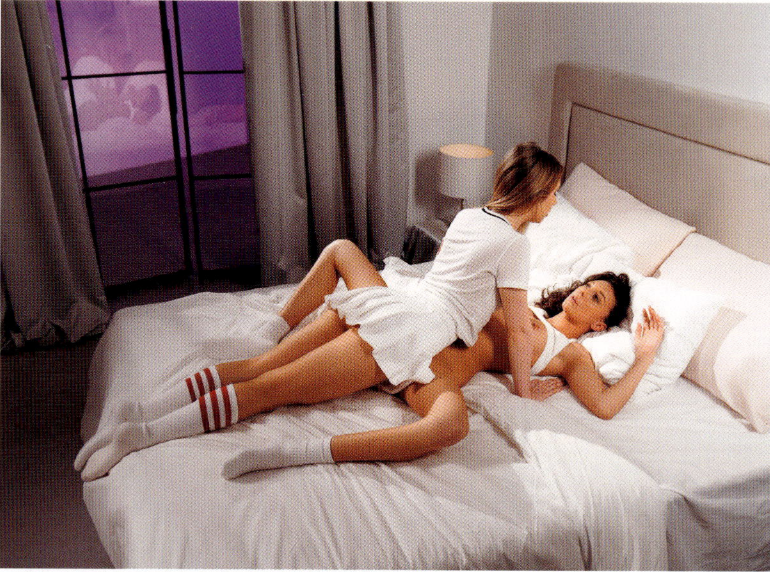
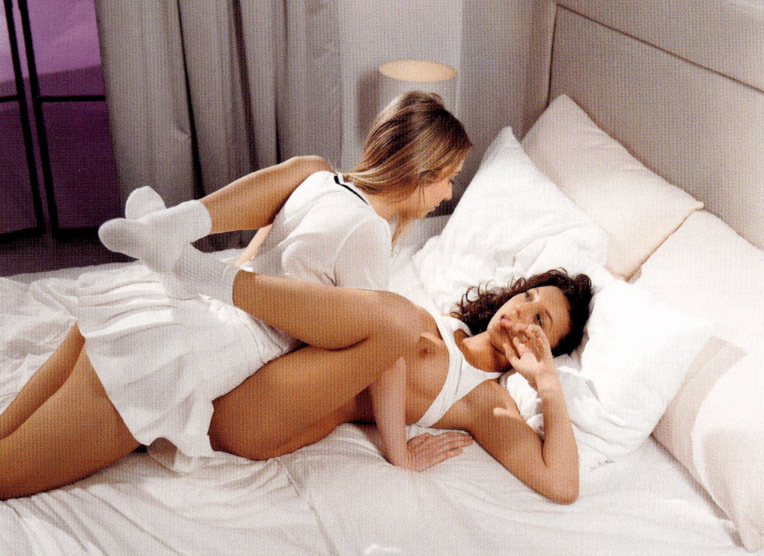
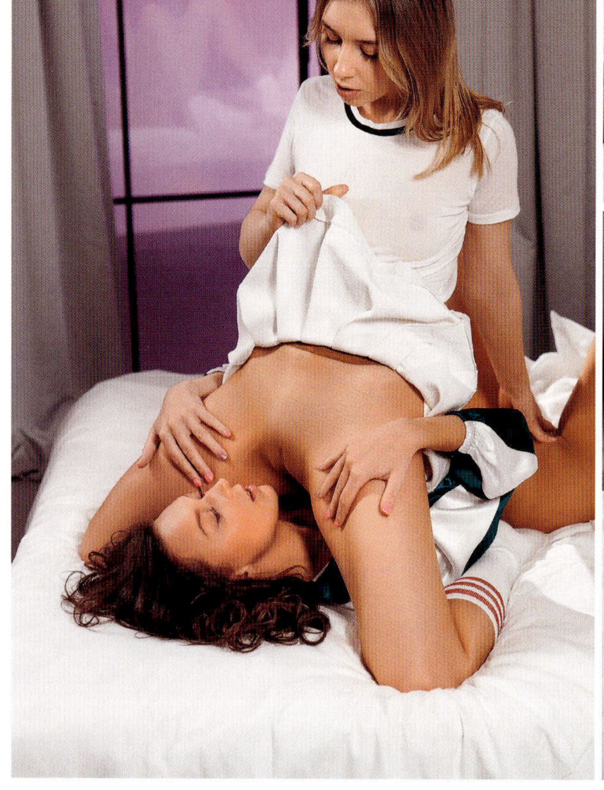
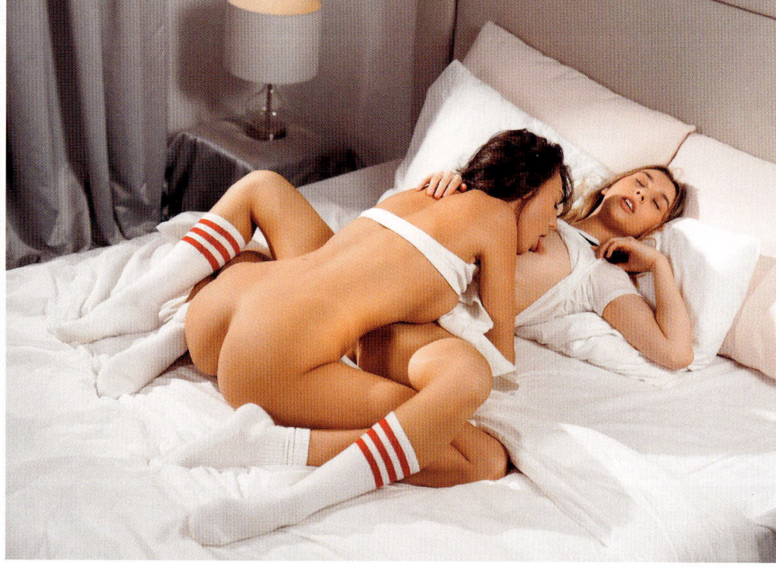

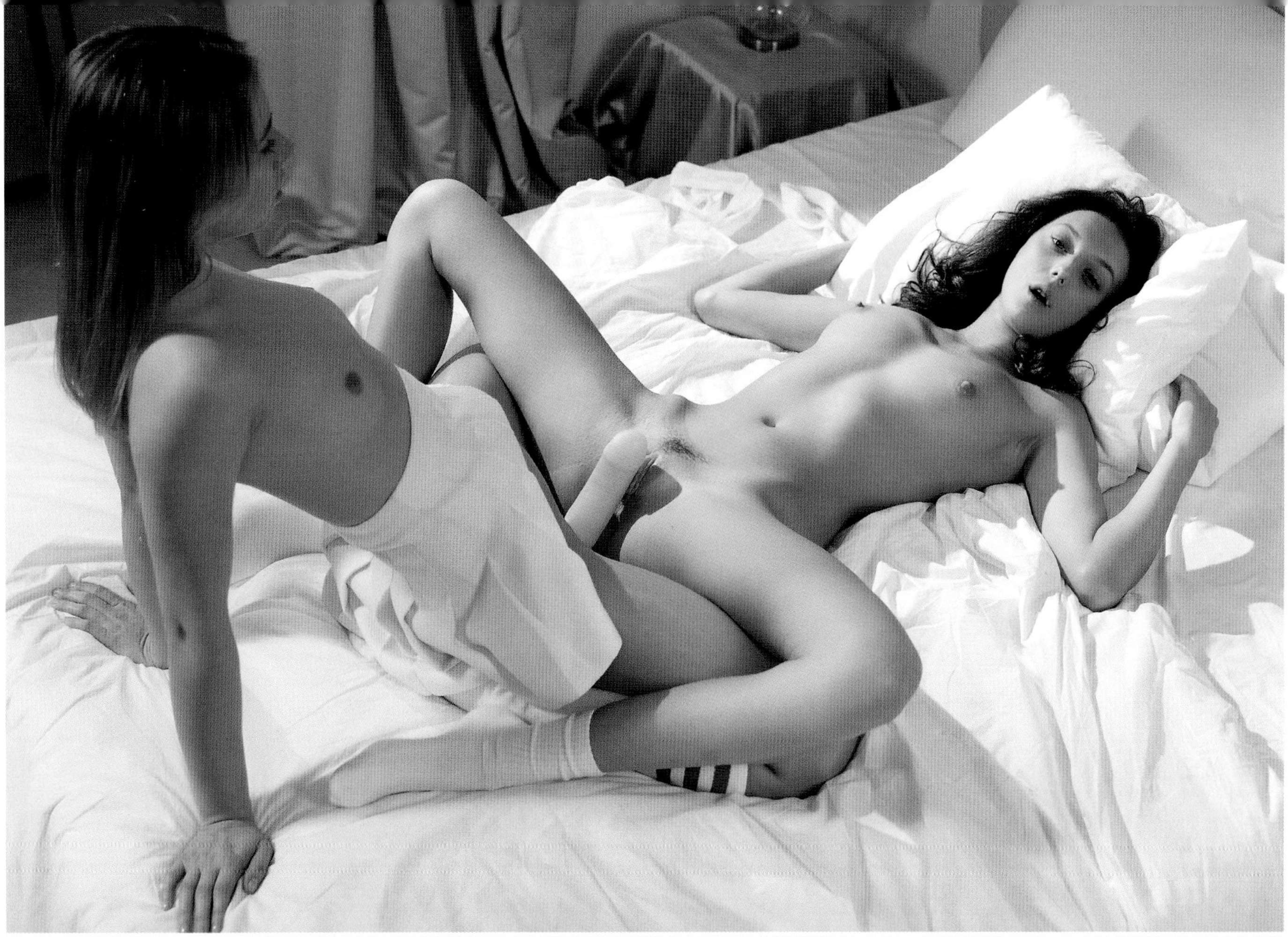

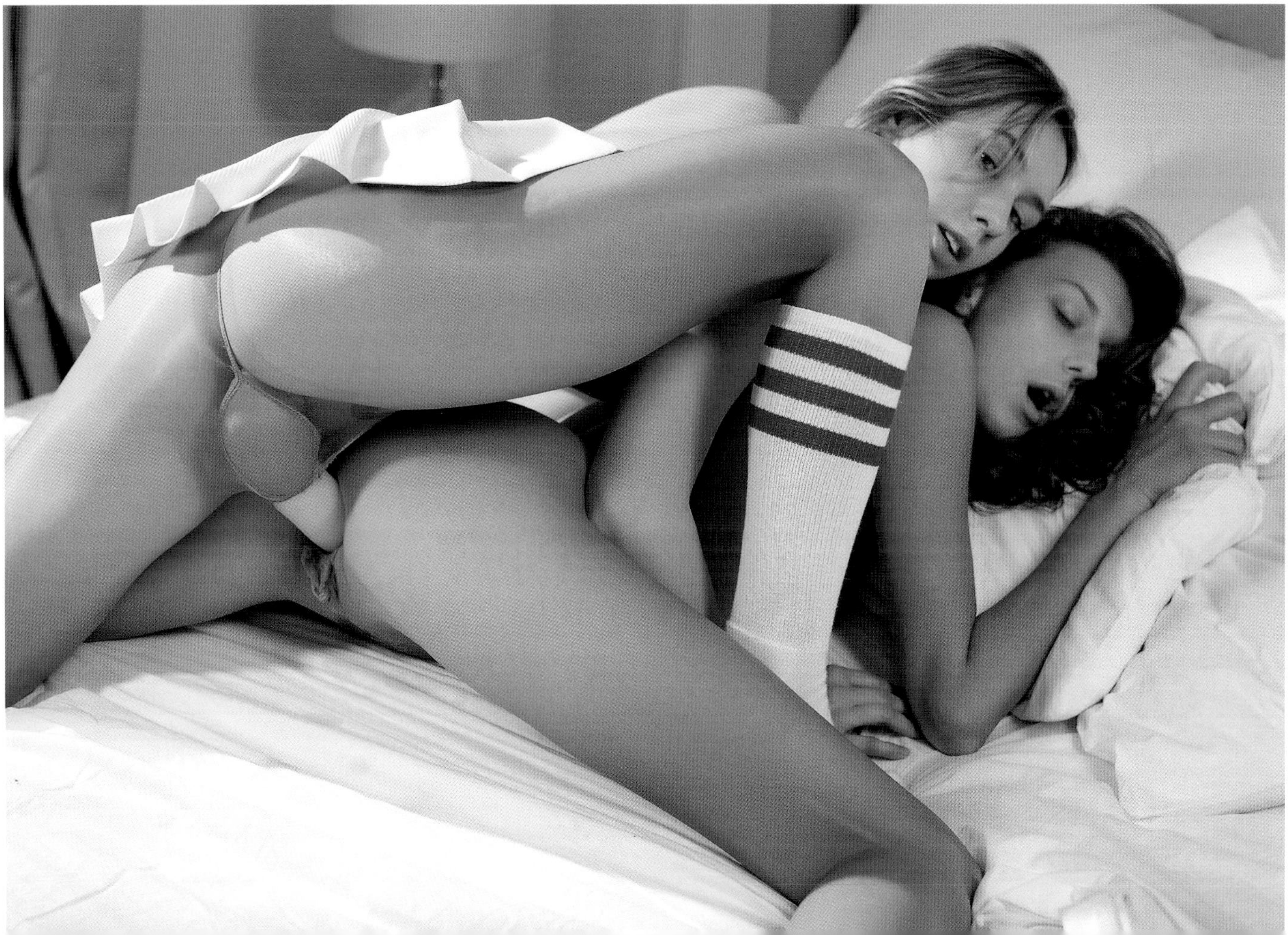

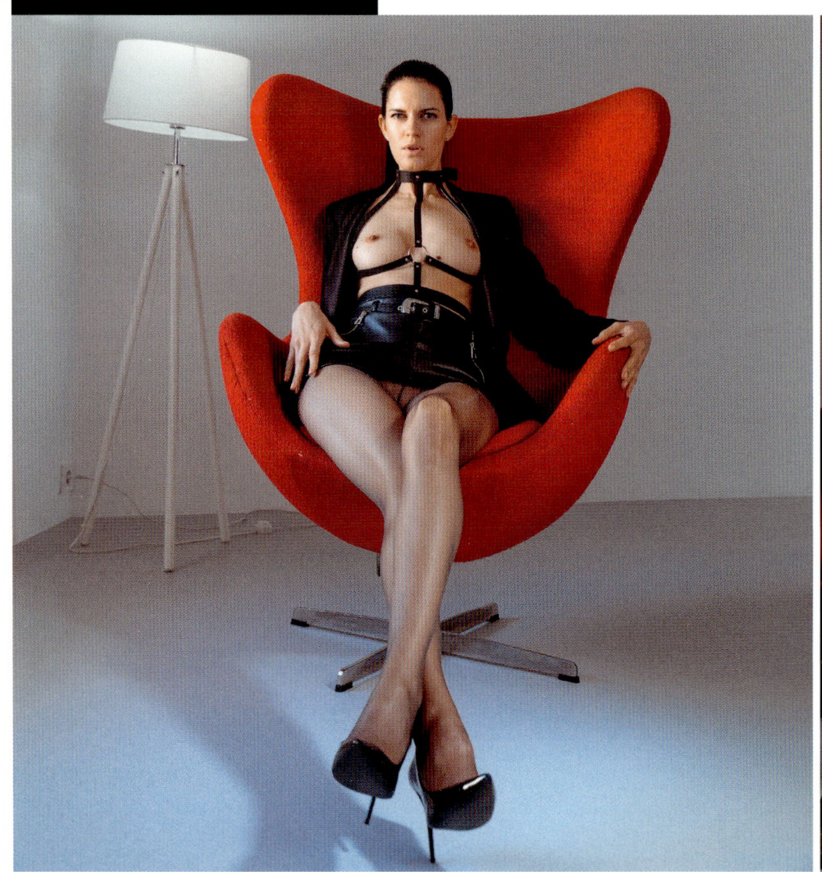
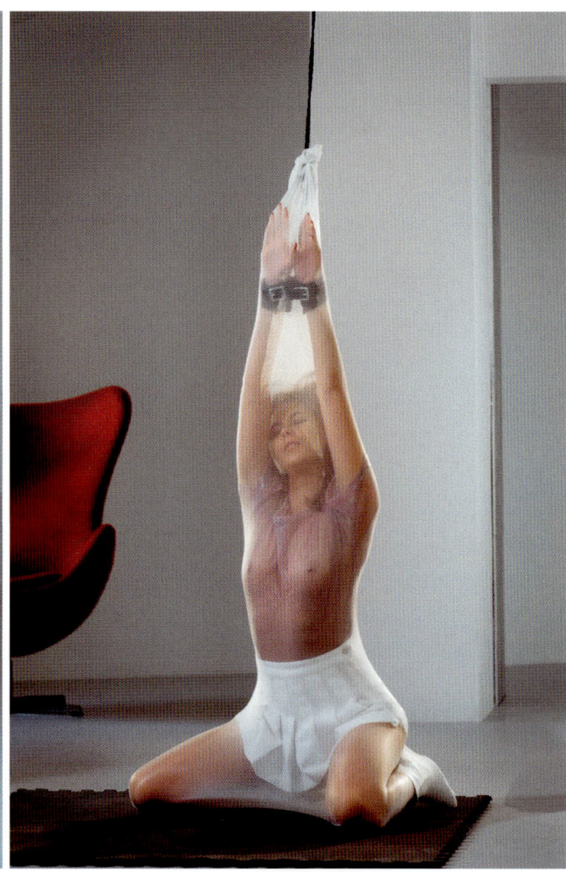
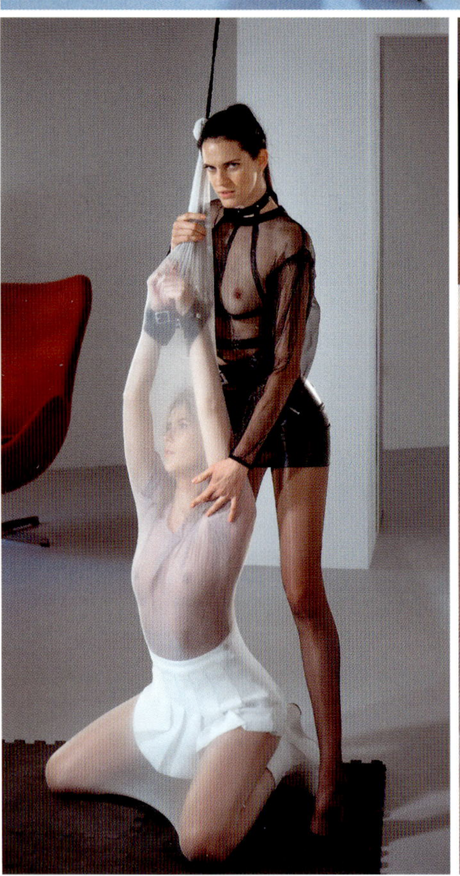
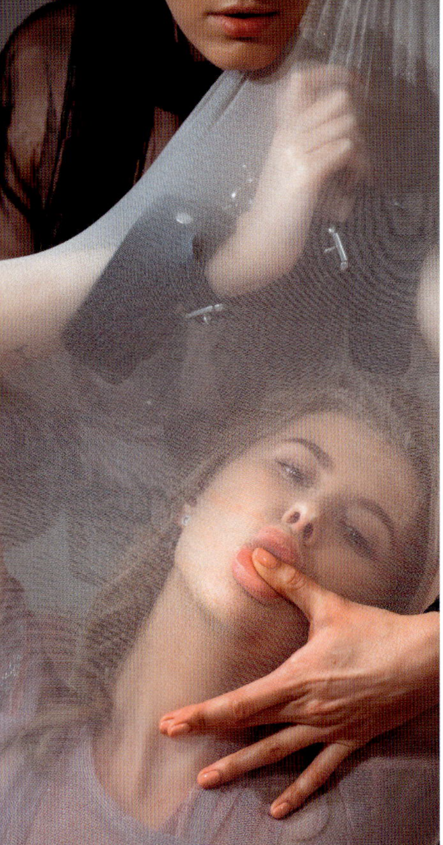
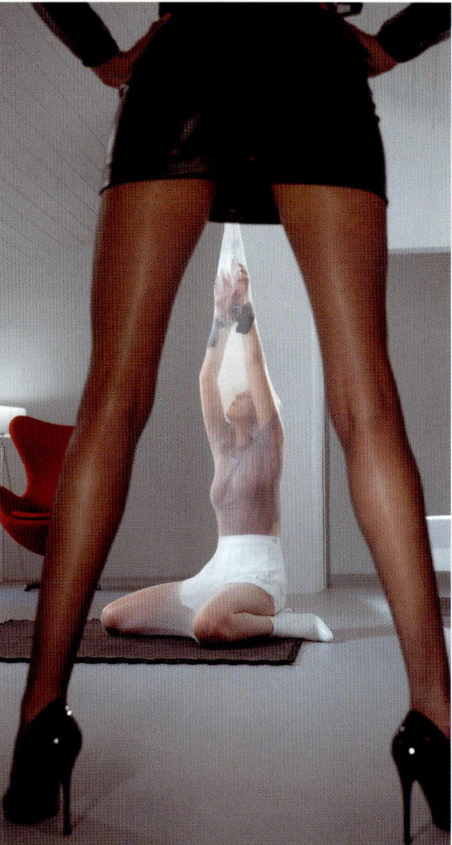

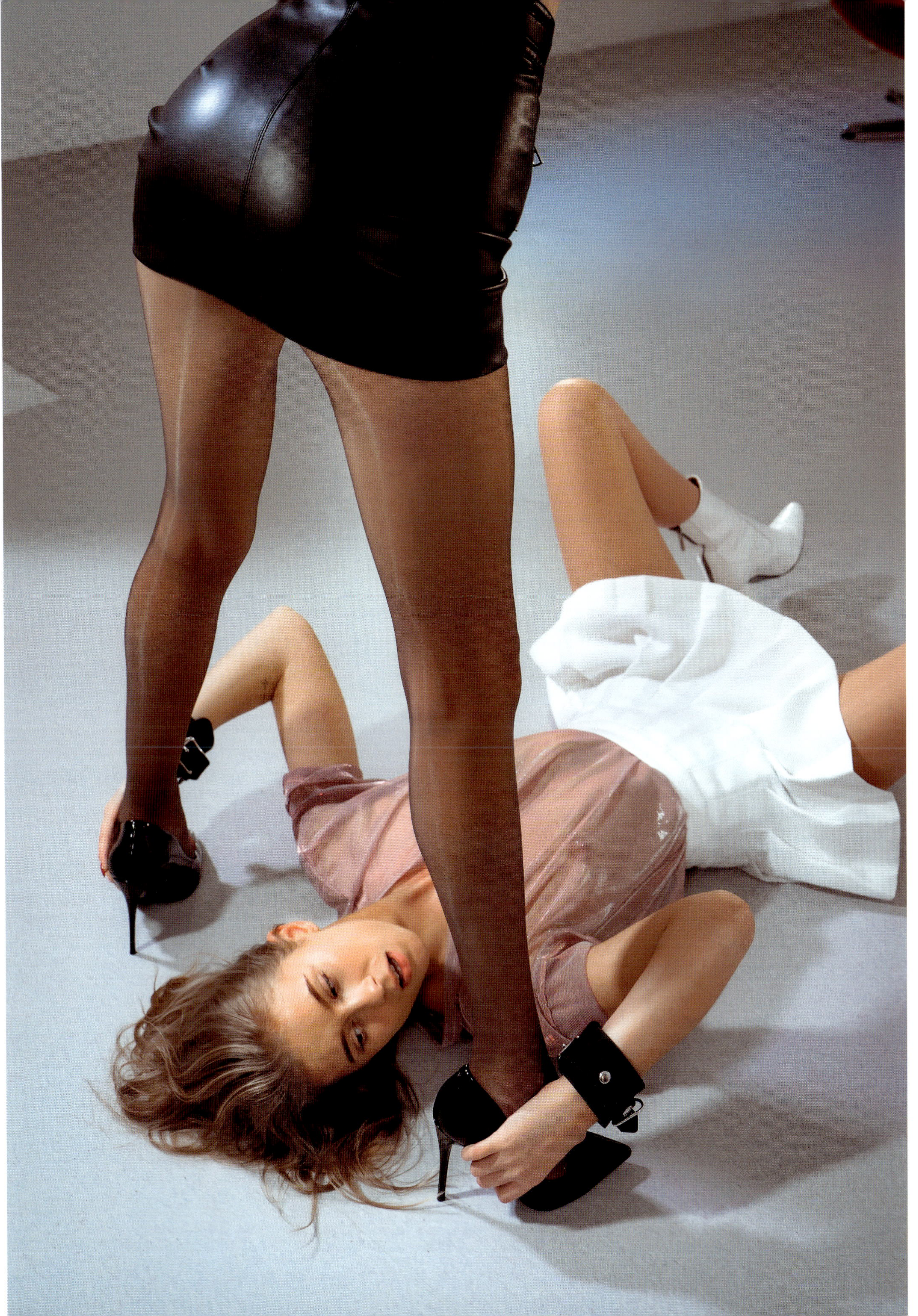

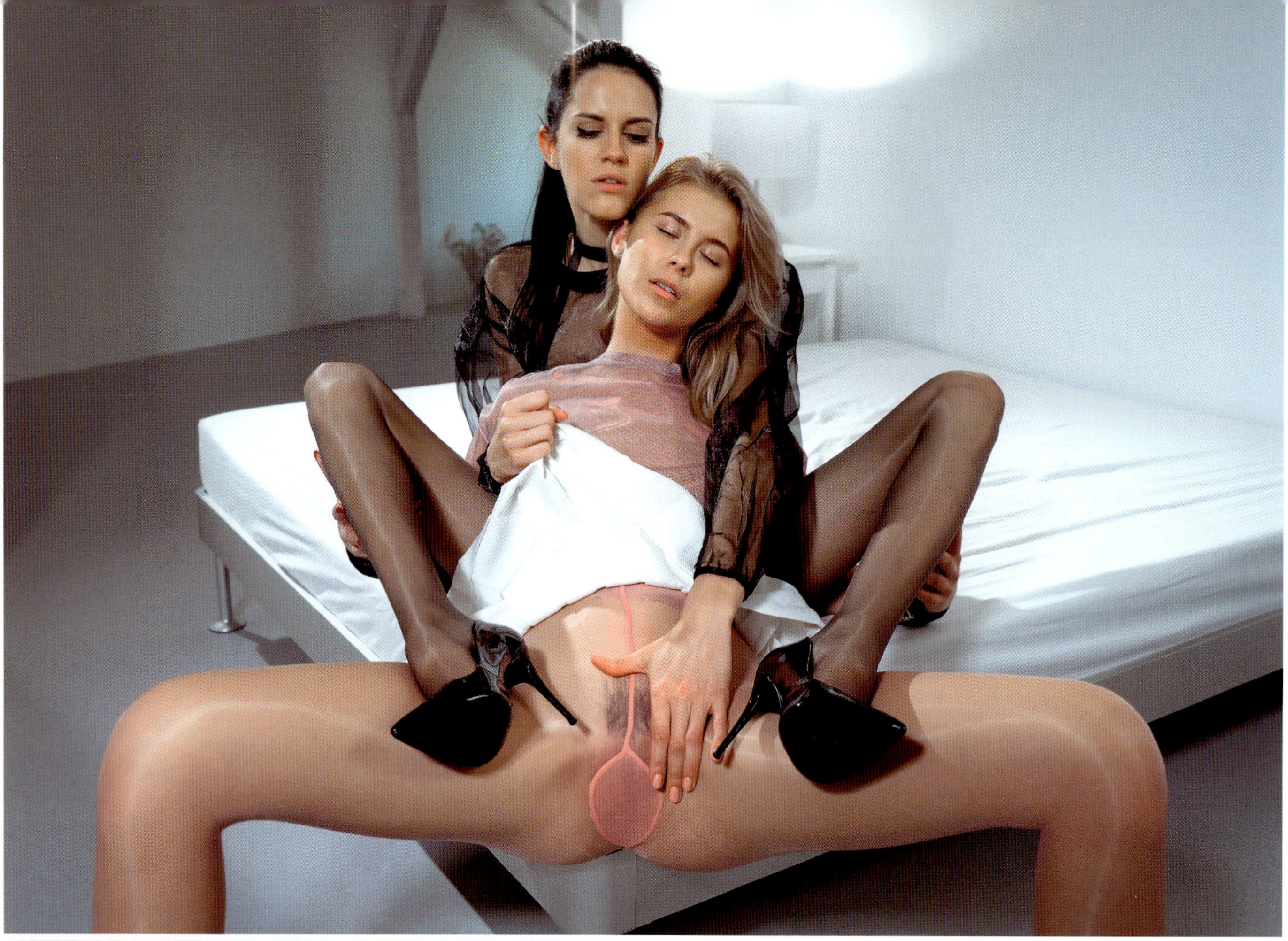

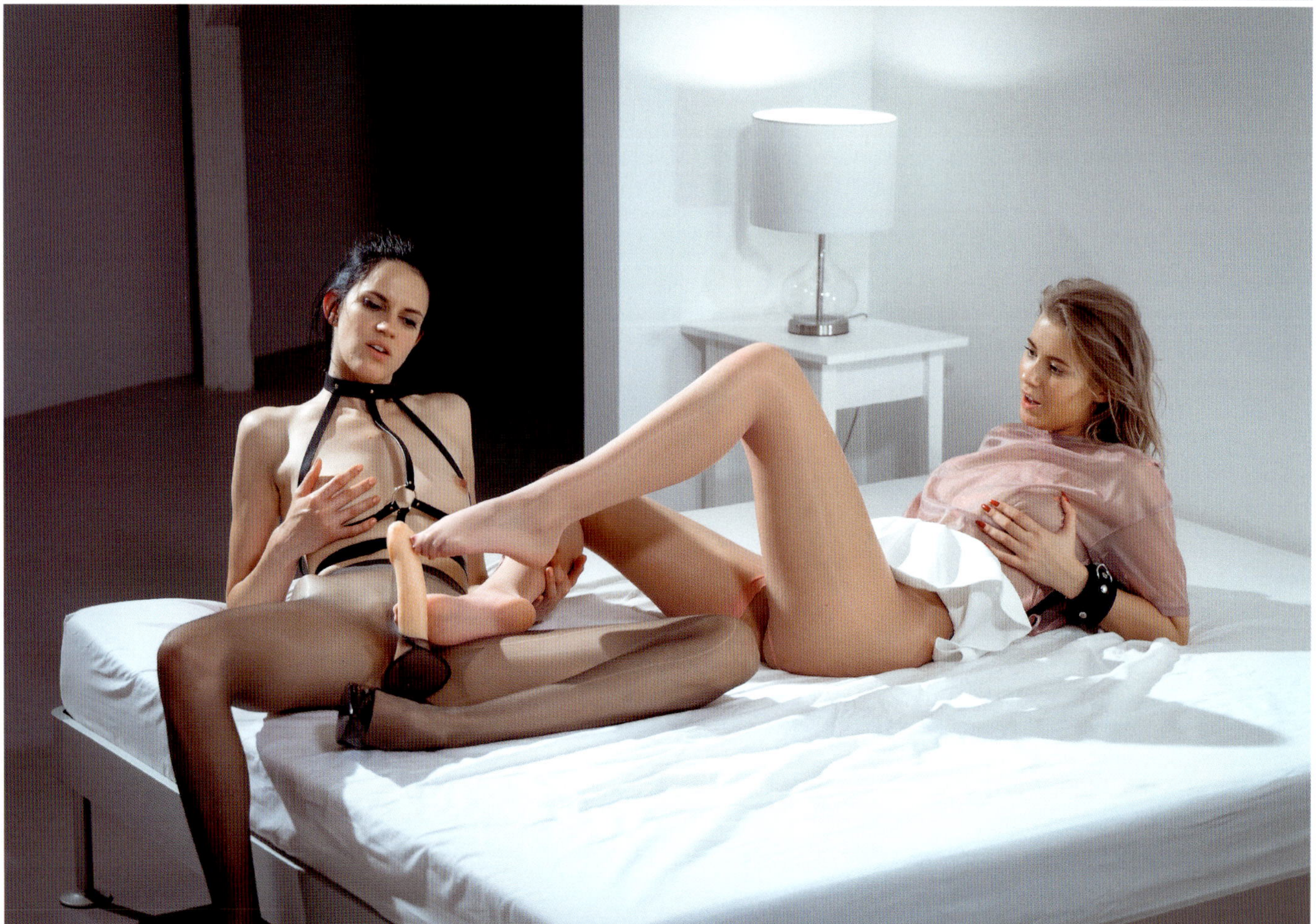

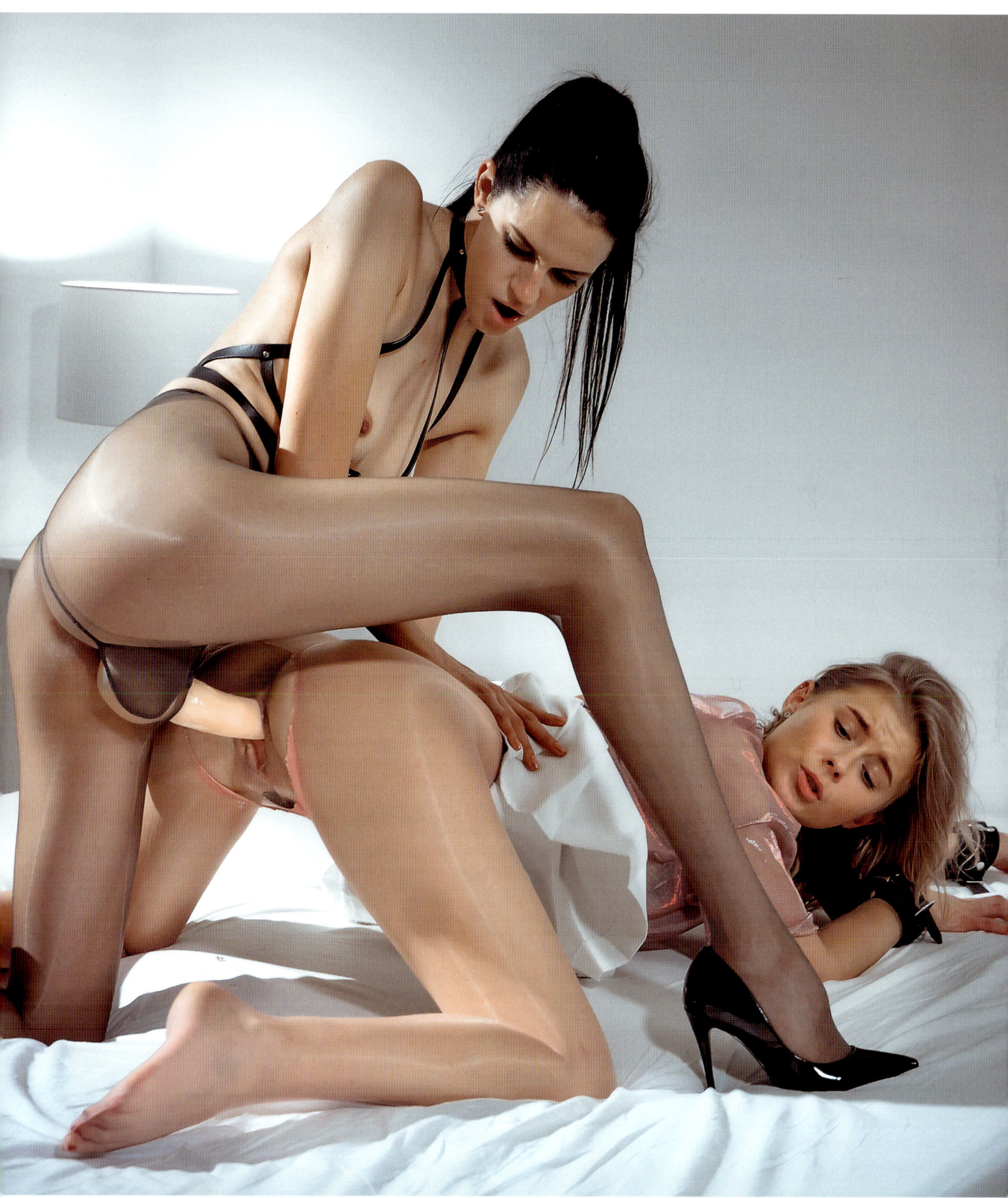

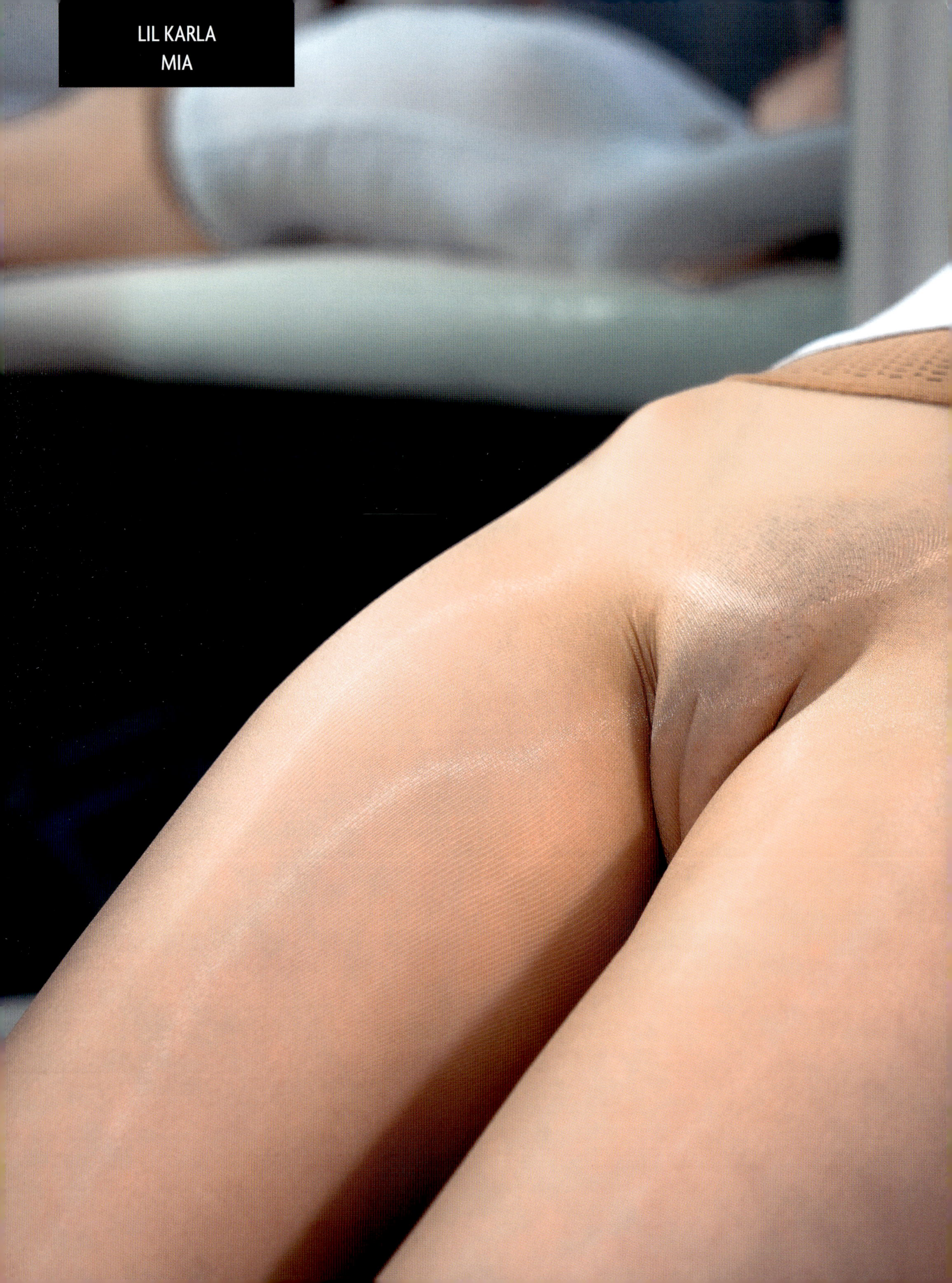
LIL KARLA
MIA

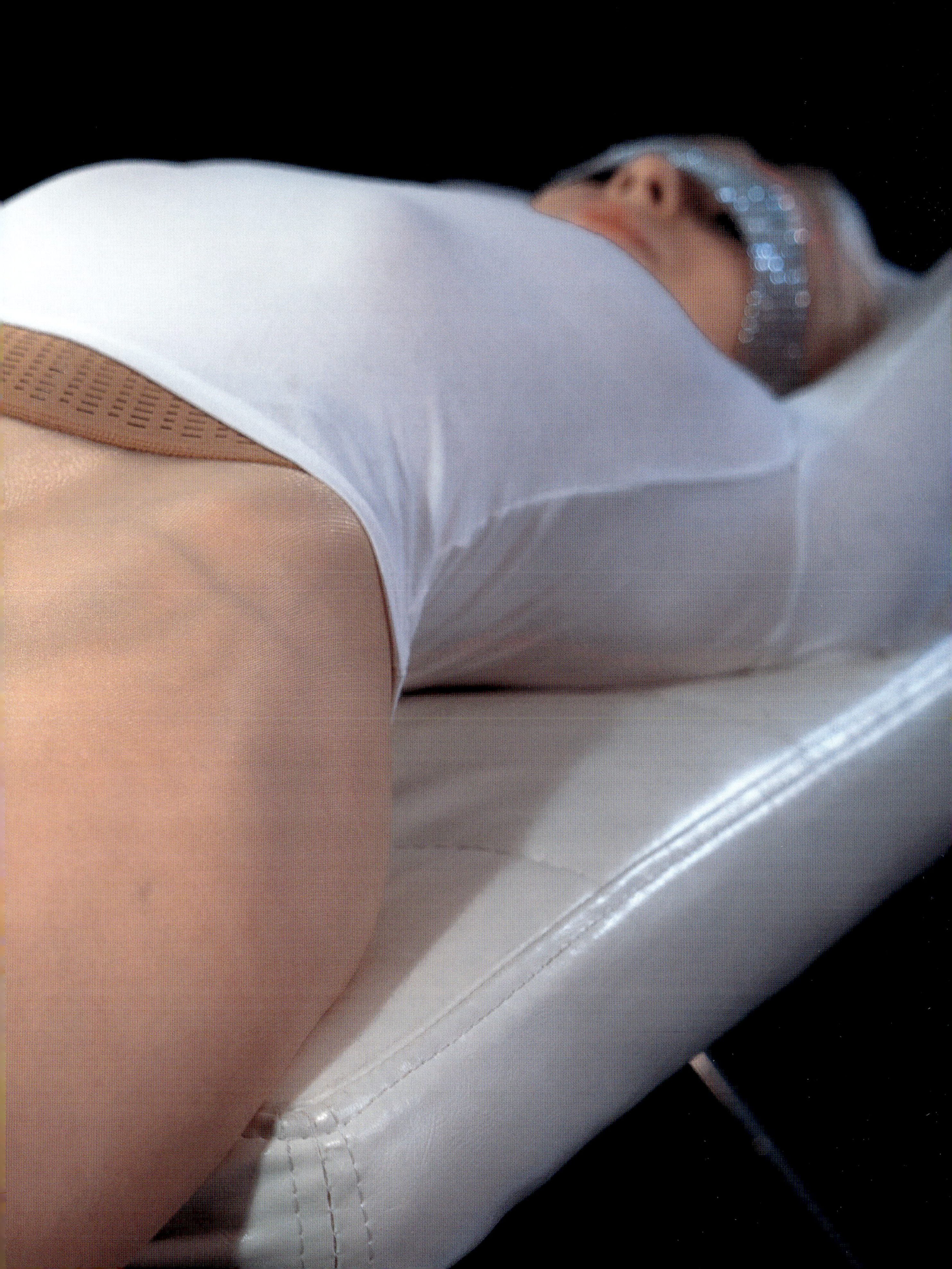

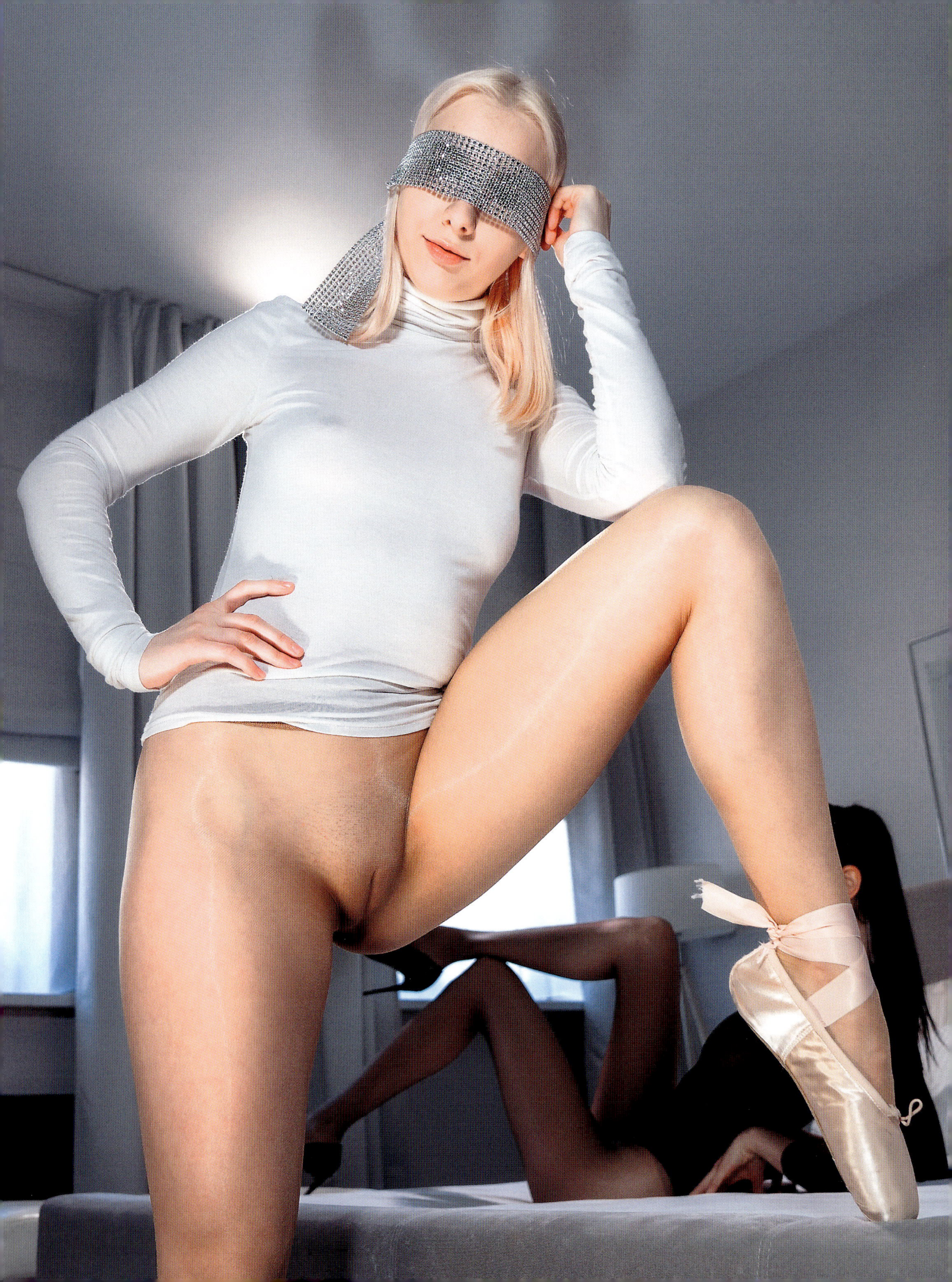

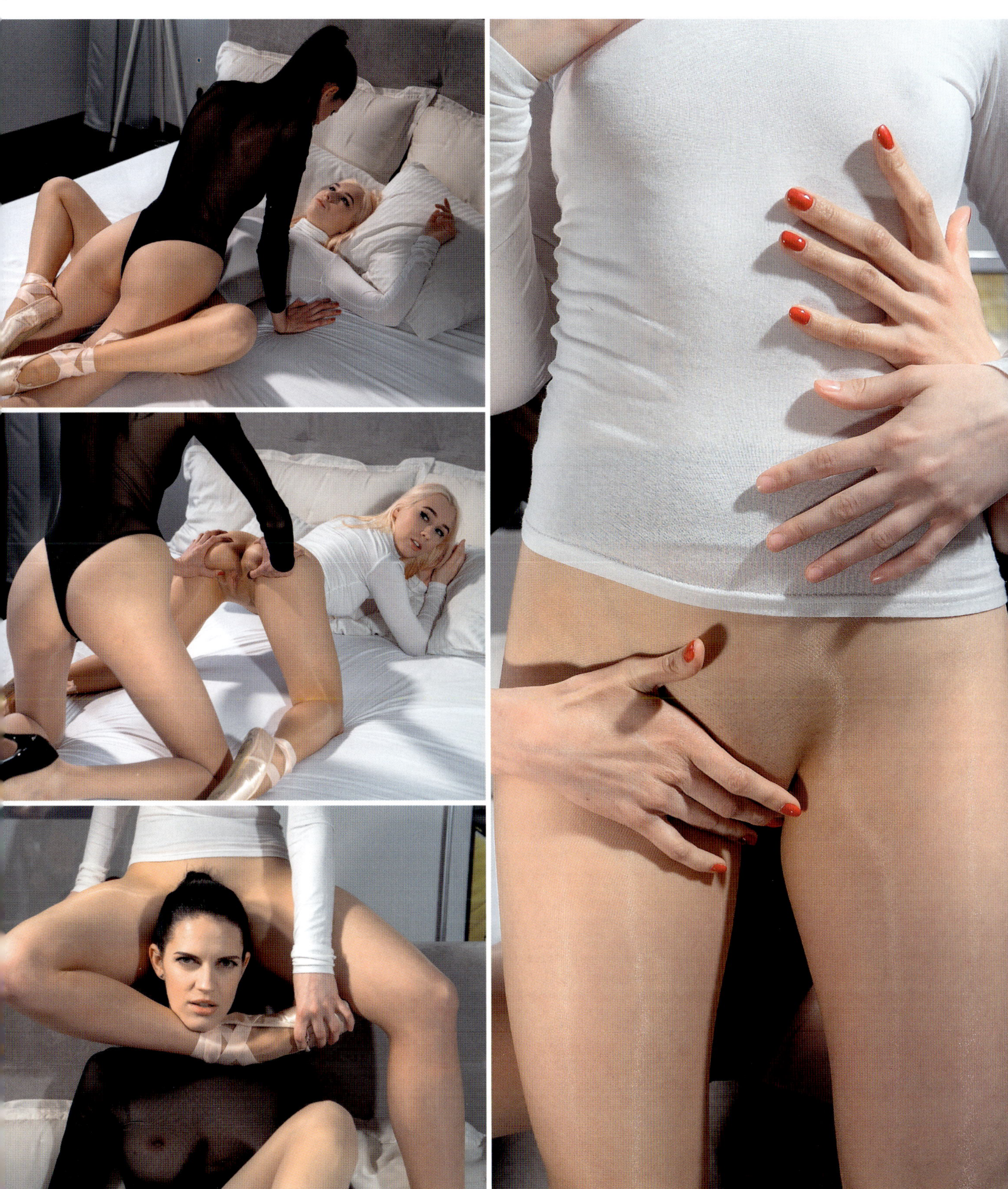

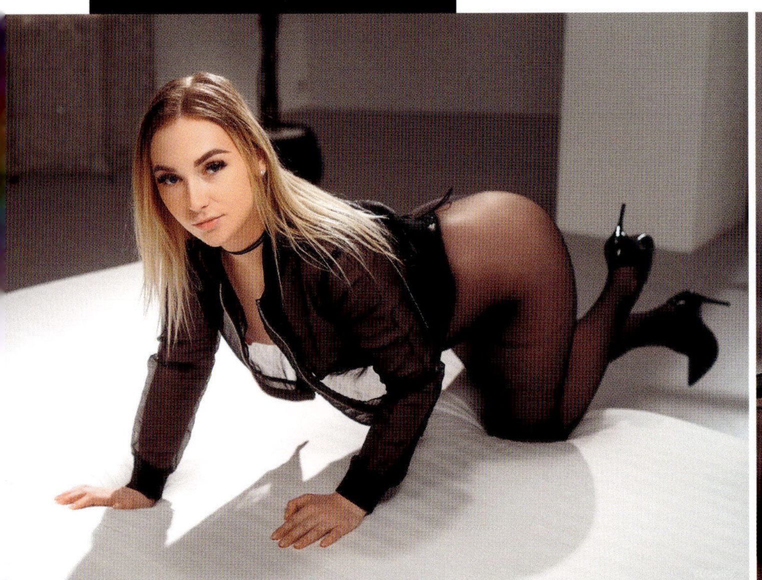

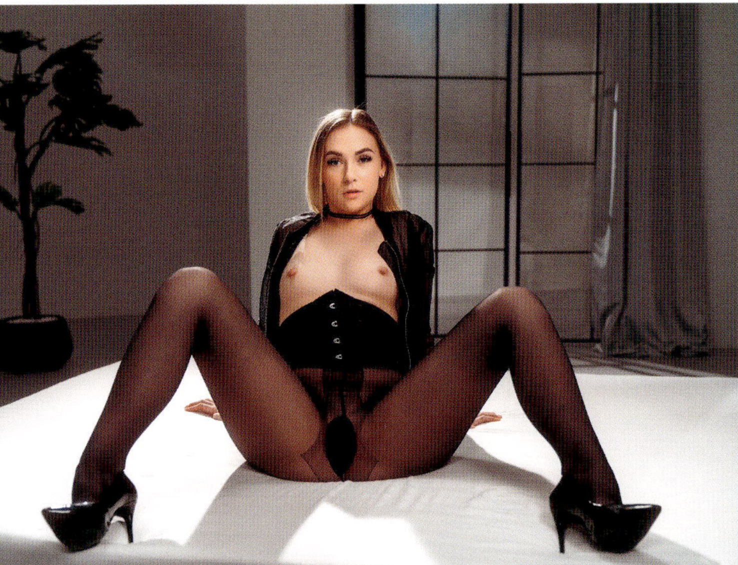

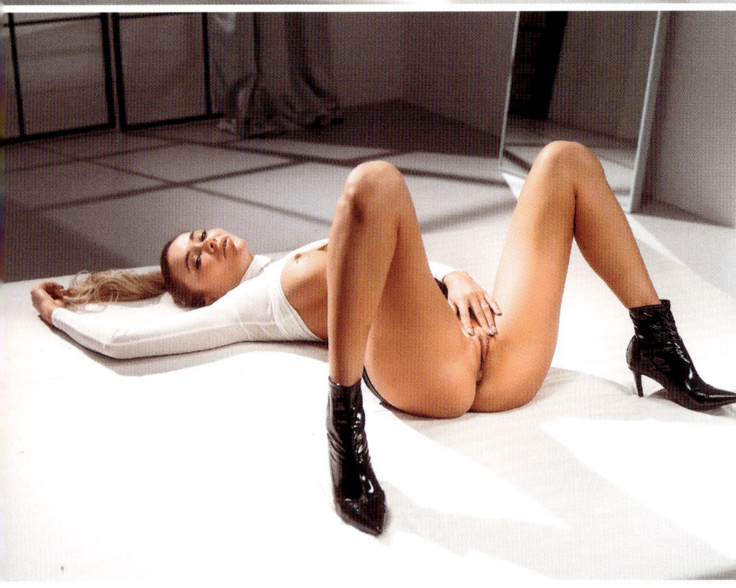

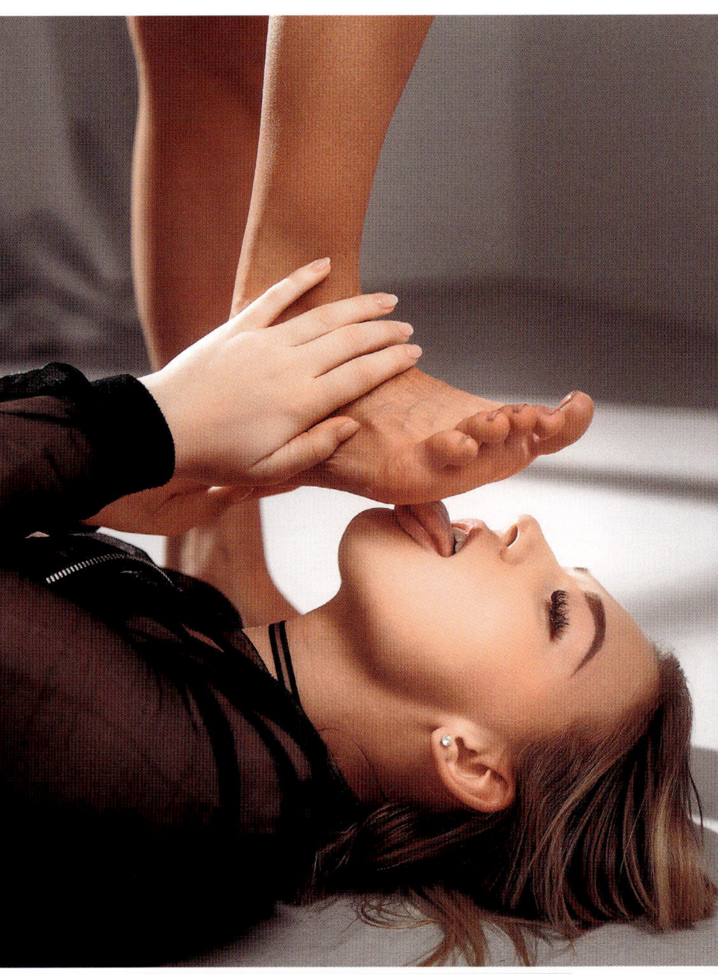

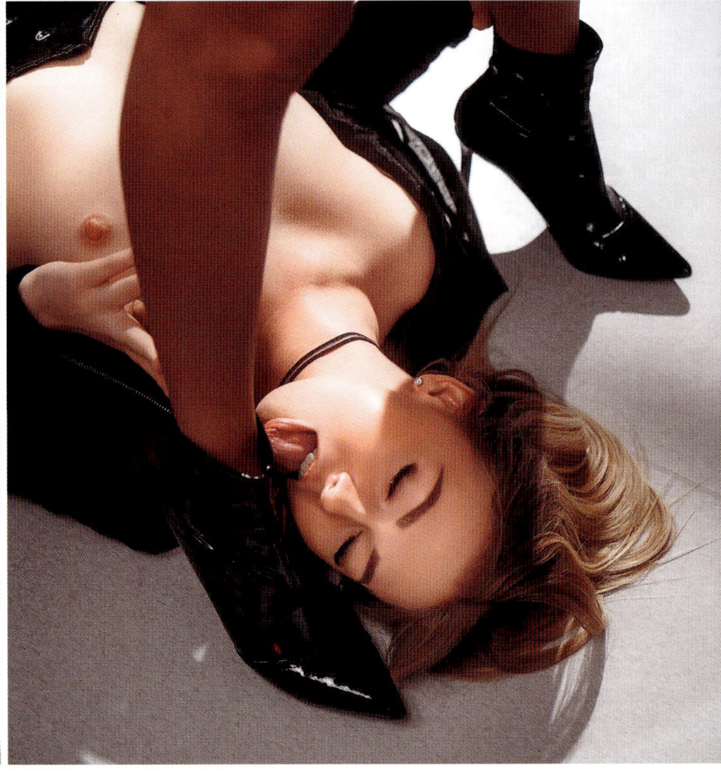

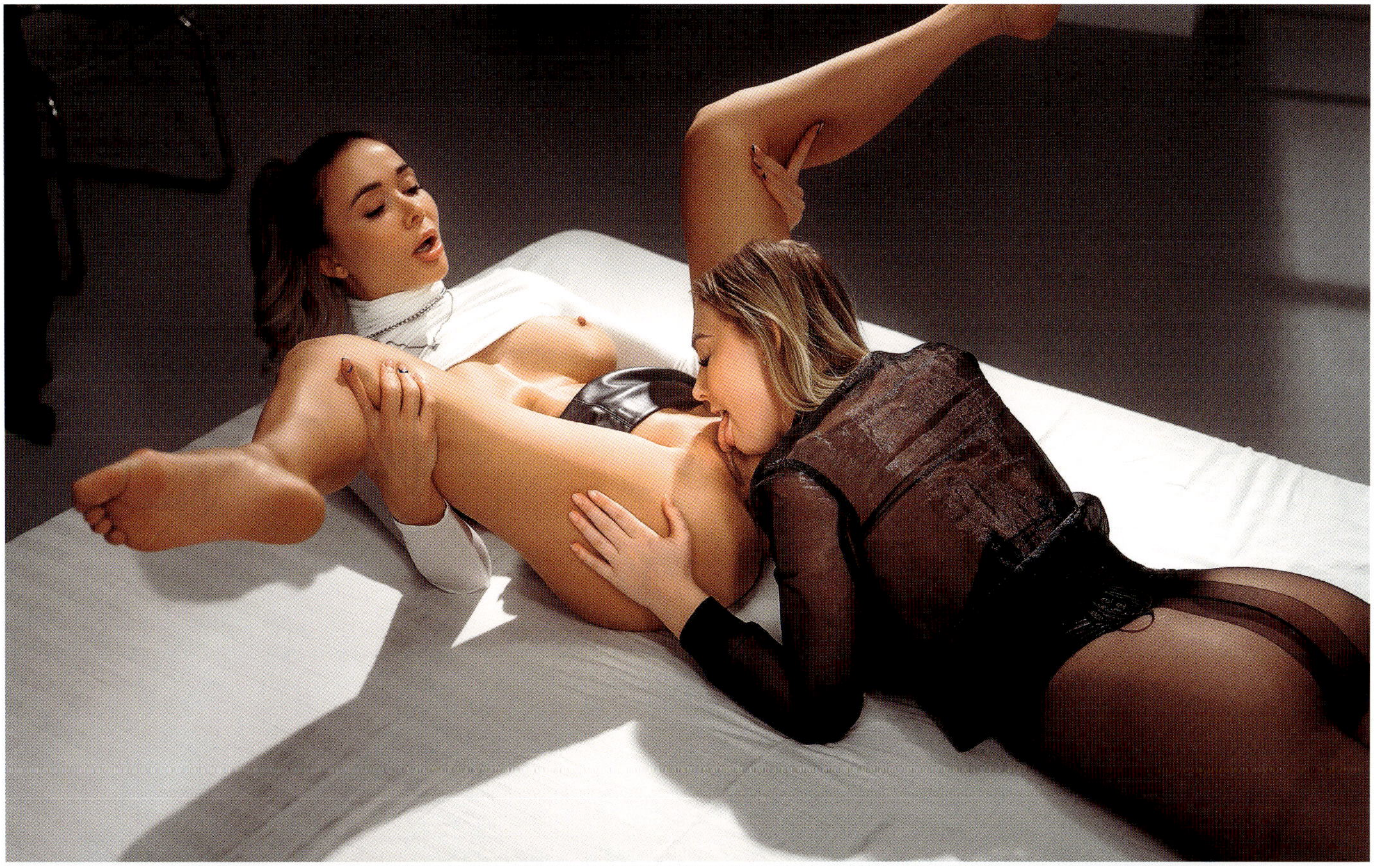

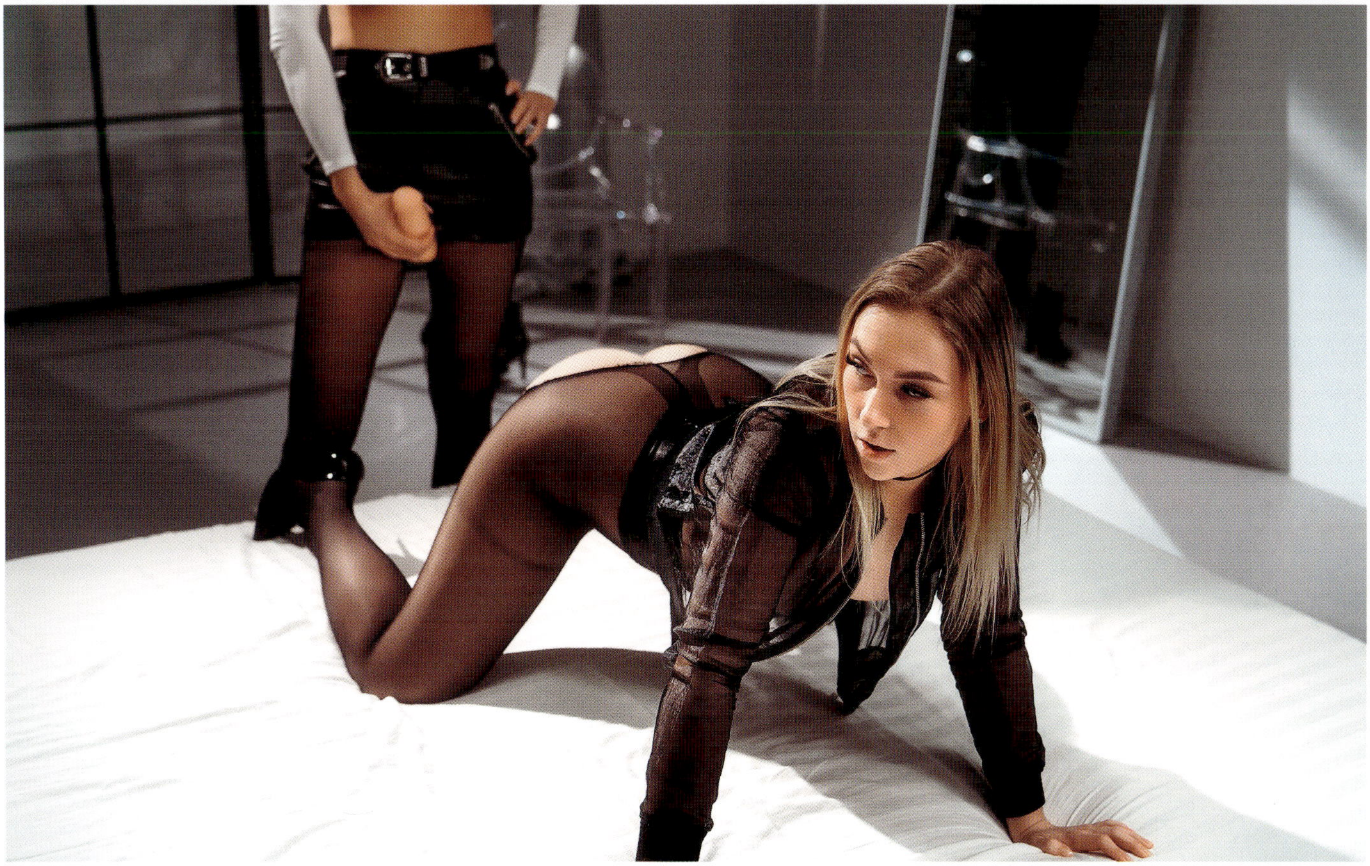

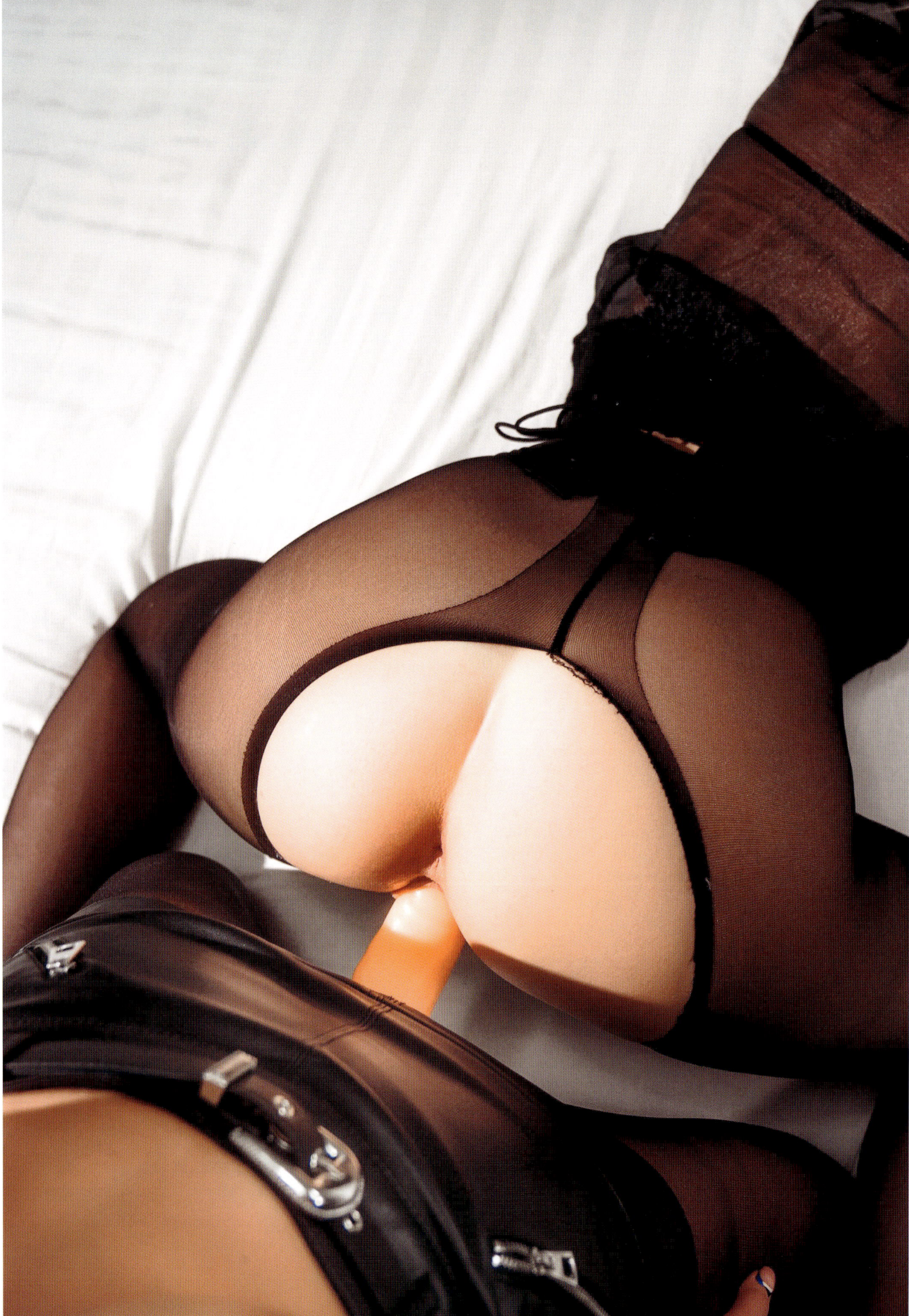

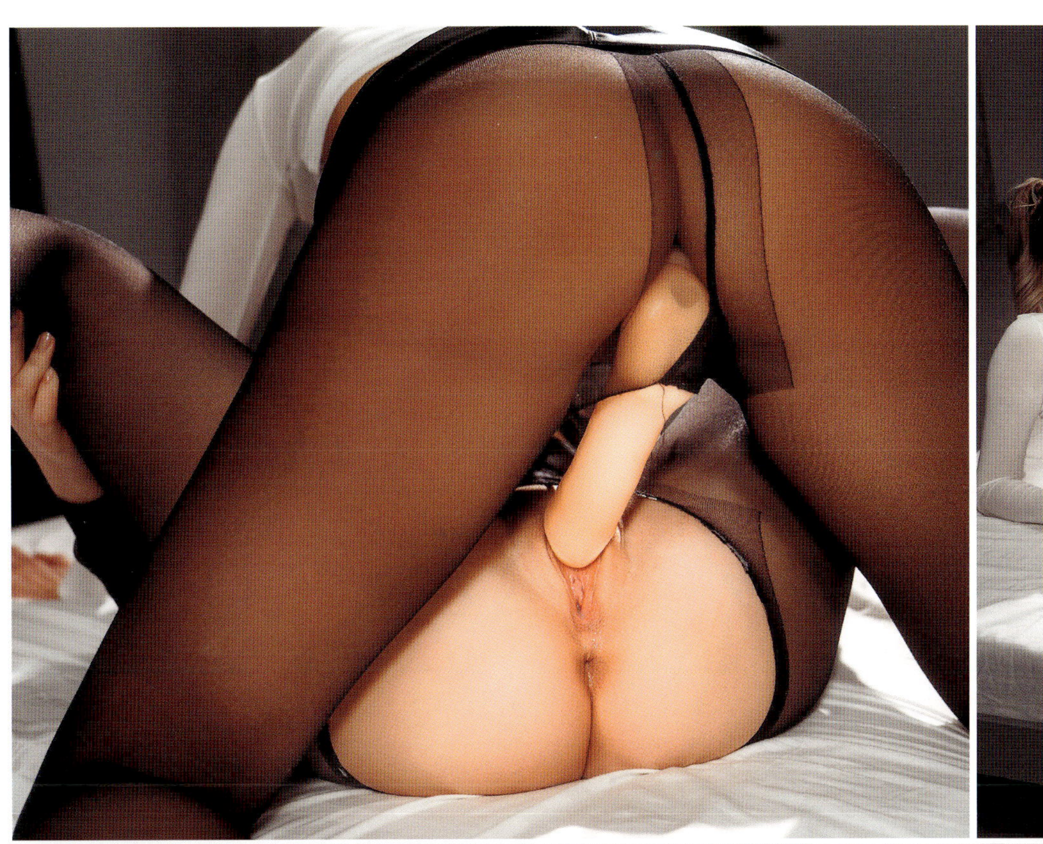
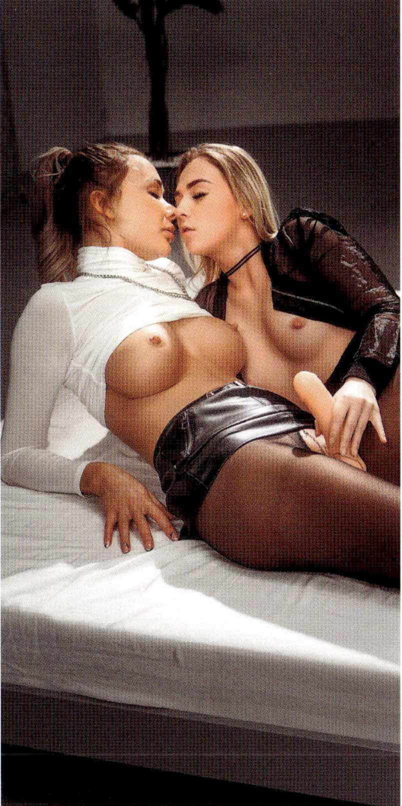

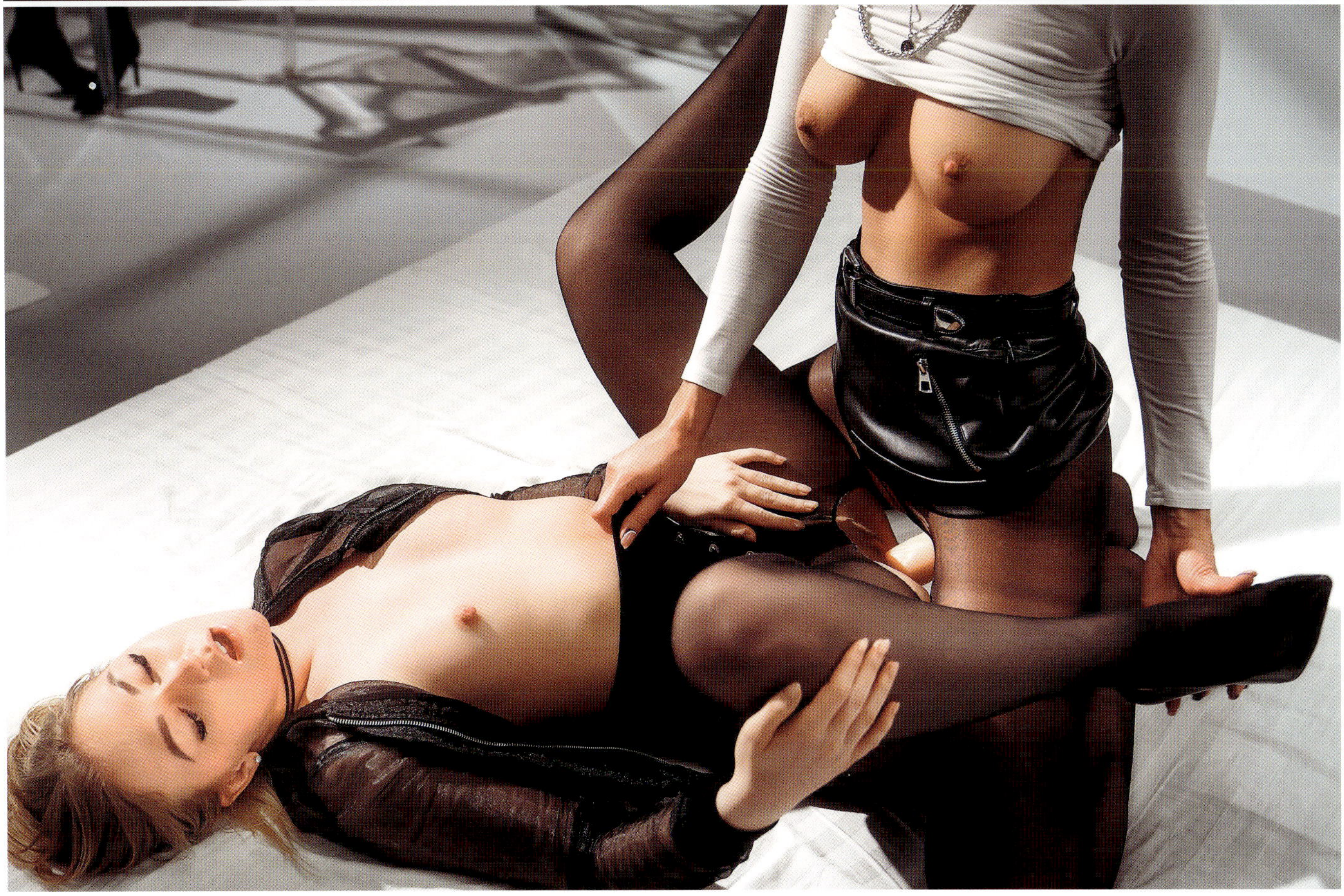

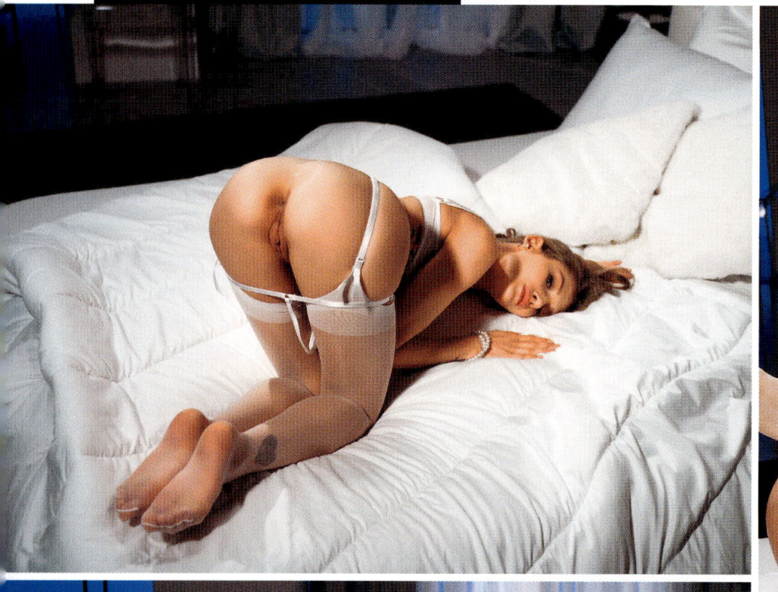

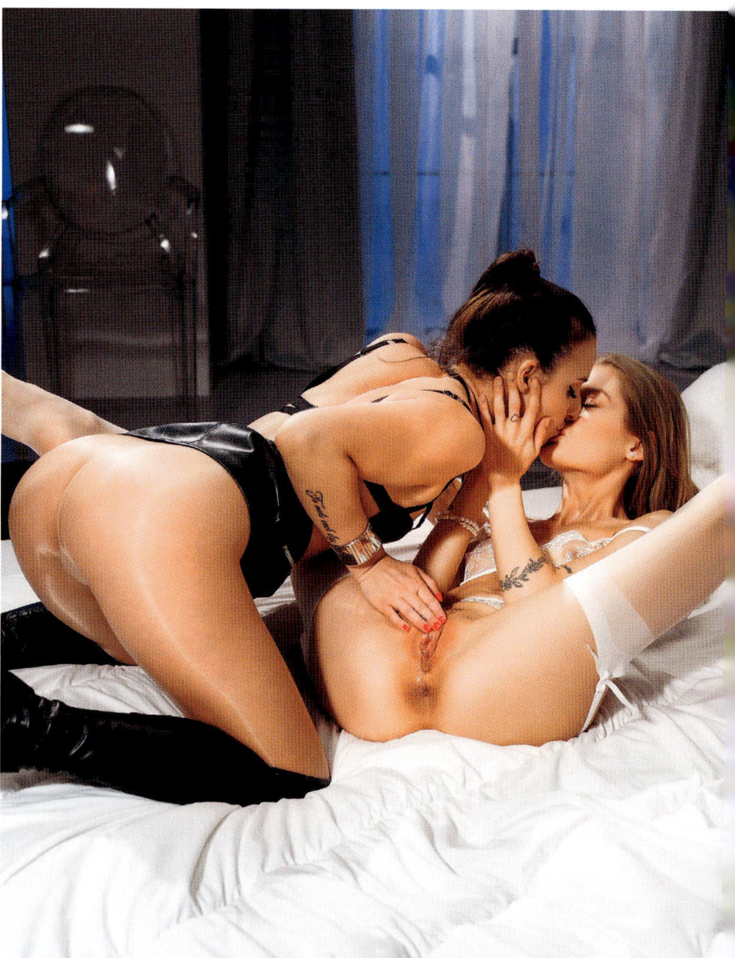

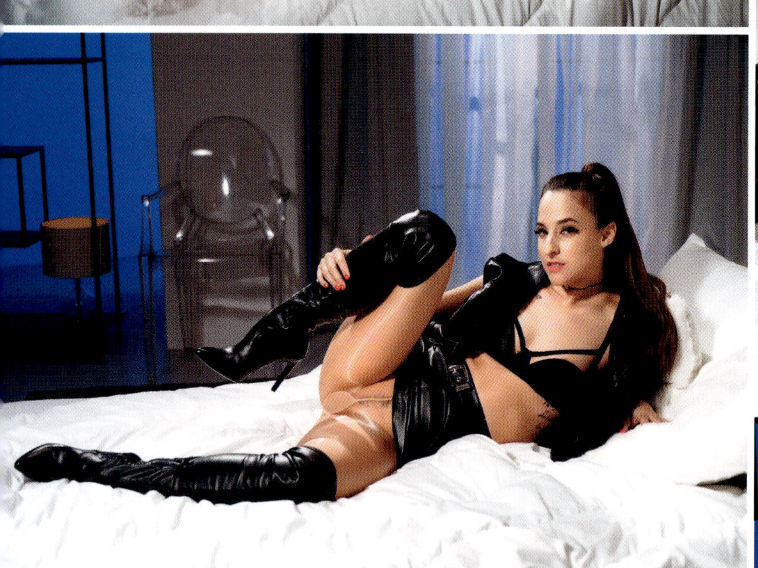

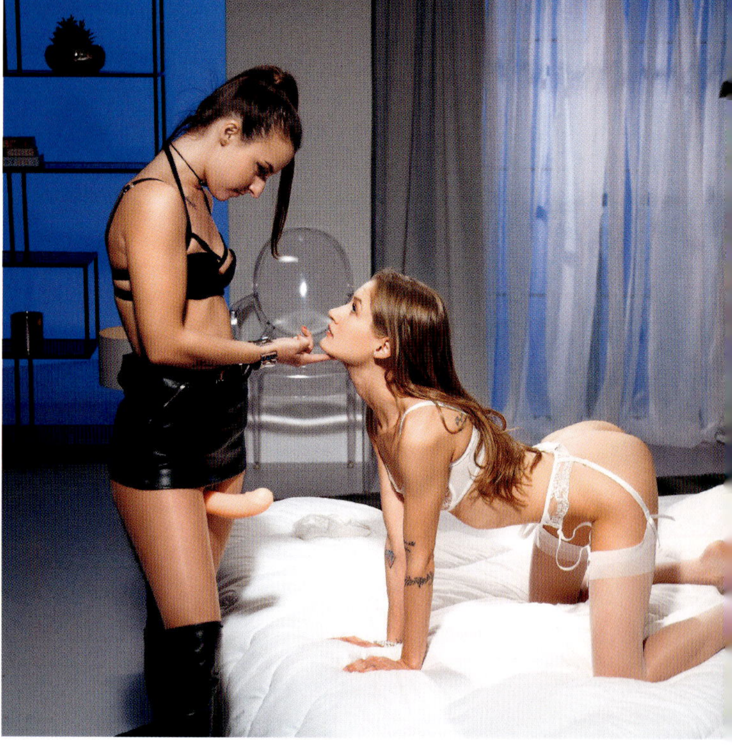

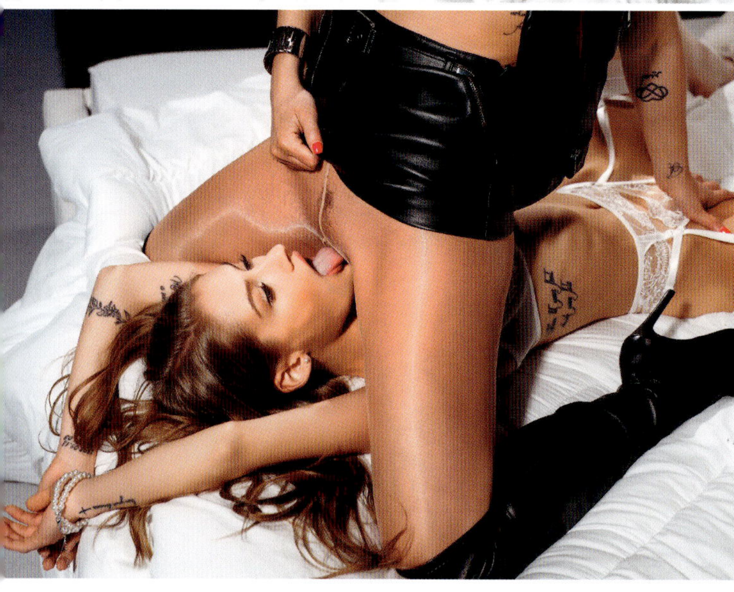

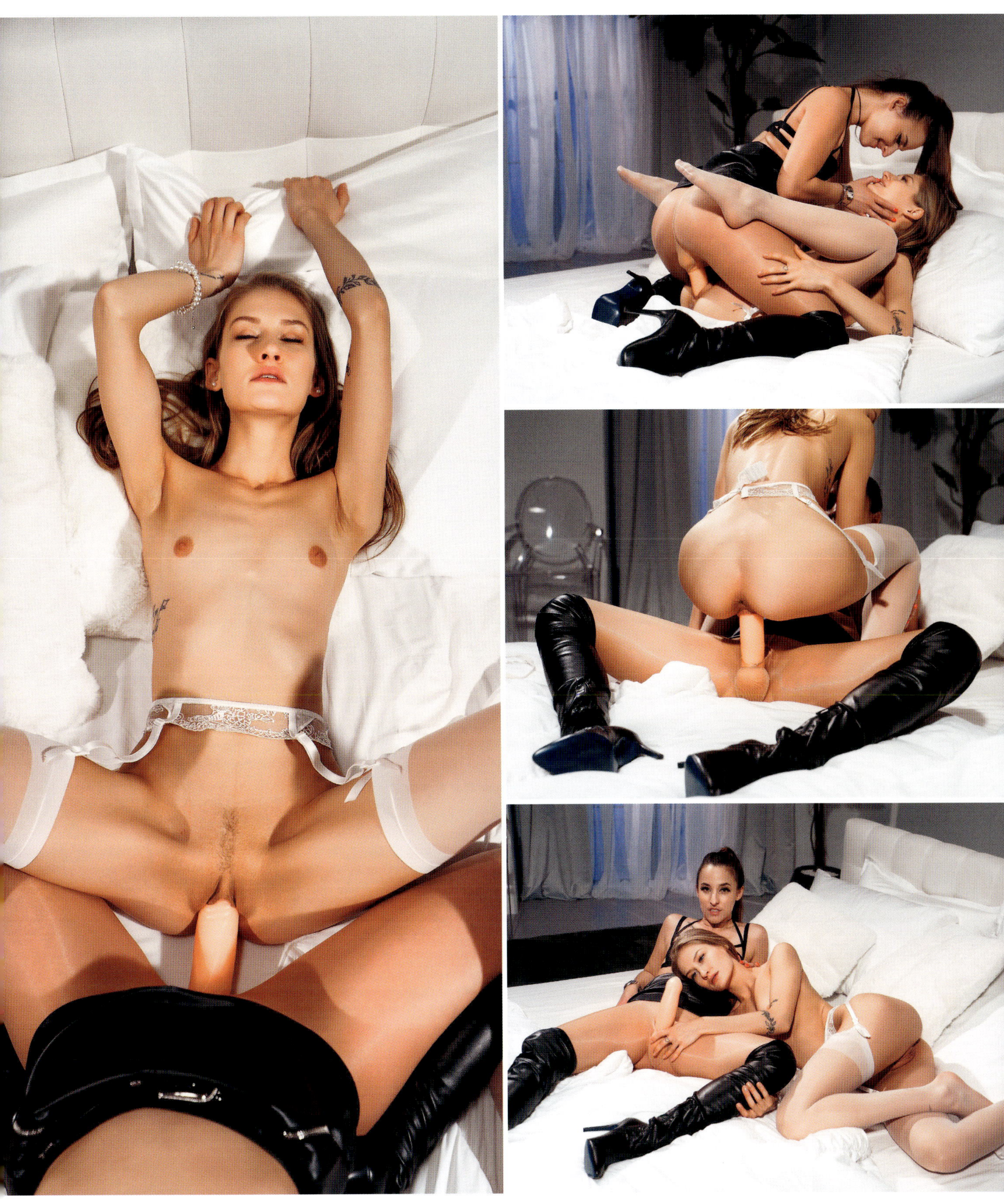

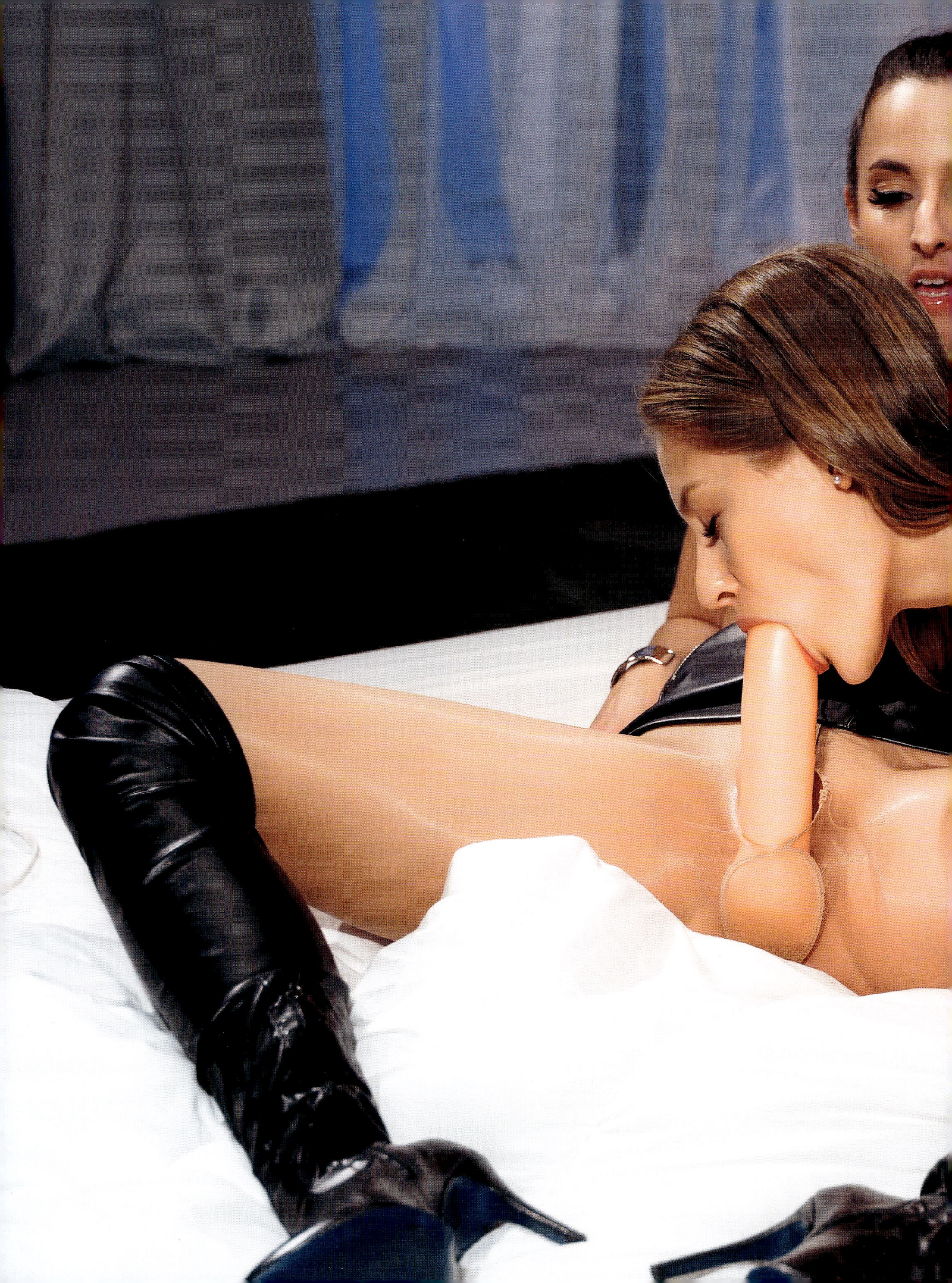

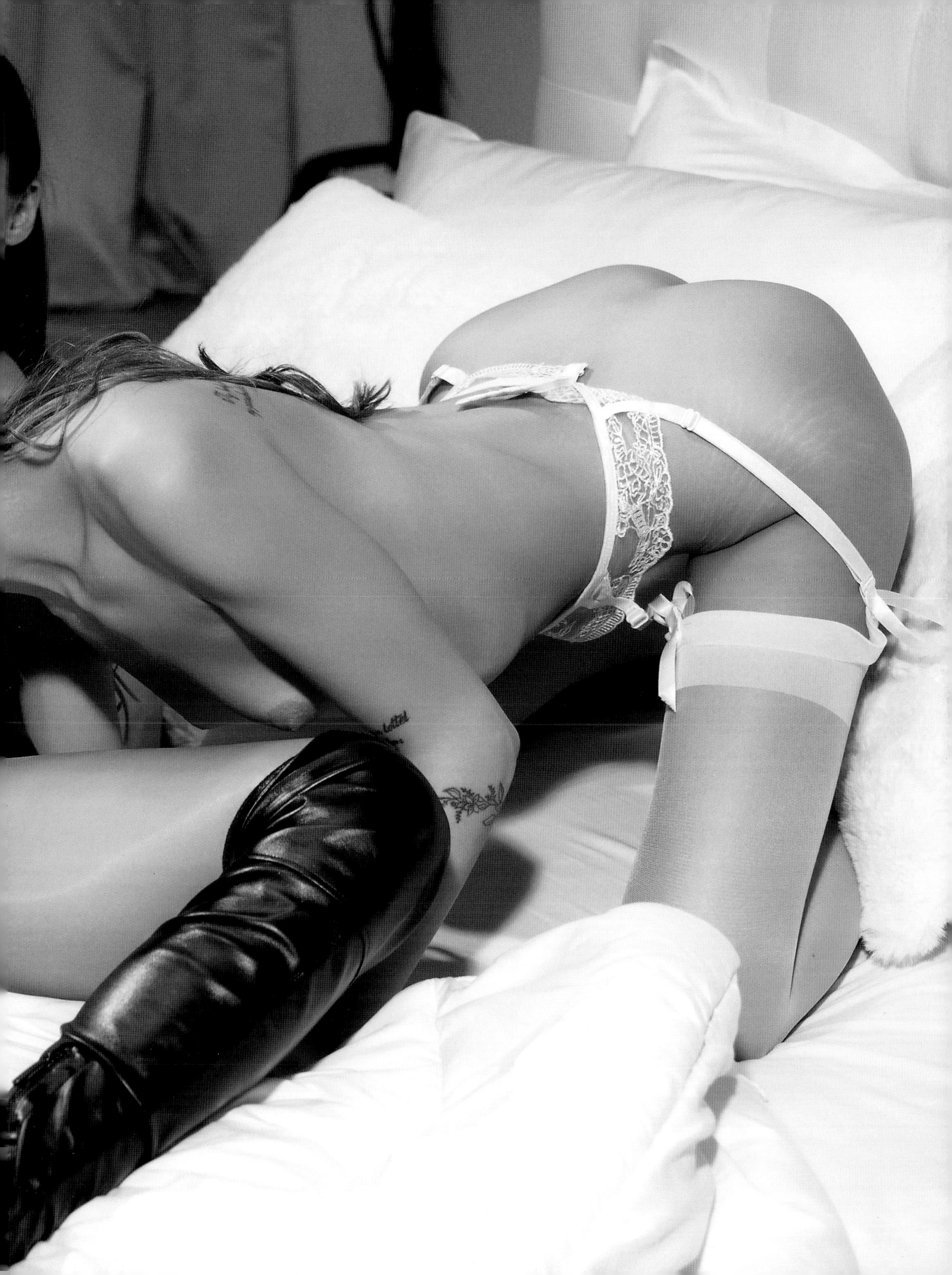

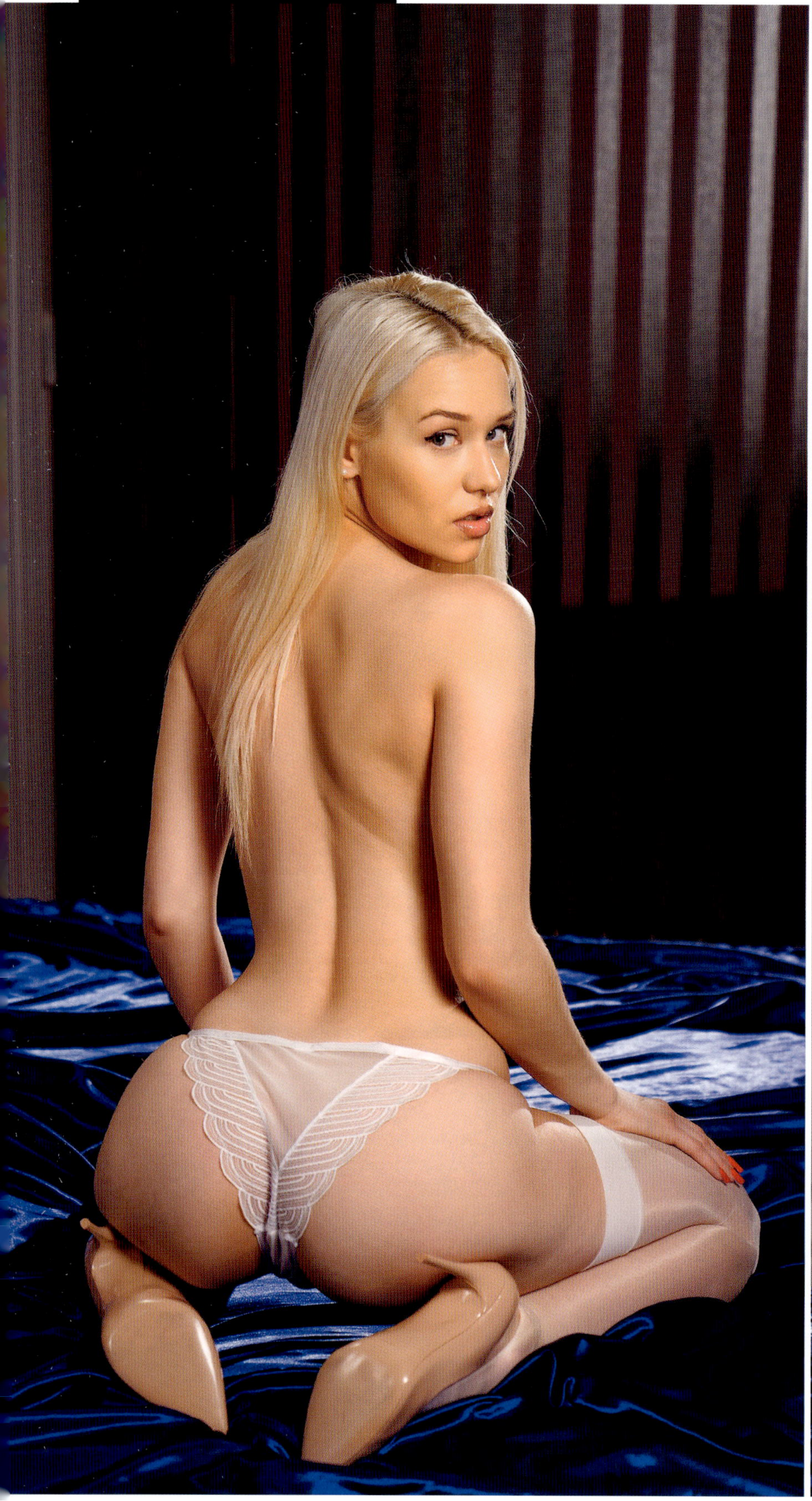

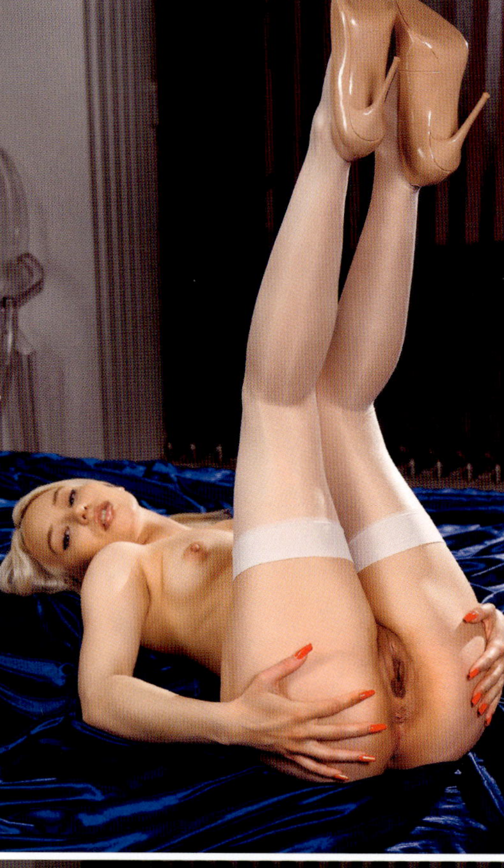

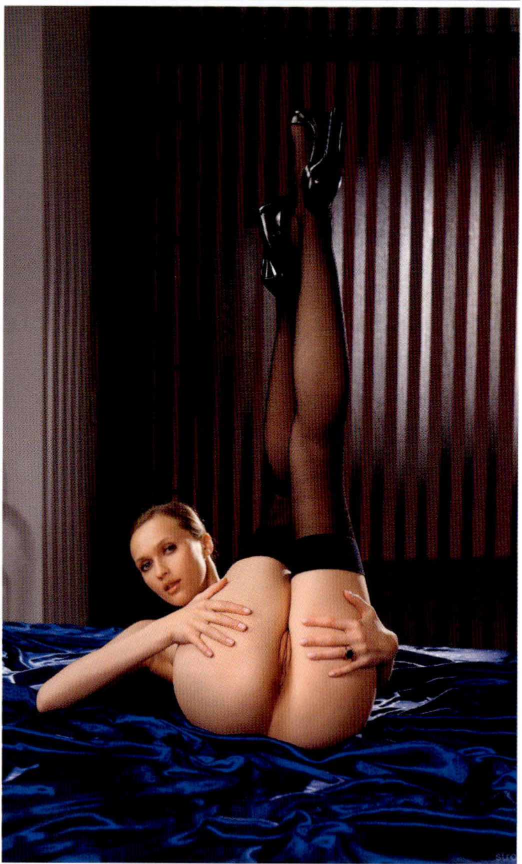

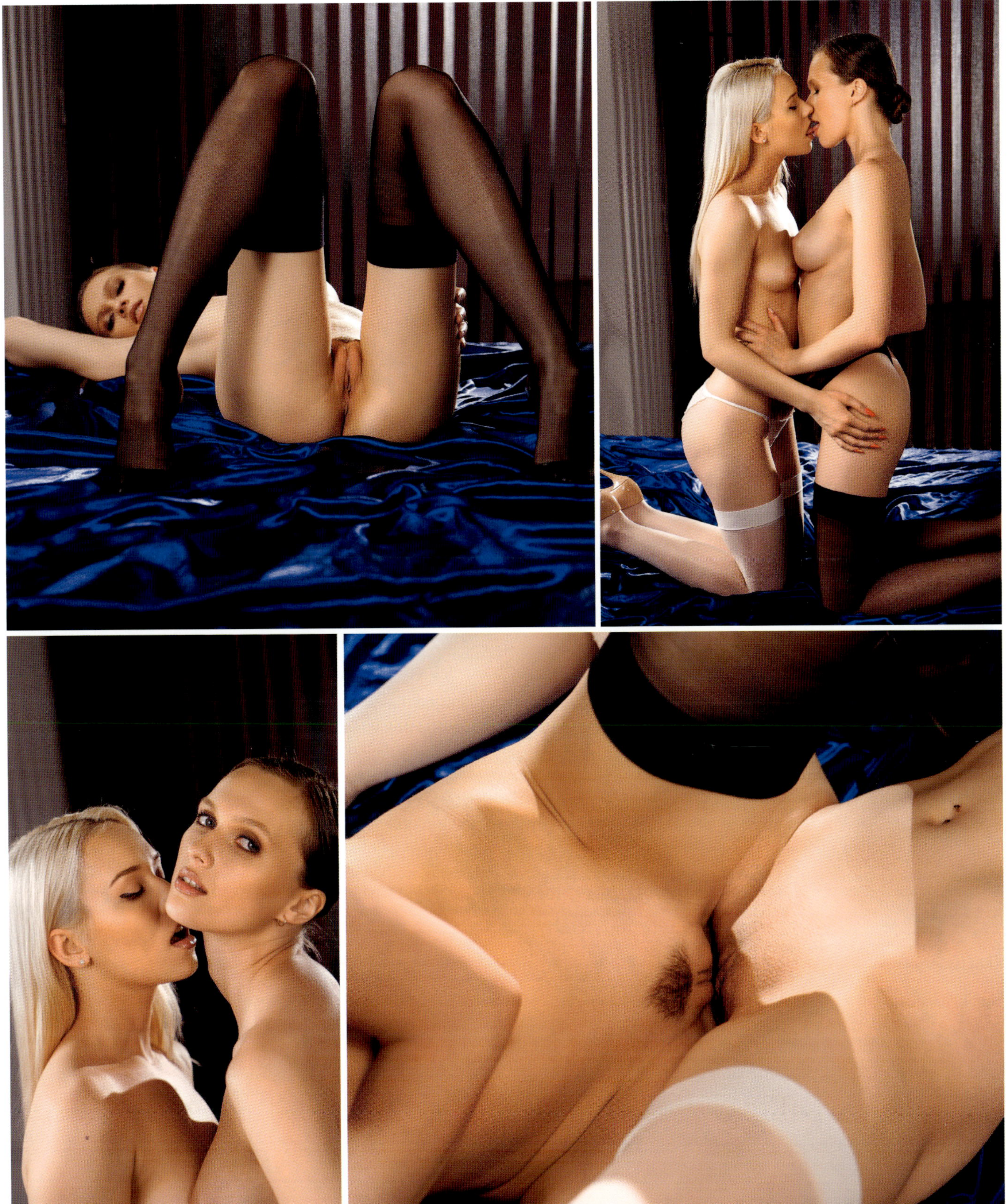

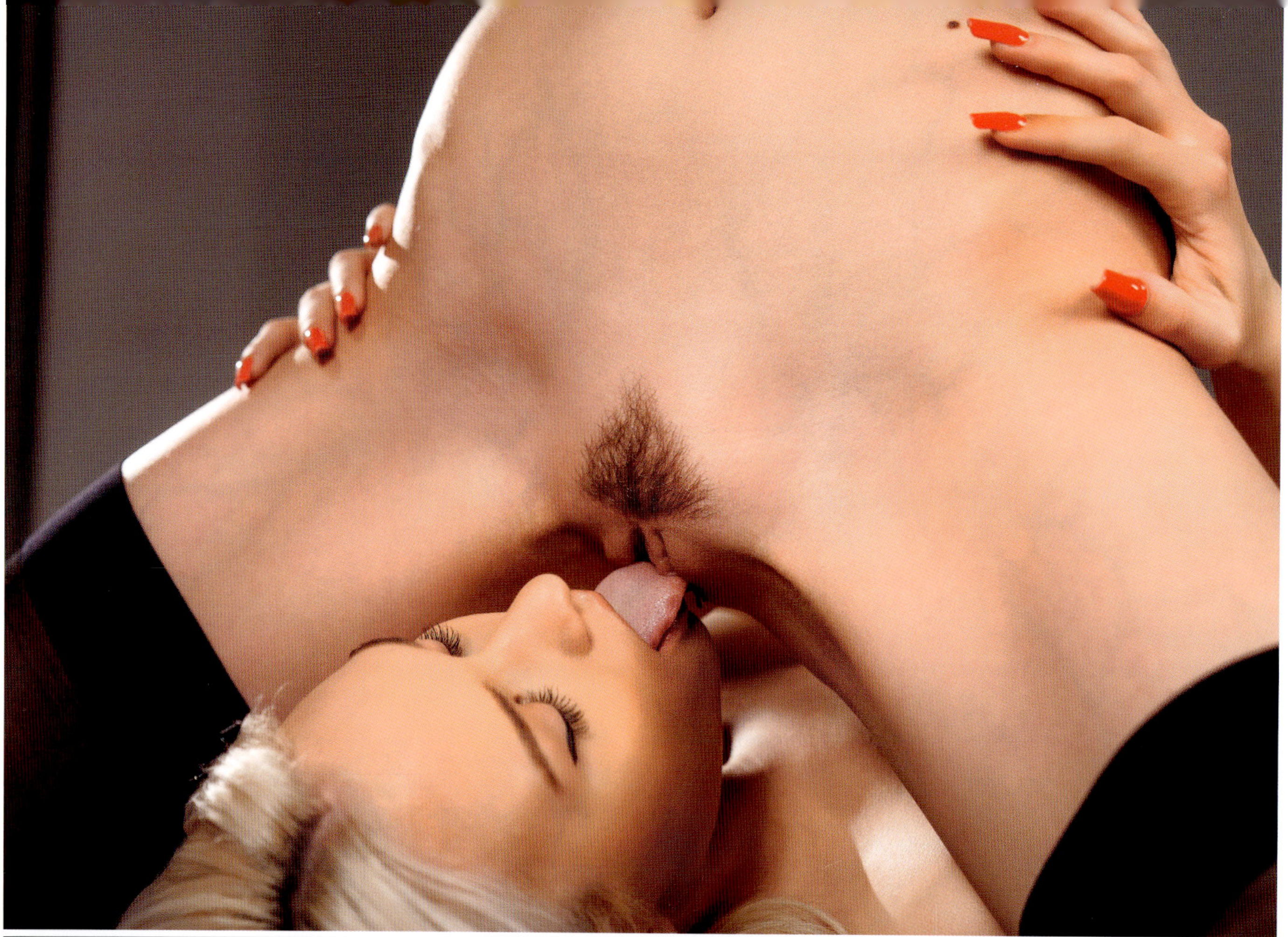

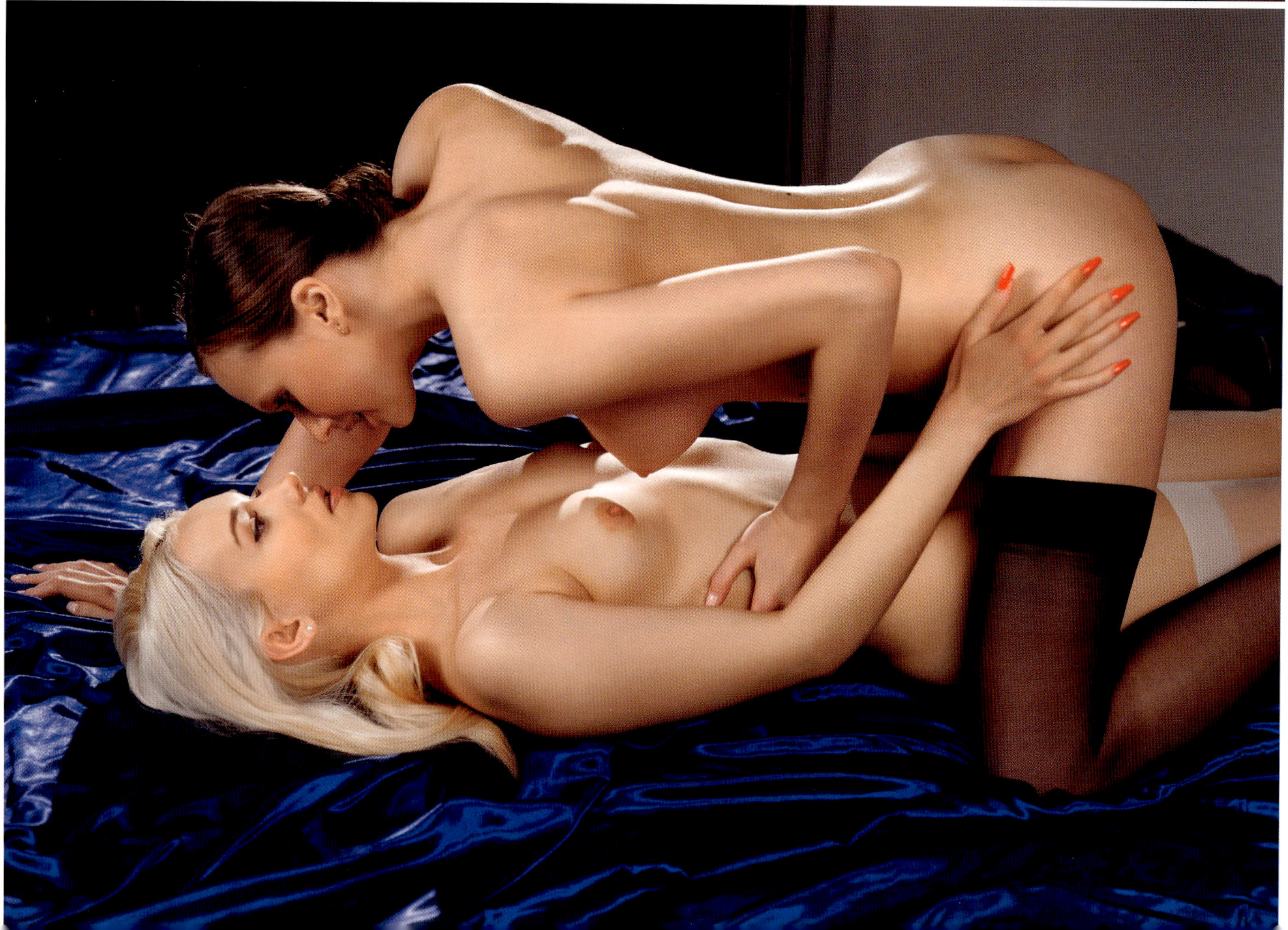

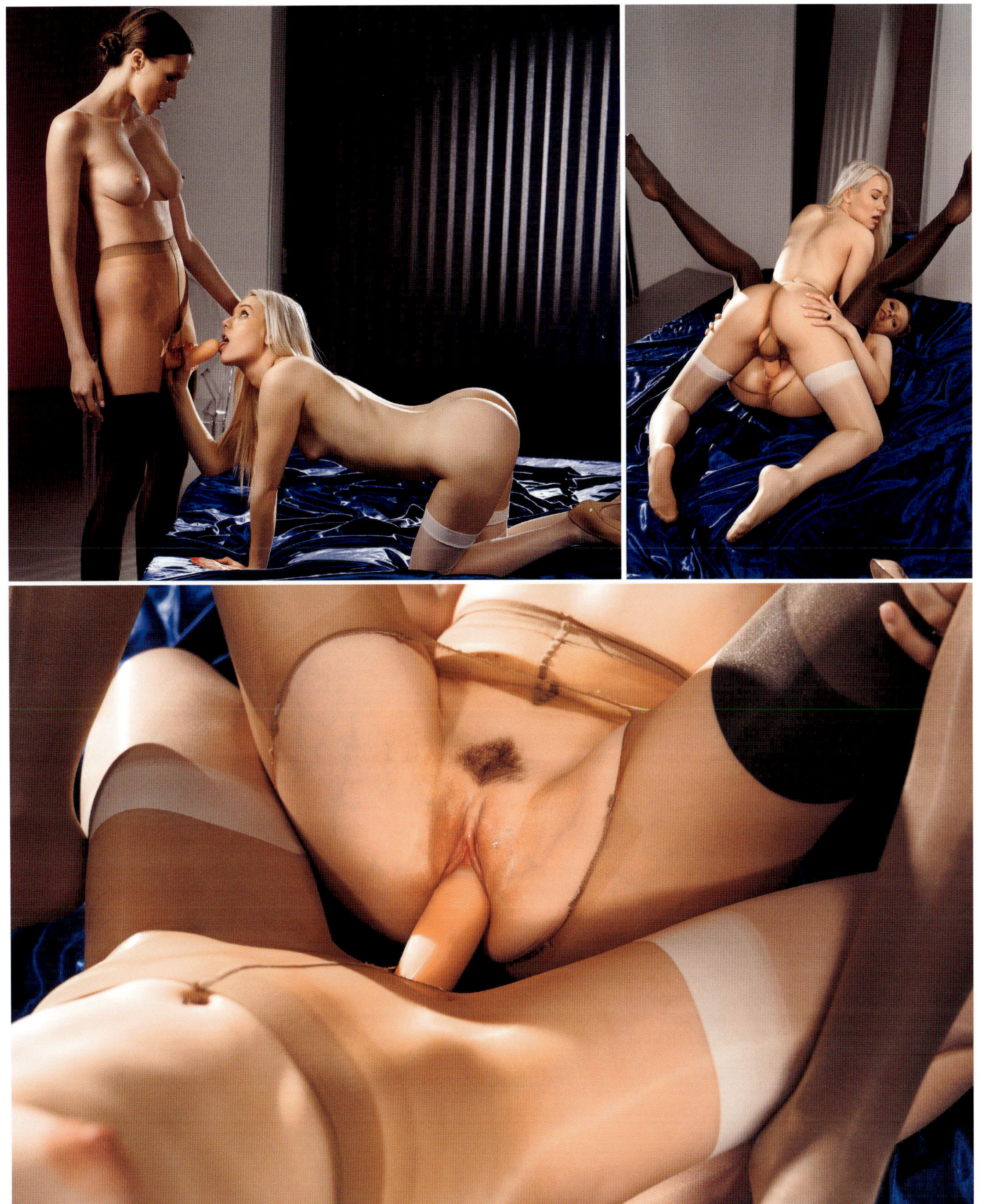

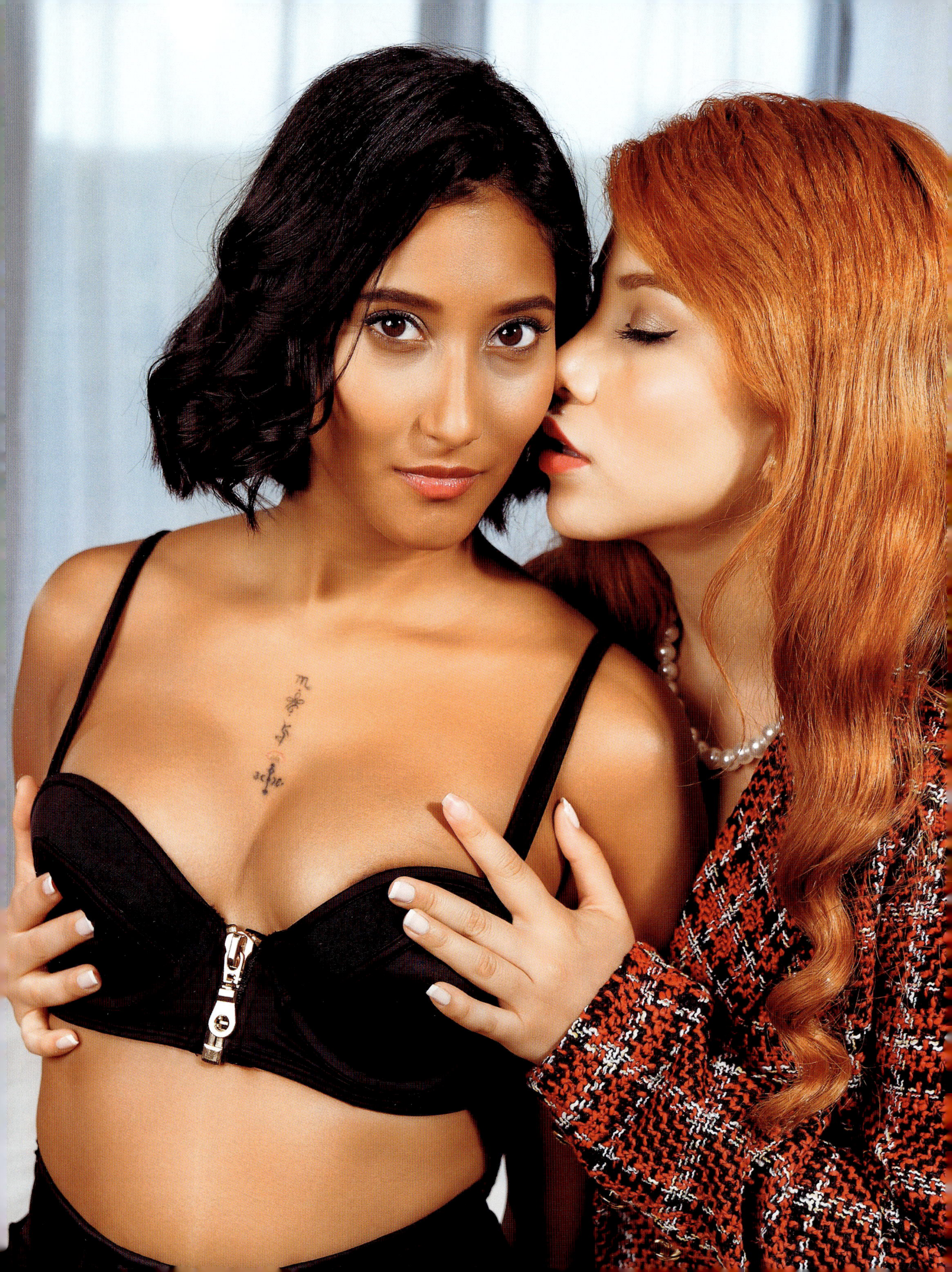

ALIKA PENAGOS
MARINA GOLD

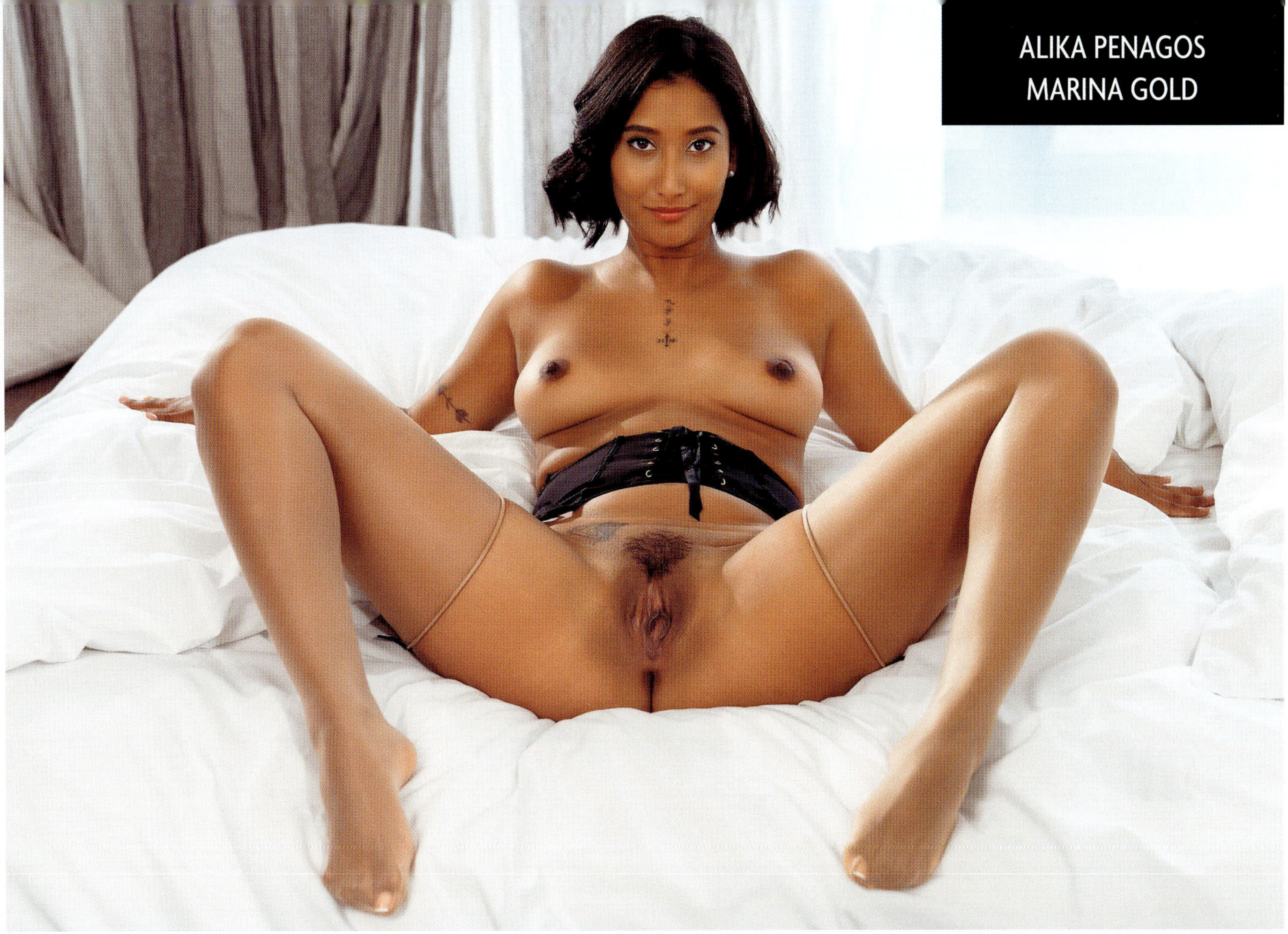

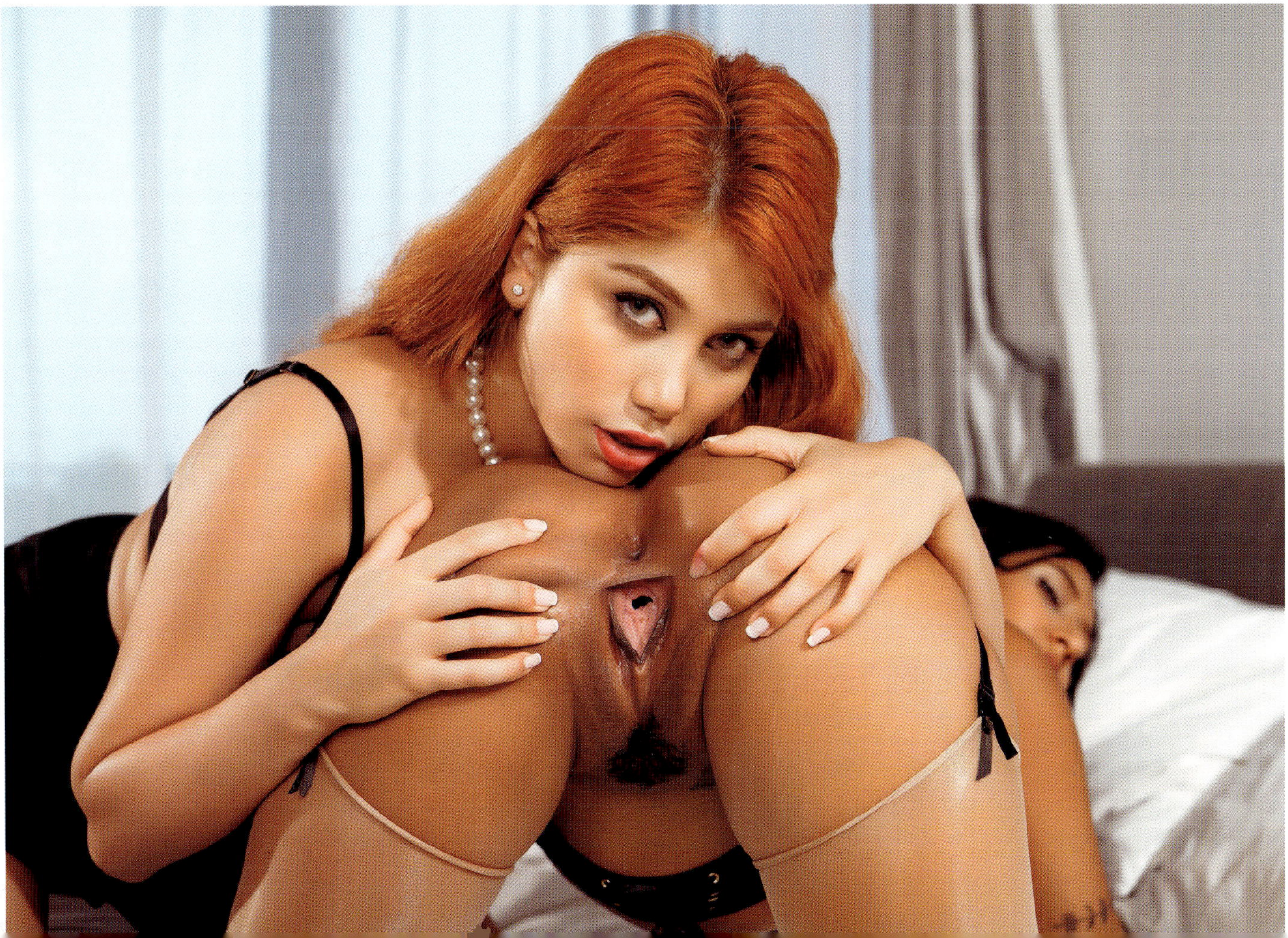

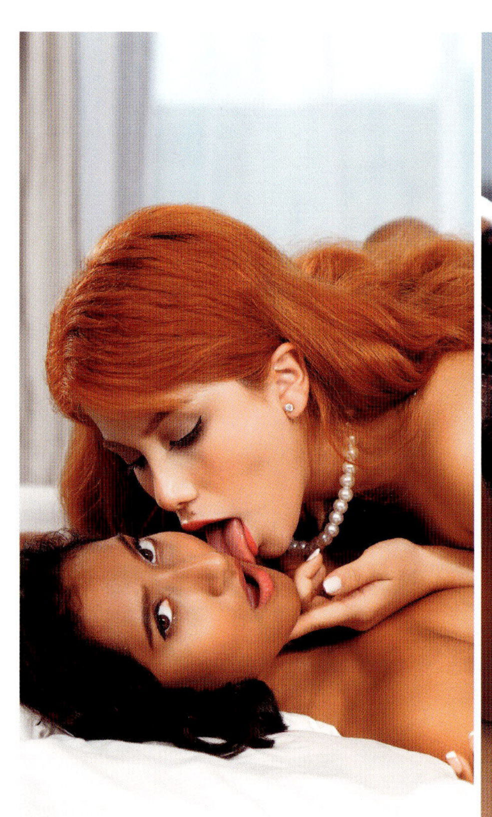
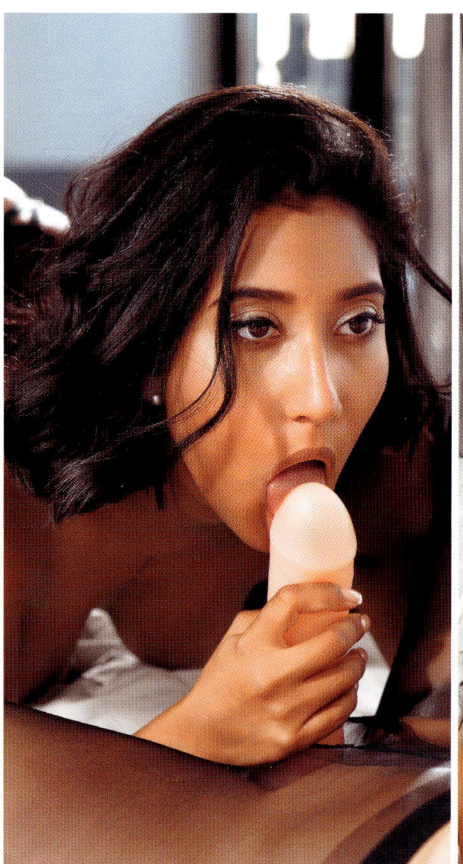
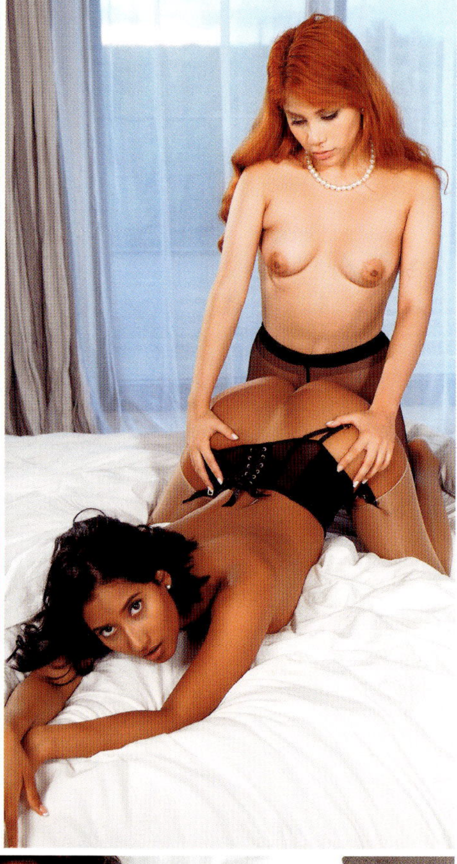

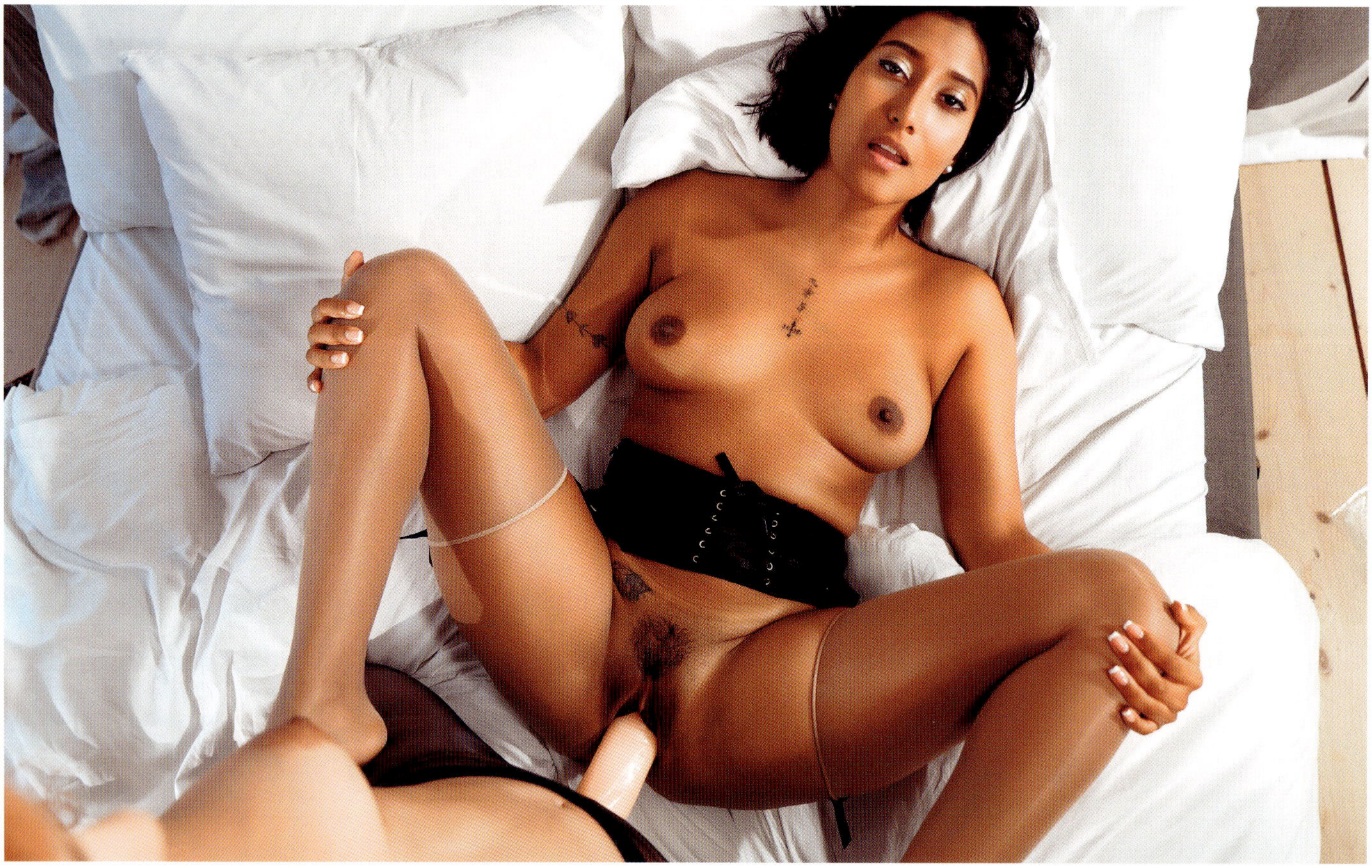

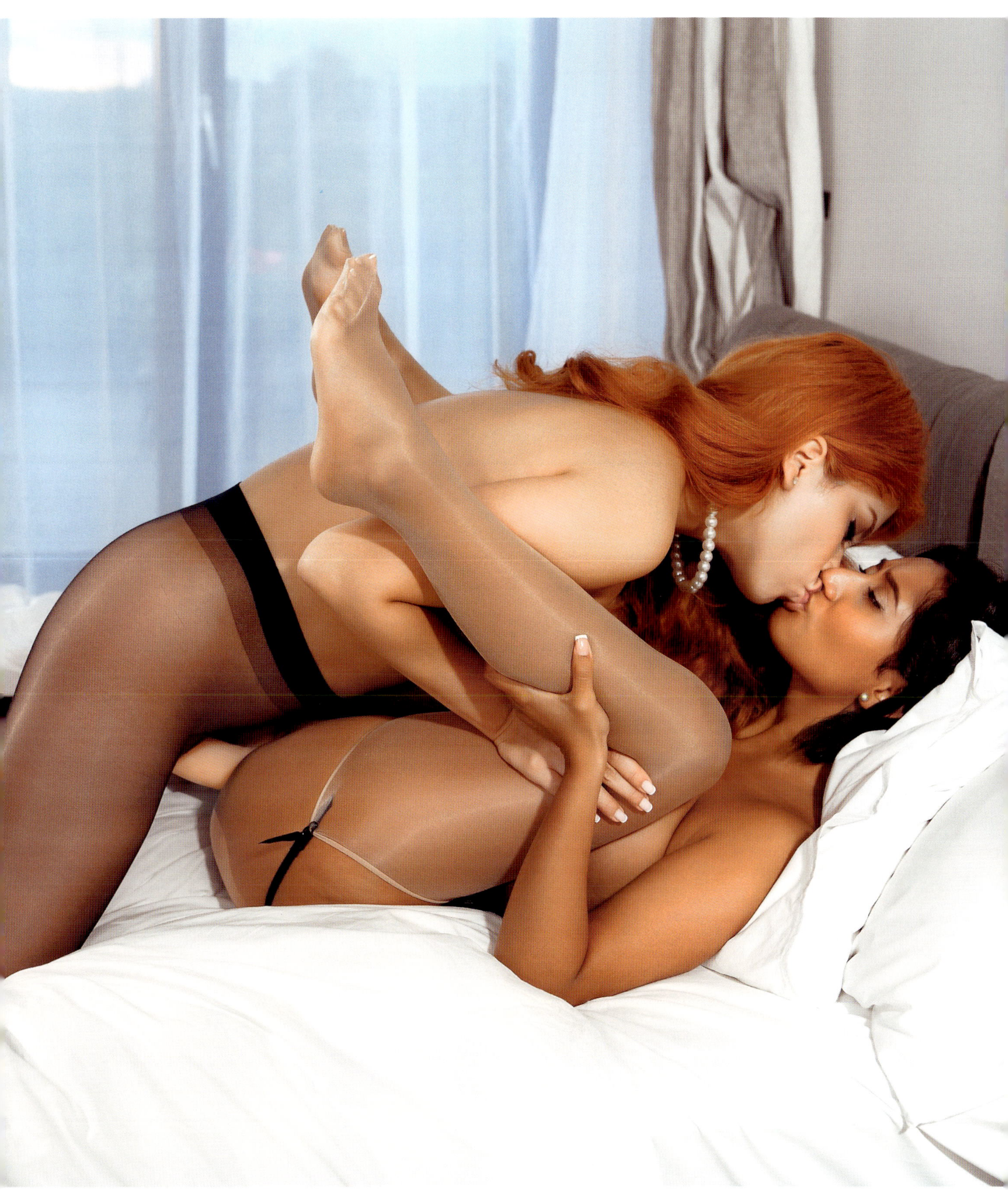

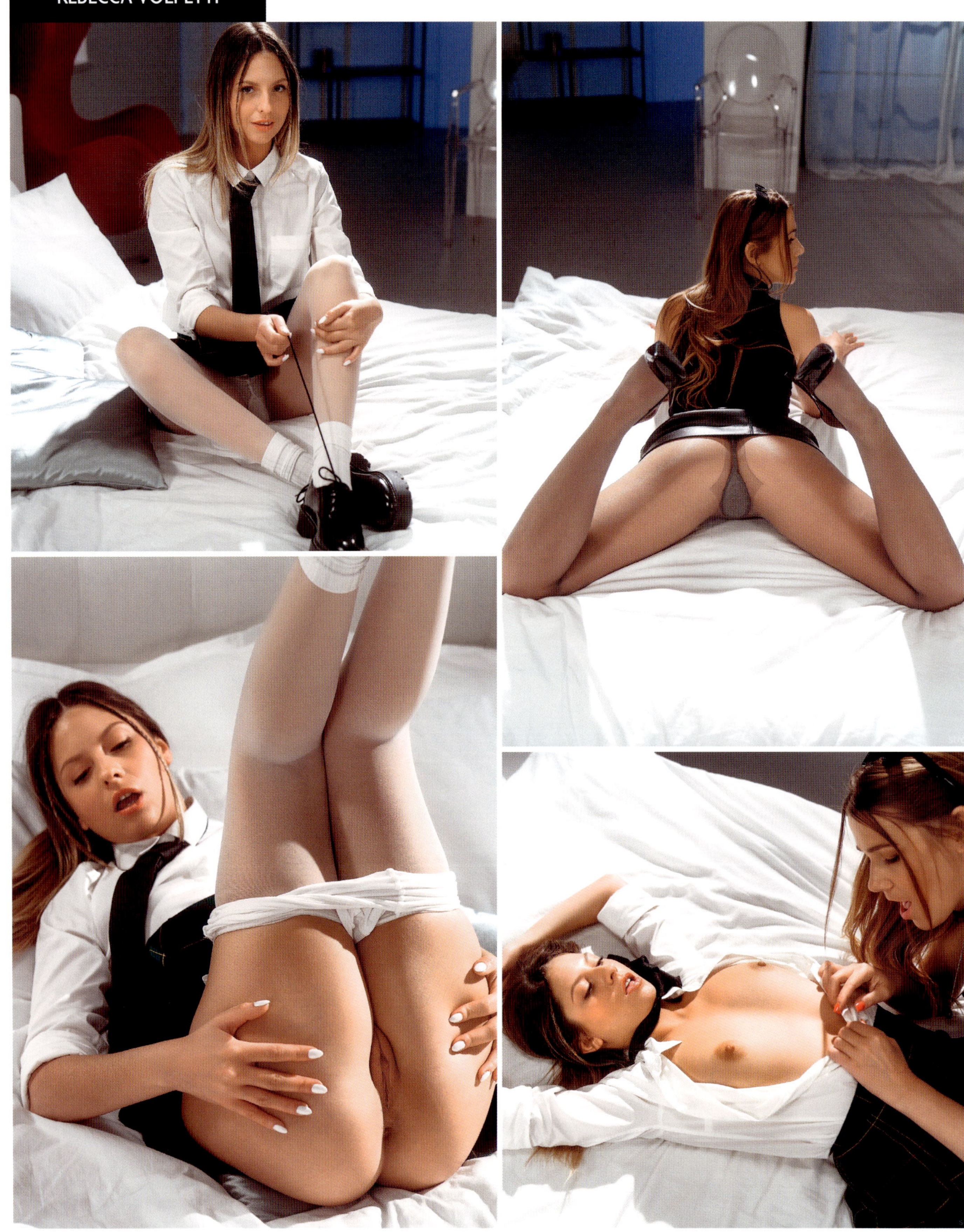

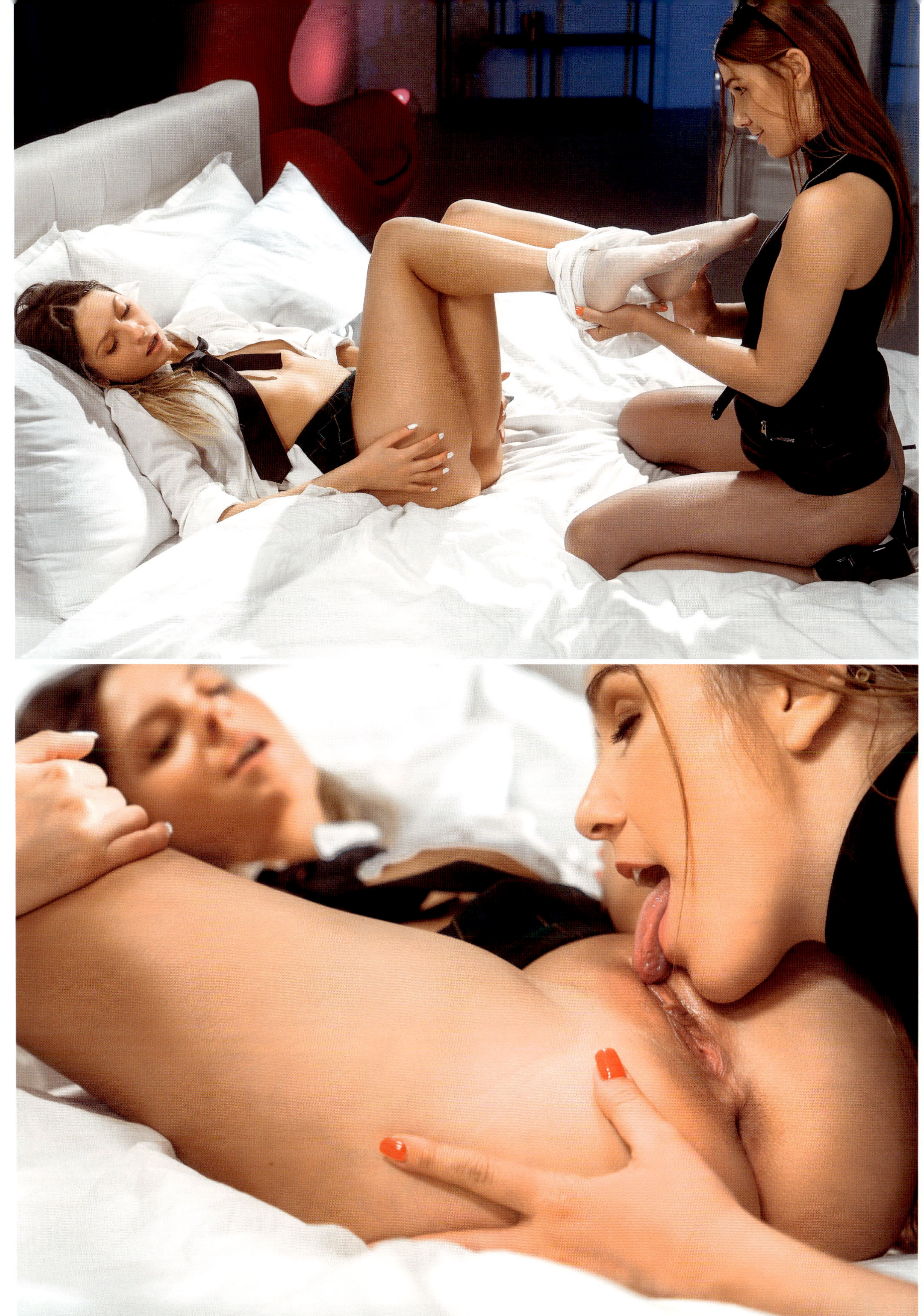

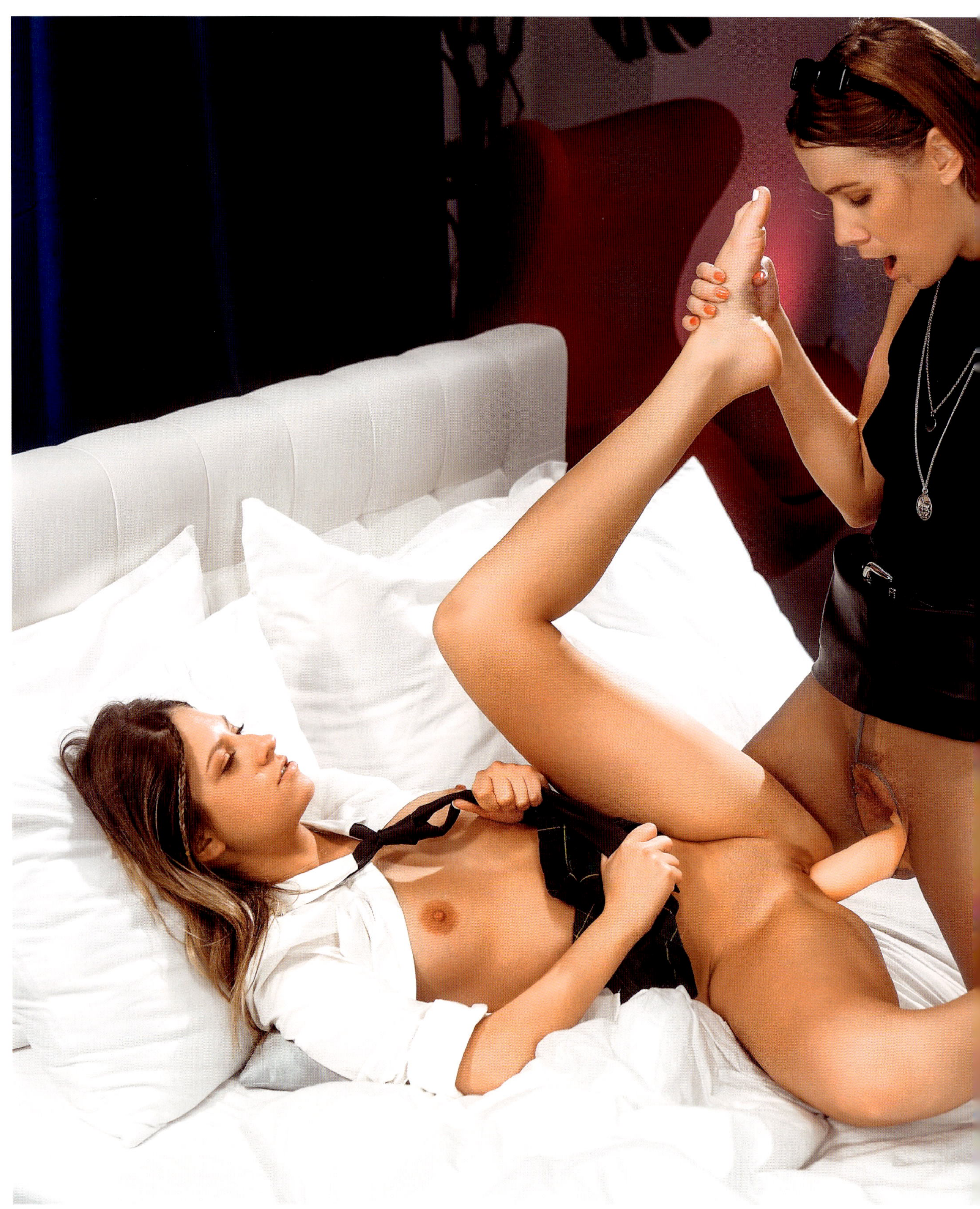

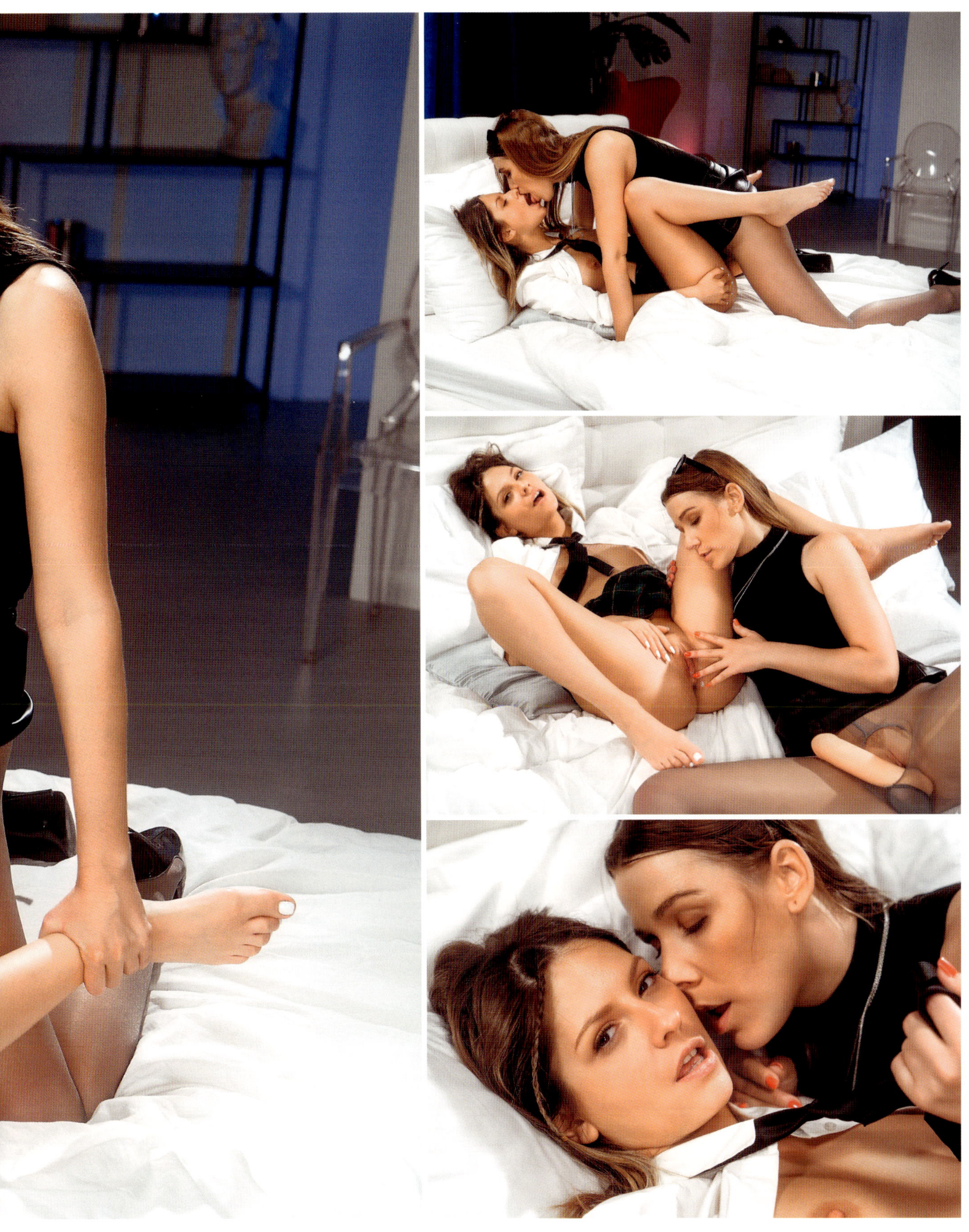

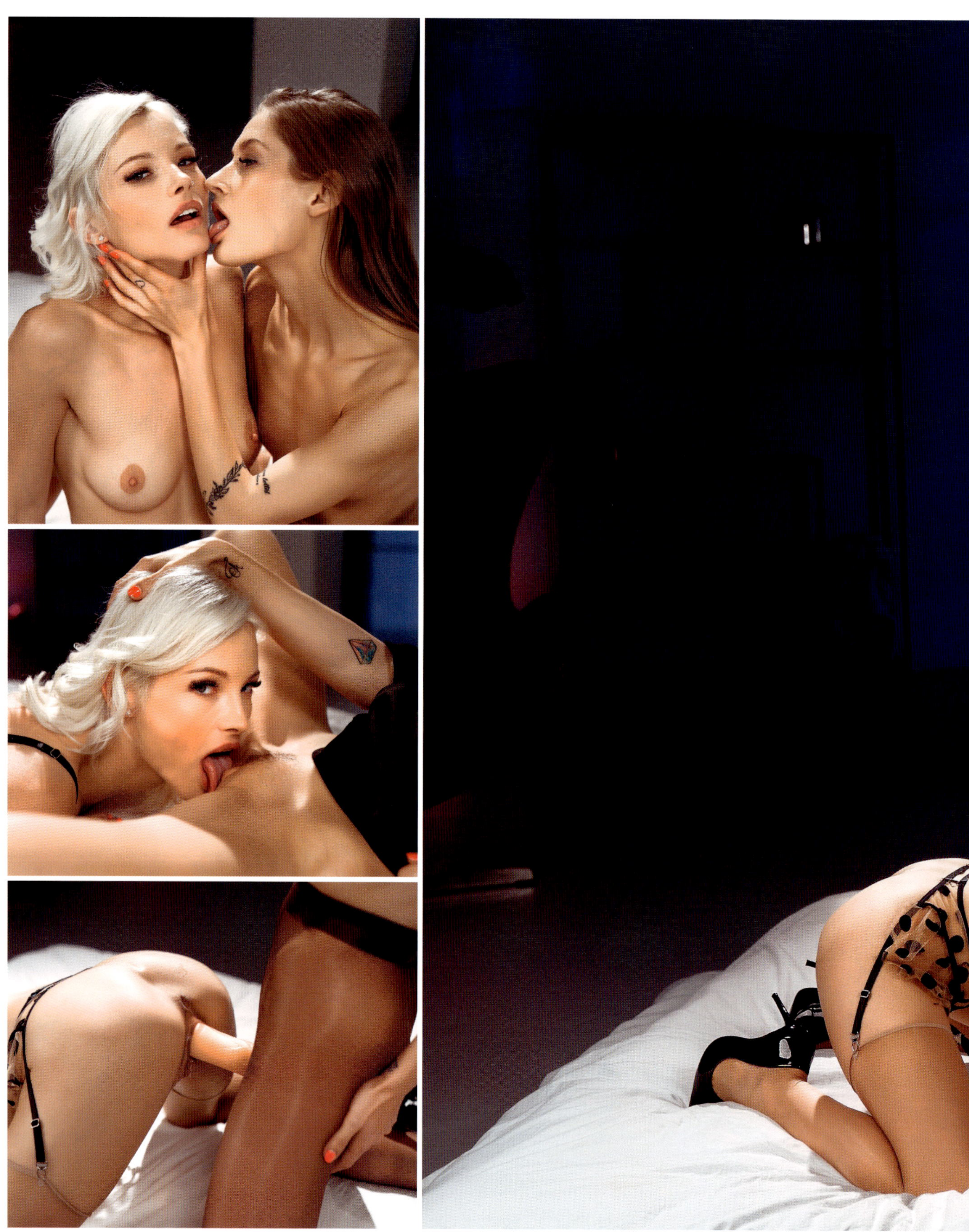

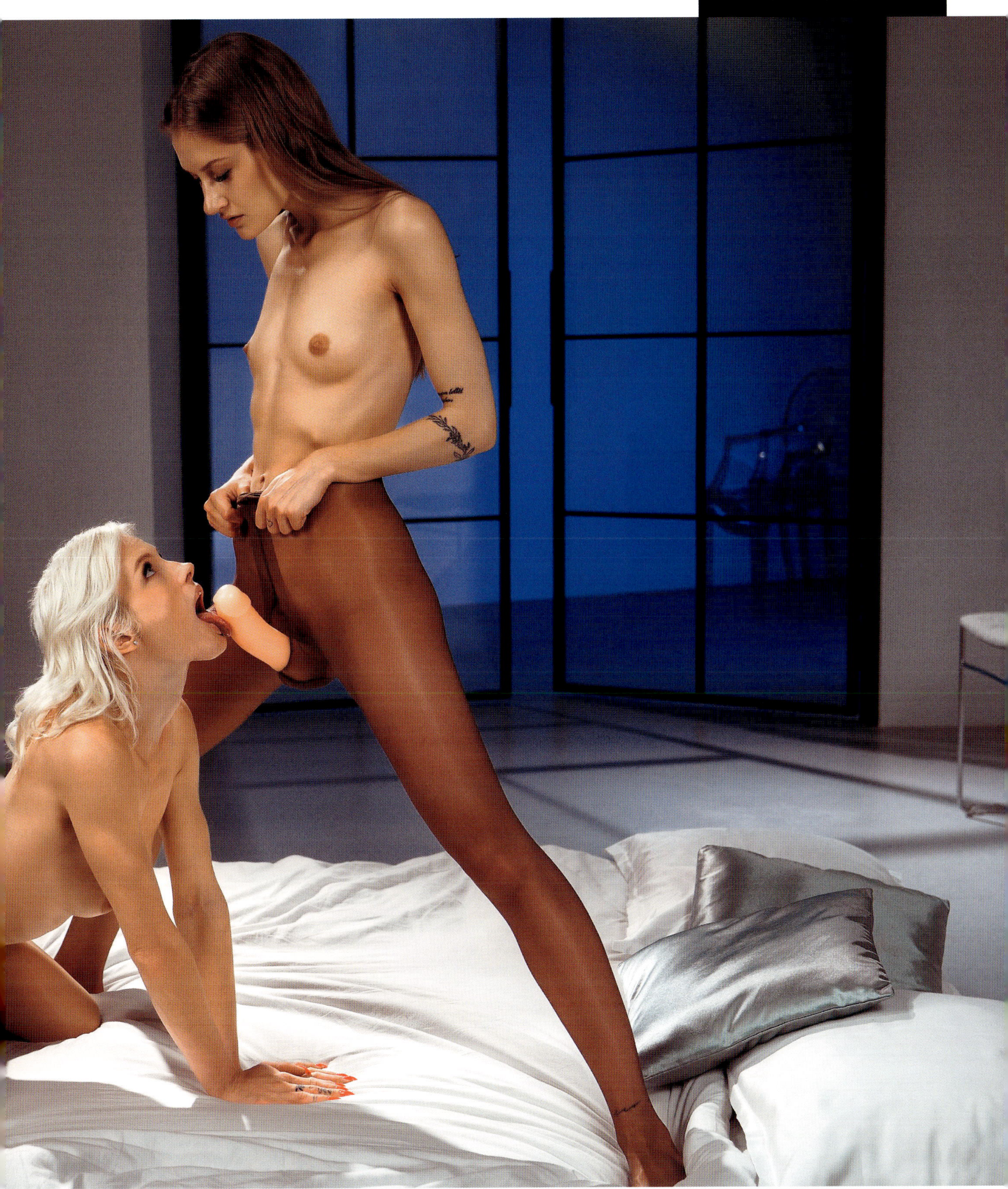

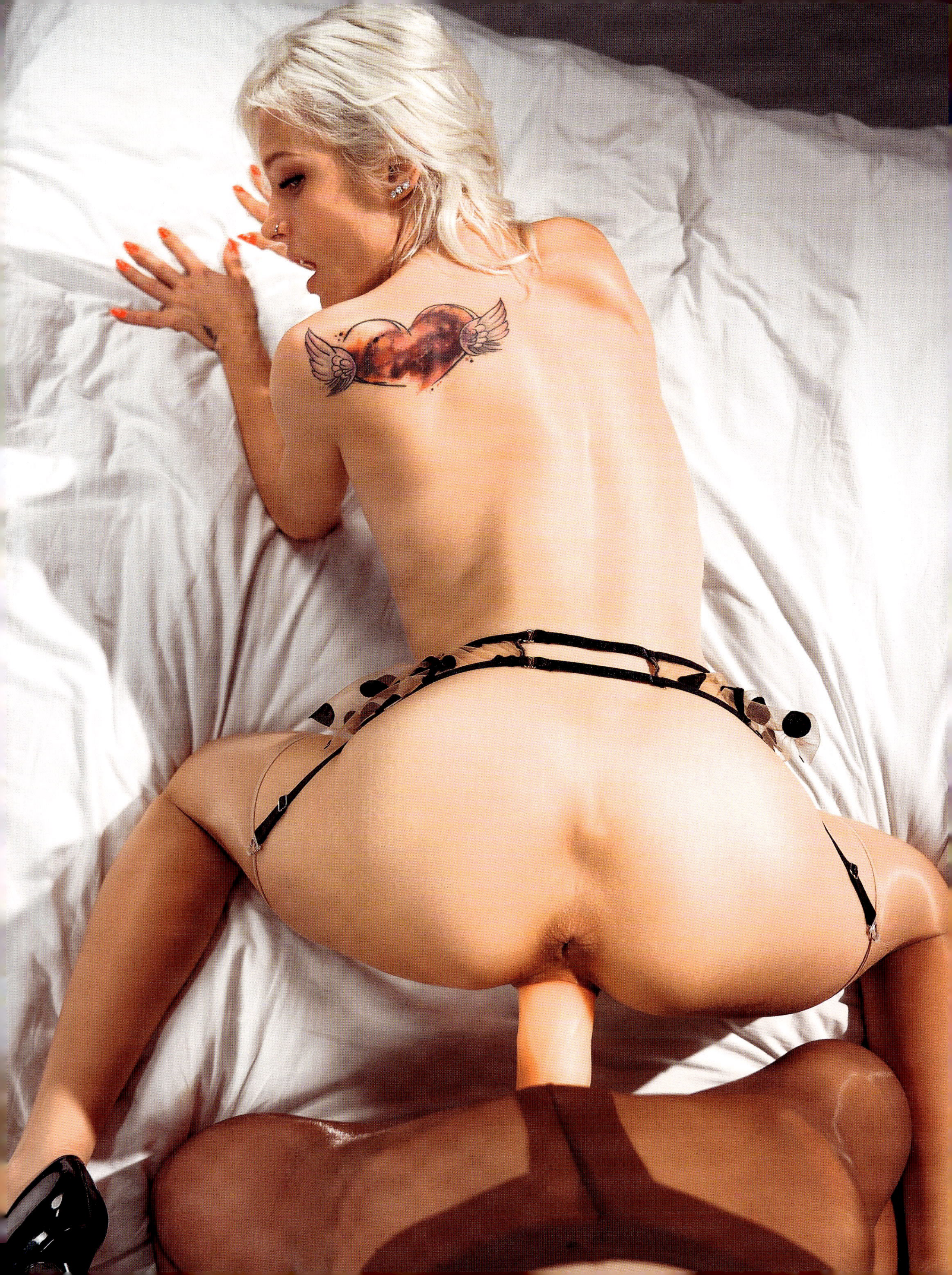

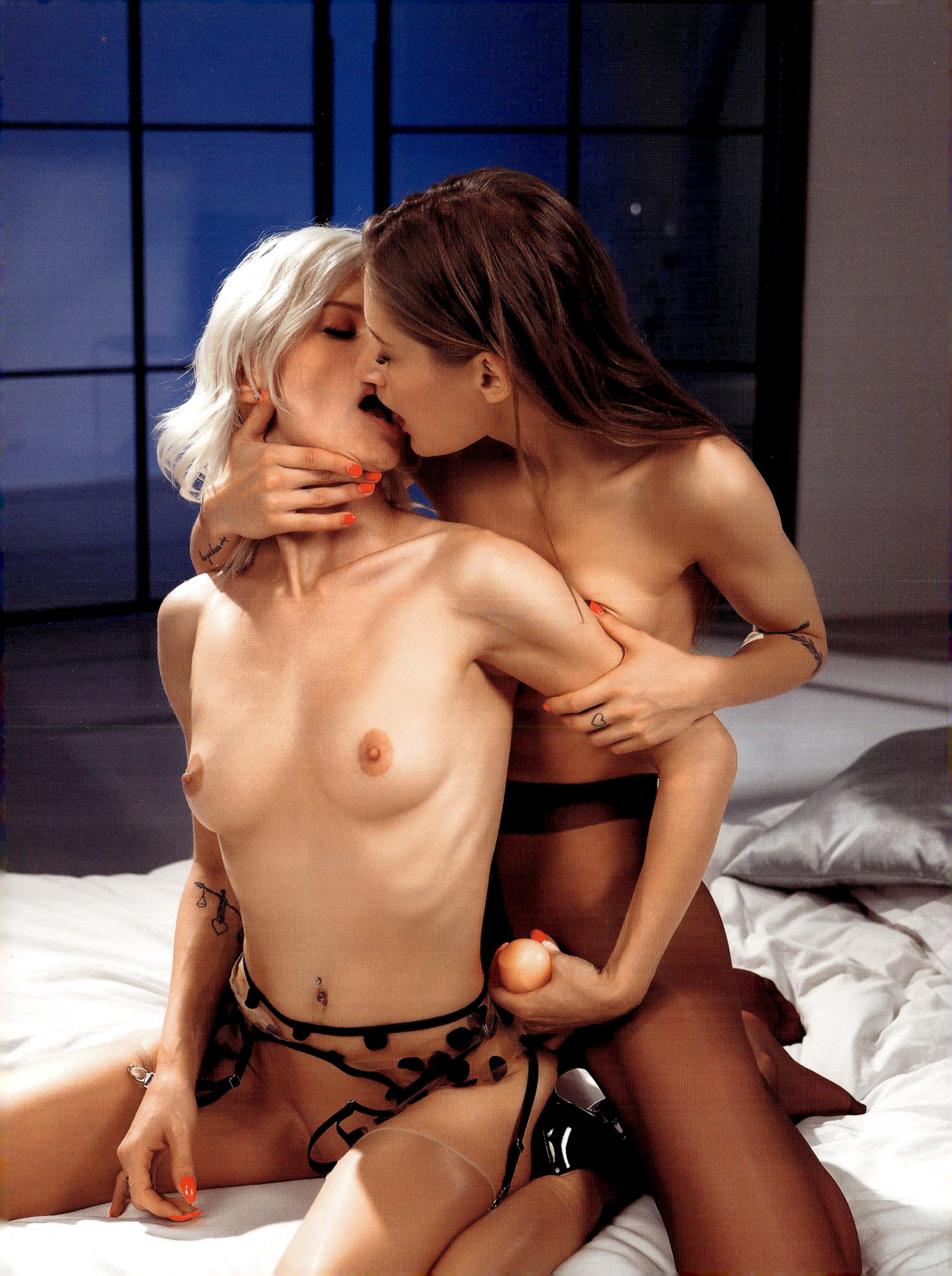

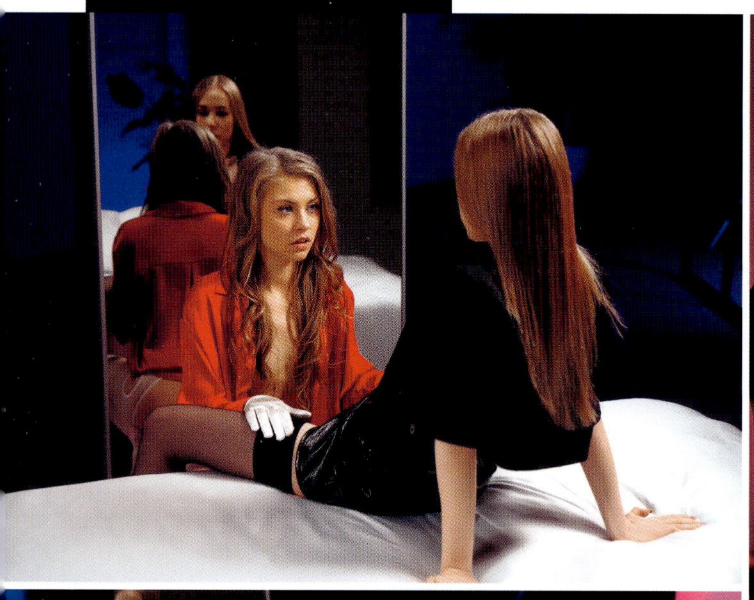

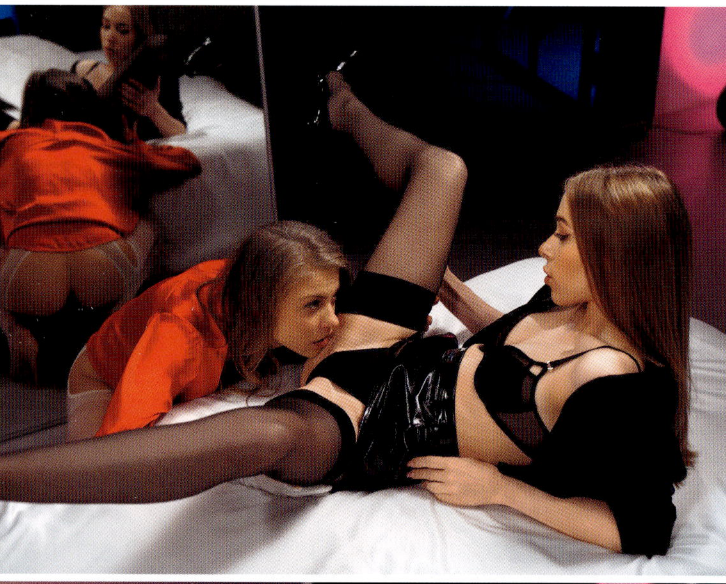

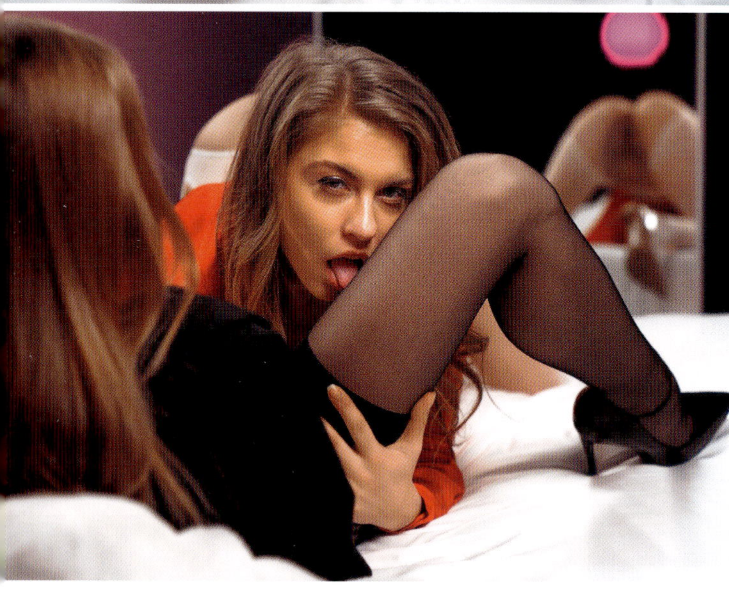

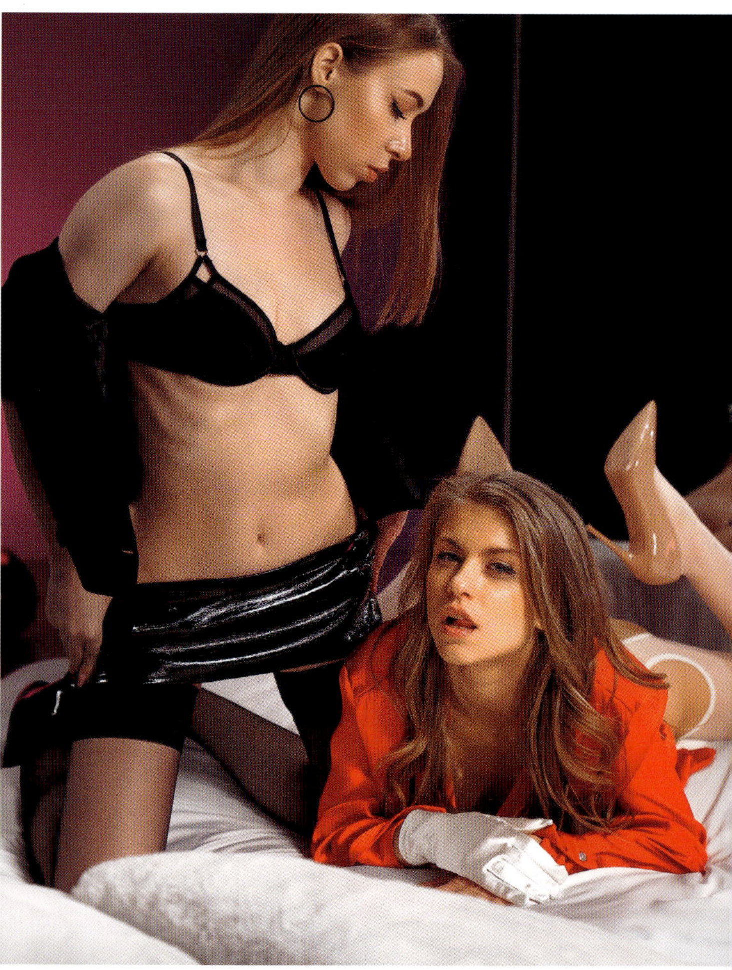

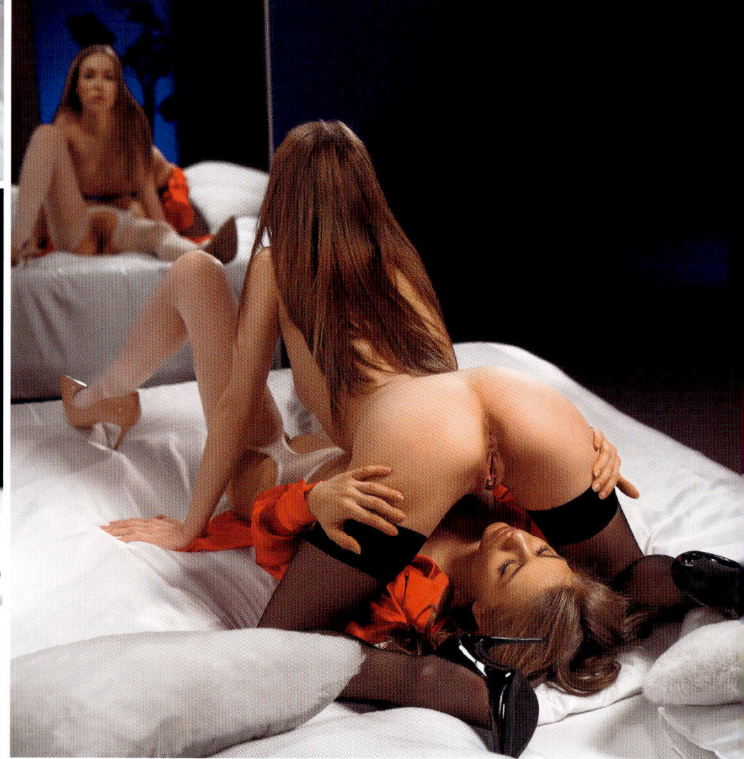

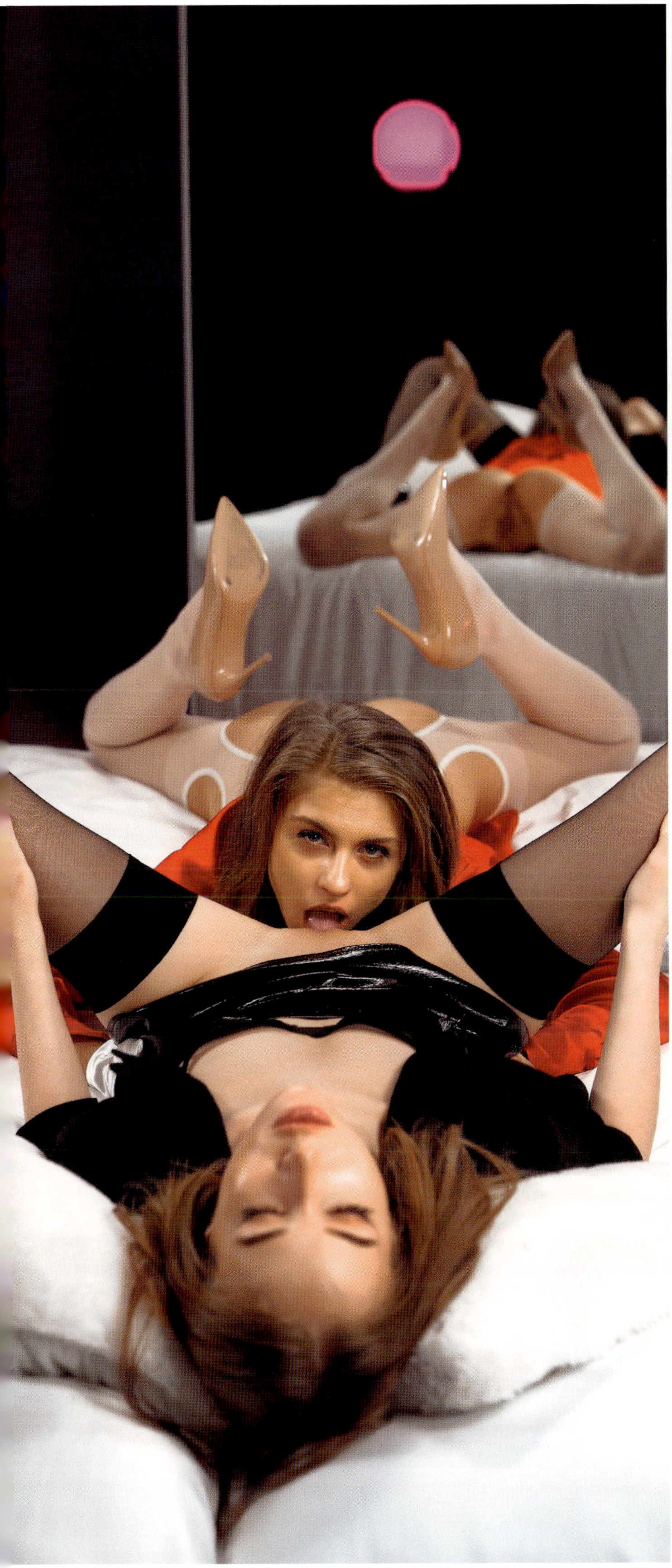

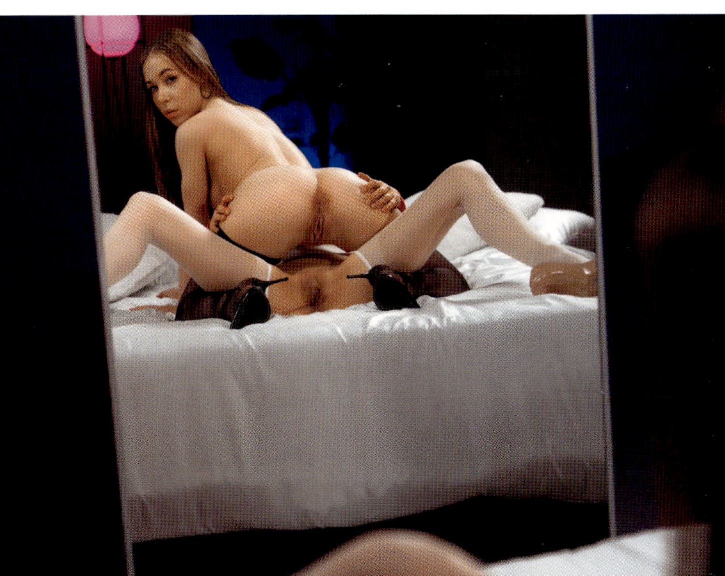
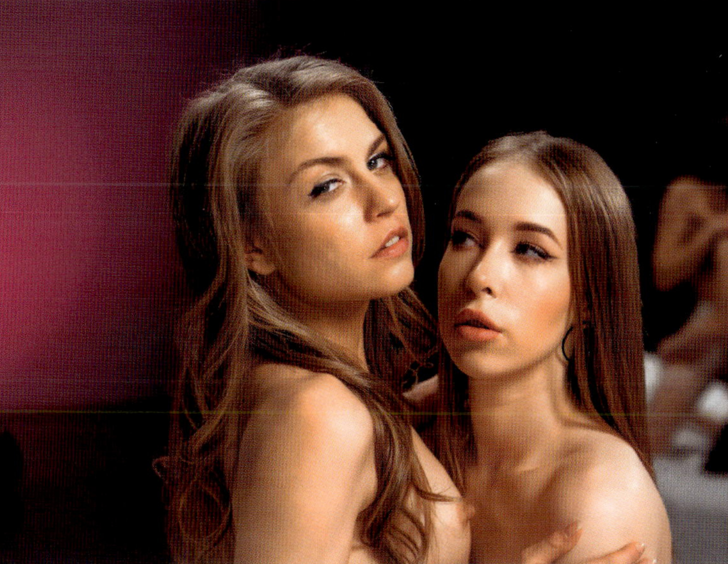
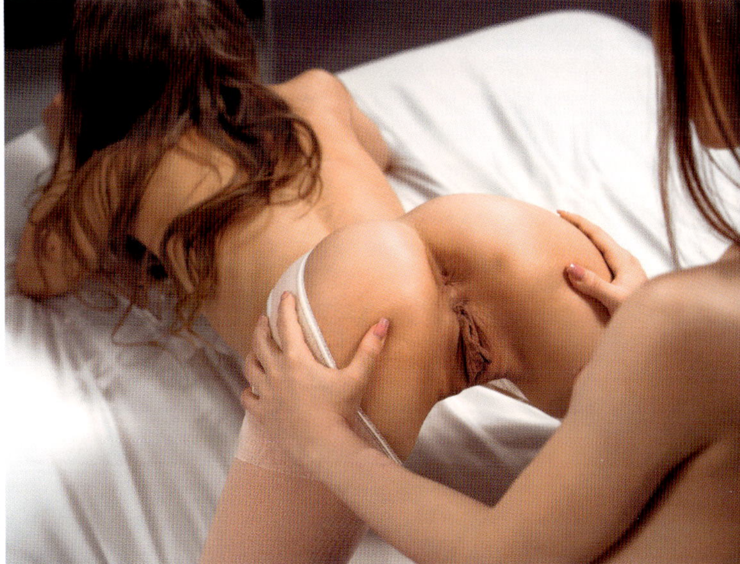

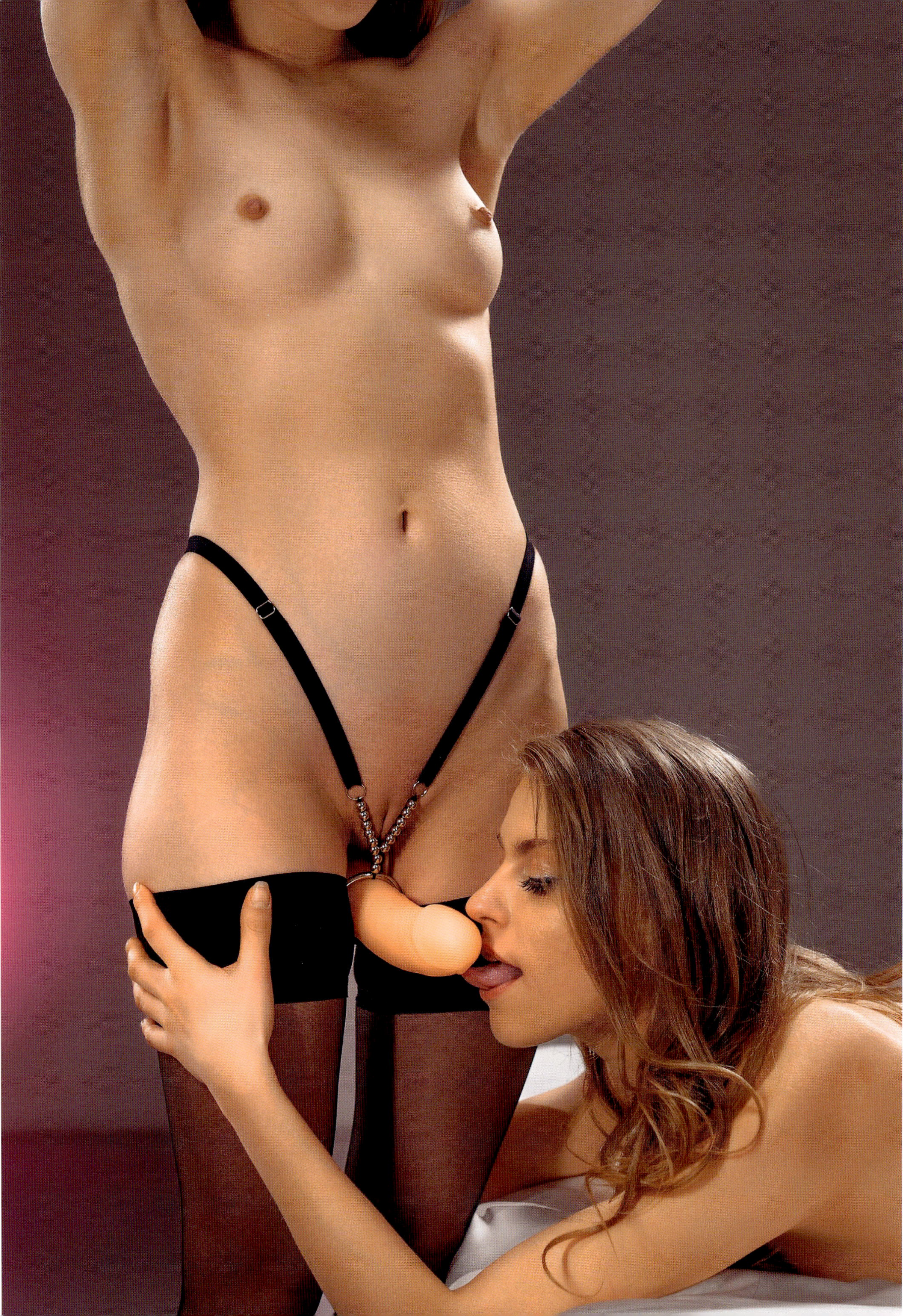

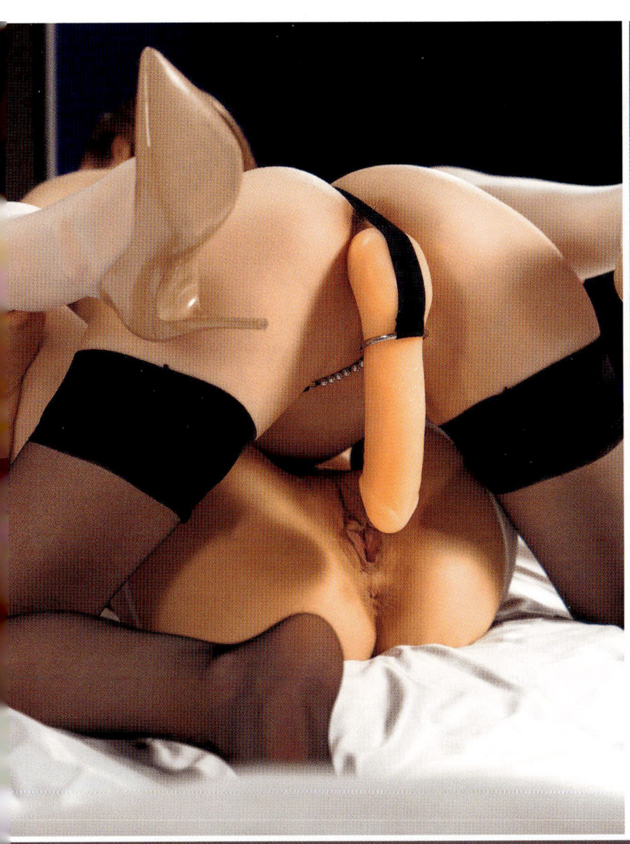
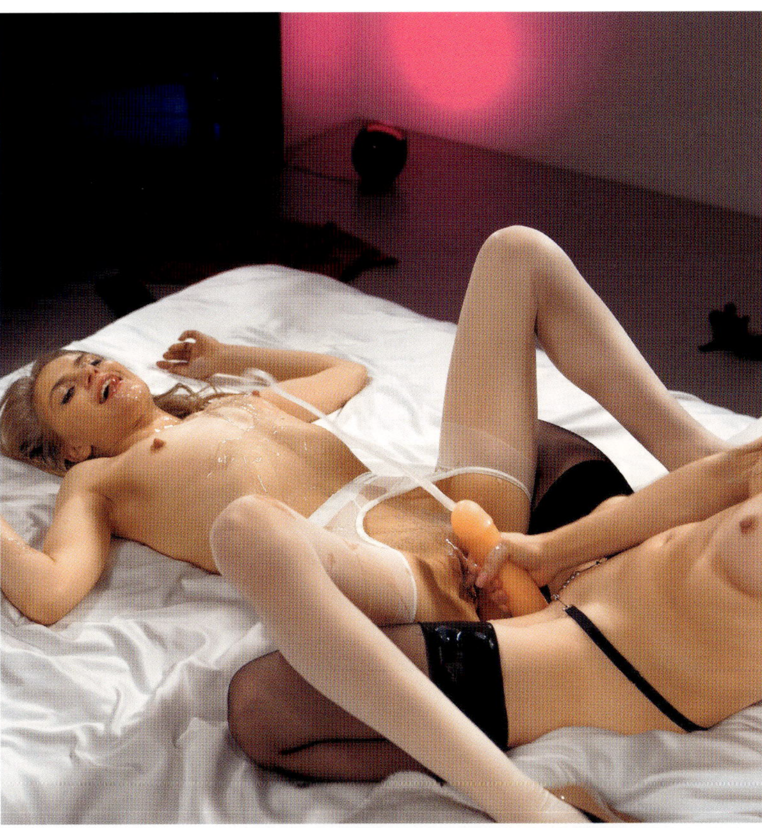

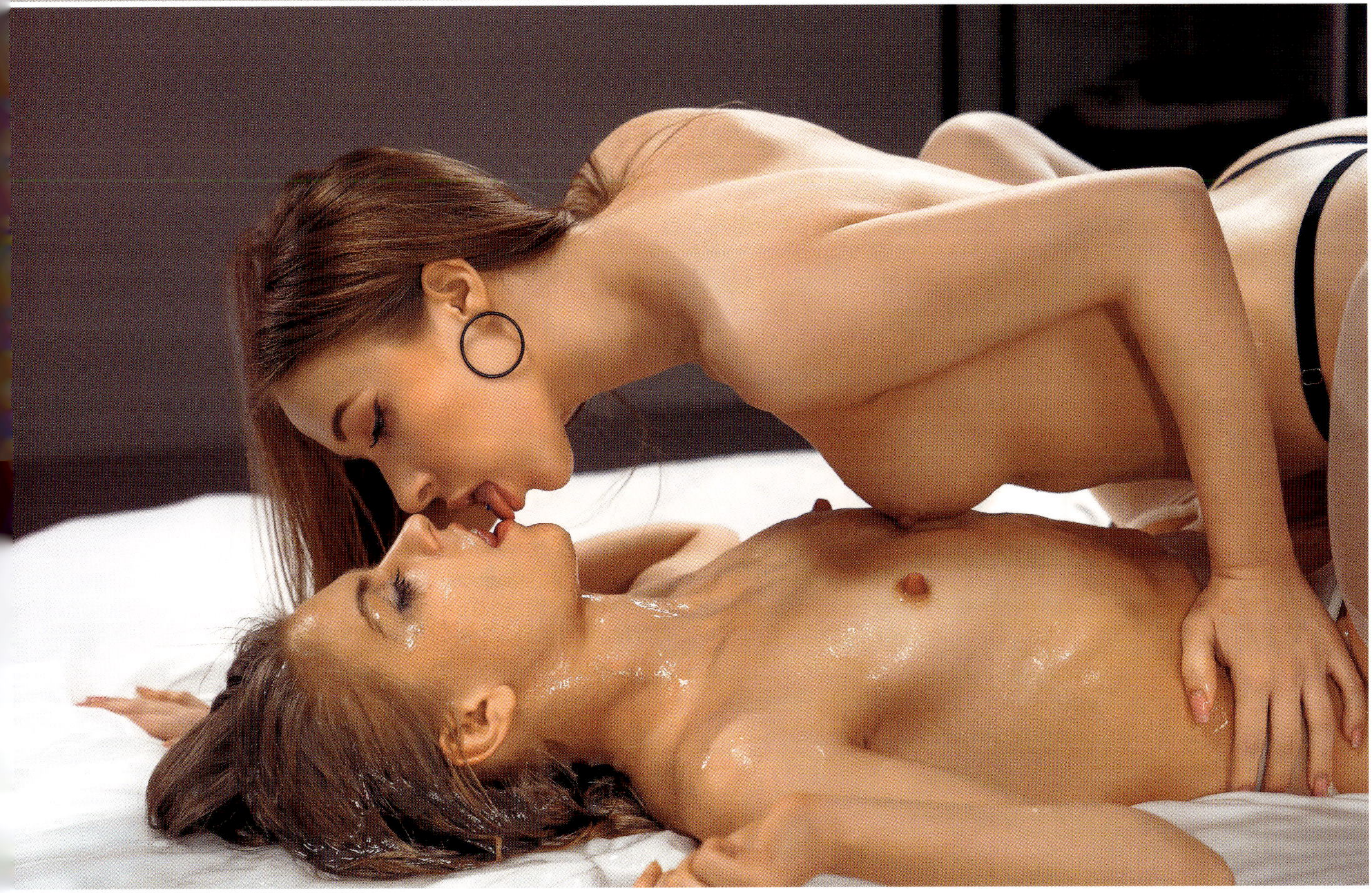

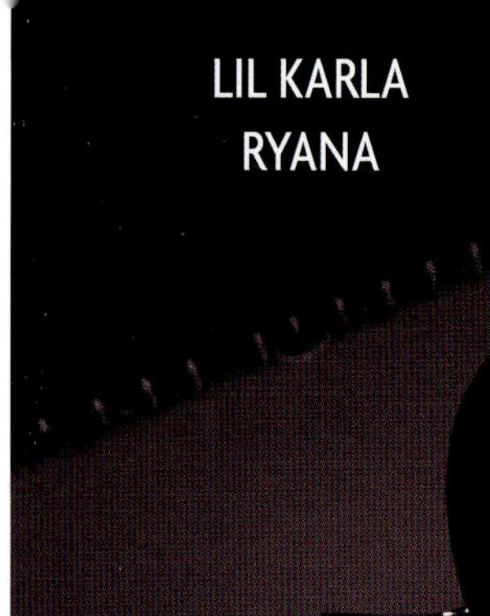
LIL KARLA
RYANA

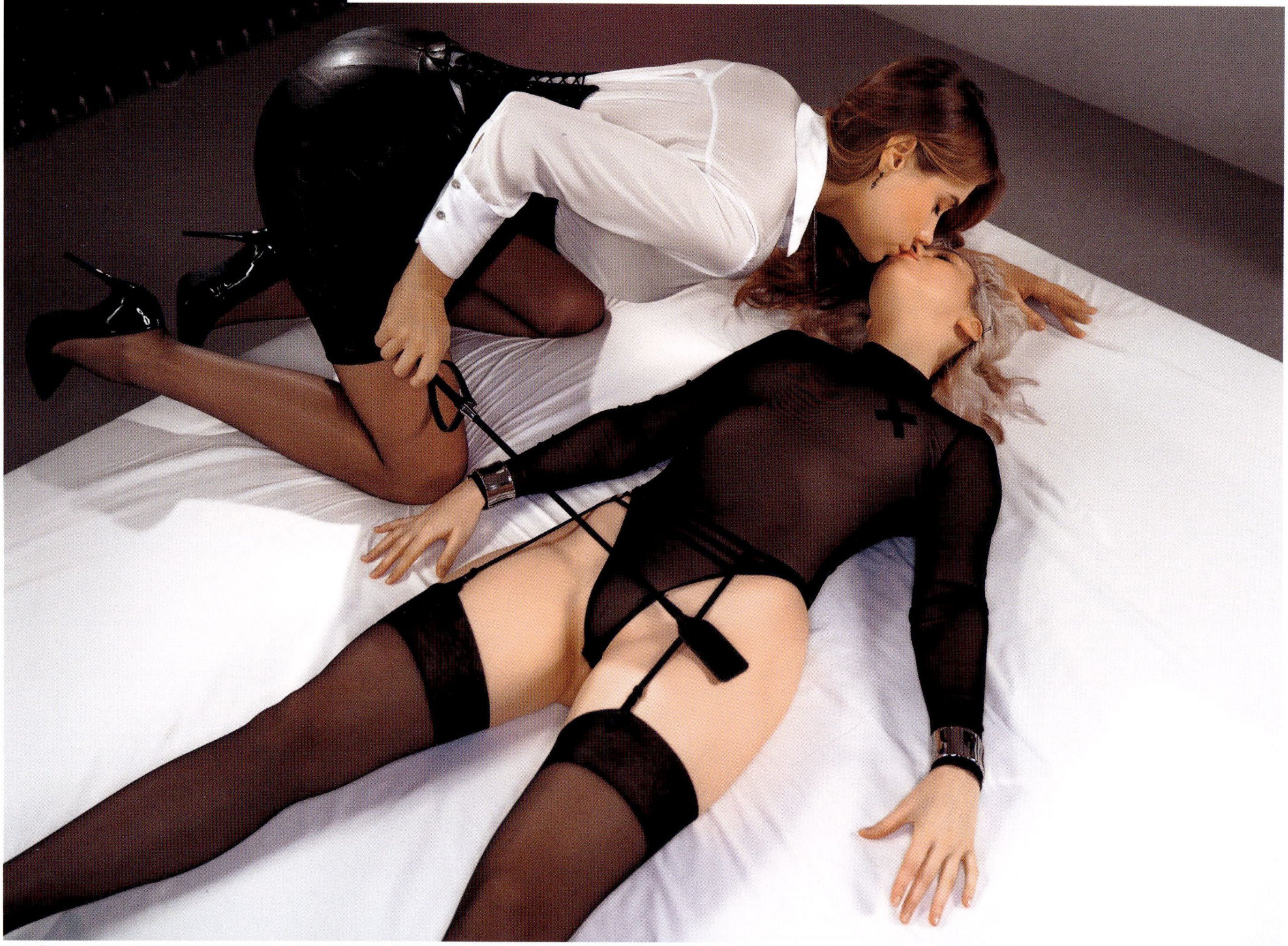

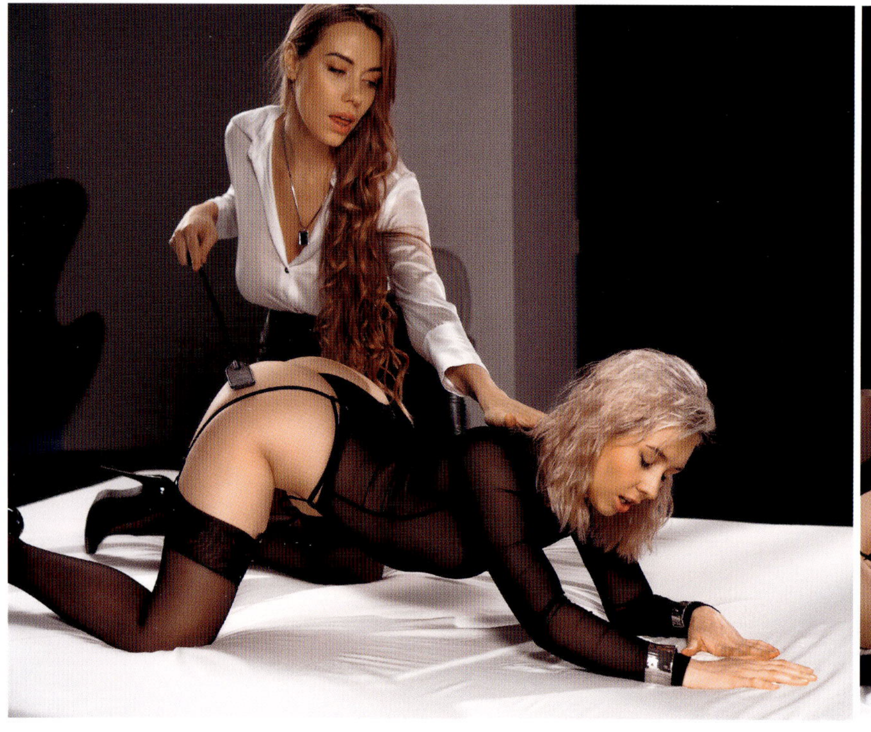

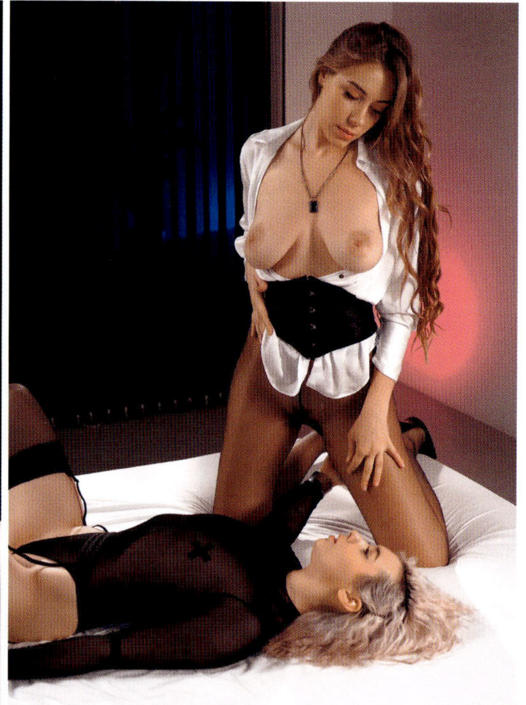

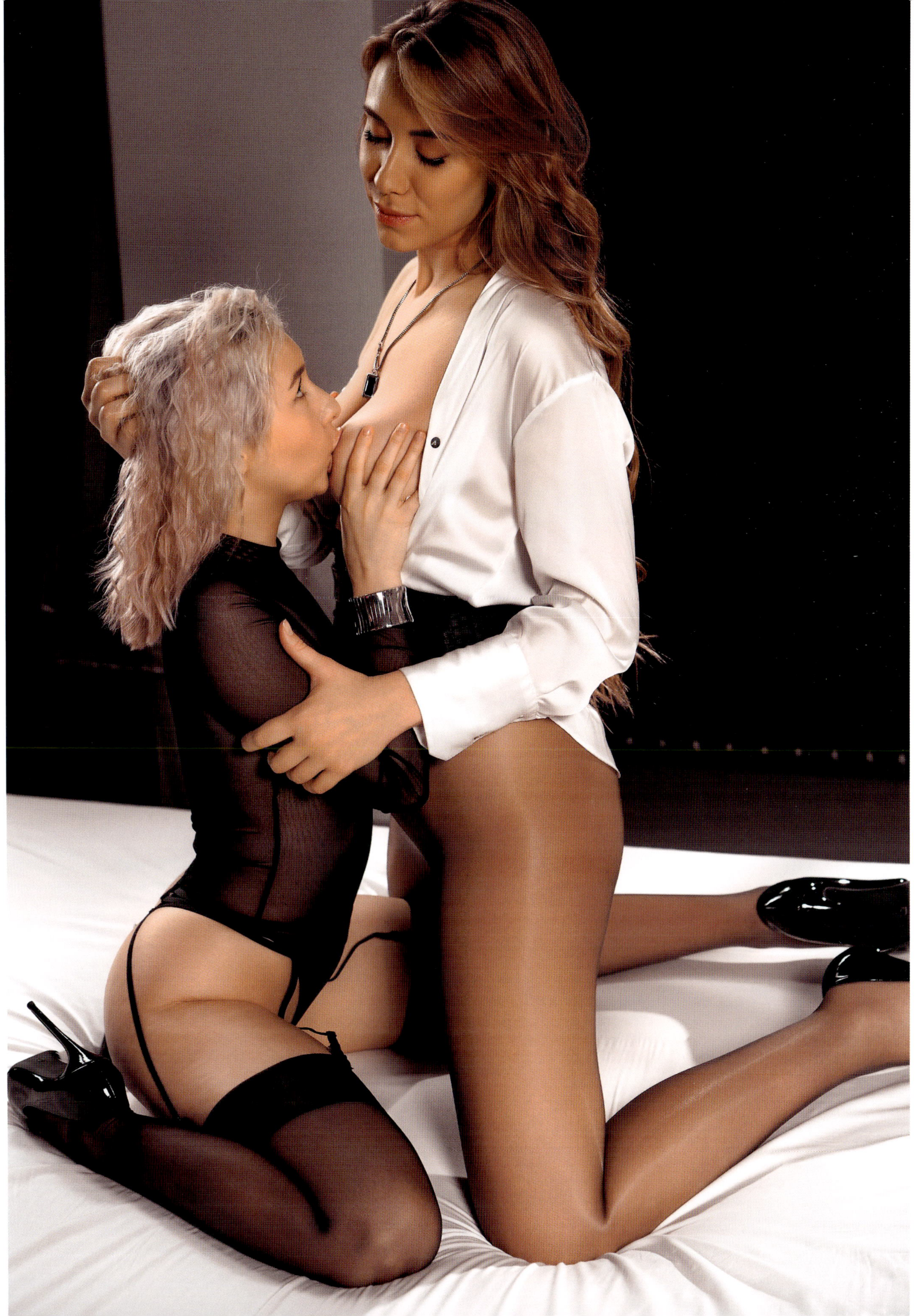

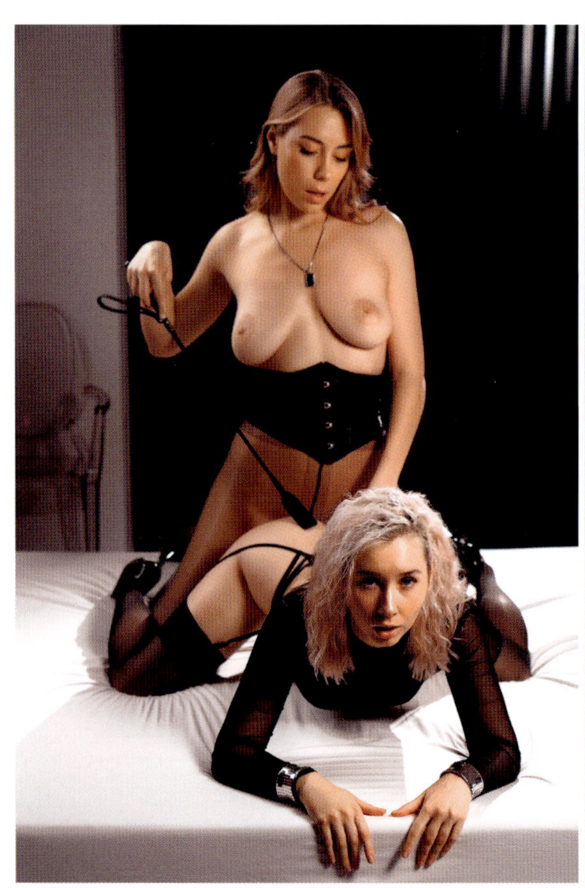
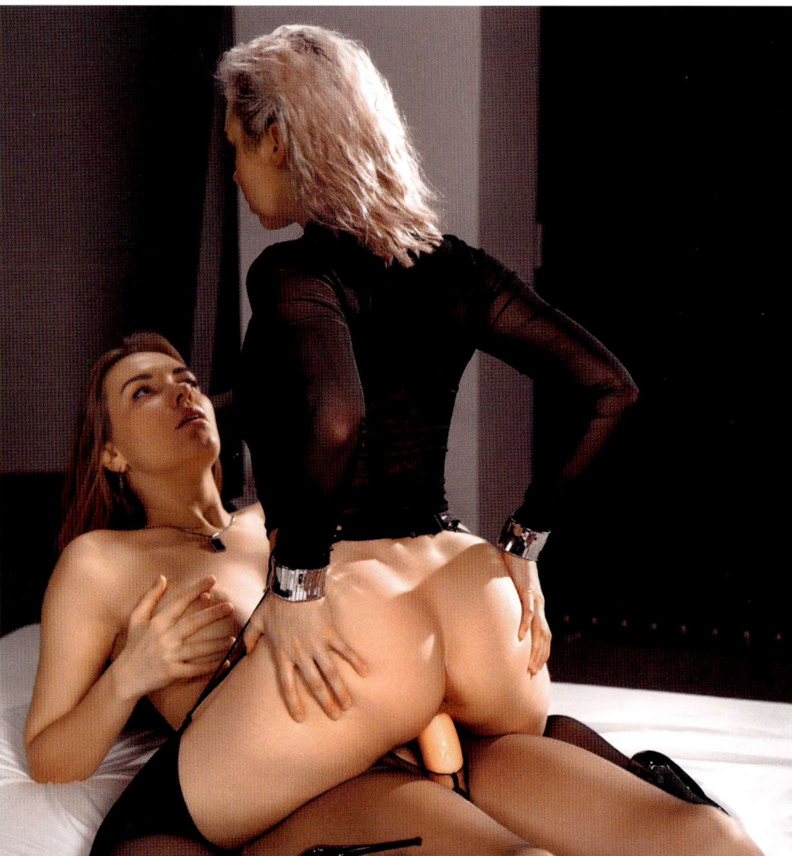

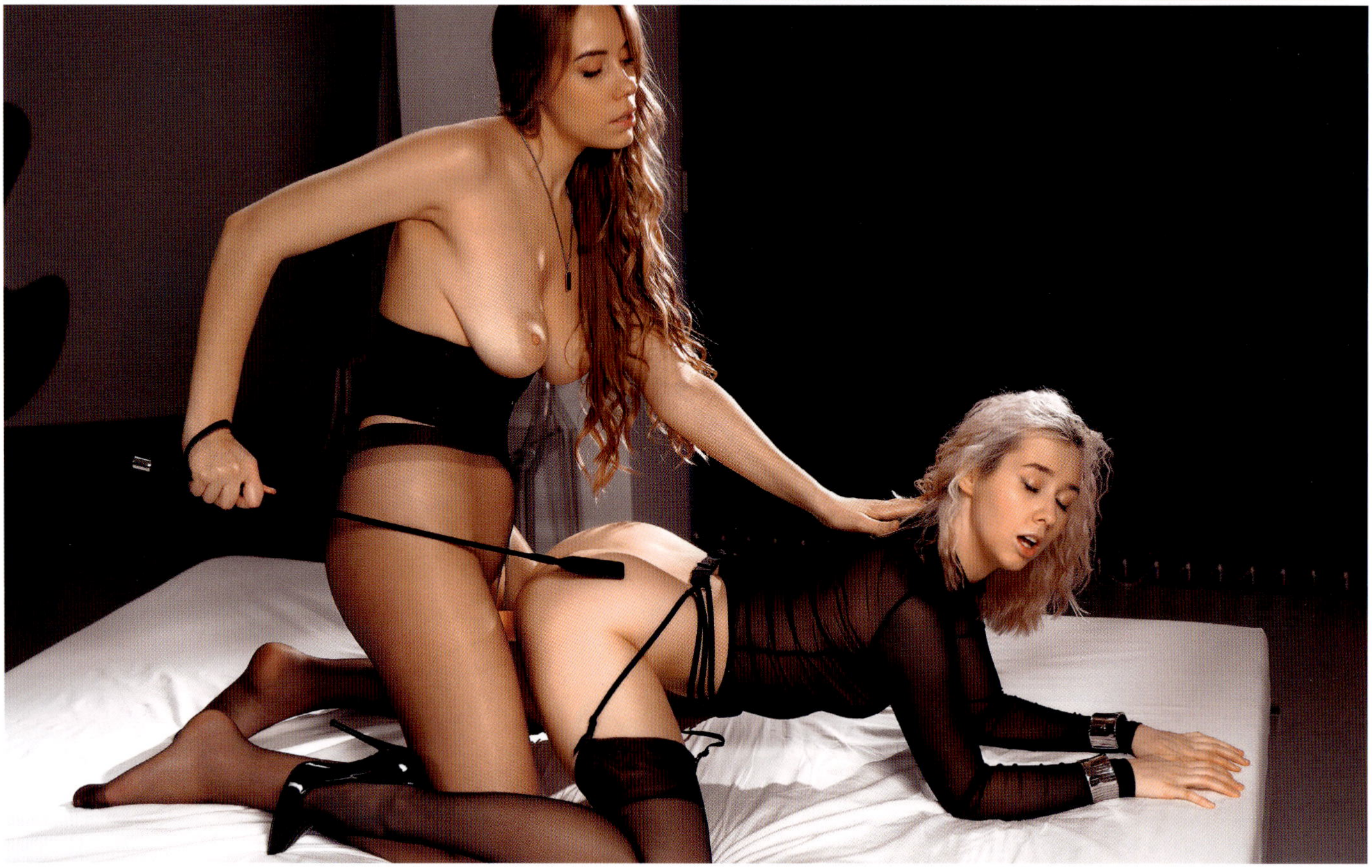

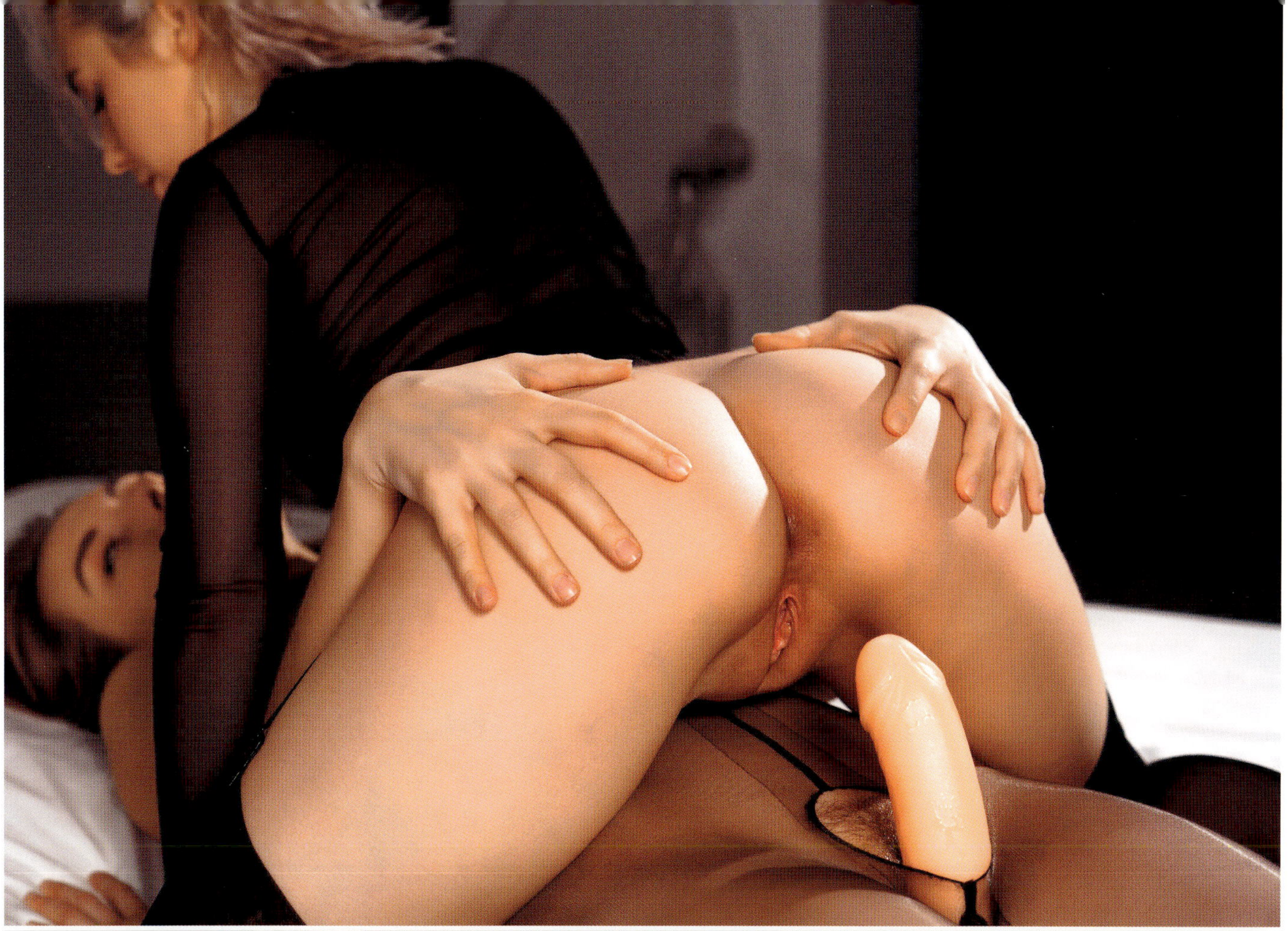

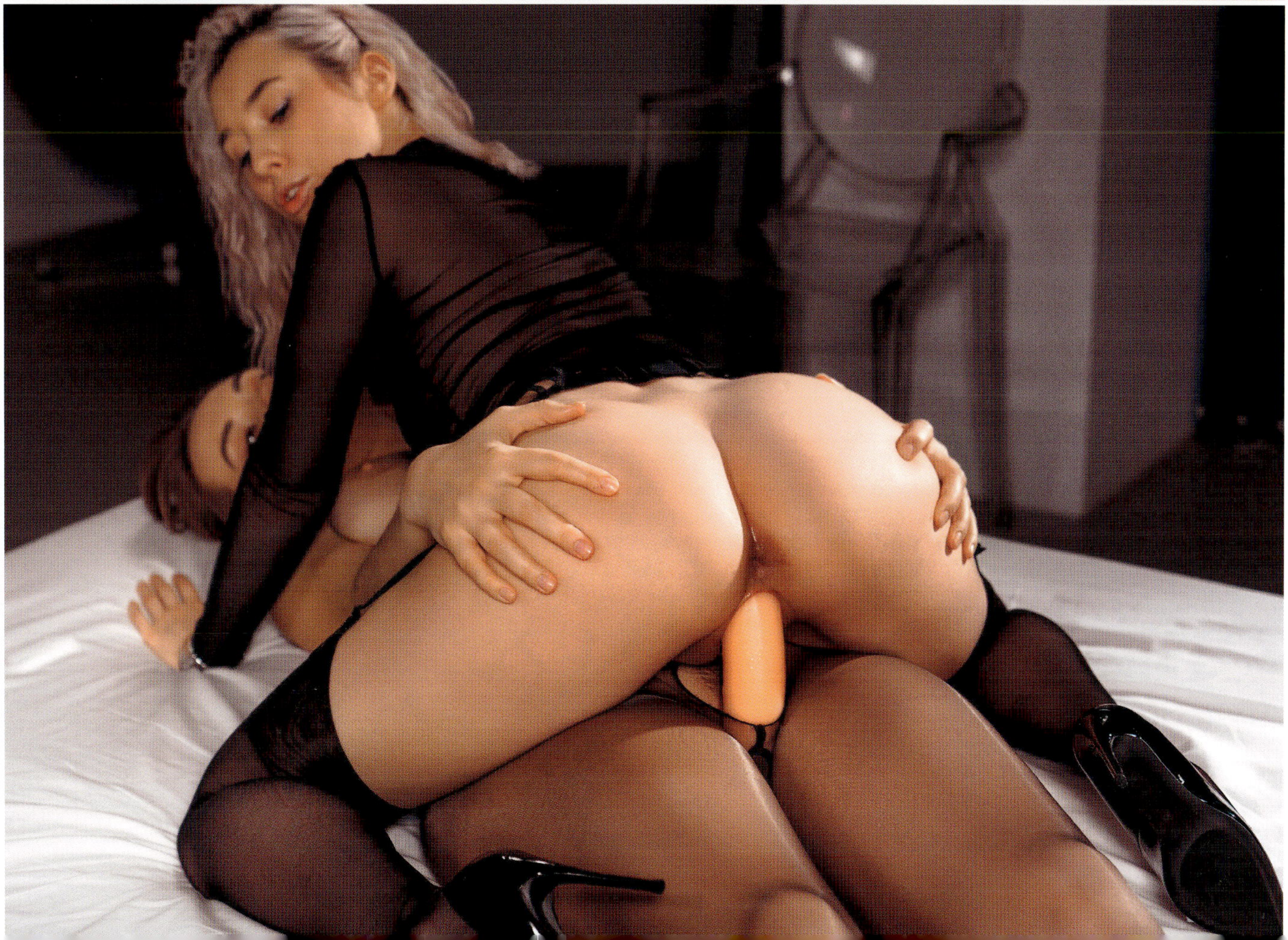

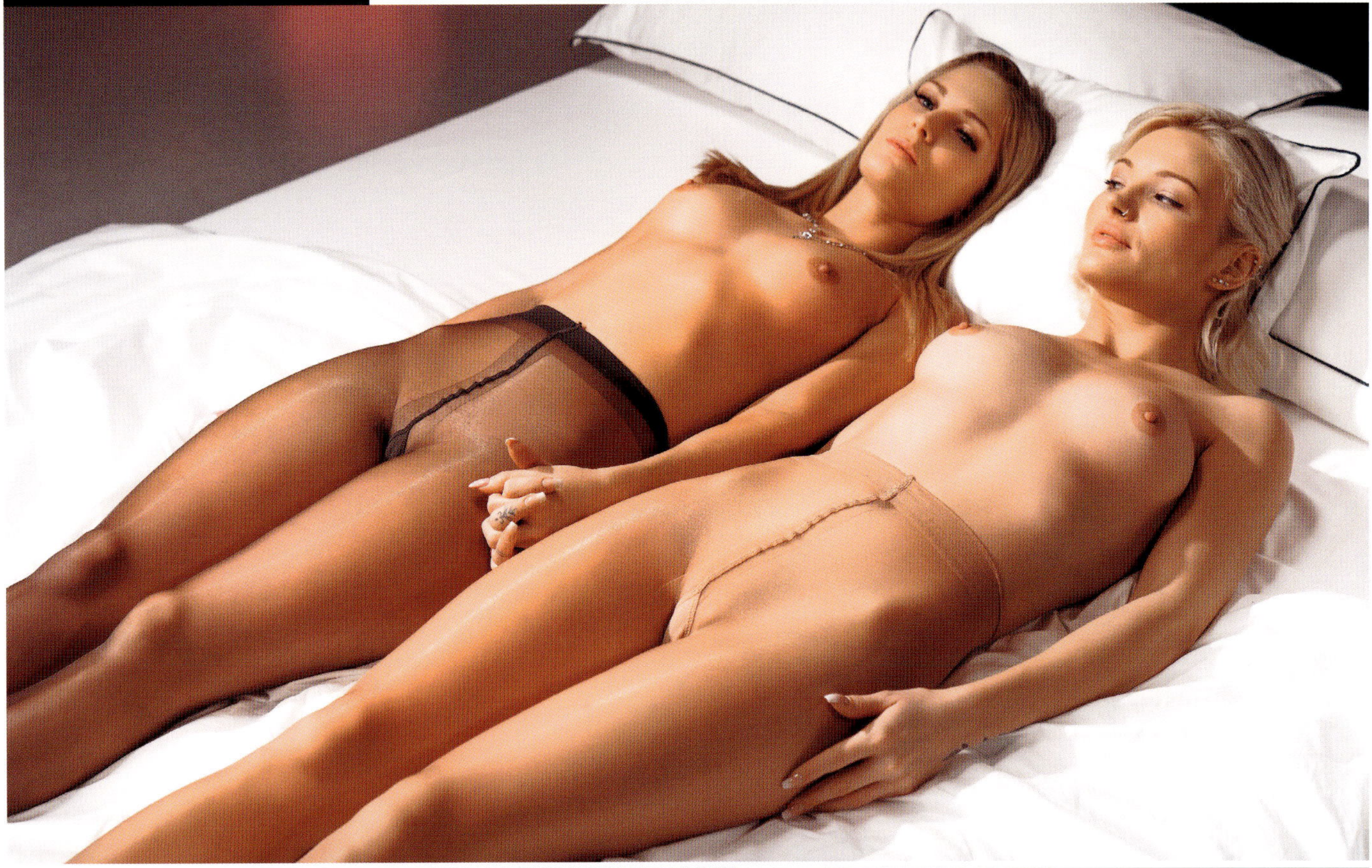

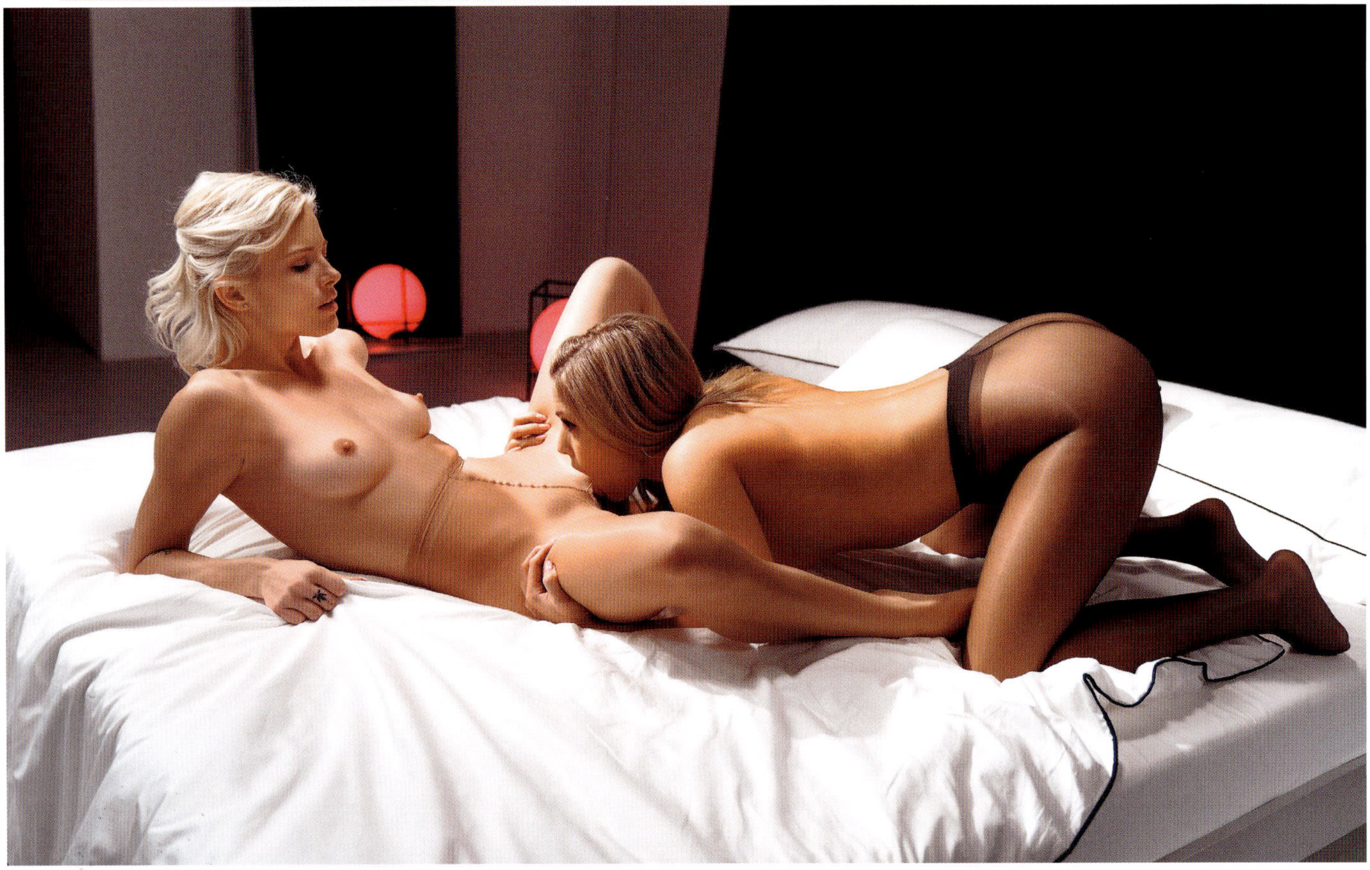

CANDEE LICIOUS
ZAZIE SKYMM

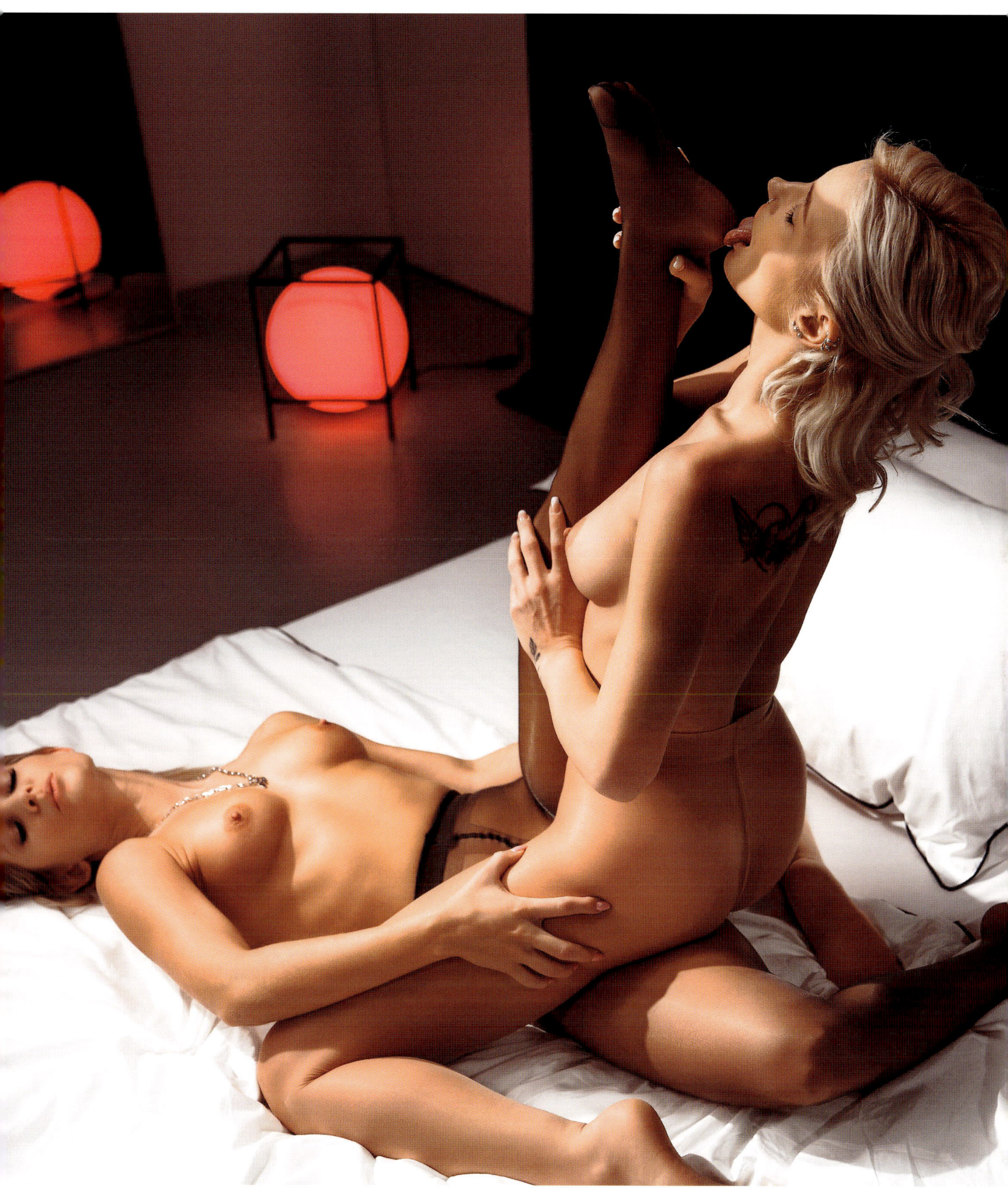

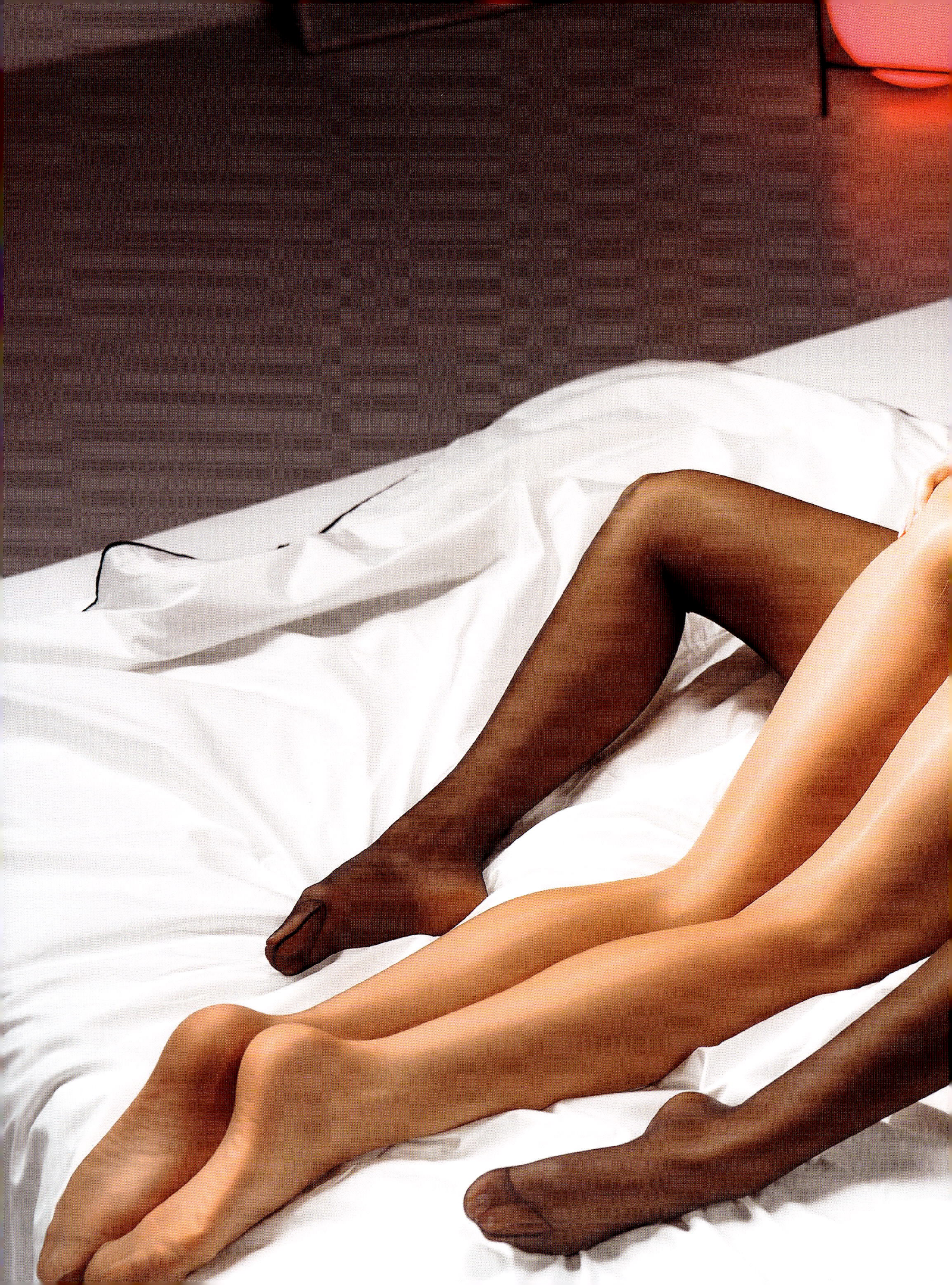

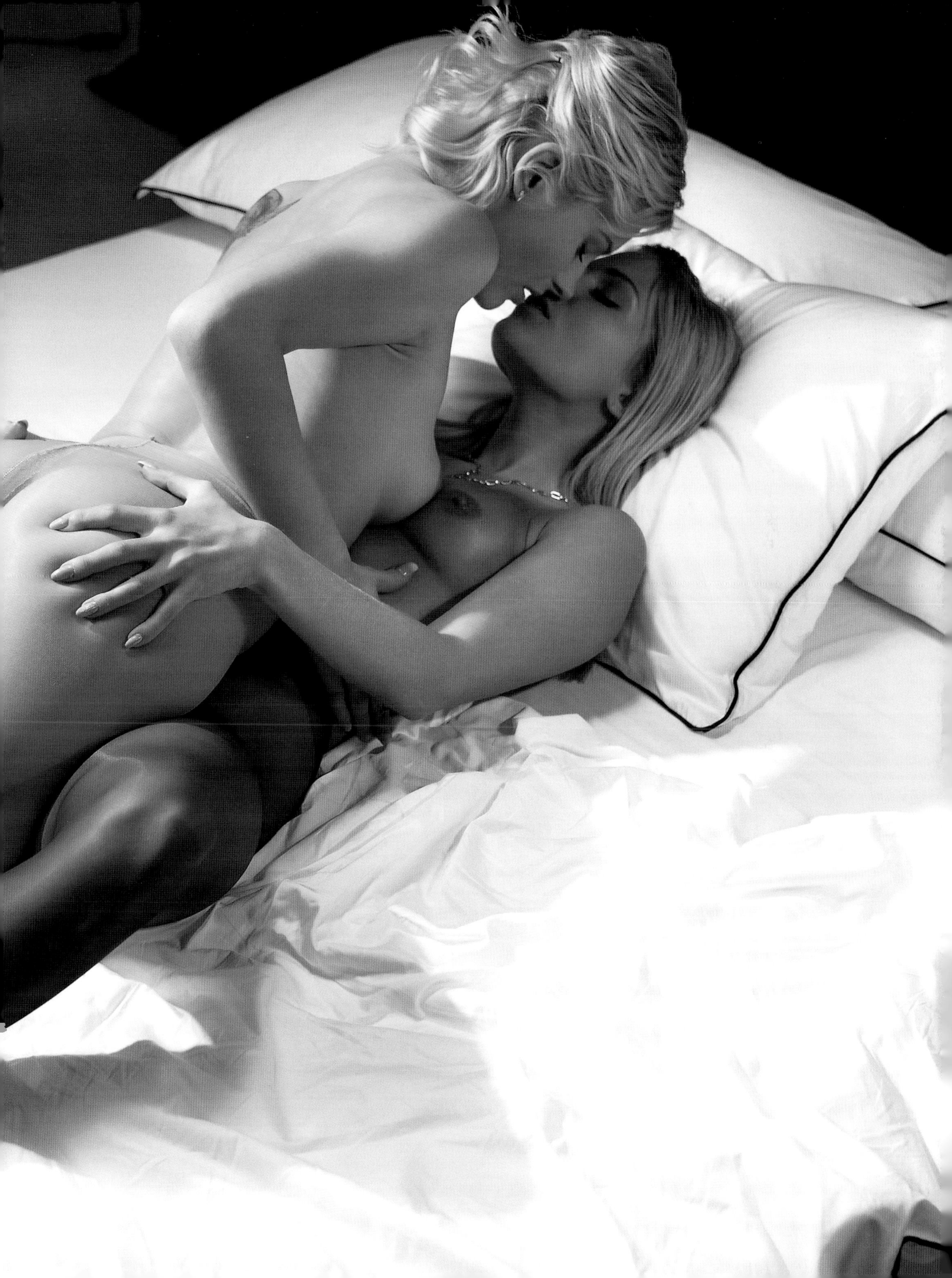

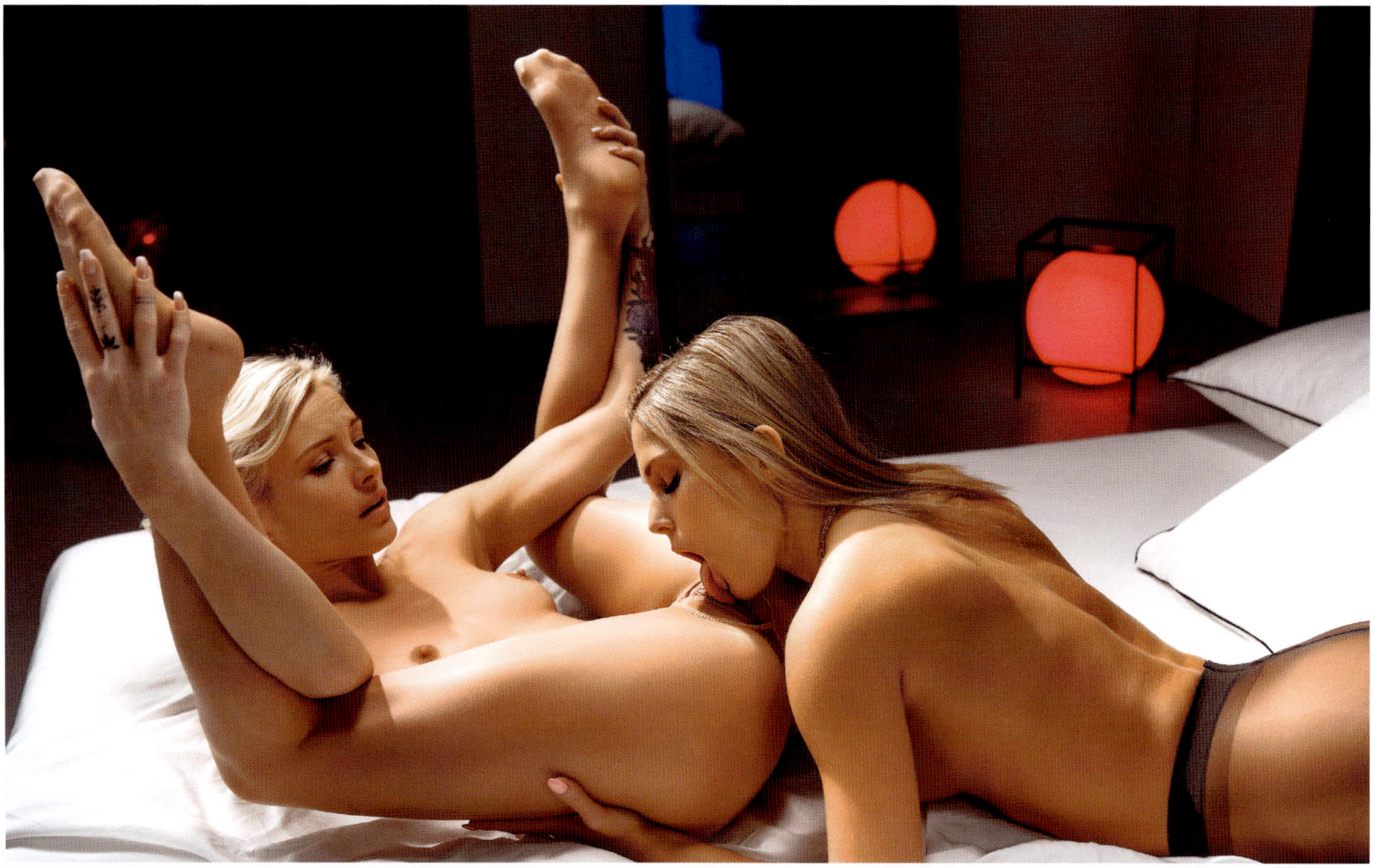

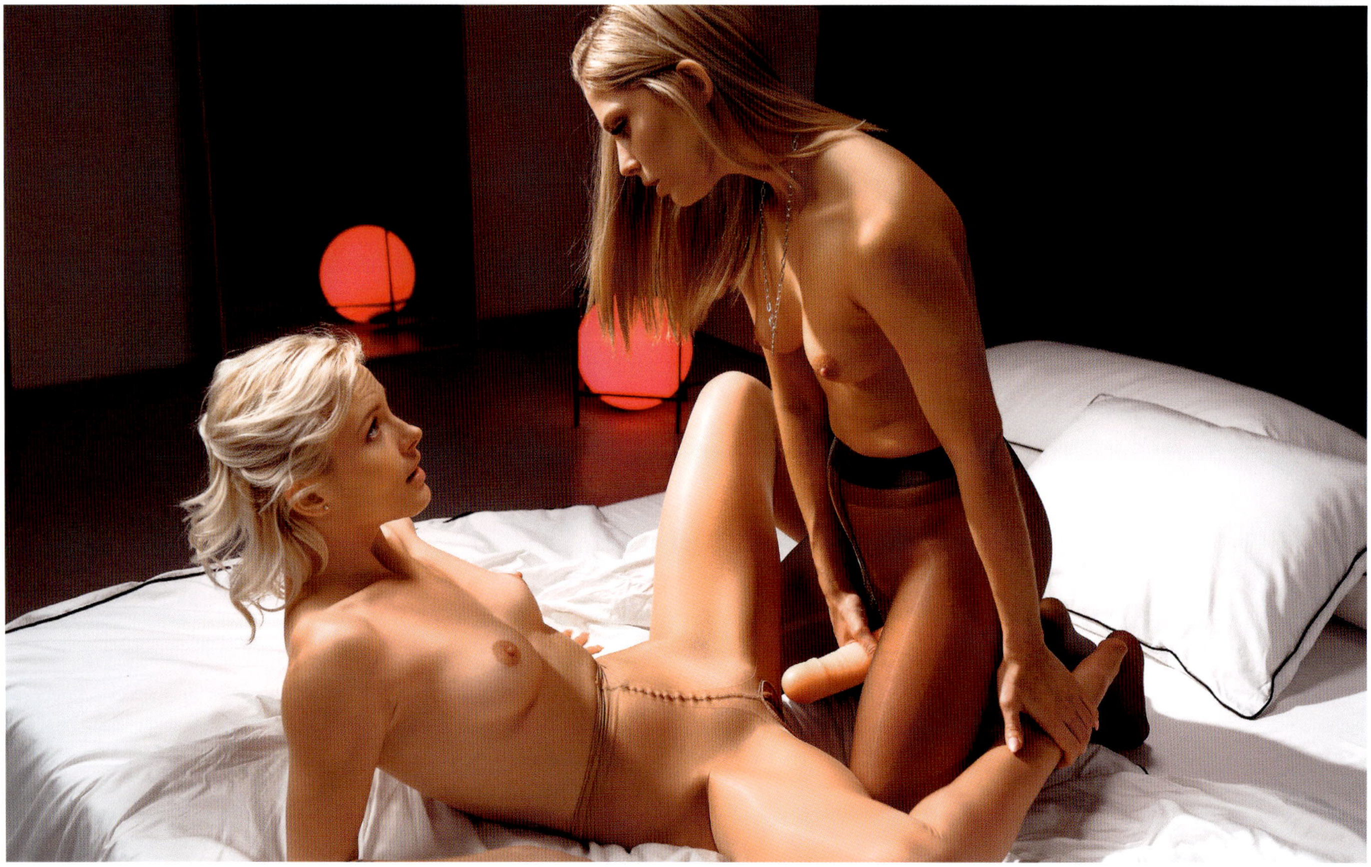

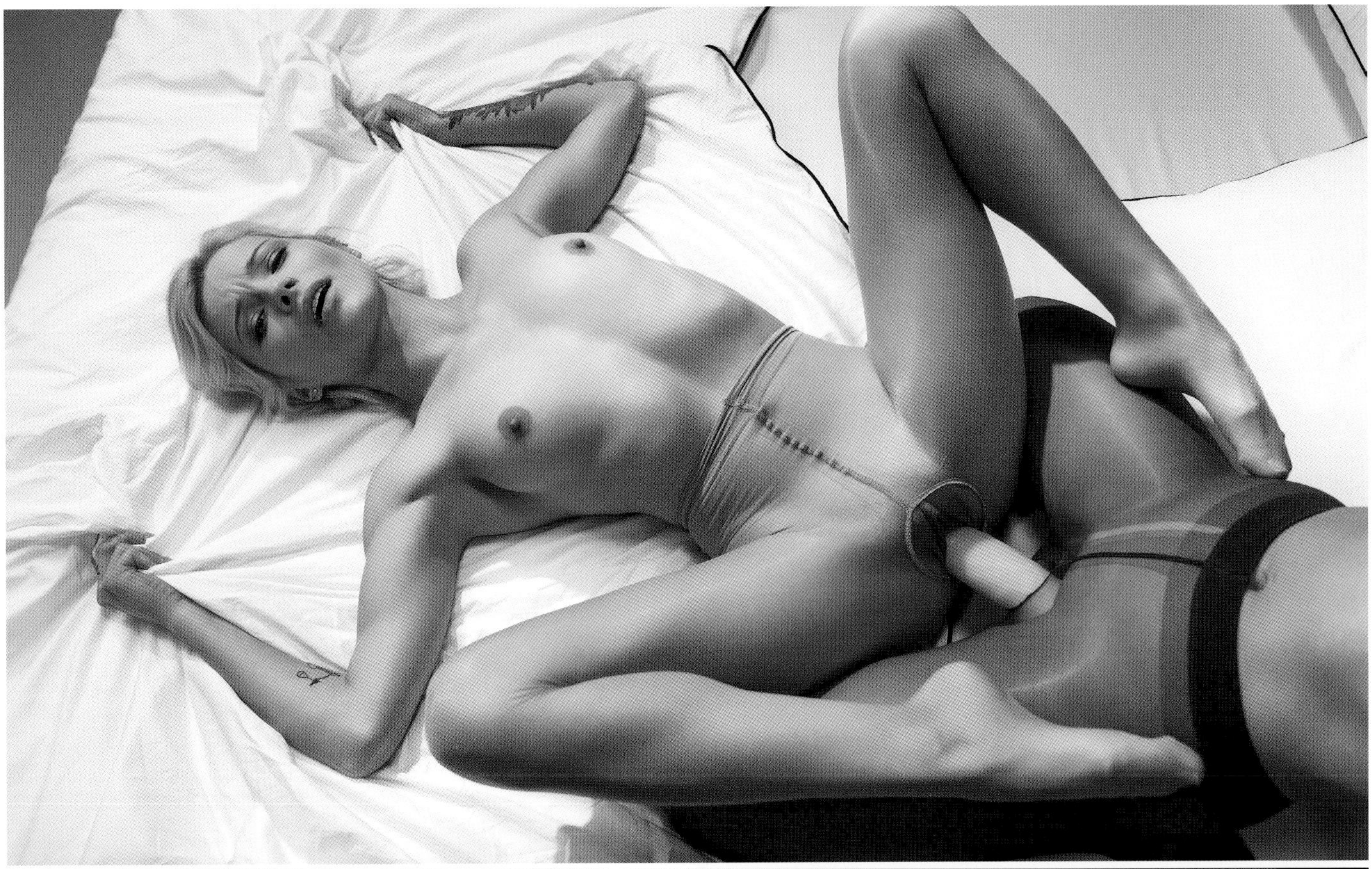

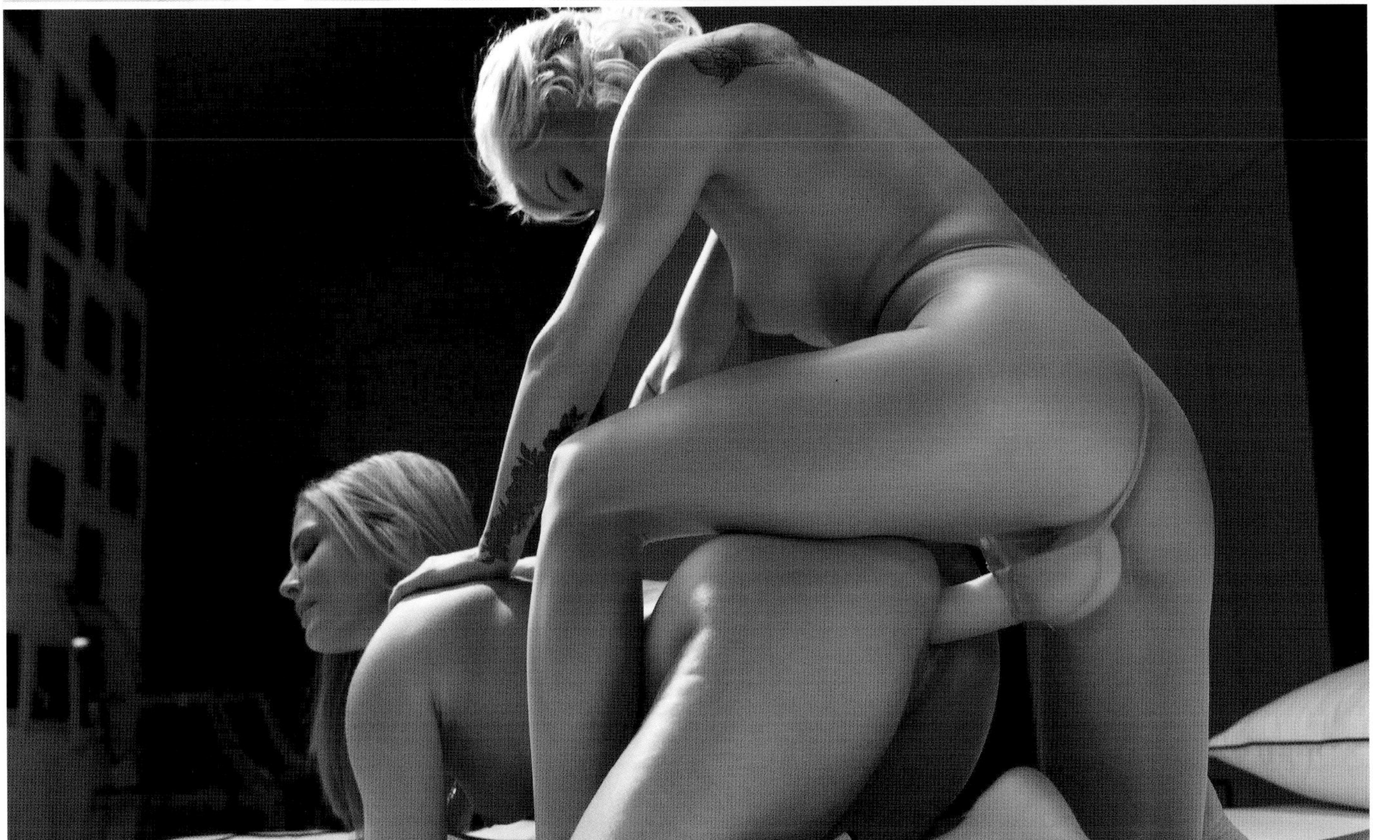

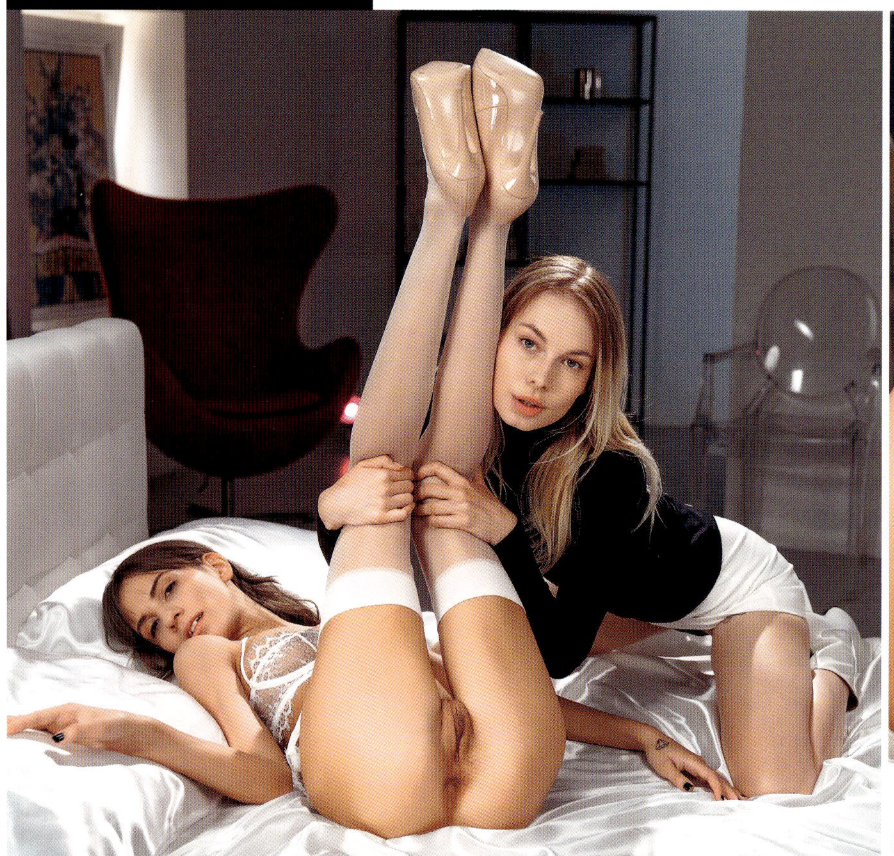

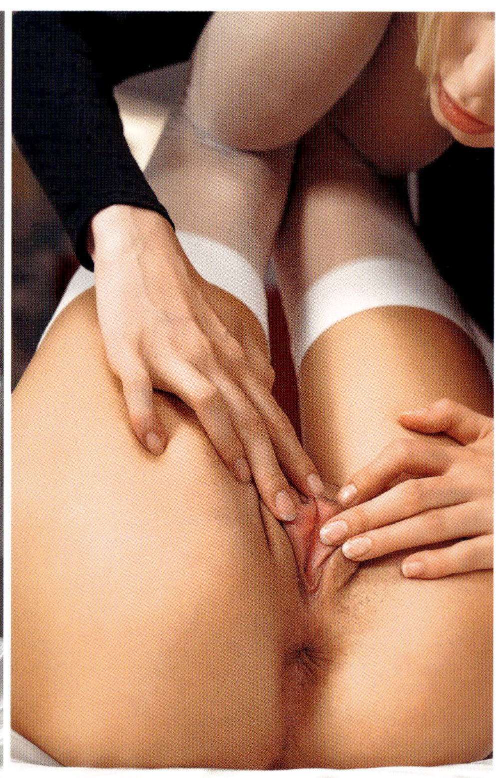

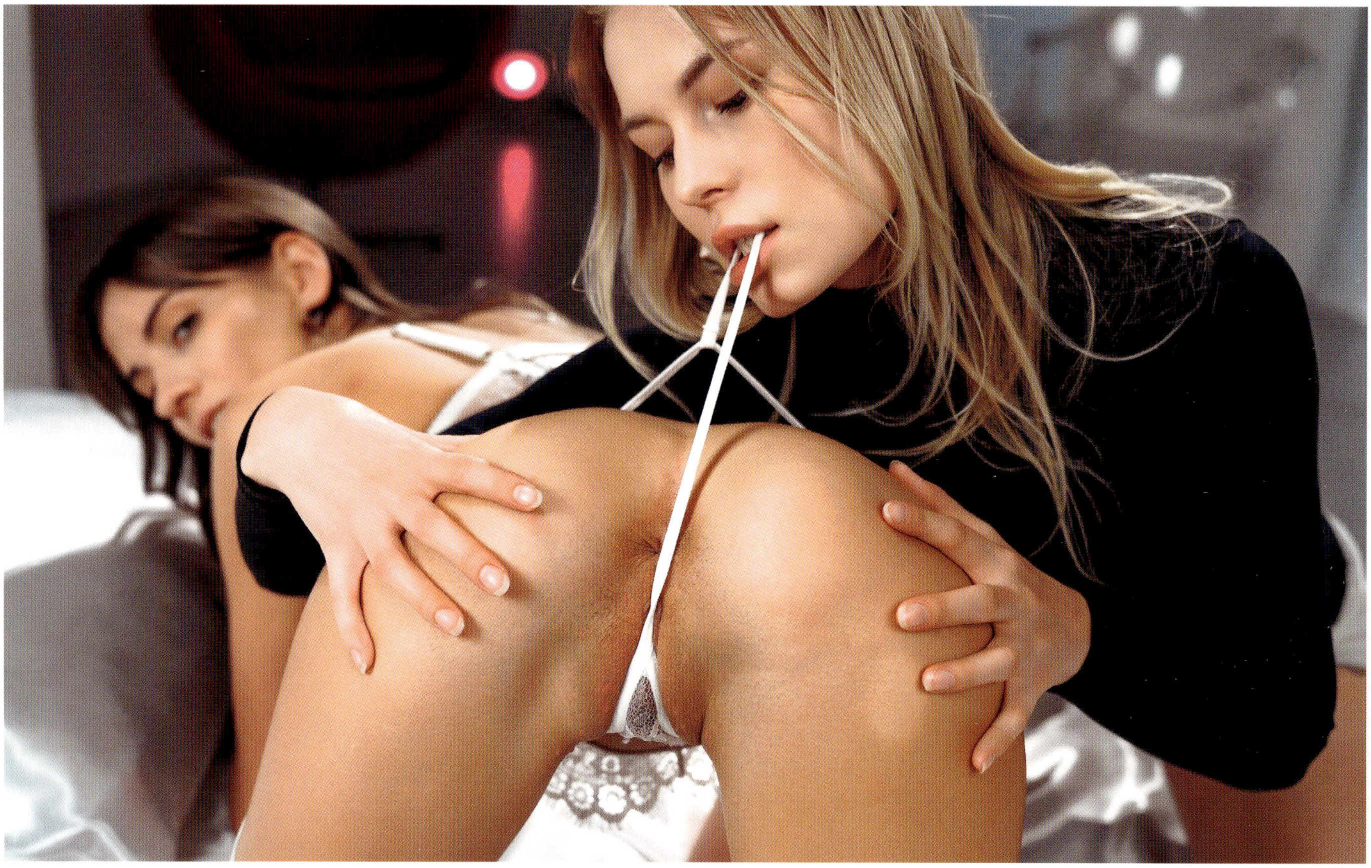

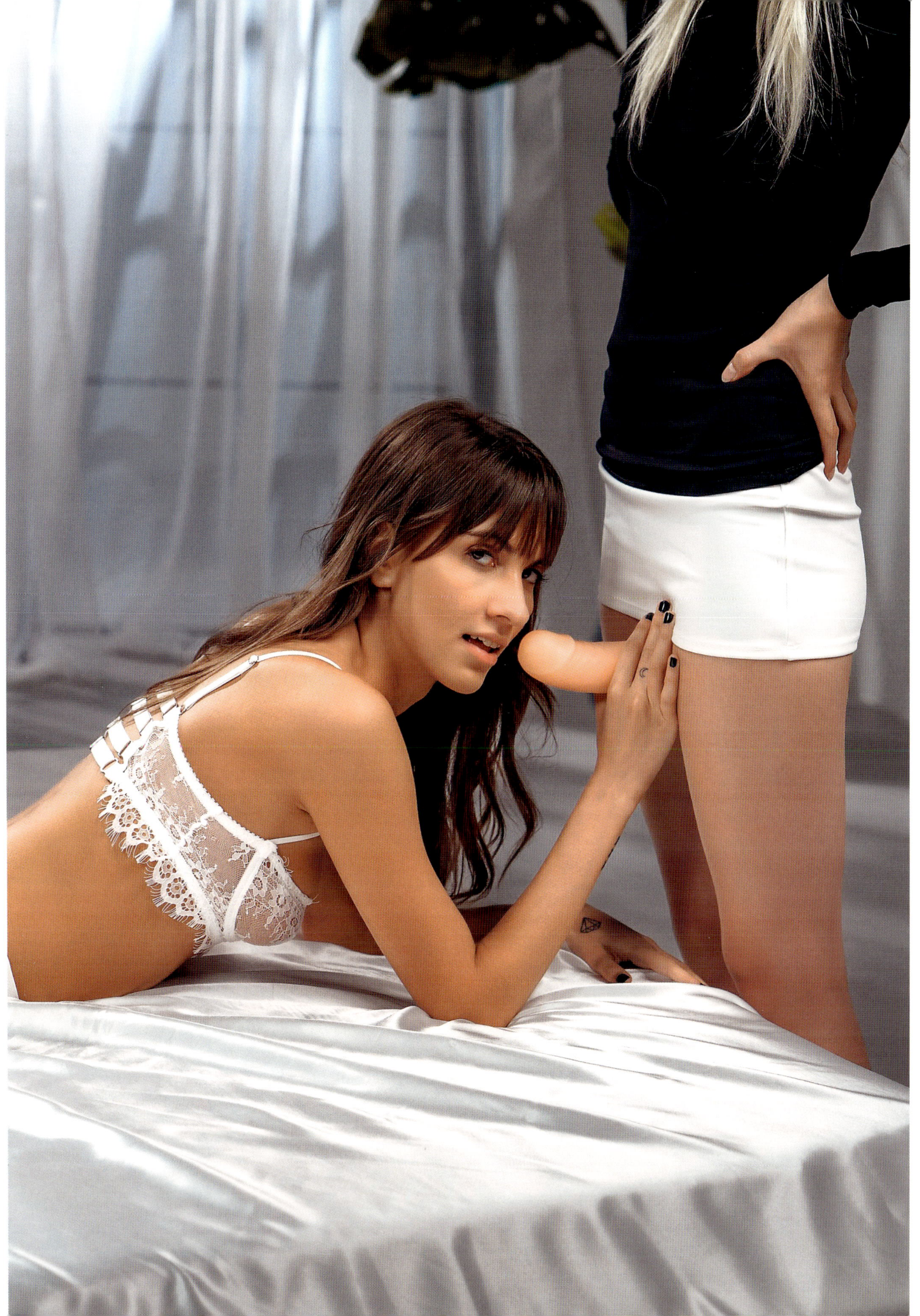

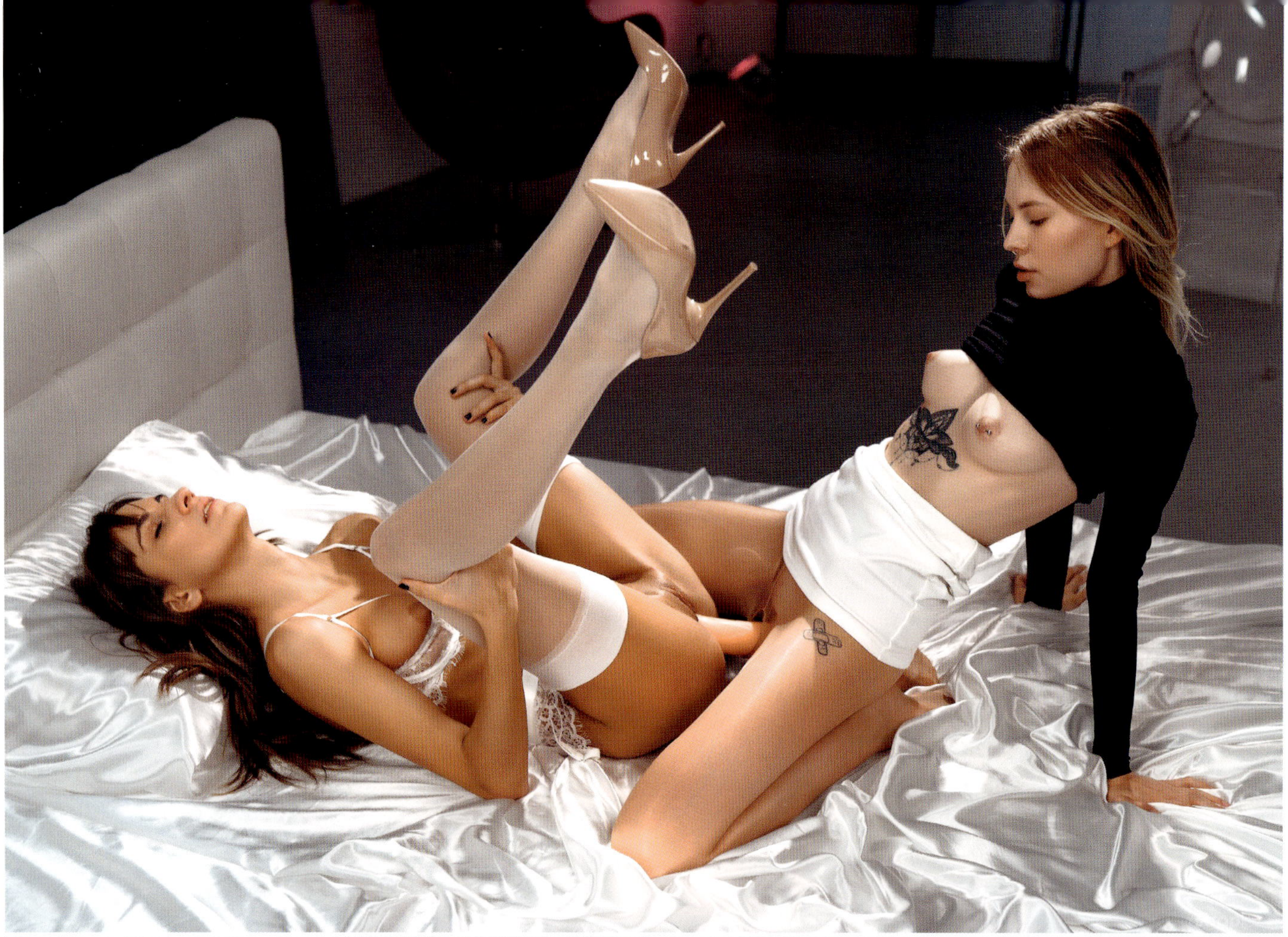

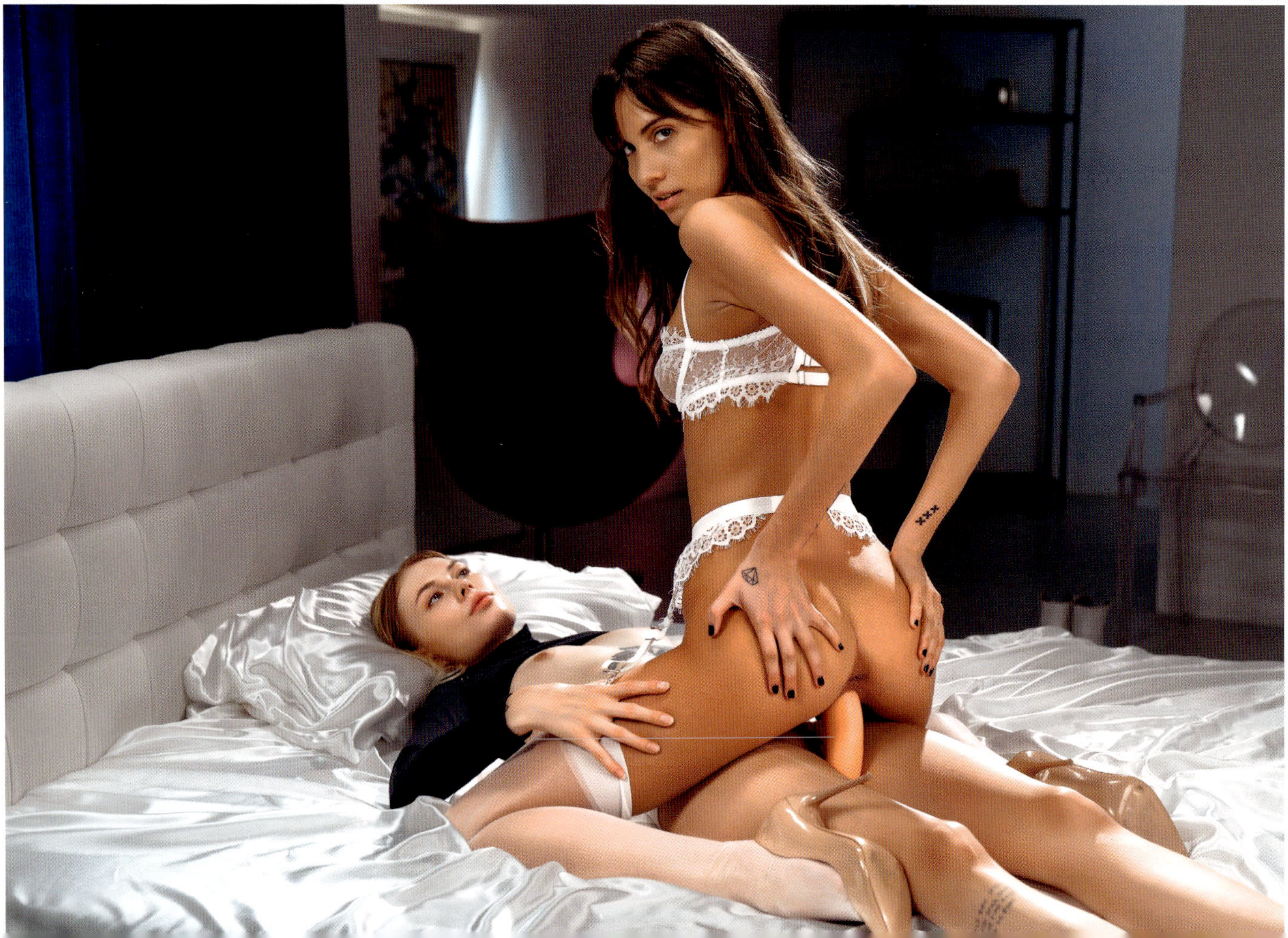

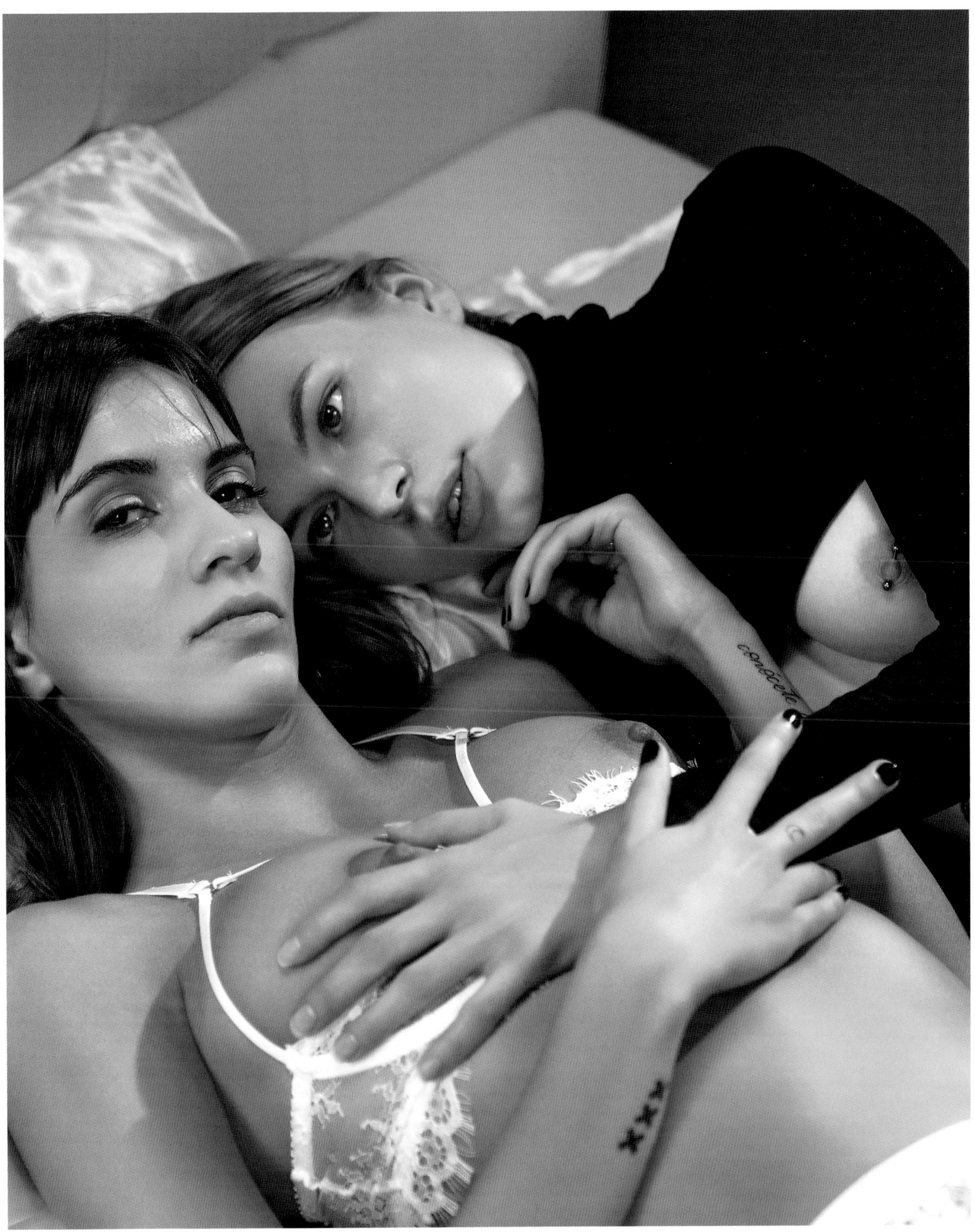

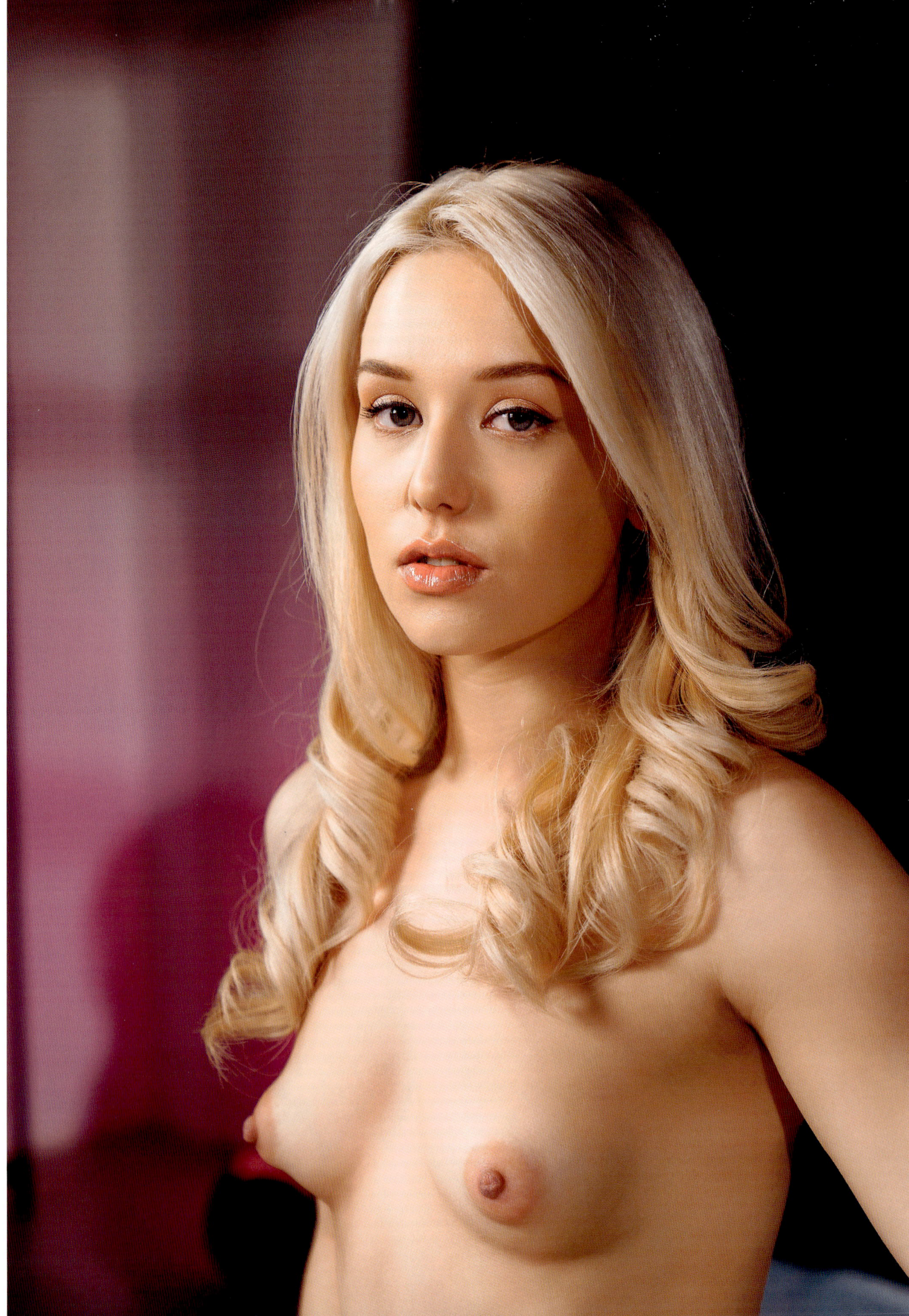

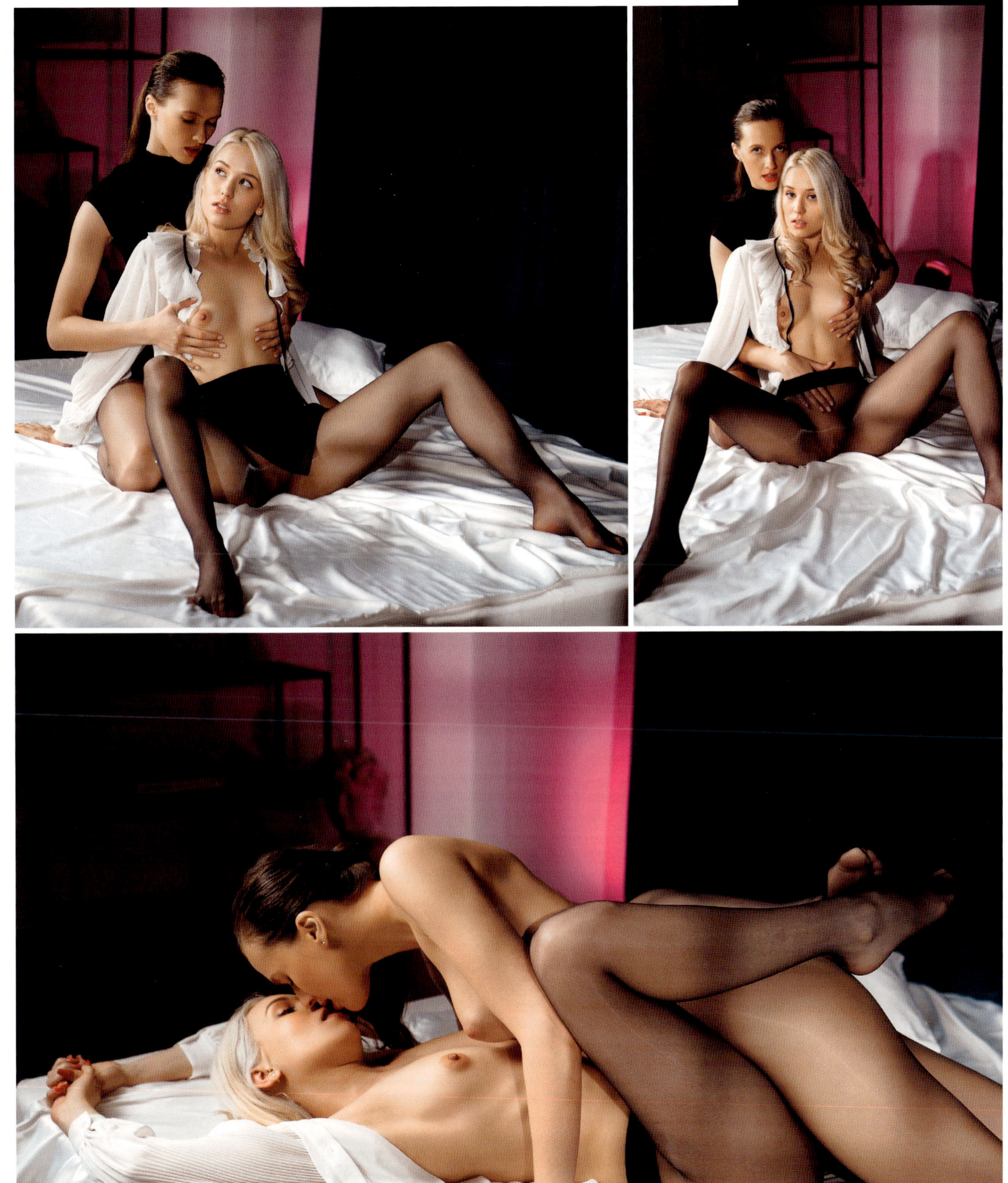

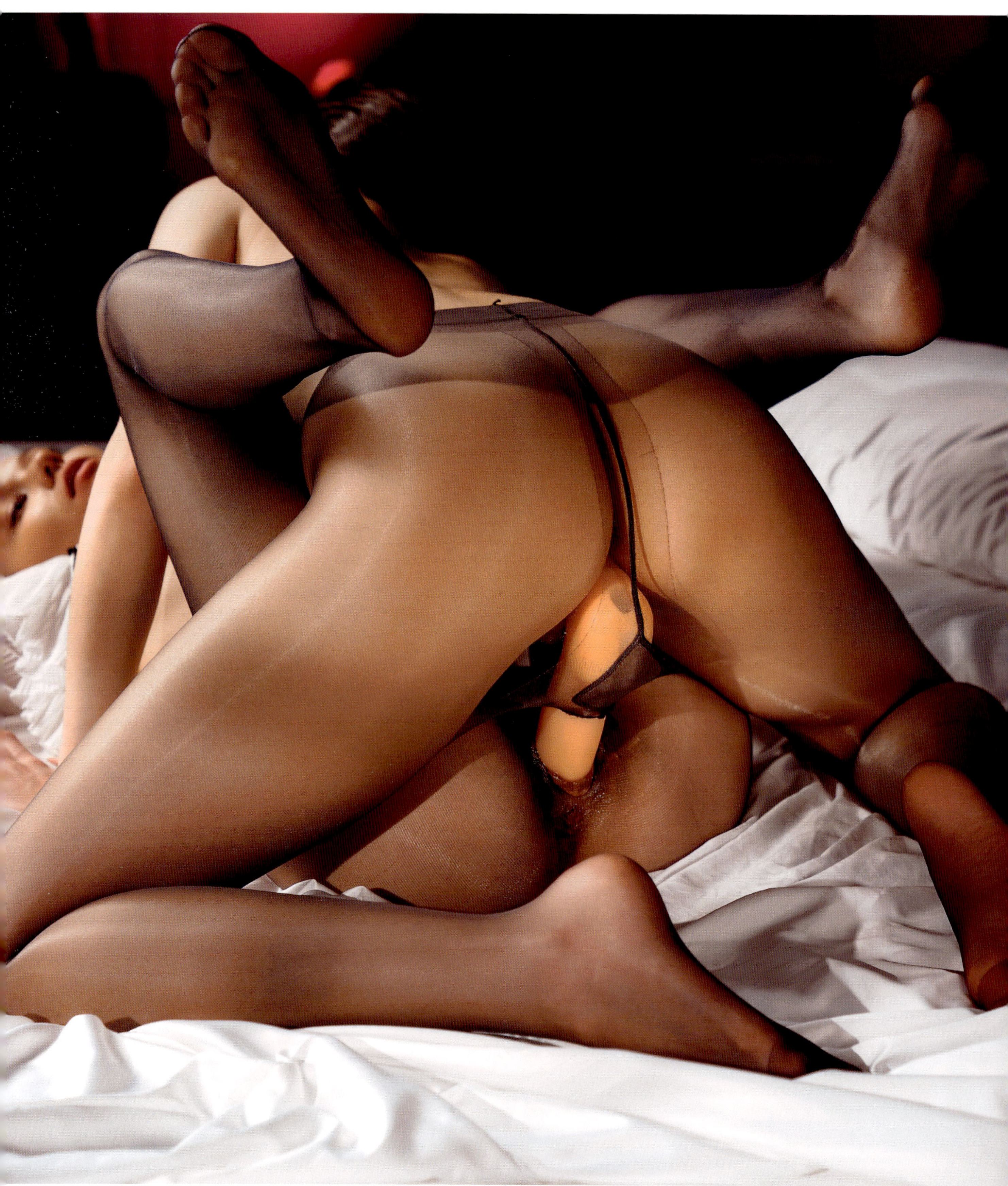

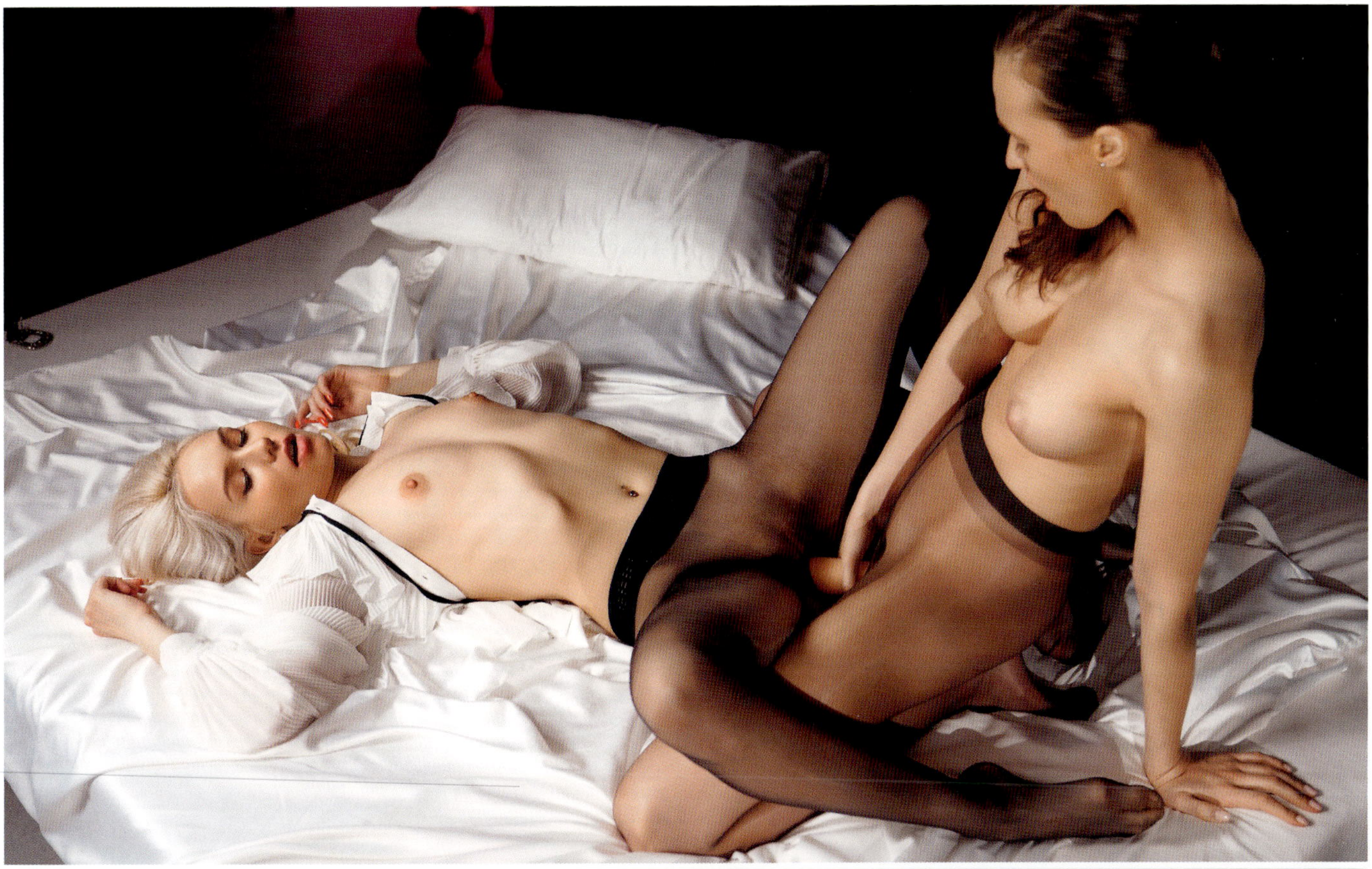

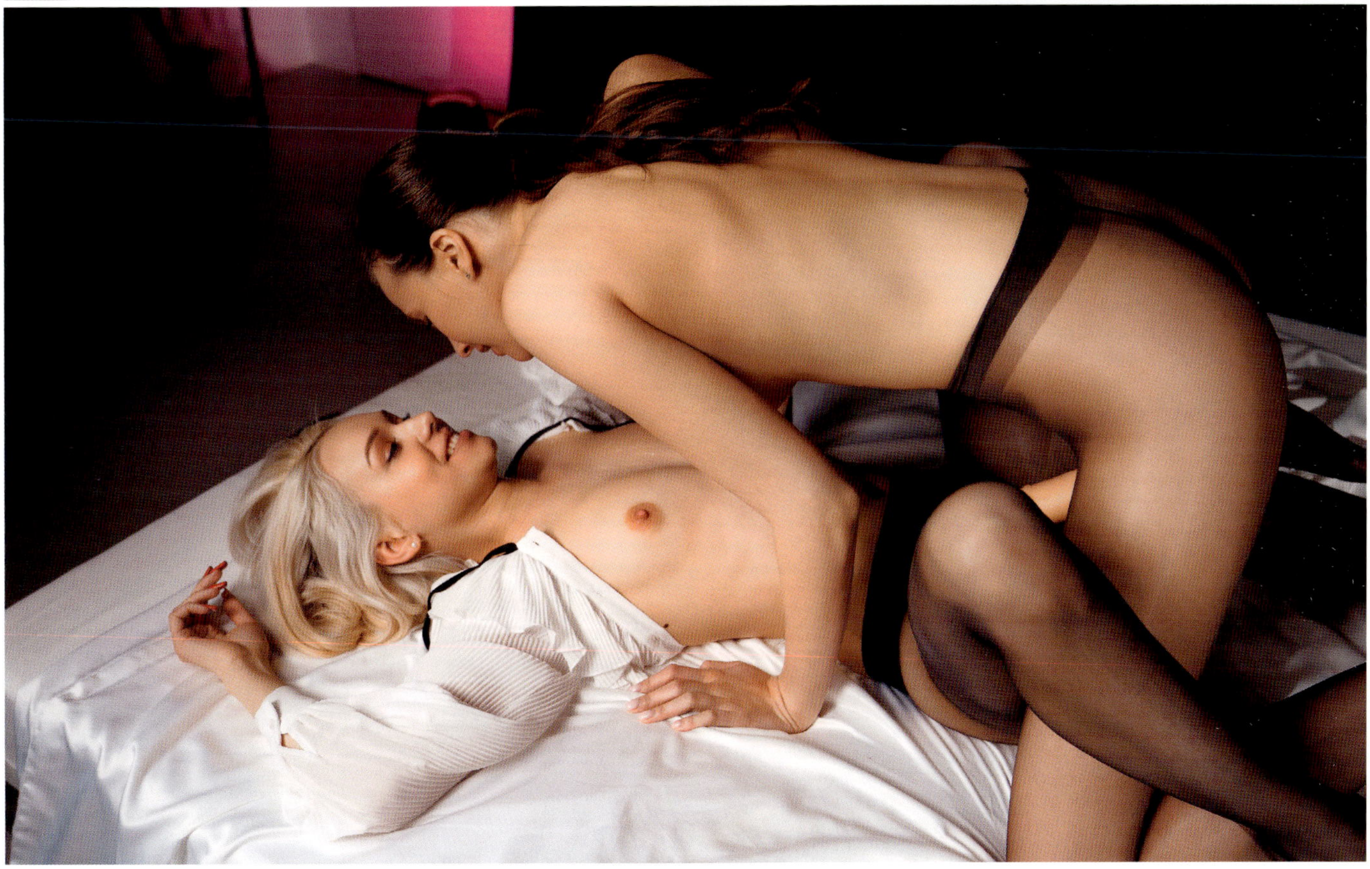

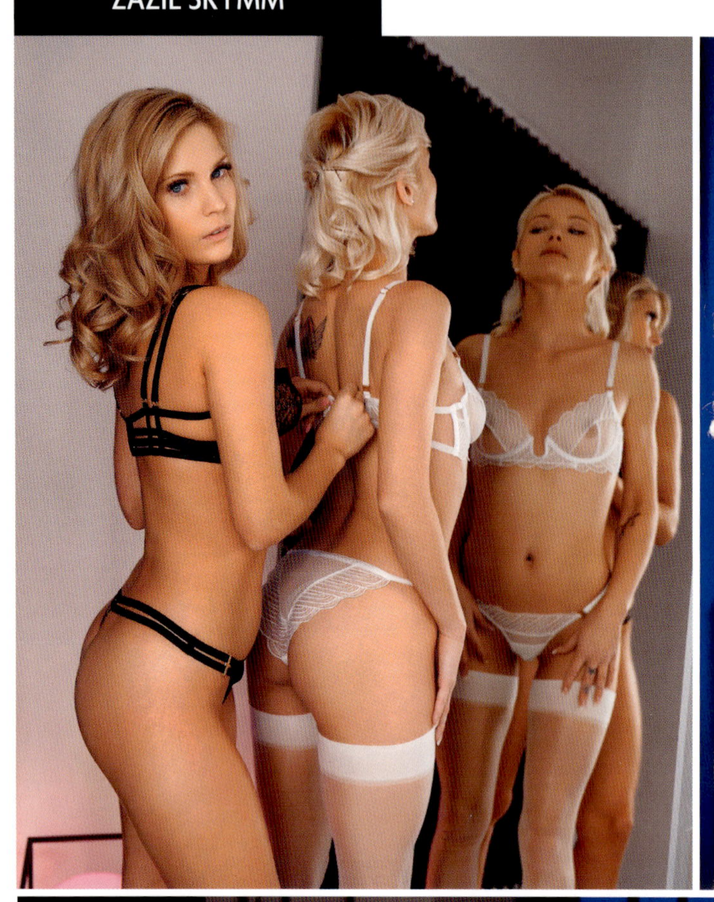
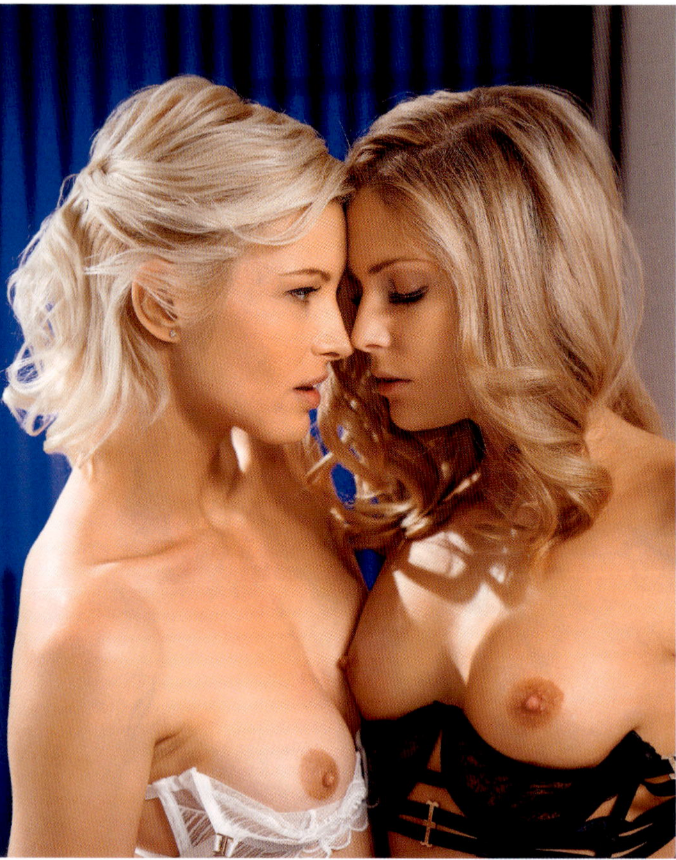

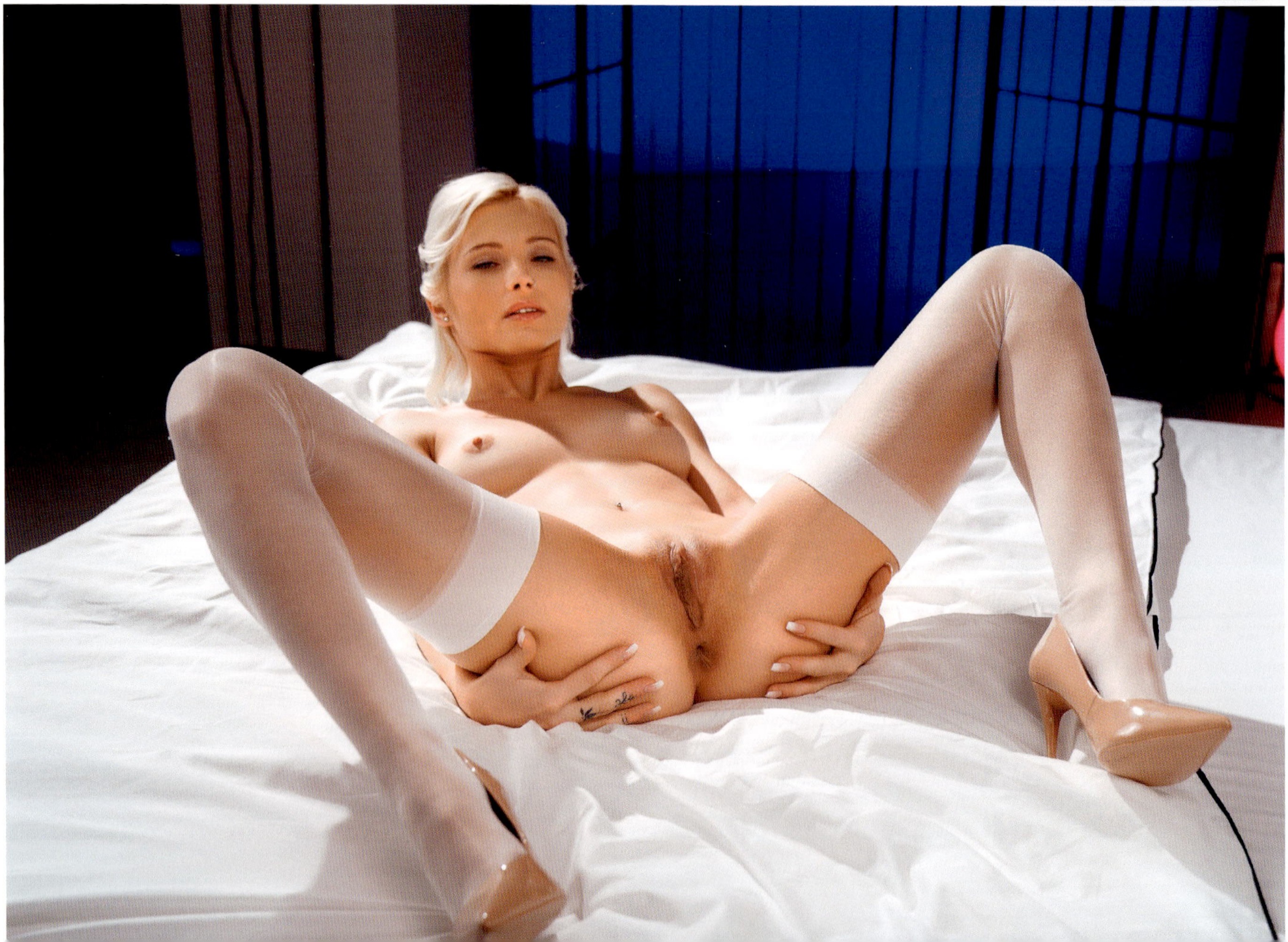

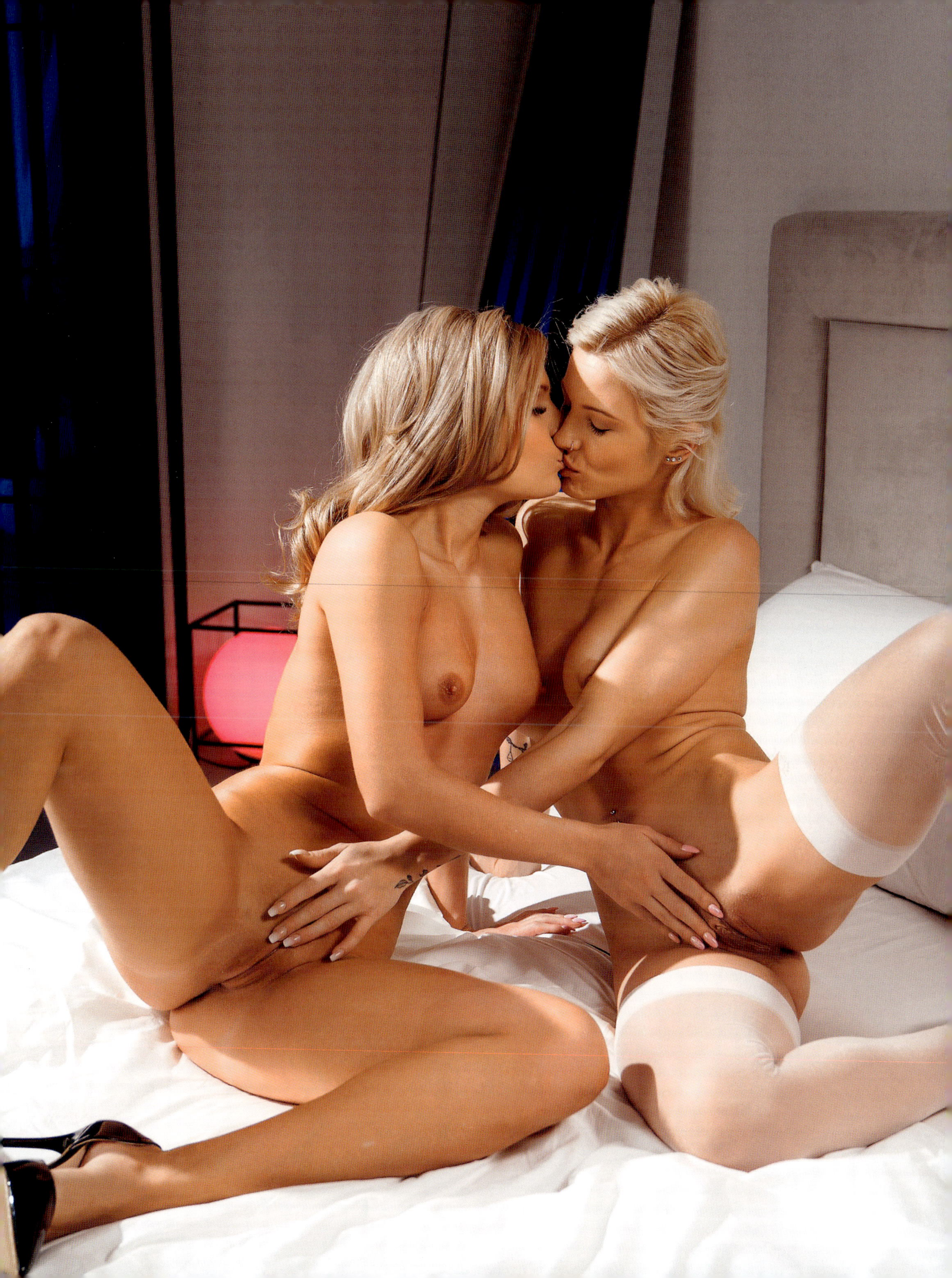

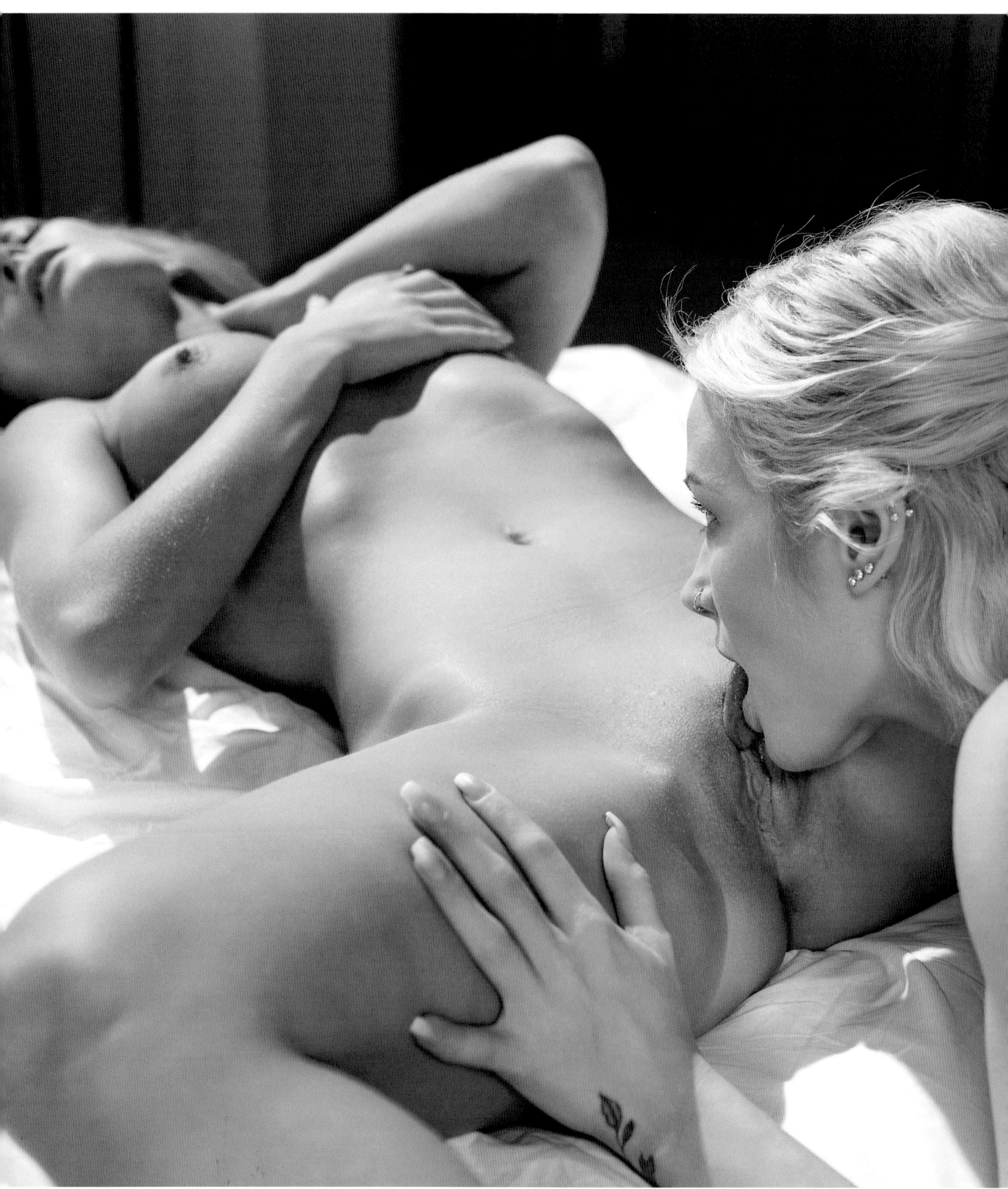

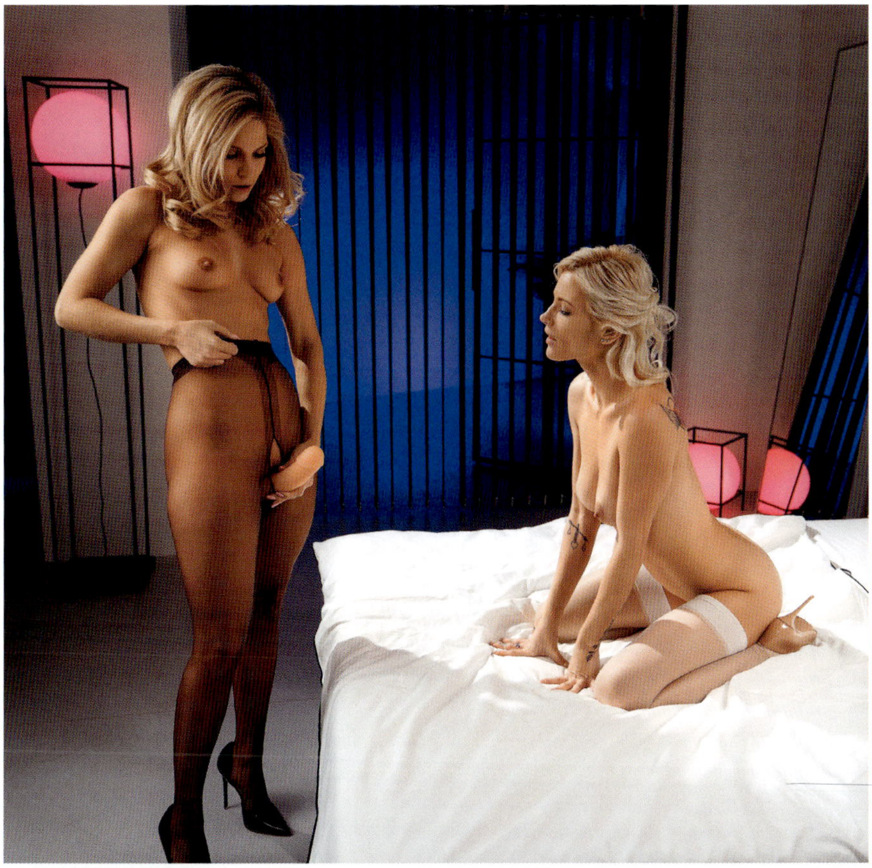

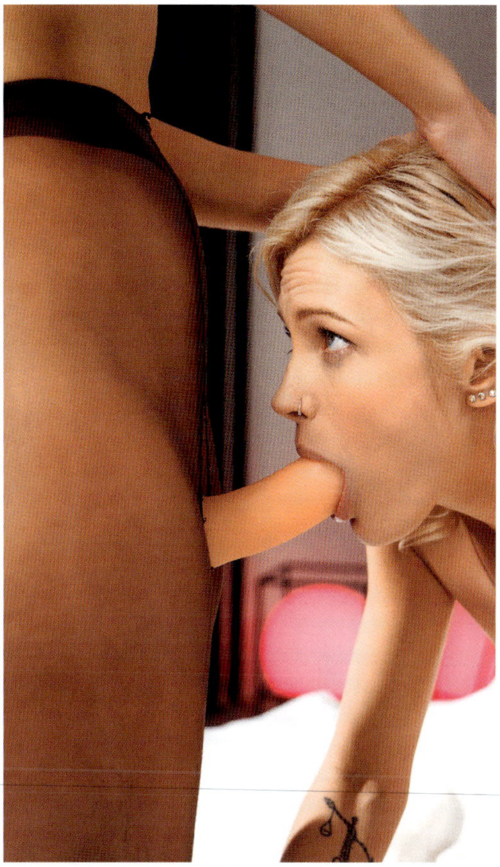

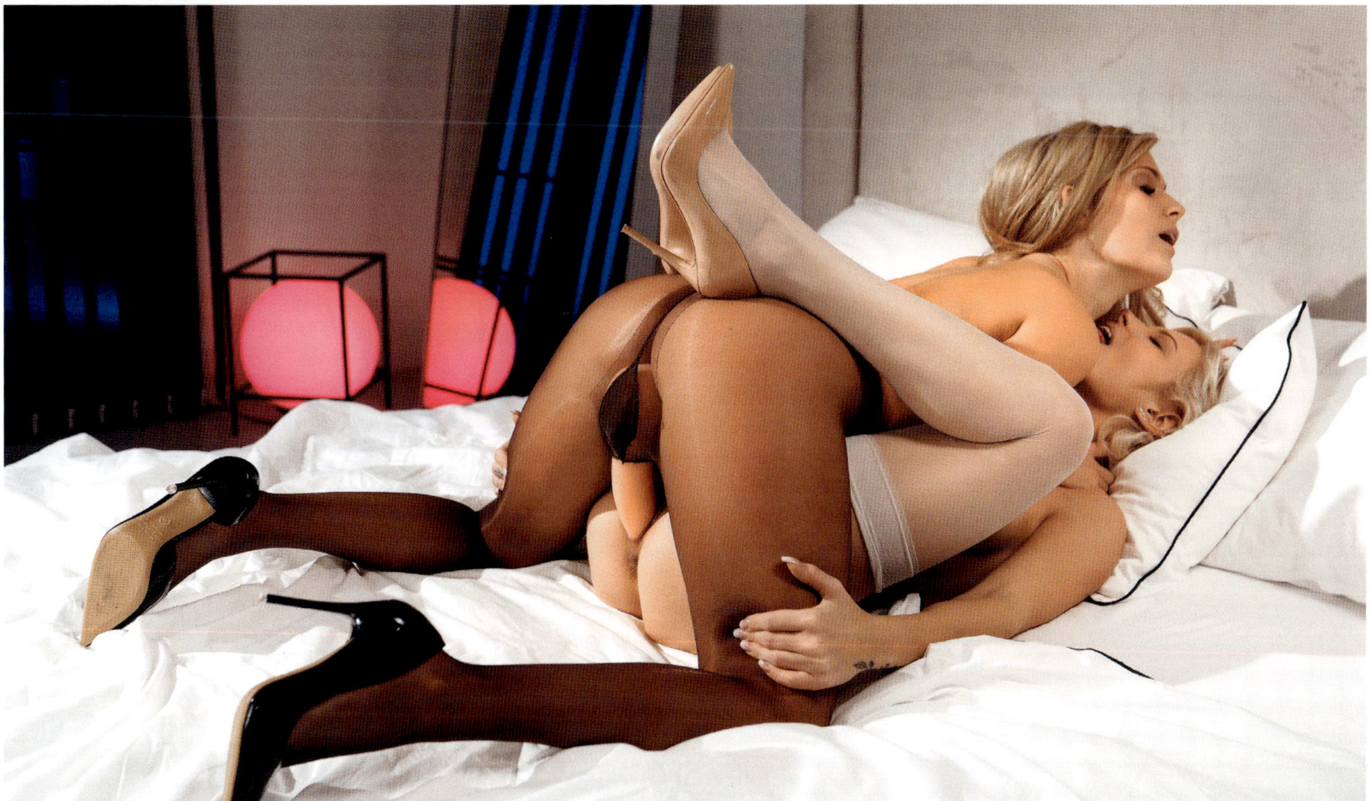

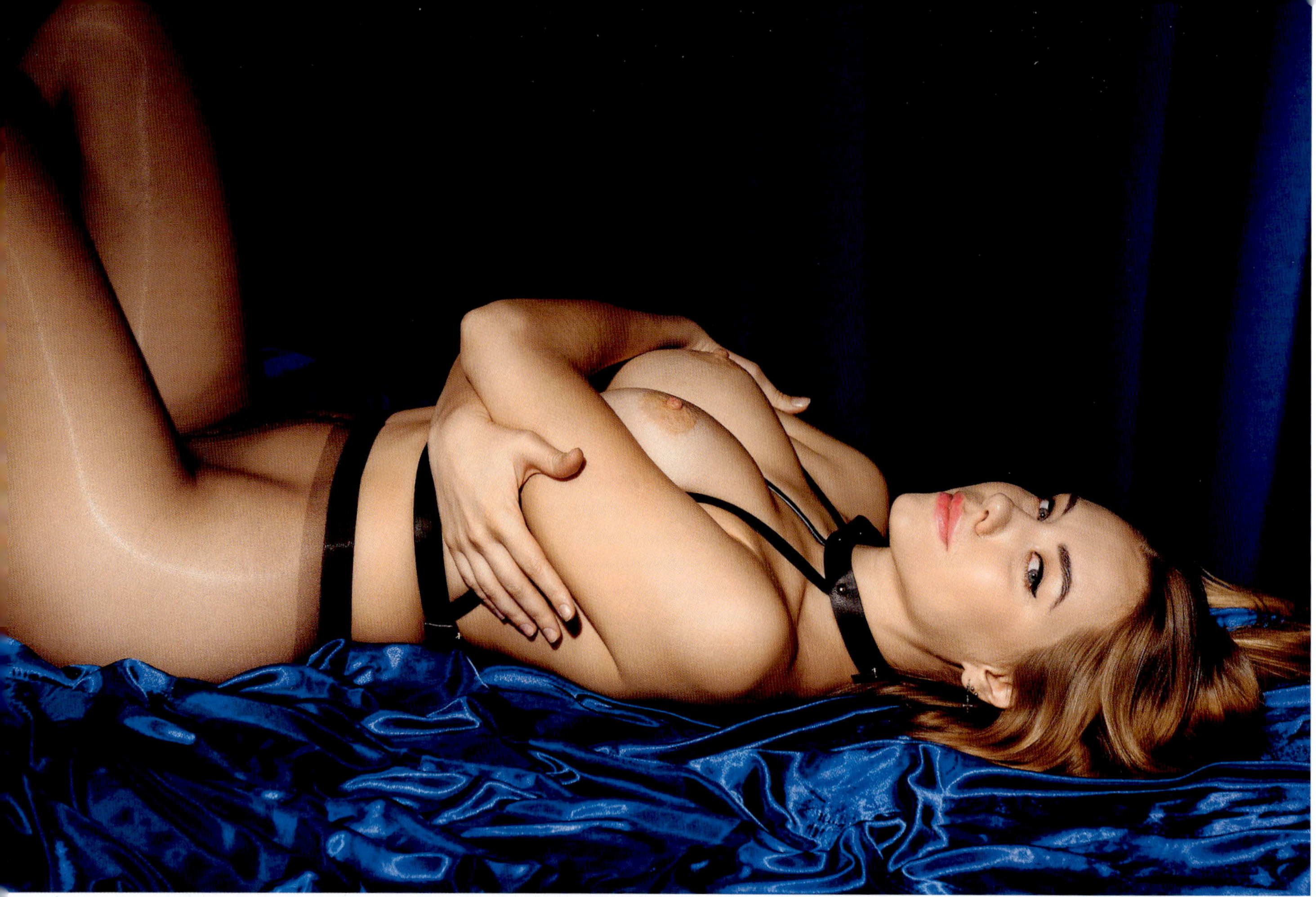

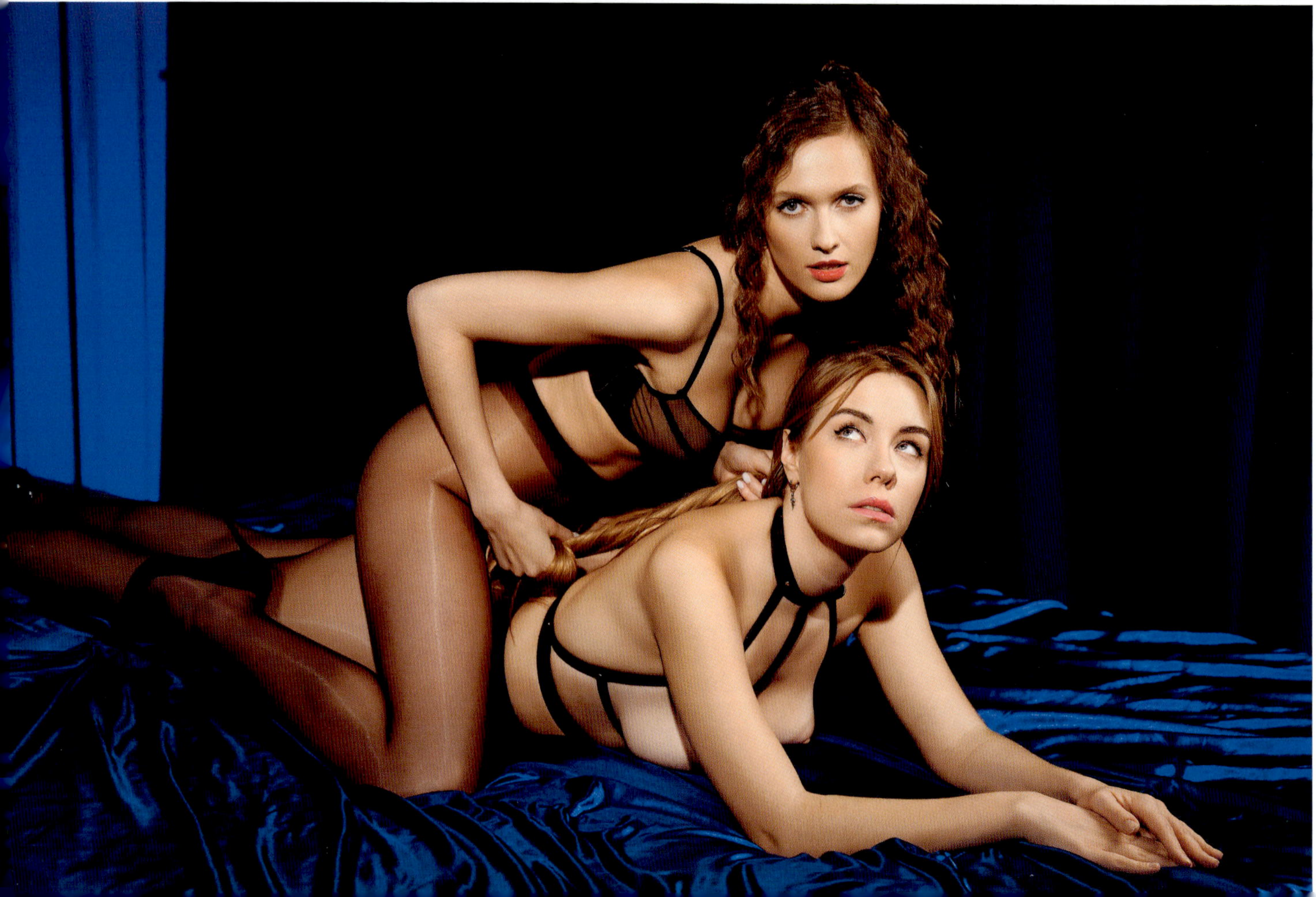

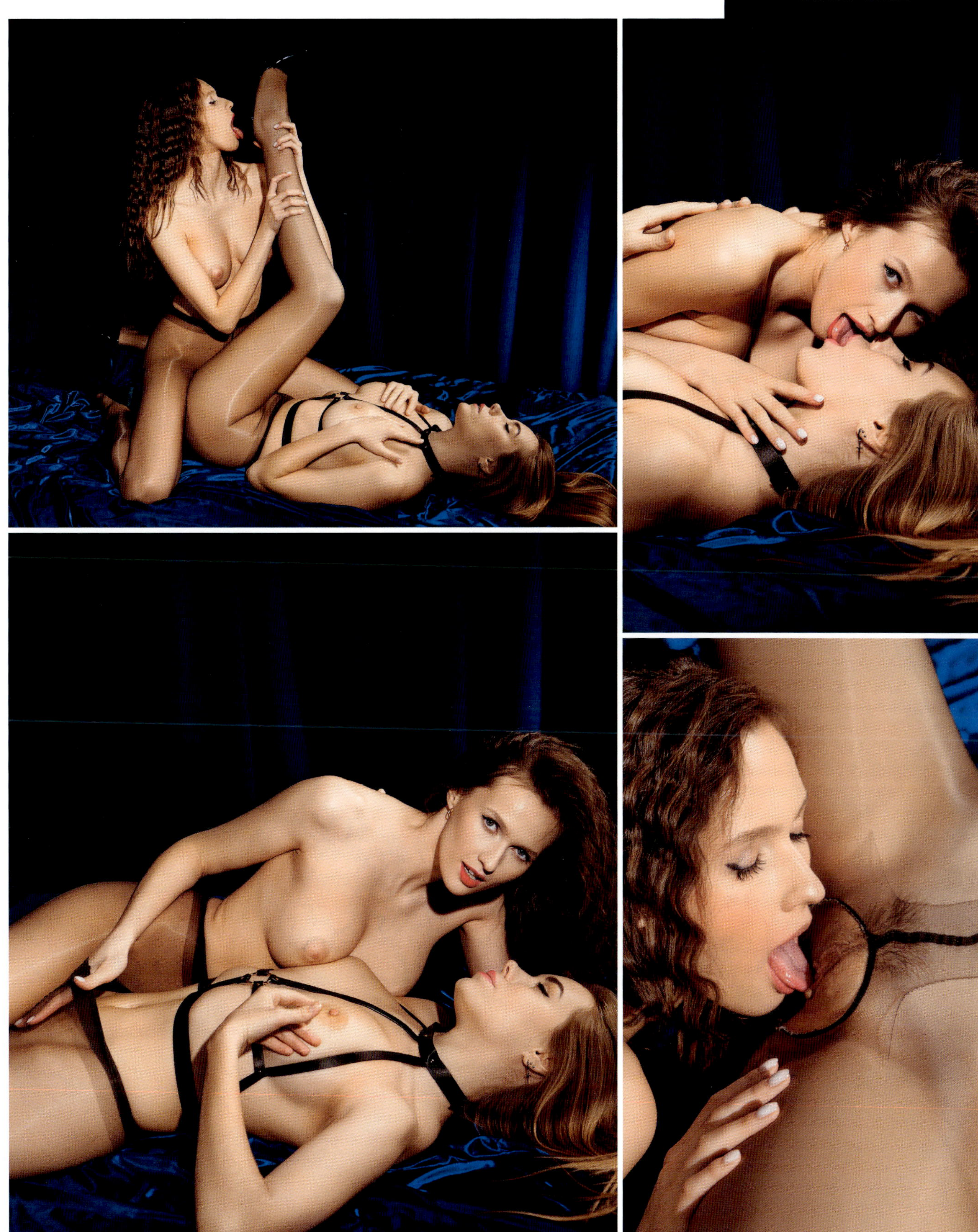
RYANA
STACY CRUZ

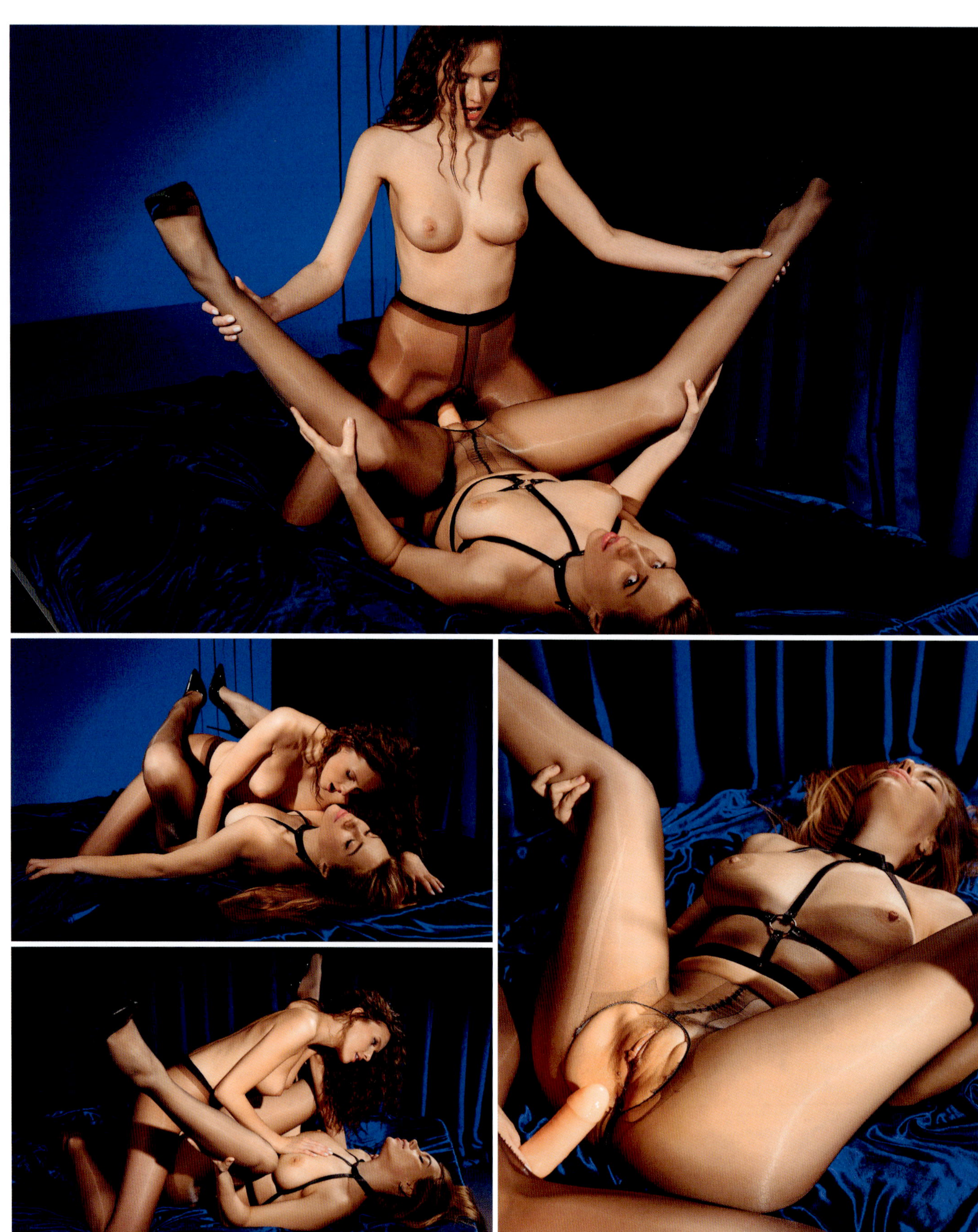

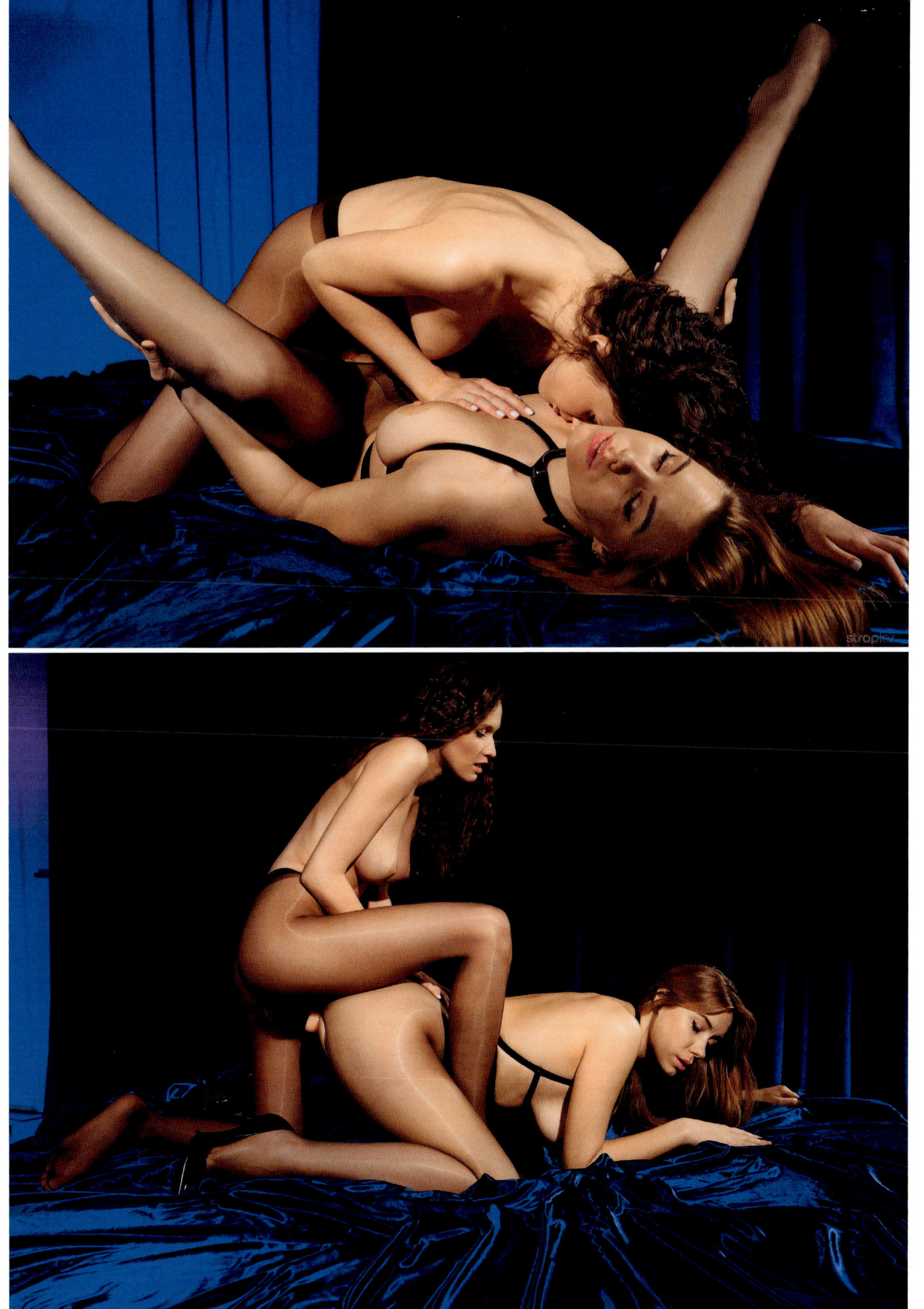

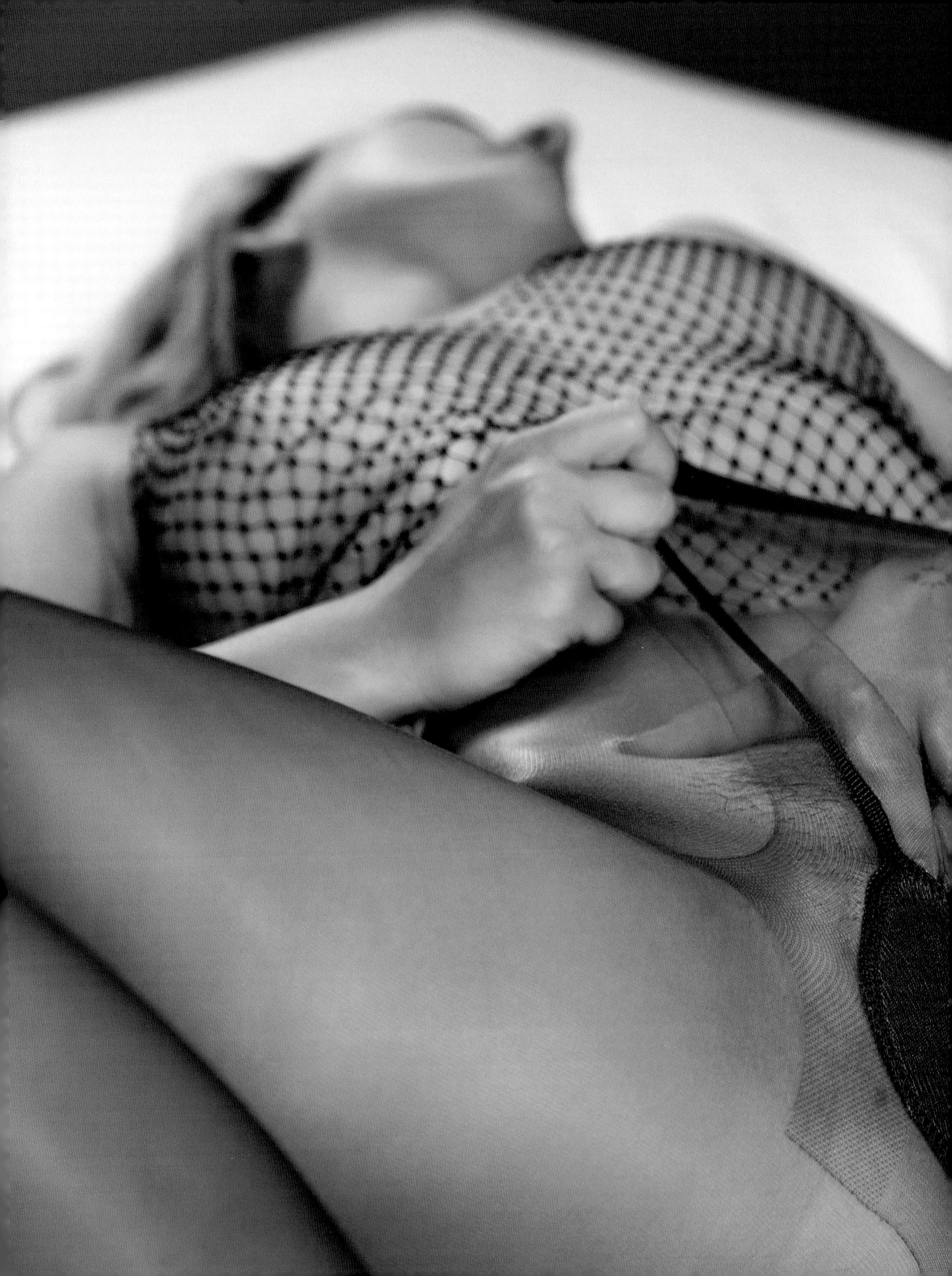

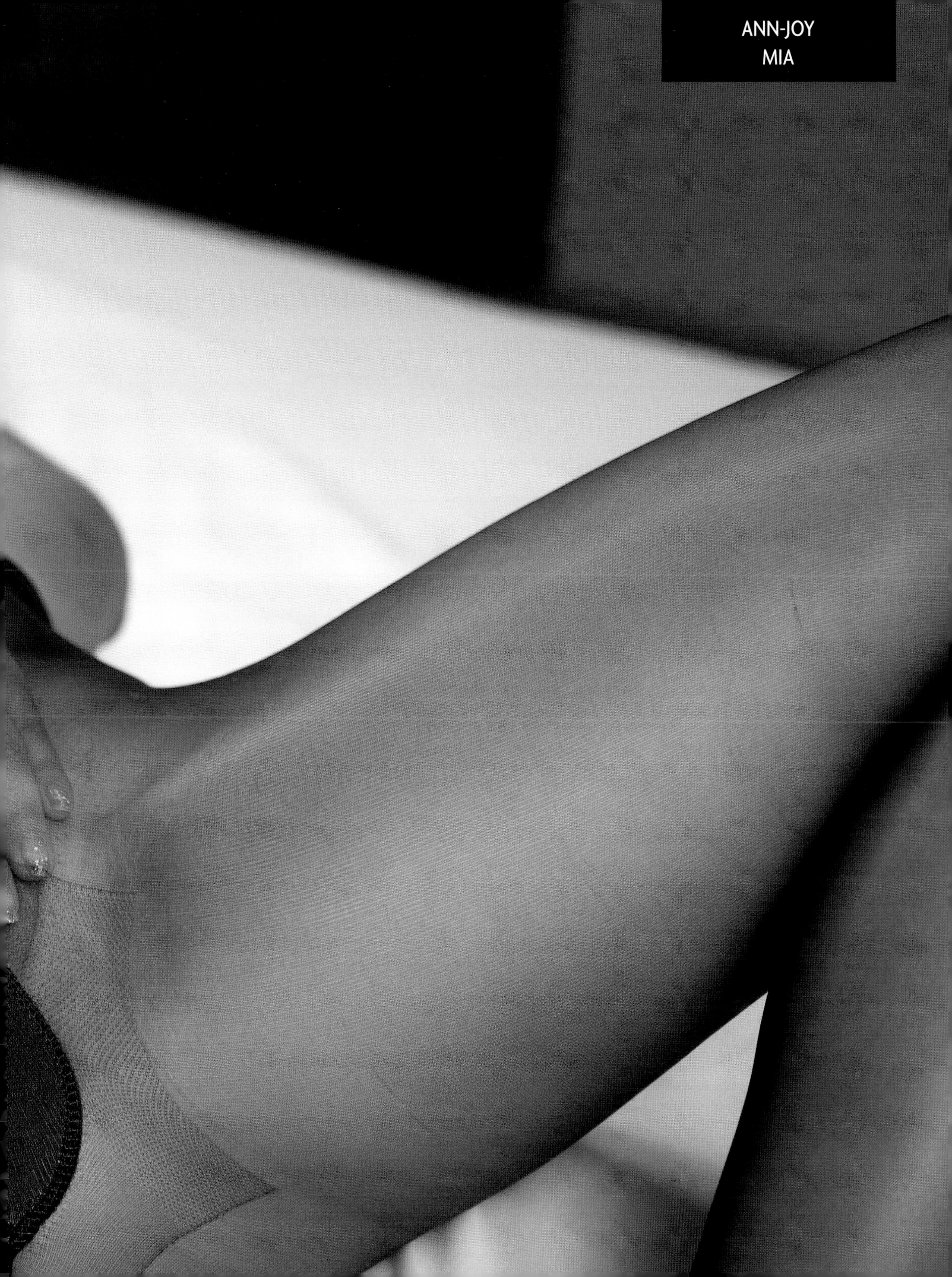
ANN-JOY
MIA

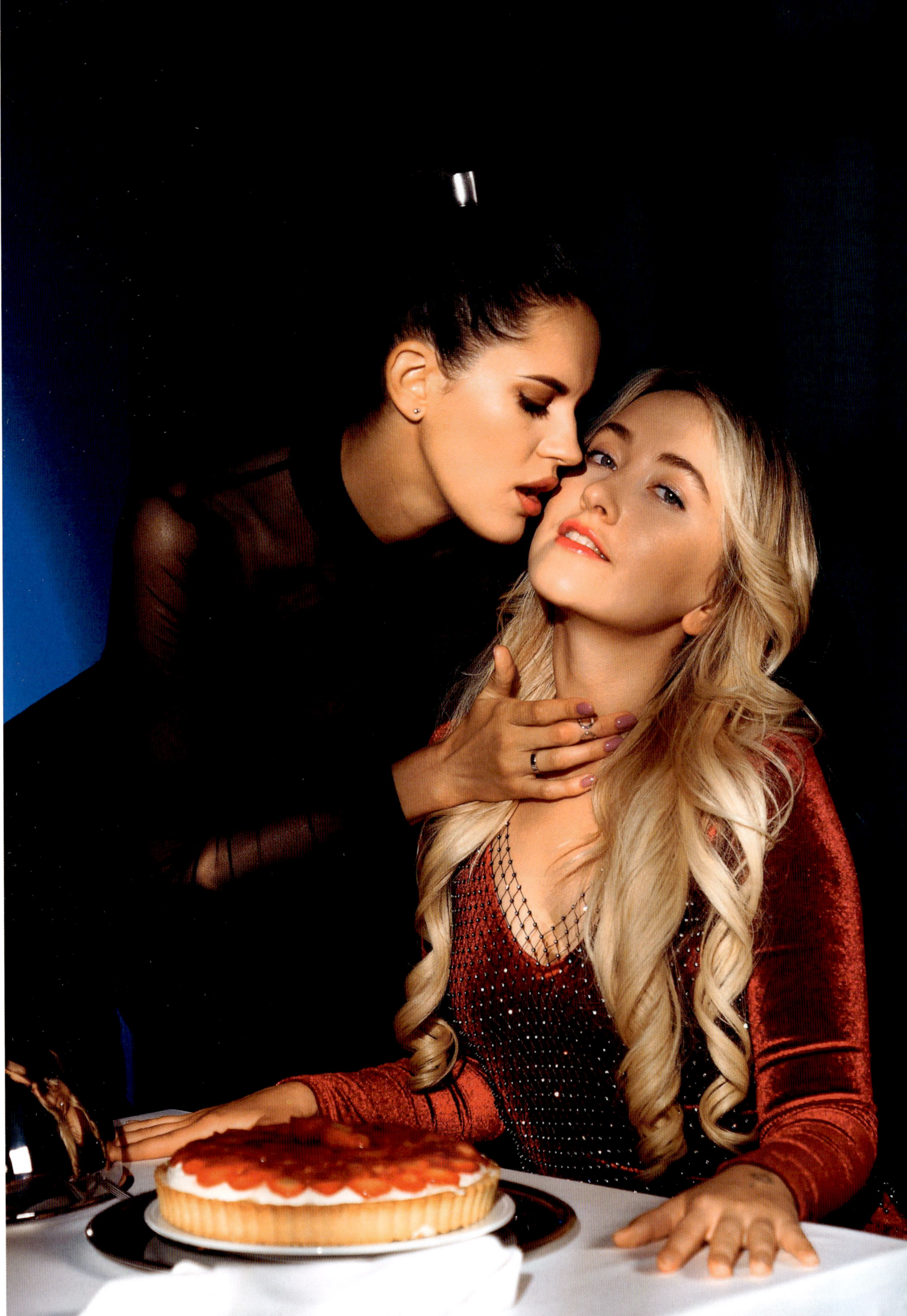

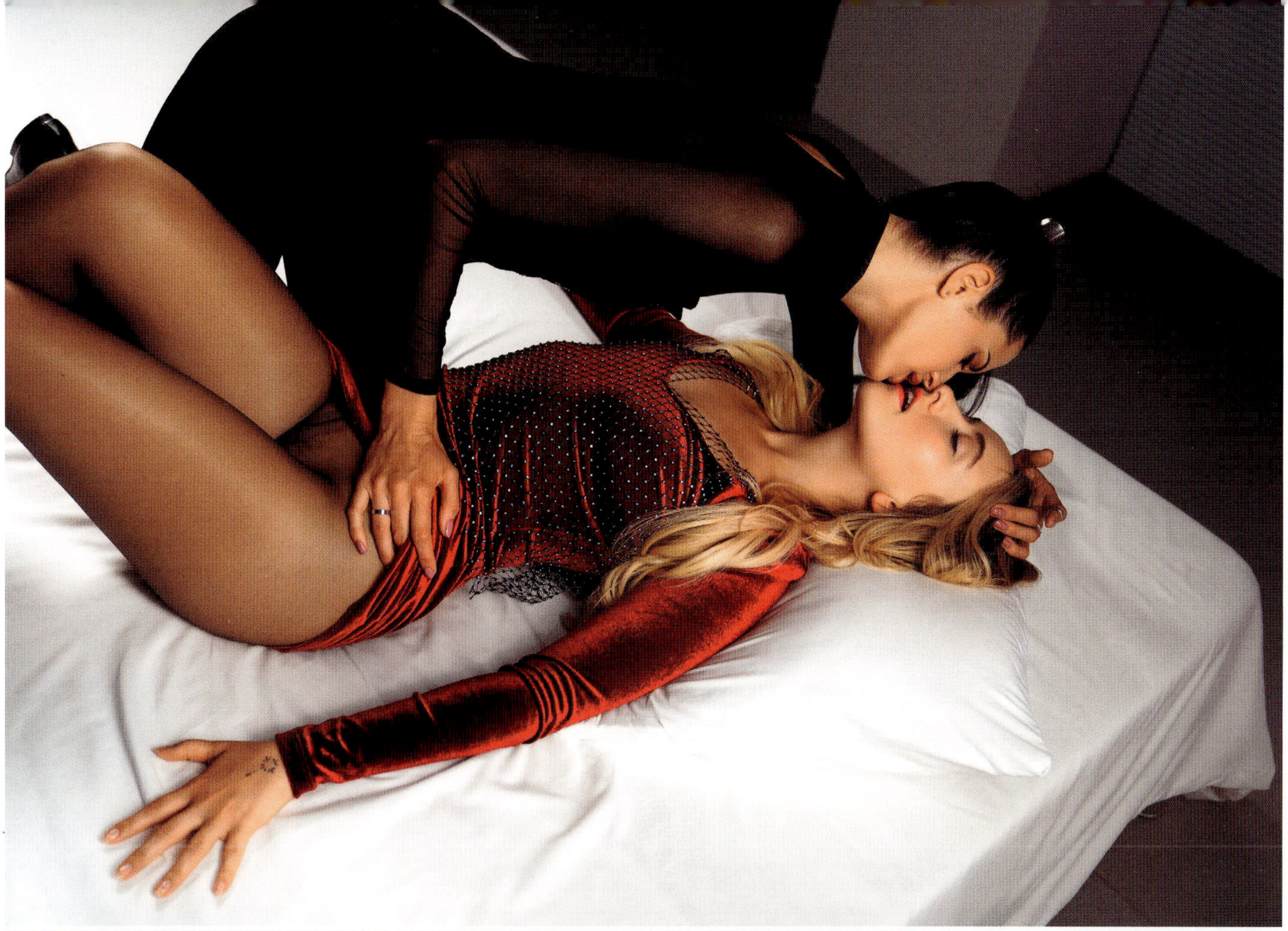

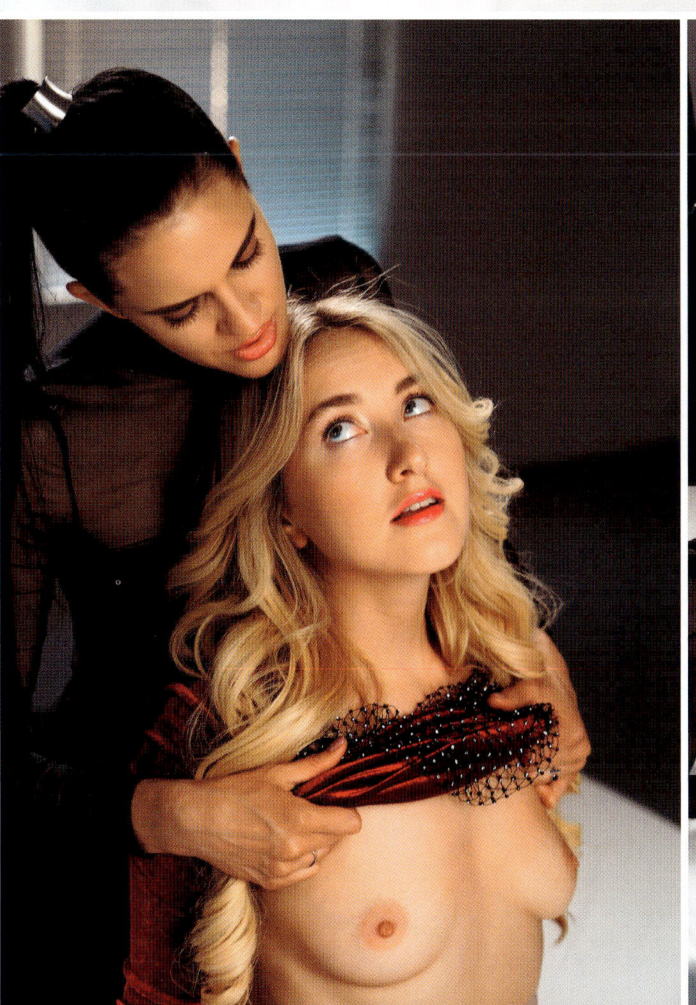
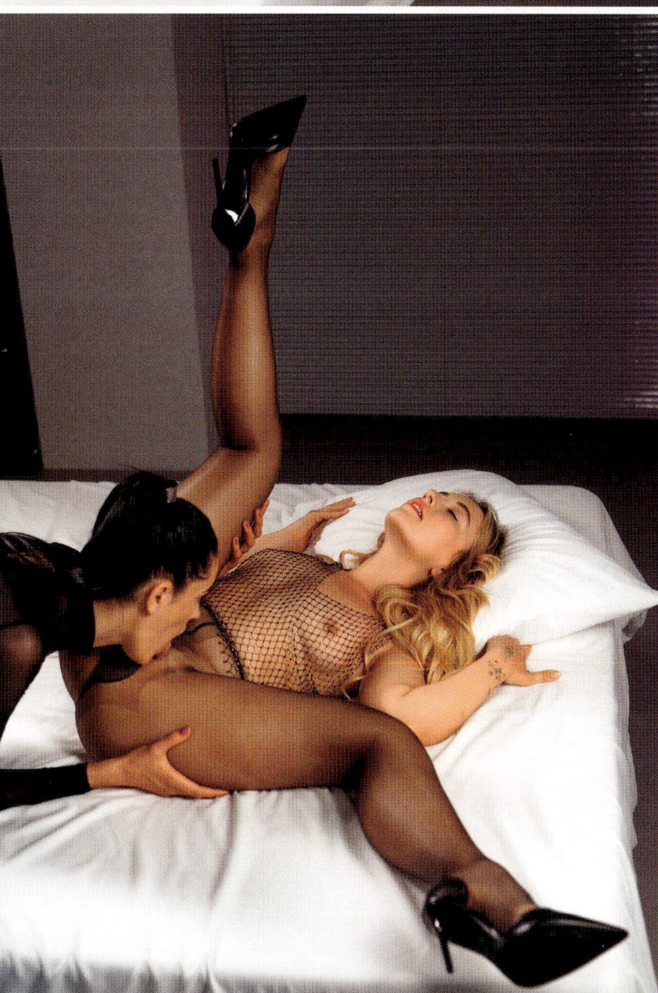

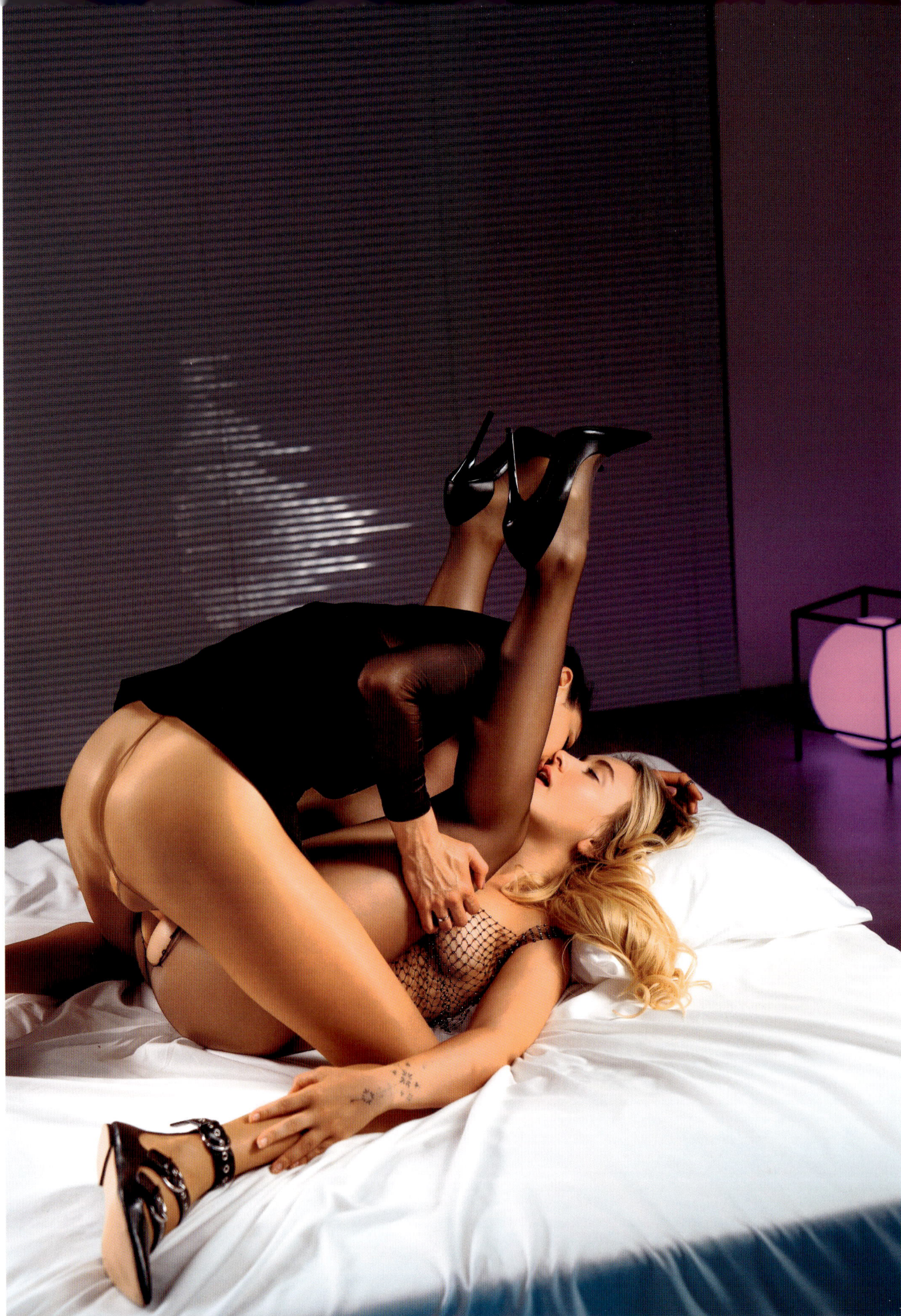

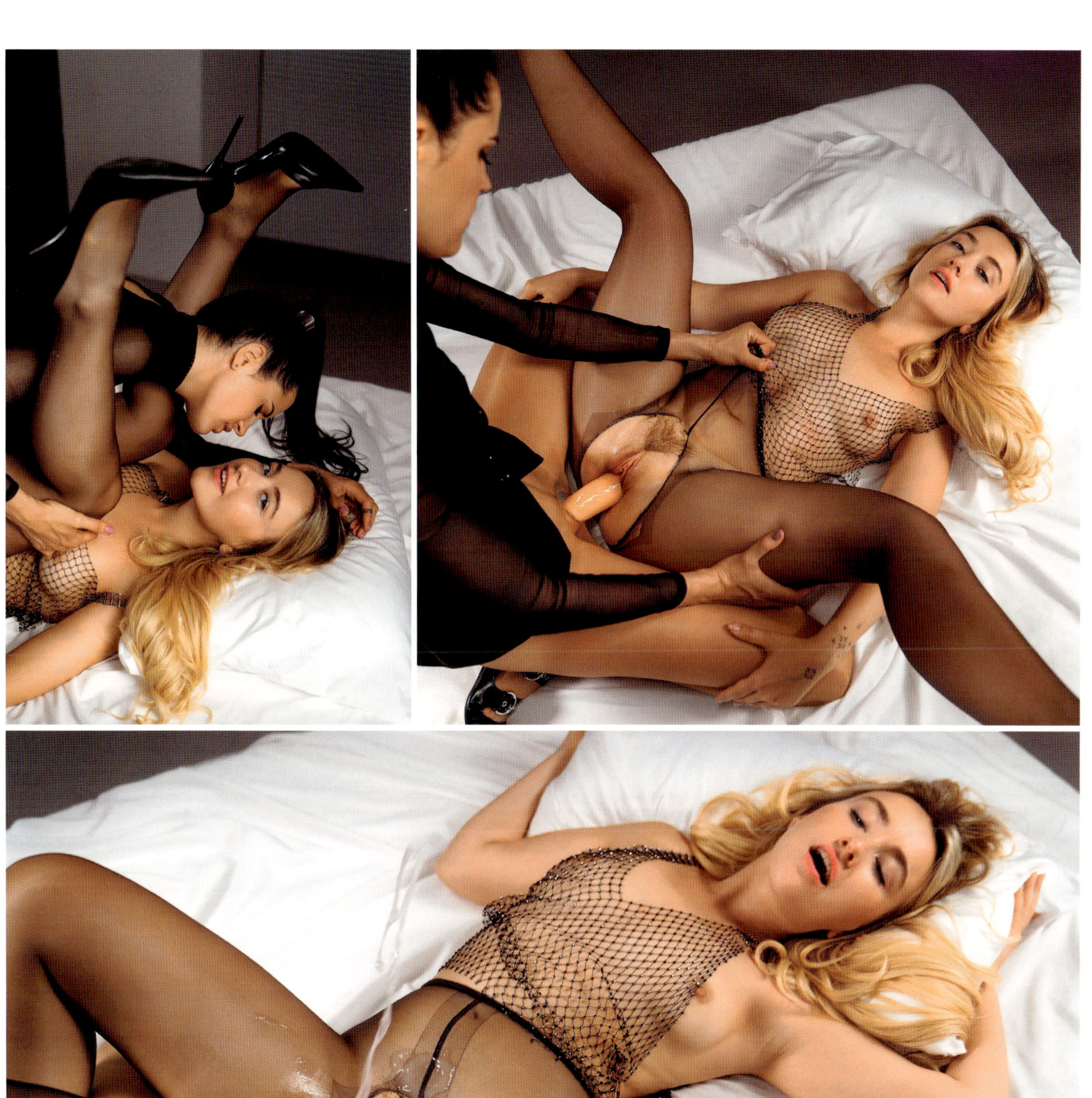

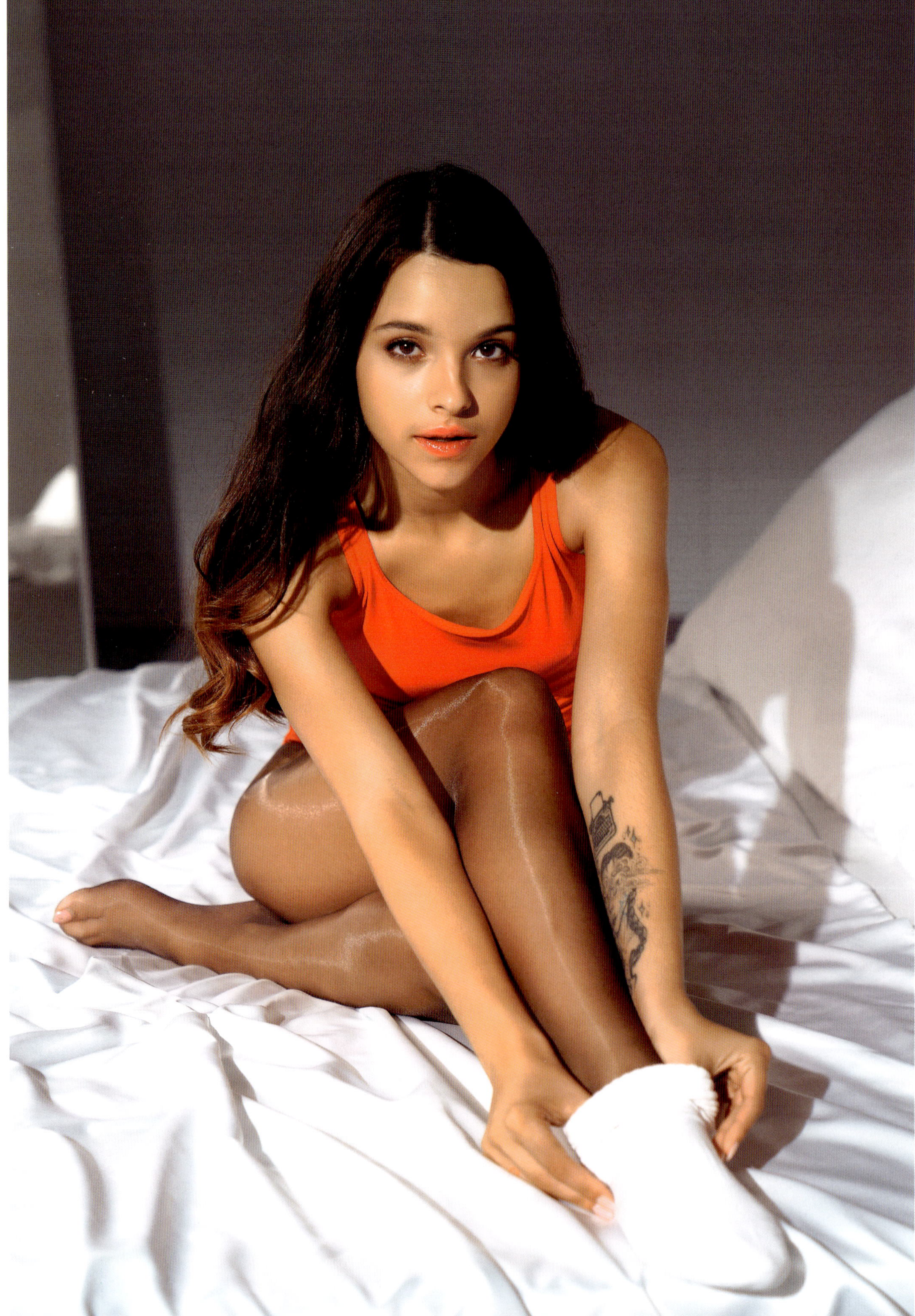

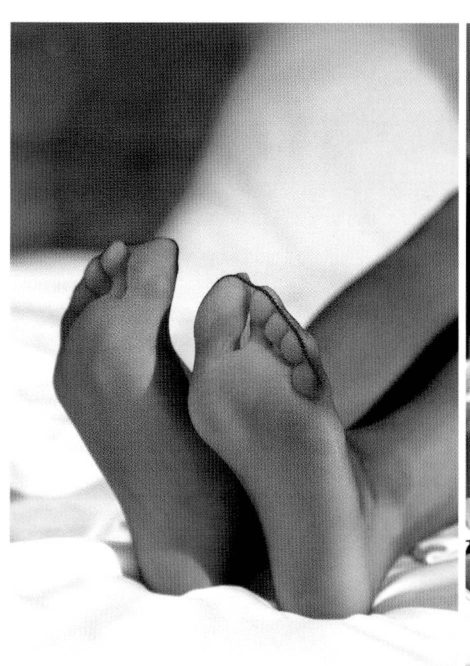
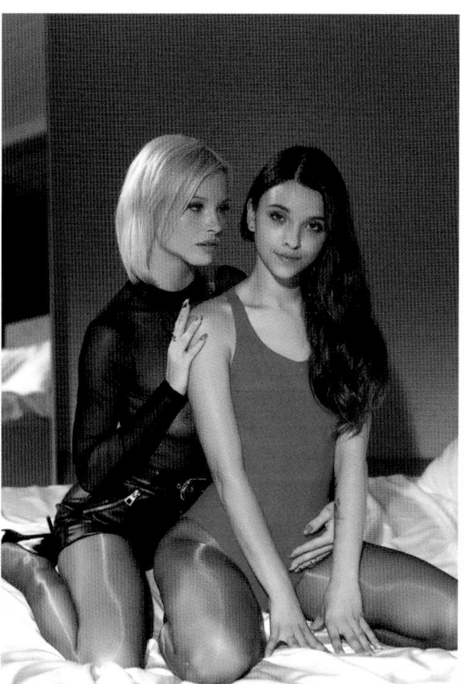
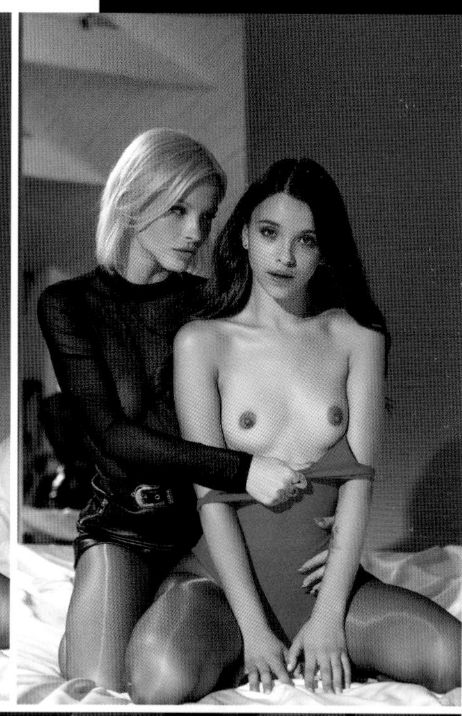
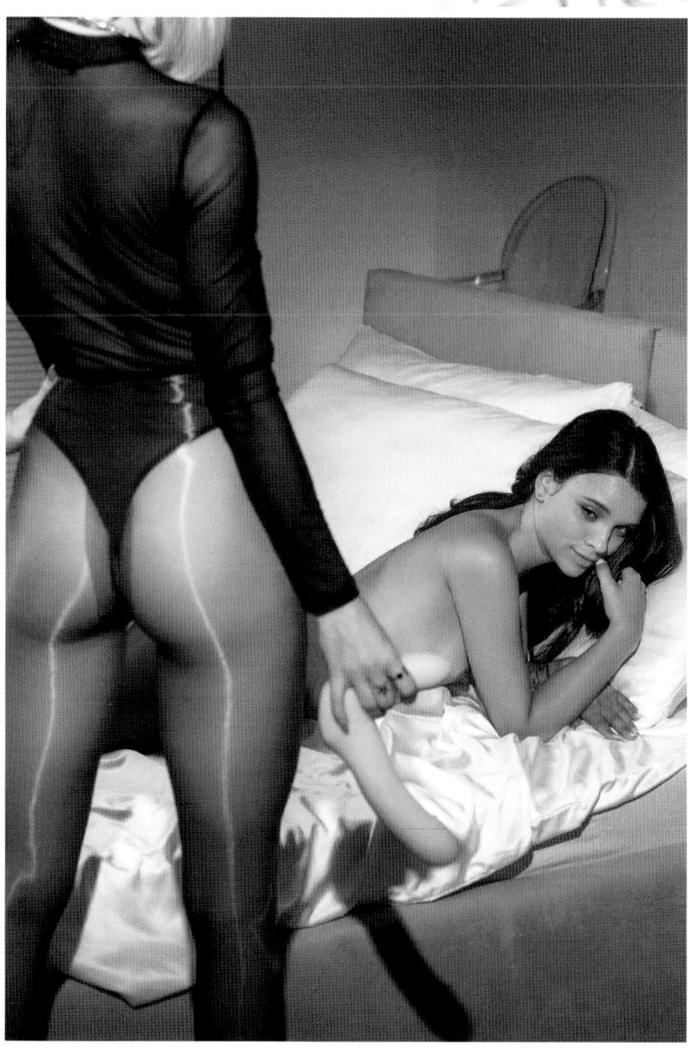
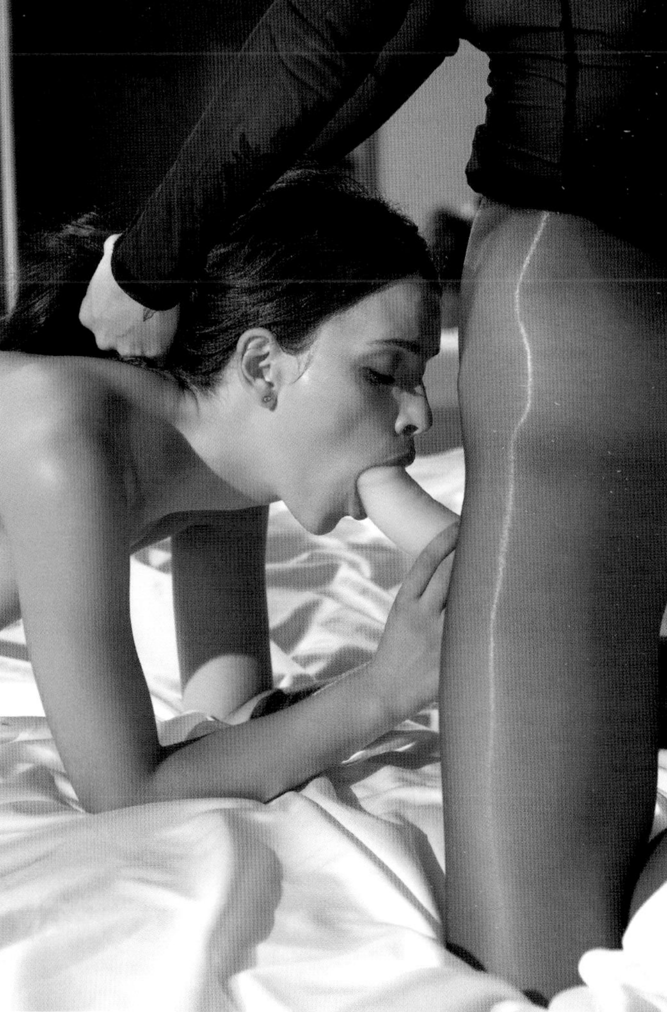

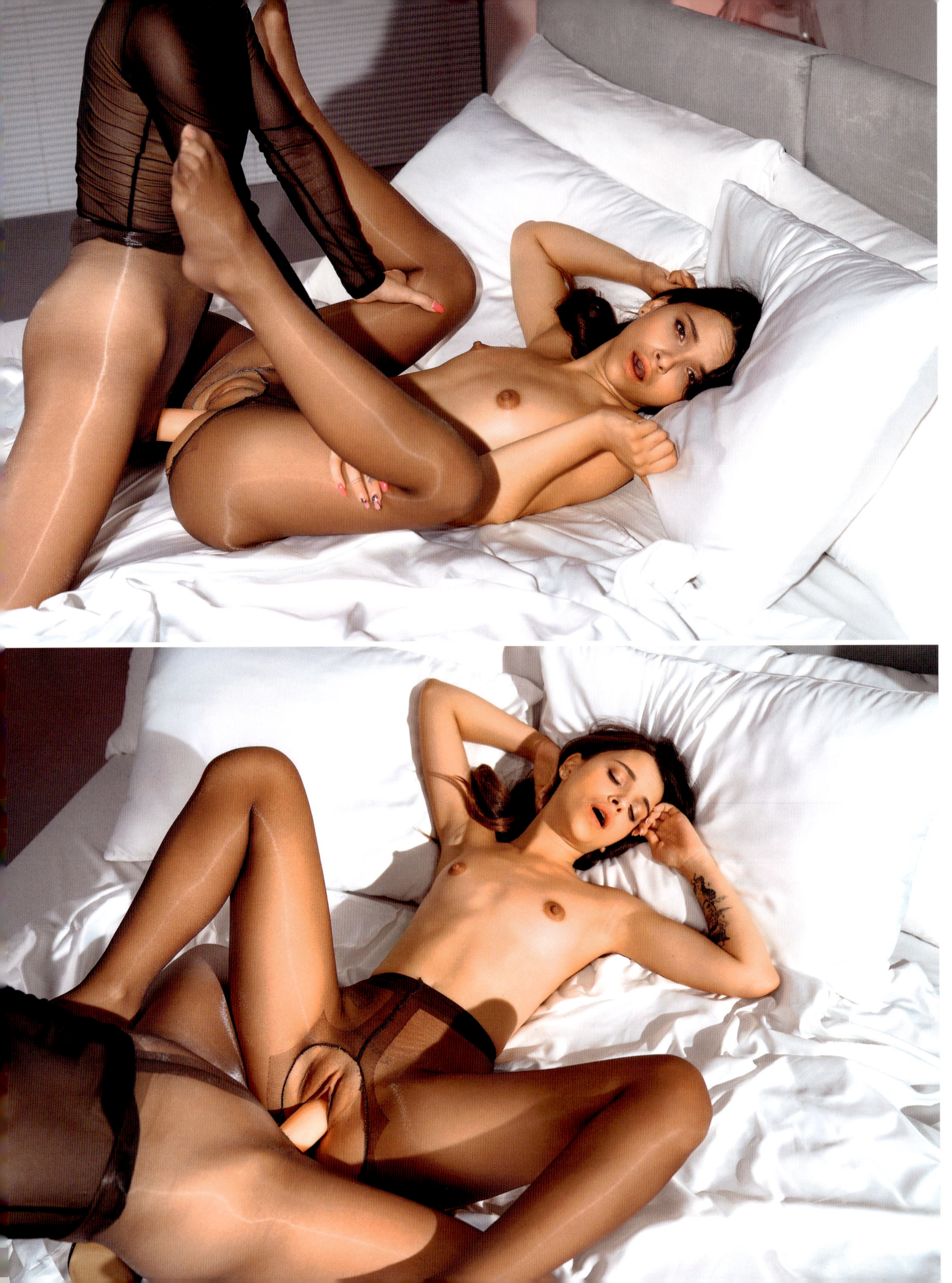

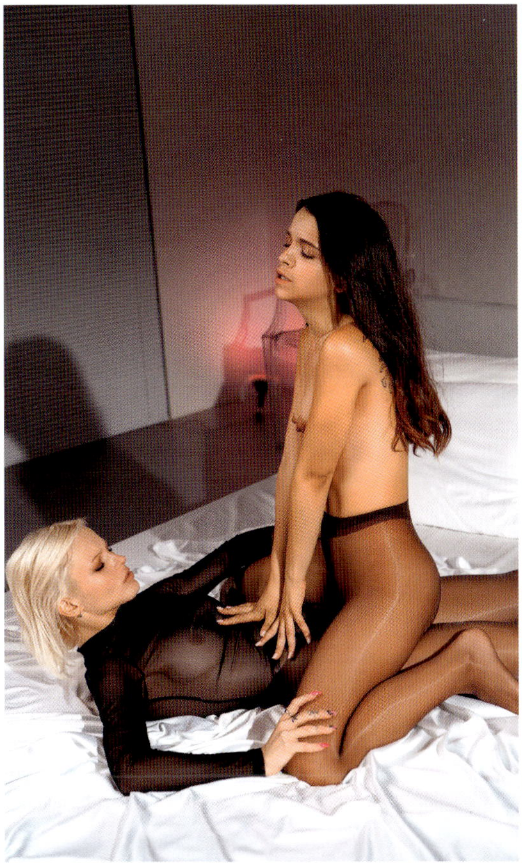

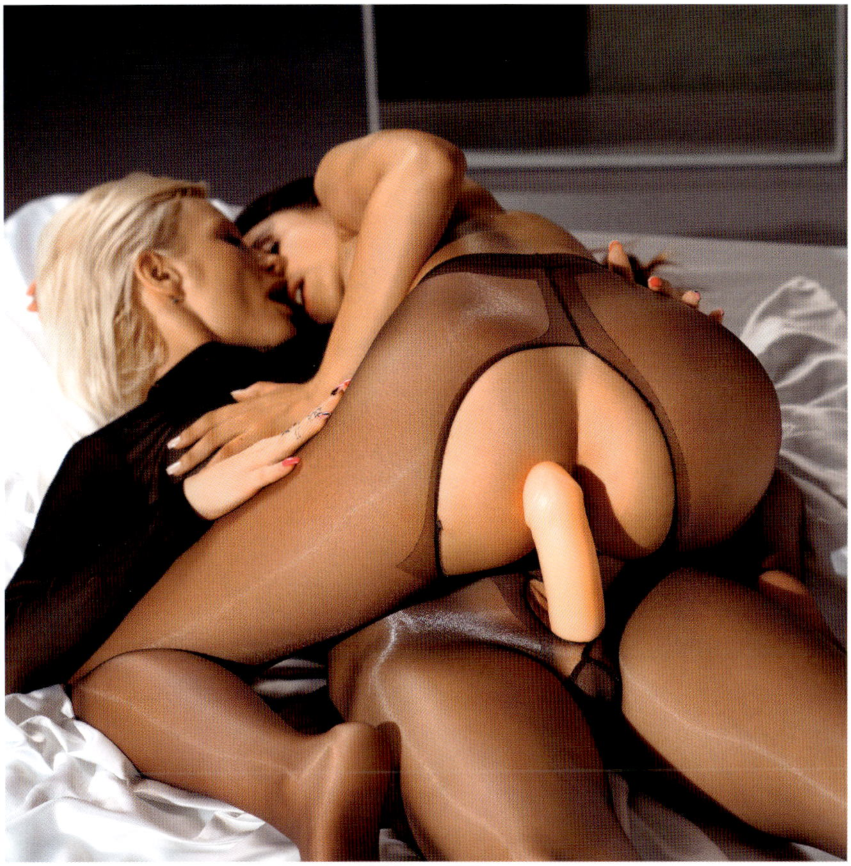

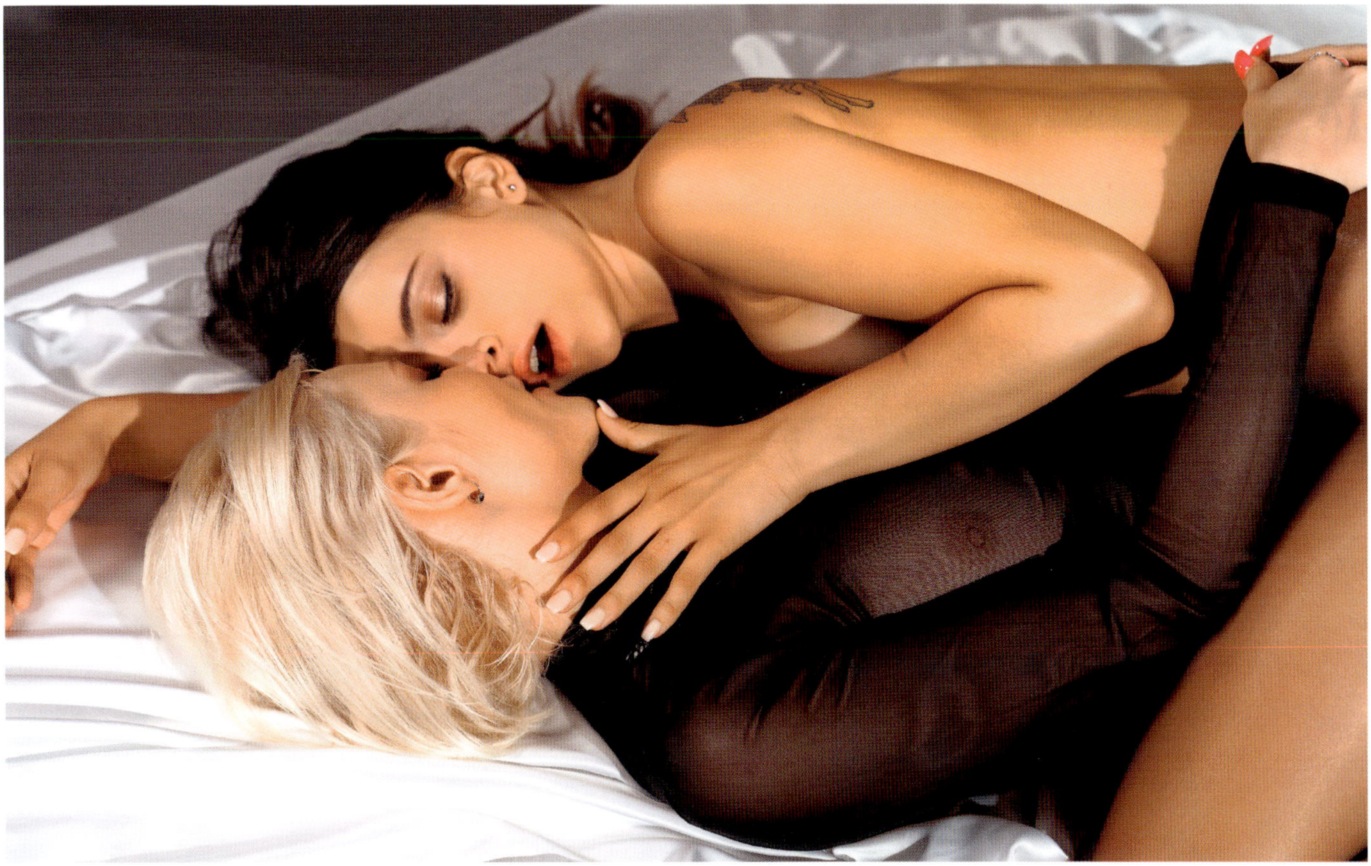

KATY ROSE
RIKA FANE

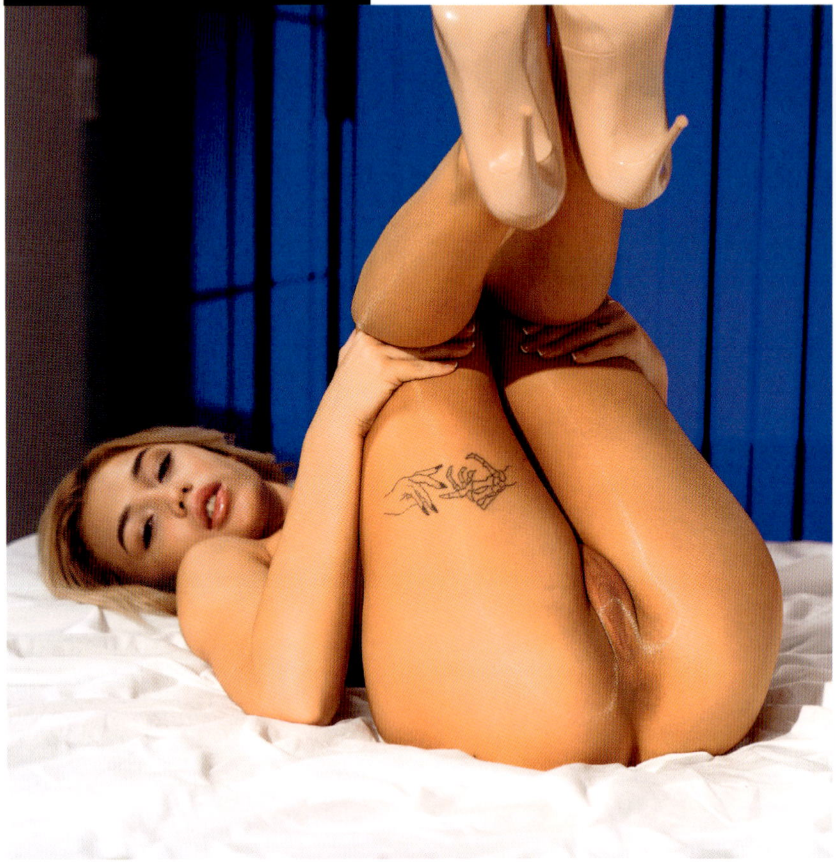

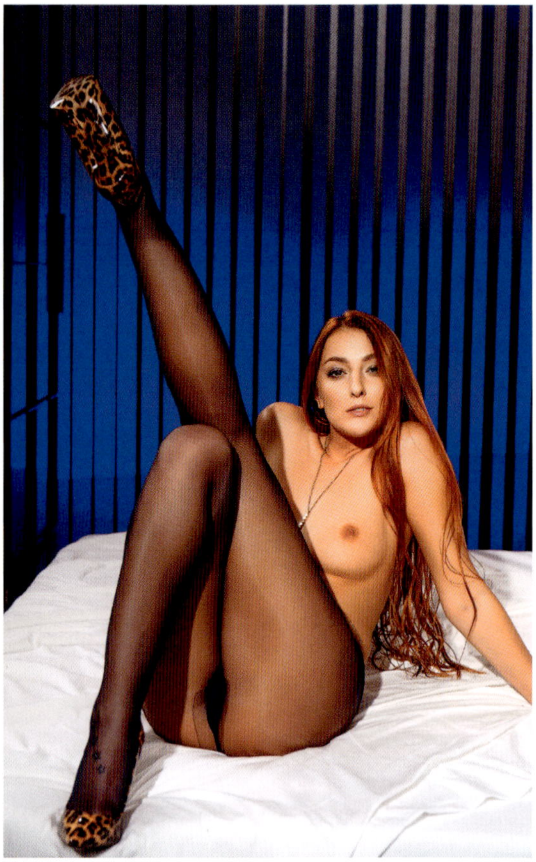

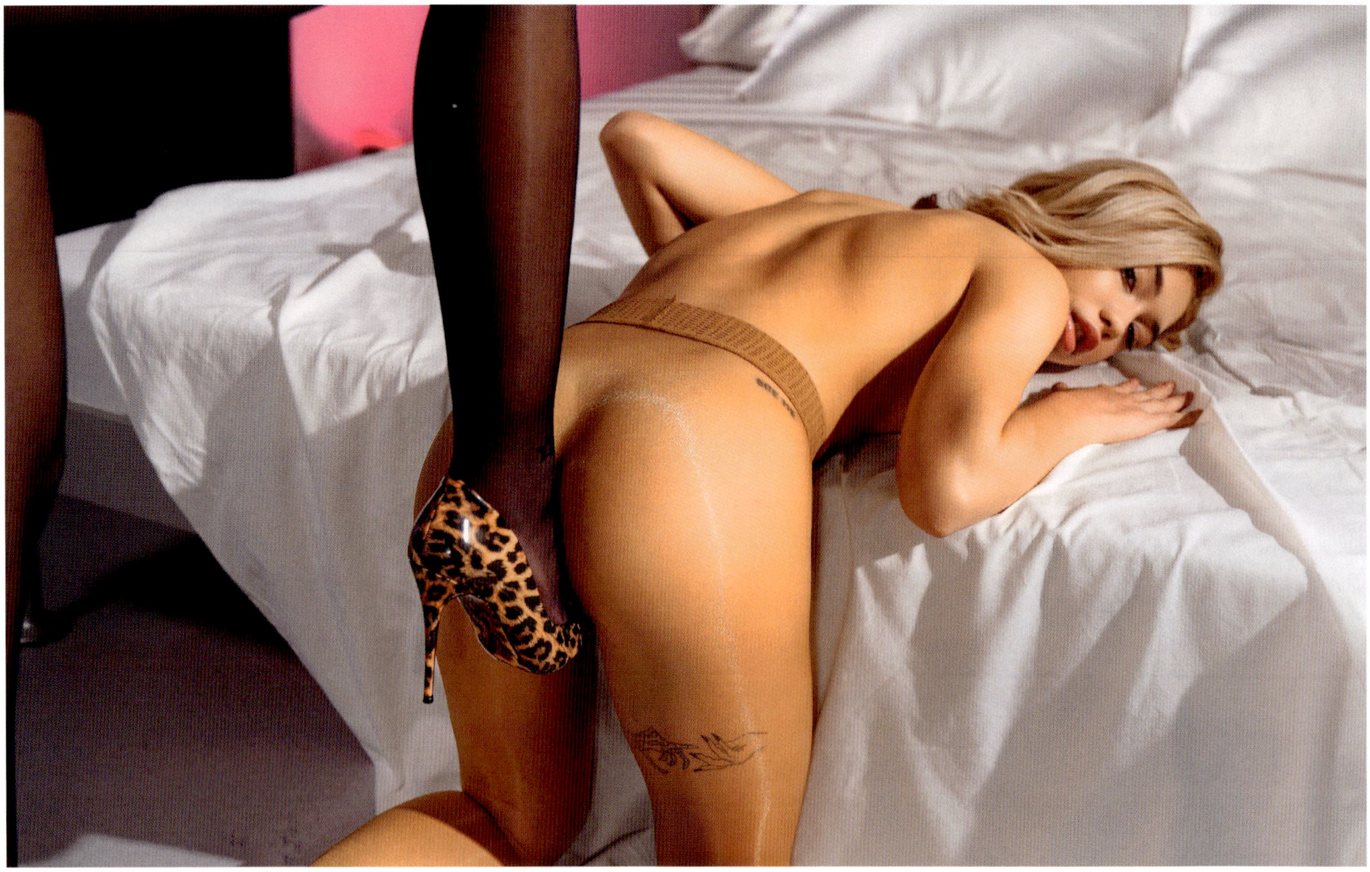

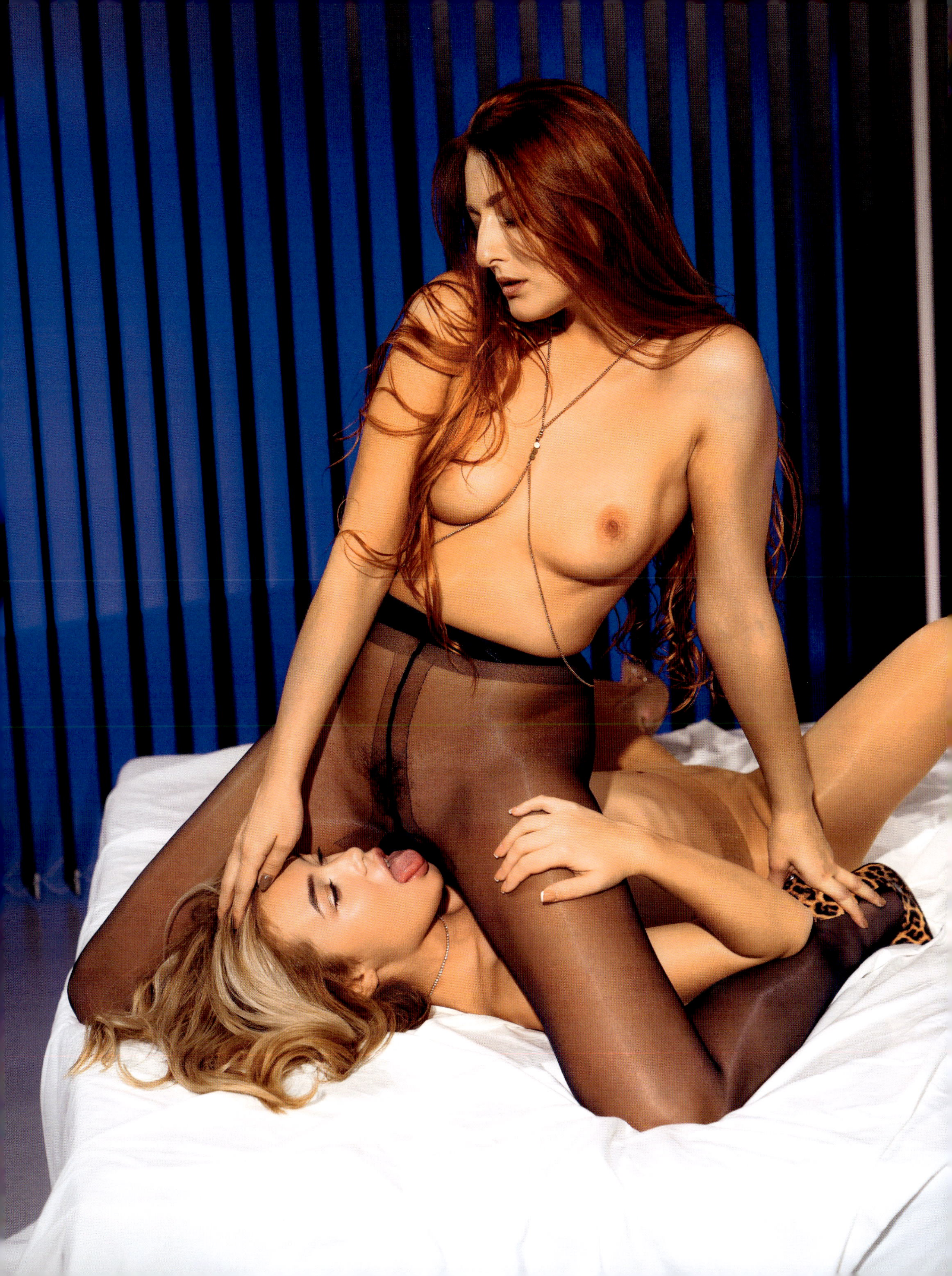

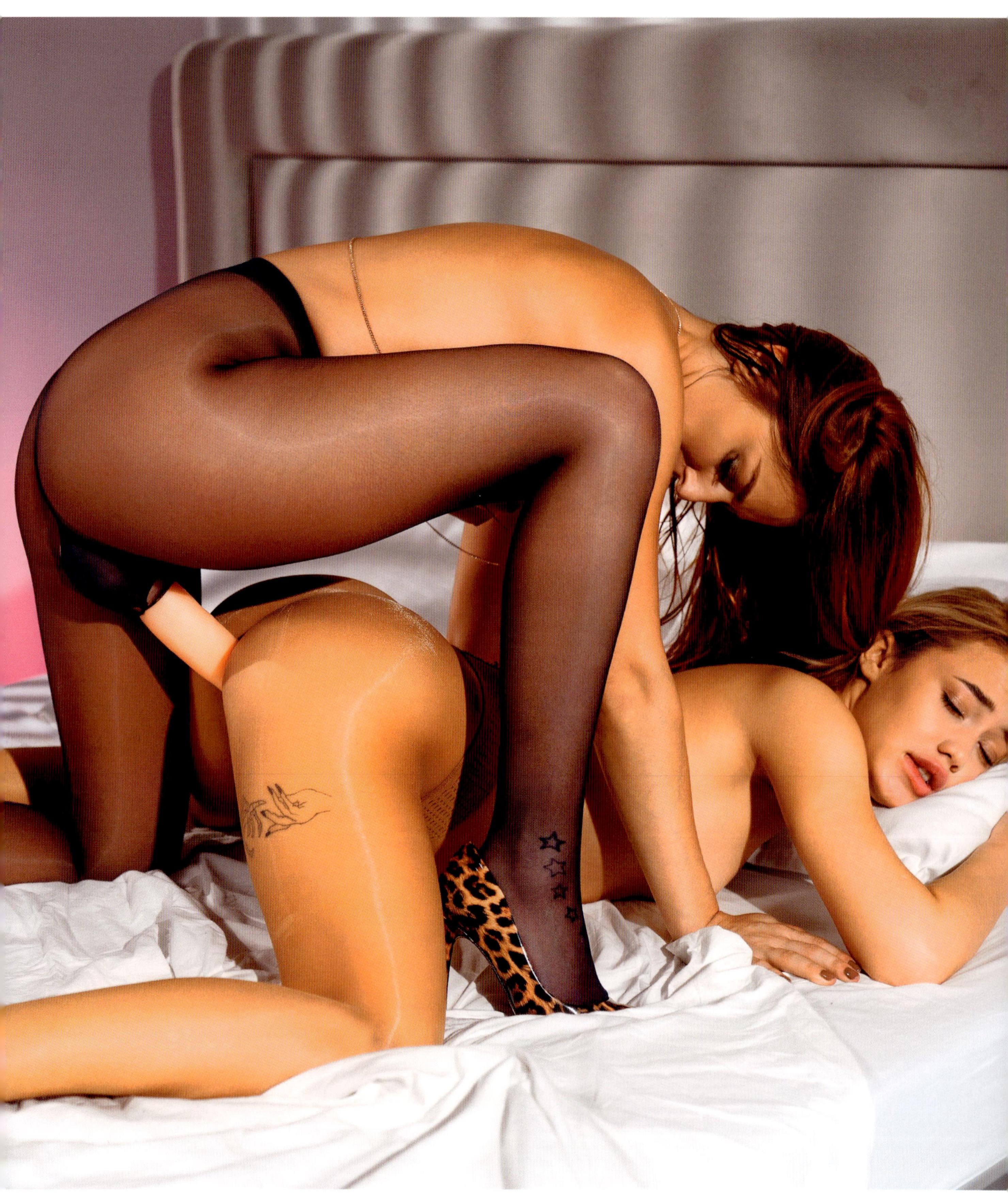

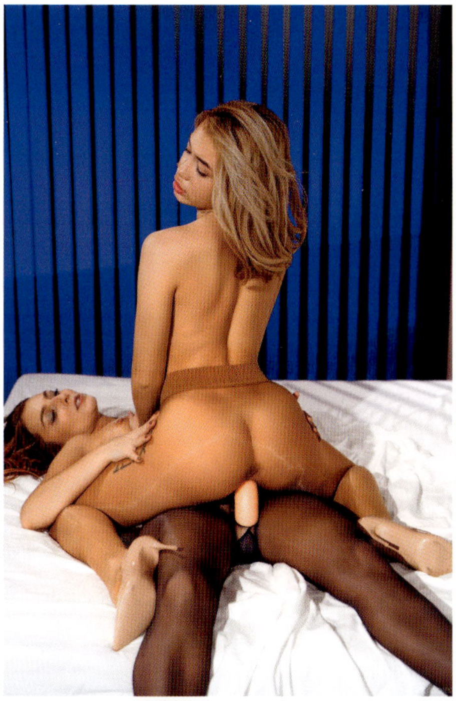

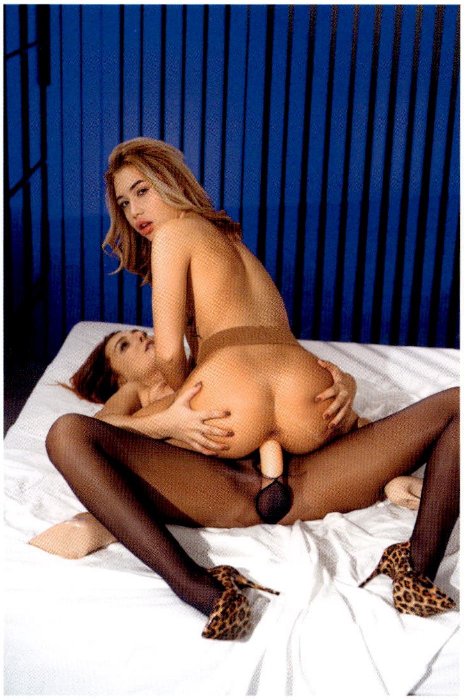

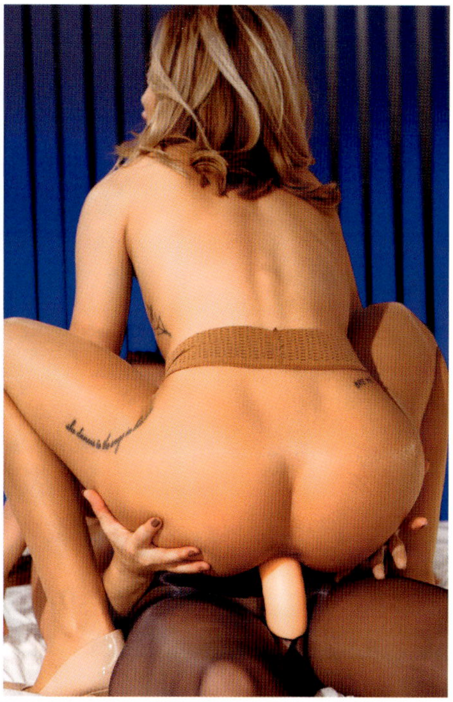

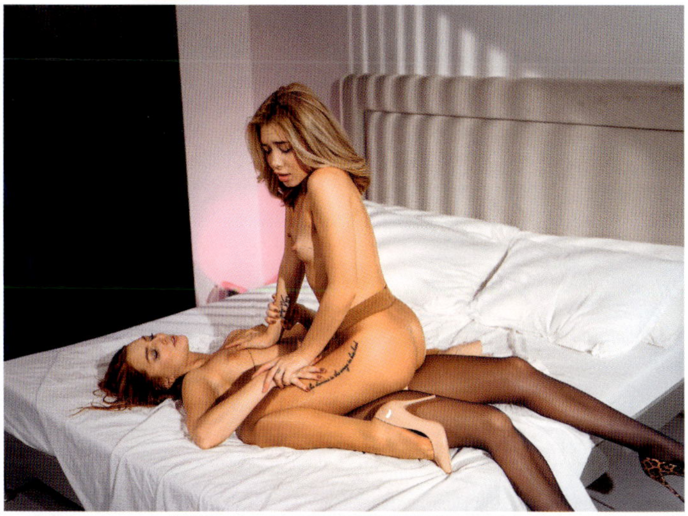

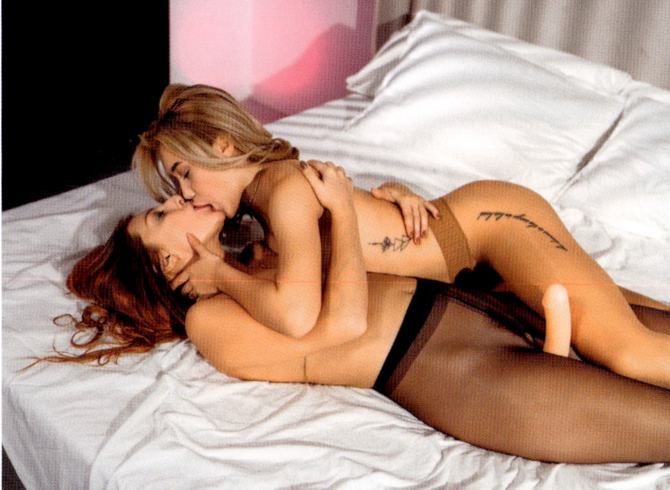
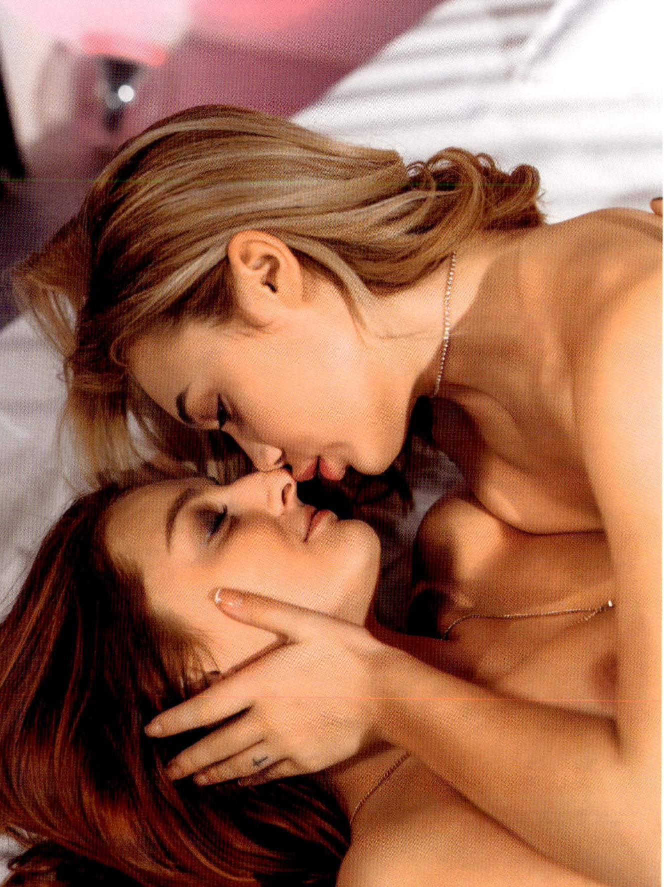

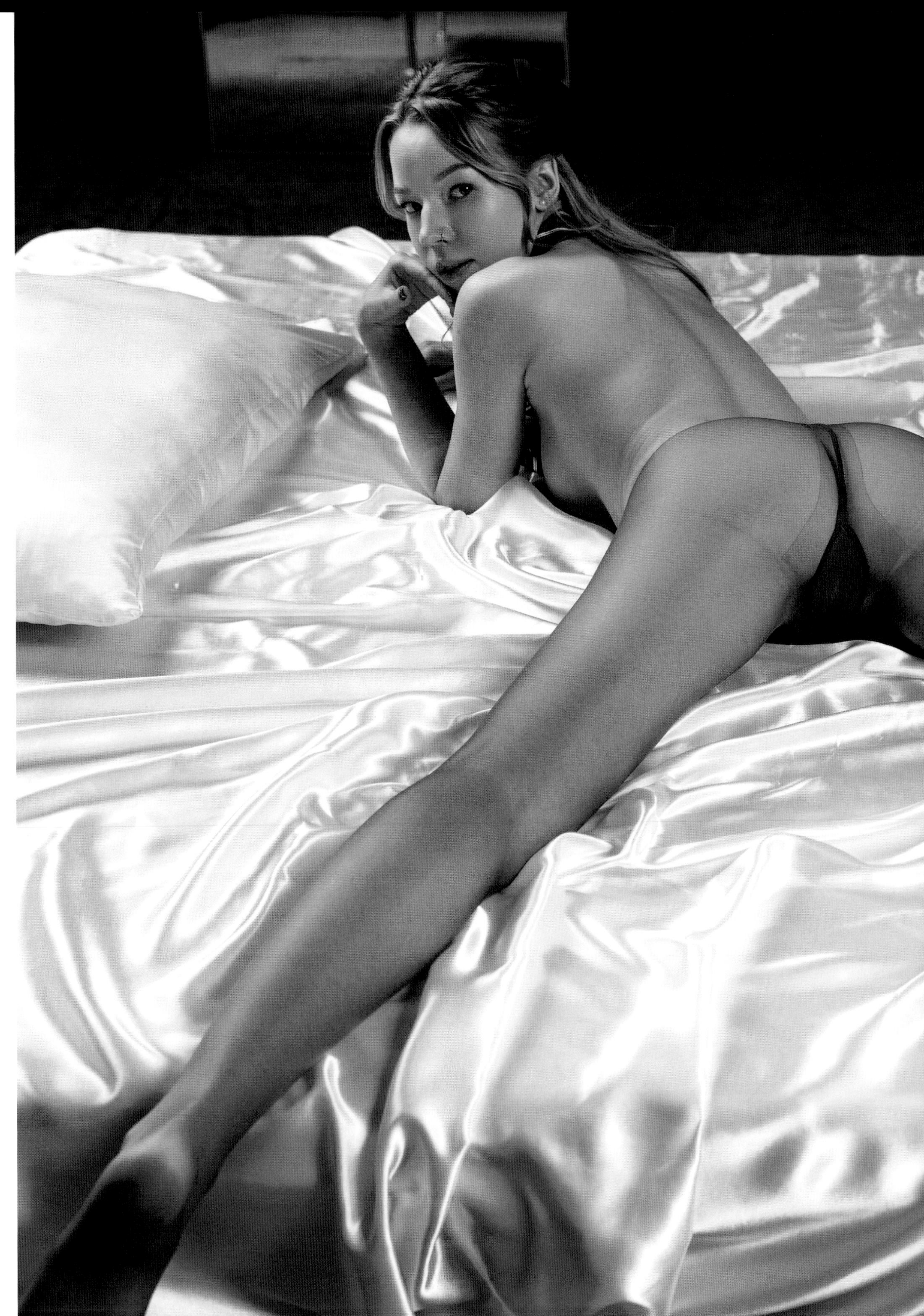

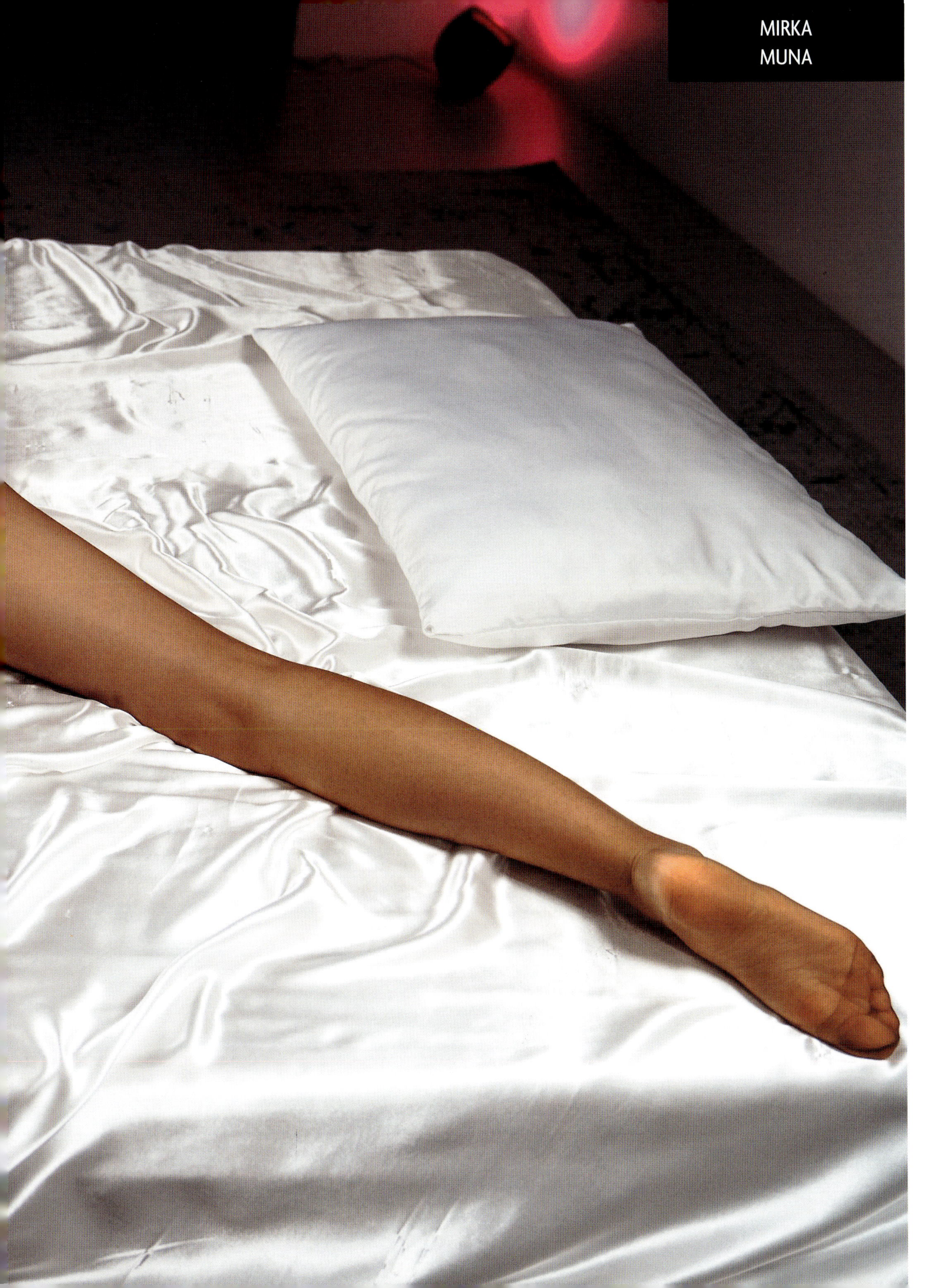
MIRKA
MUNA

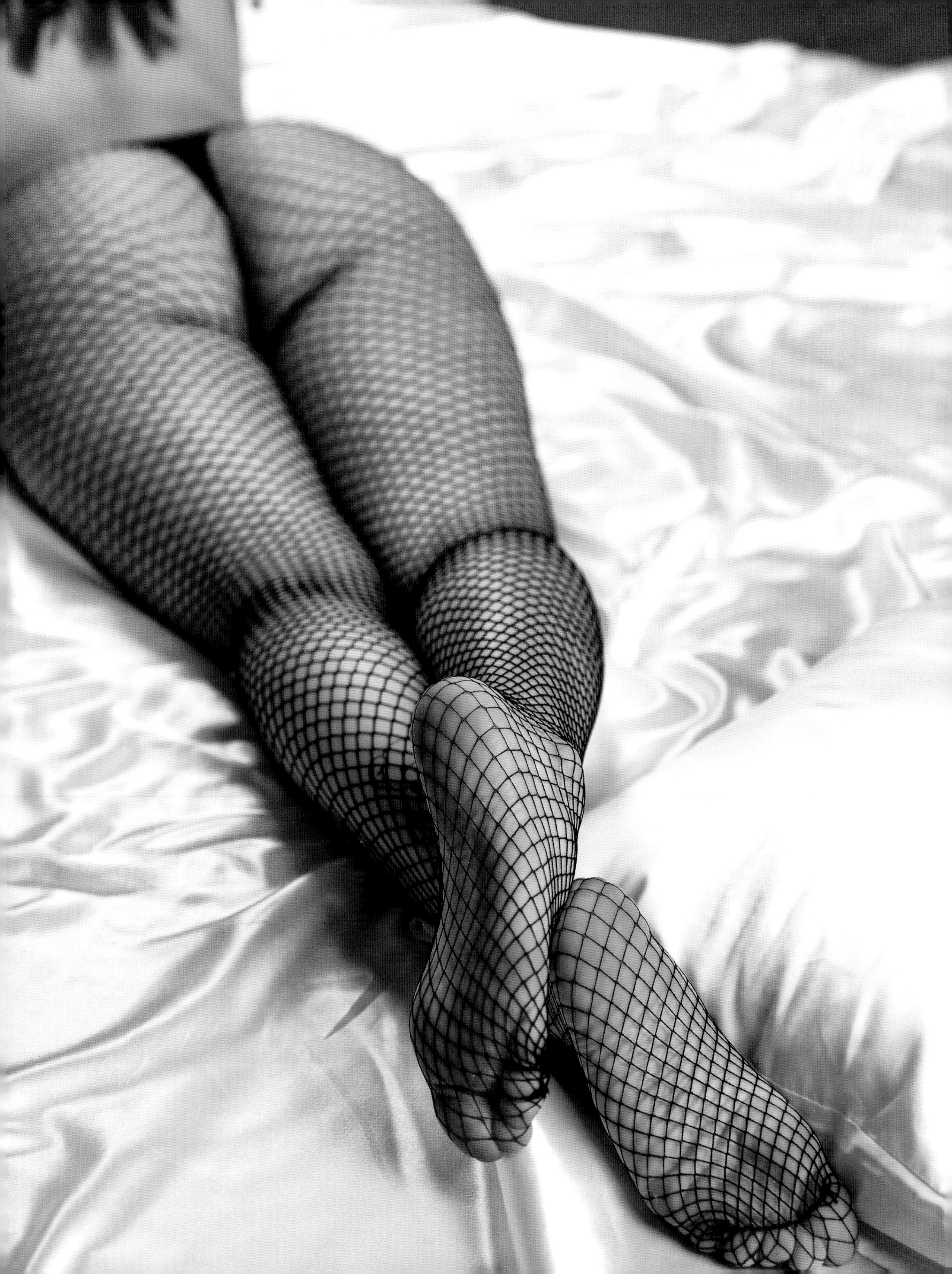

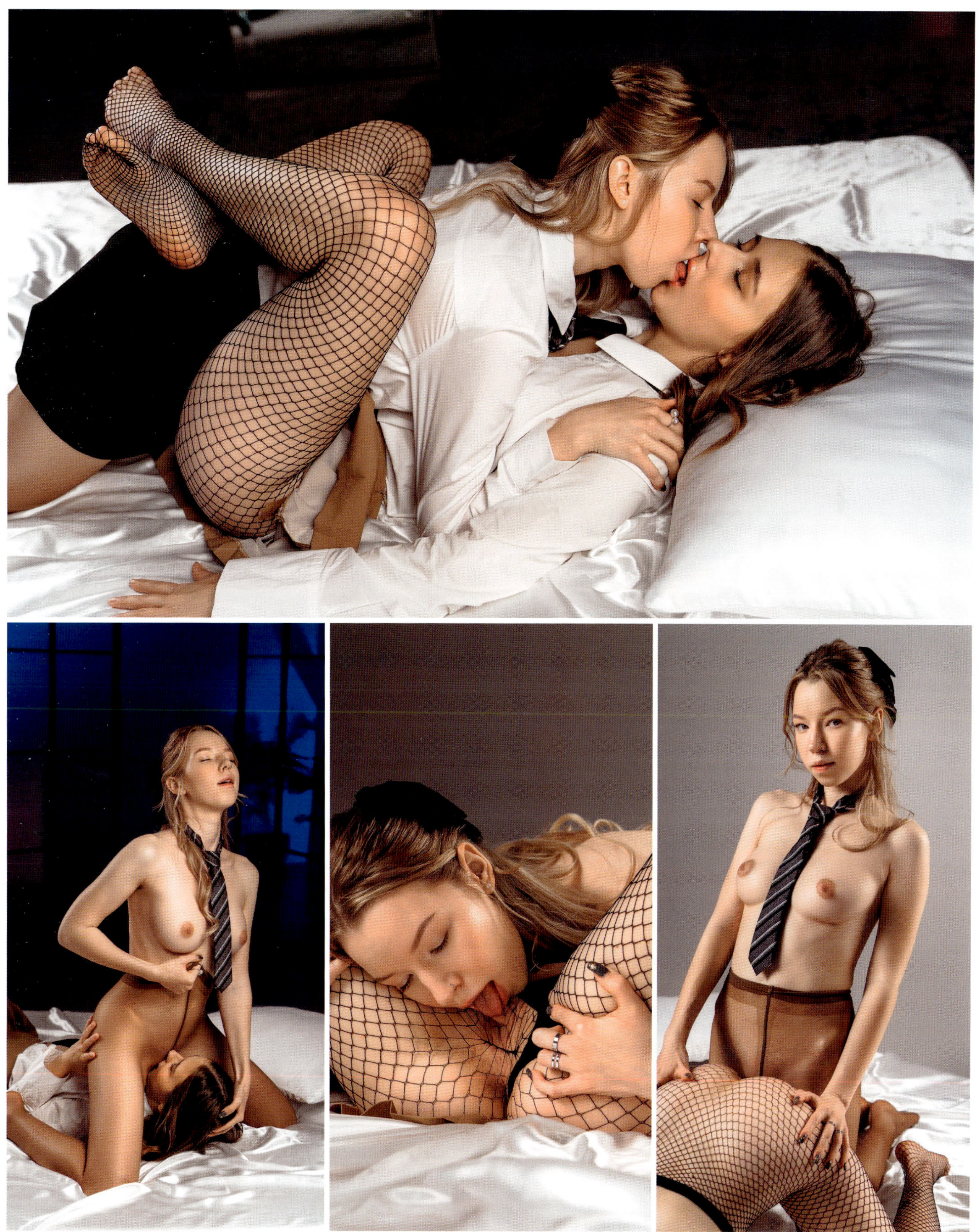

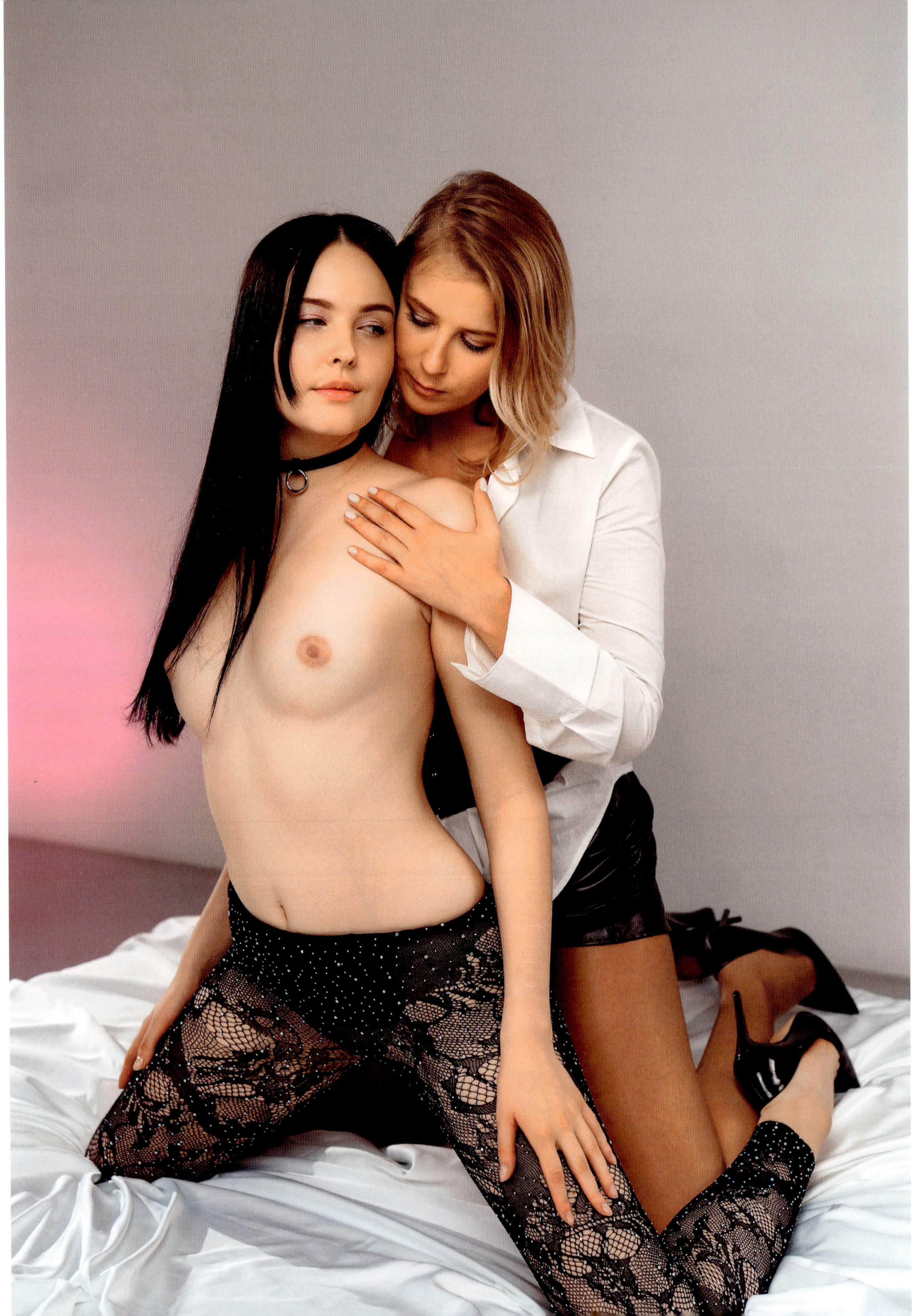

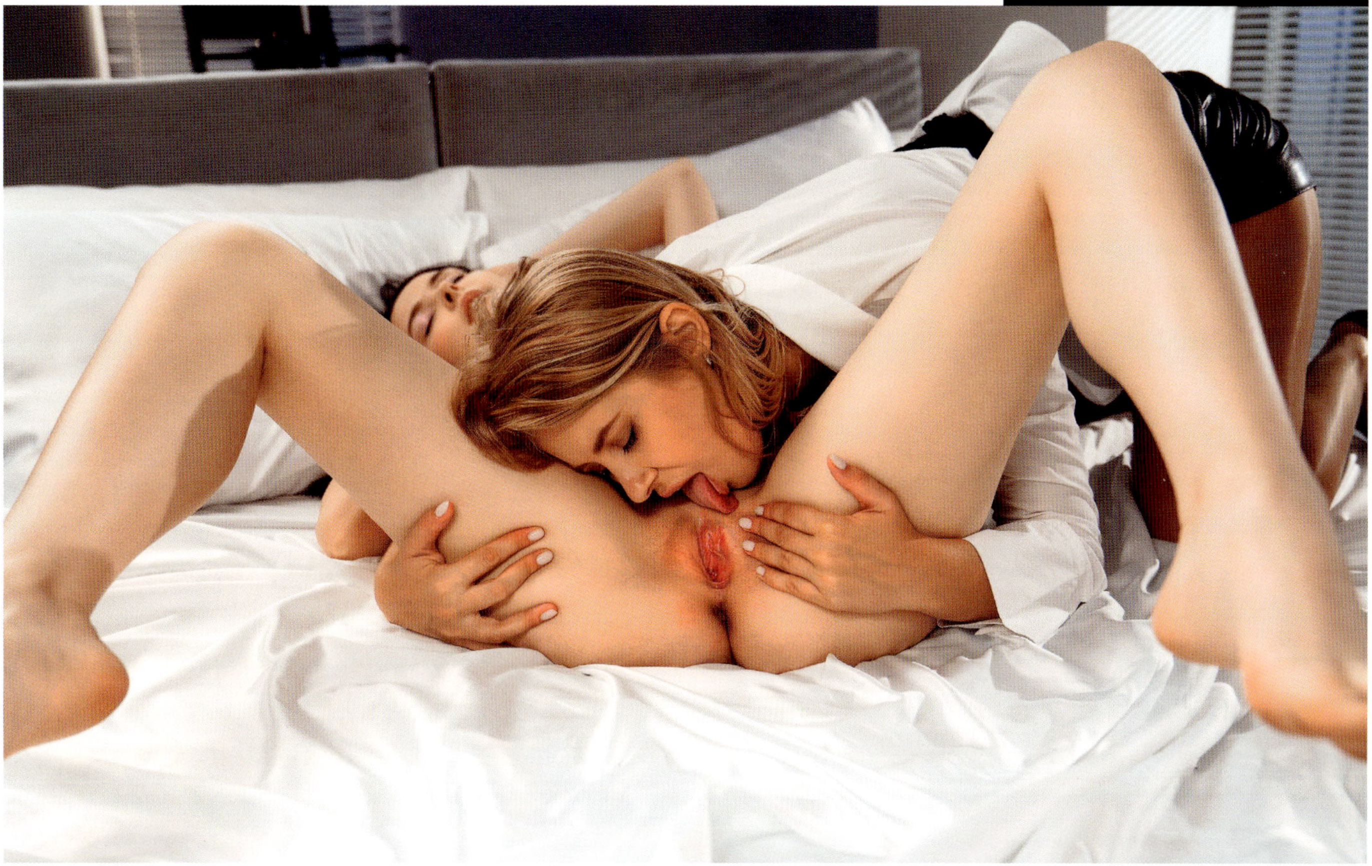

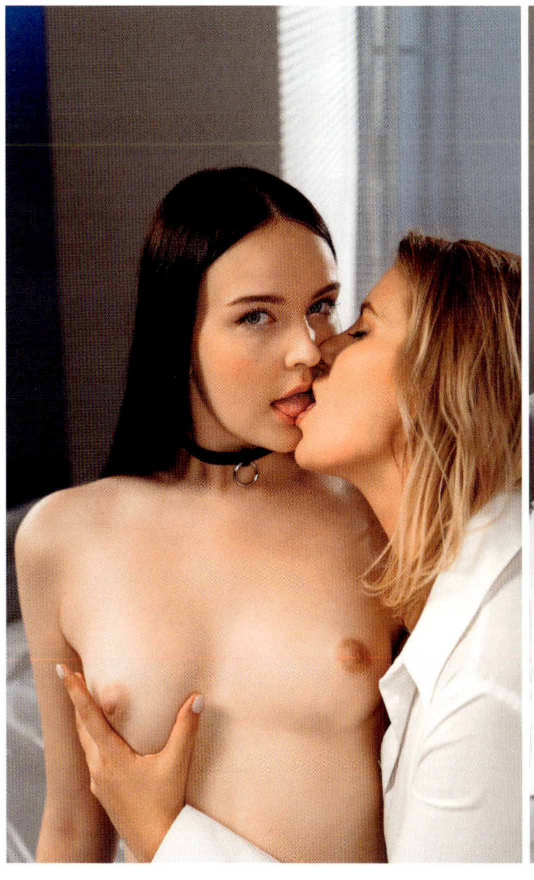

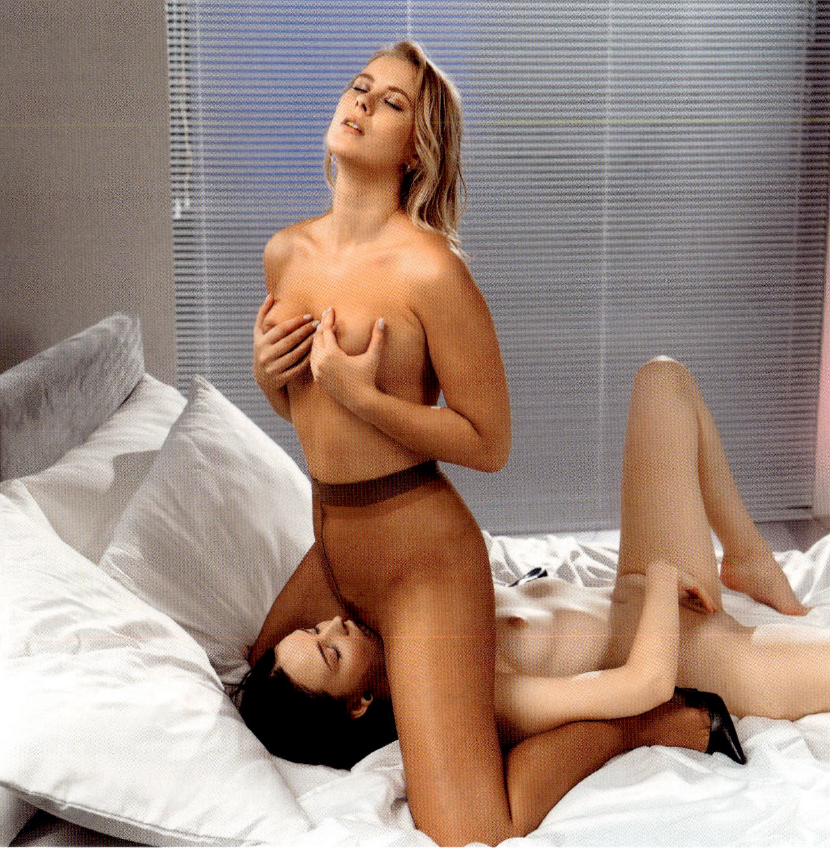

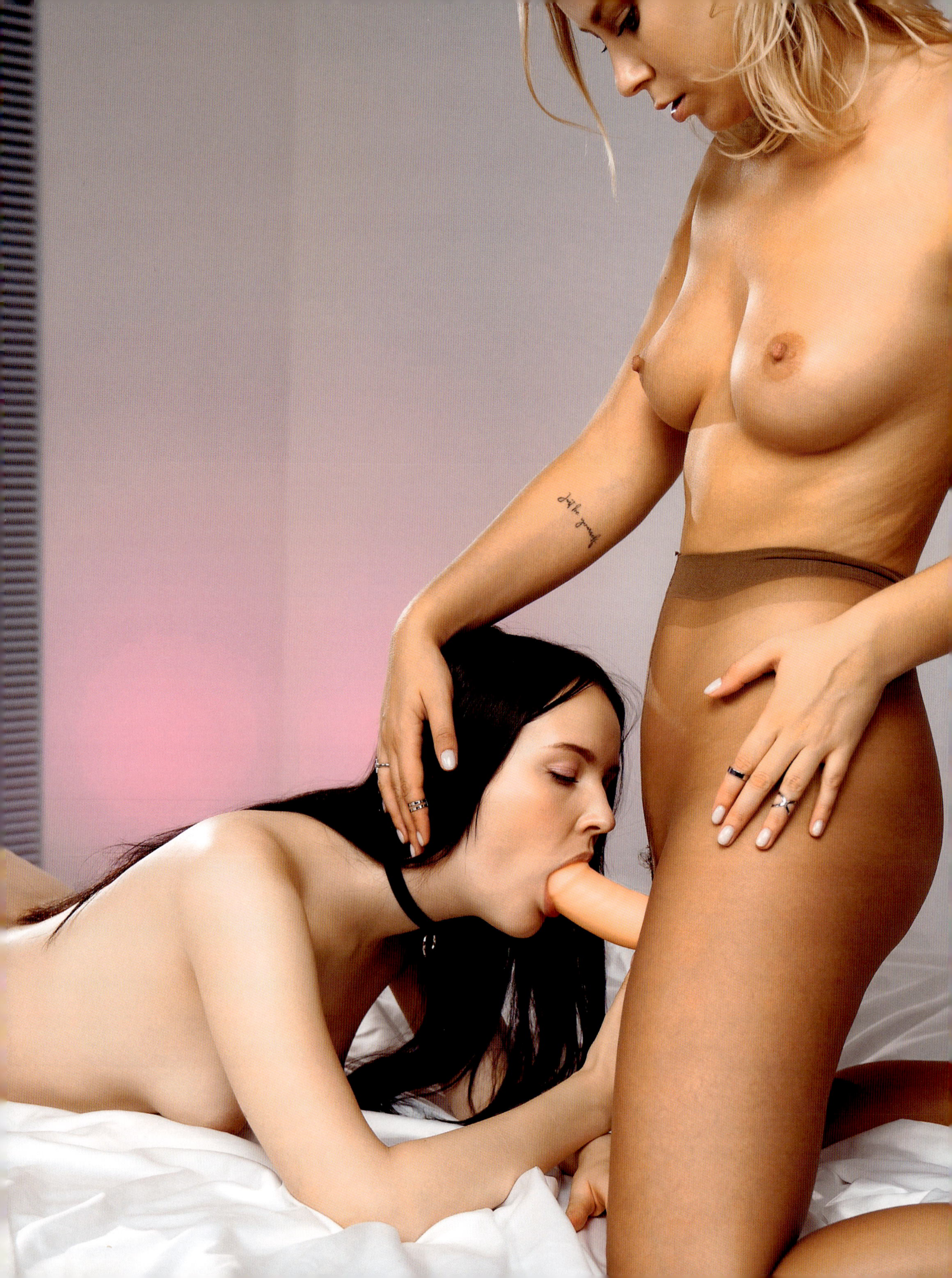

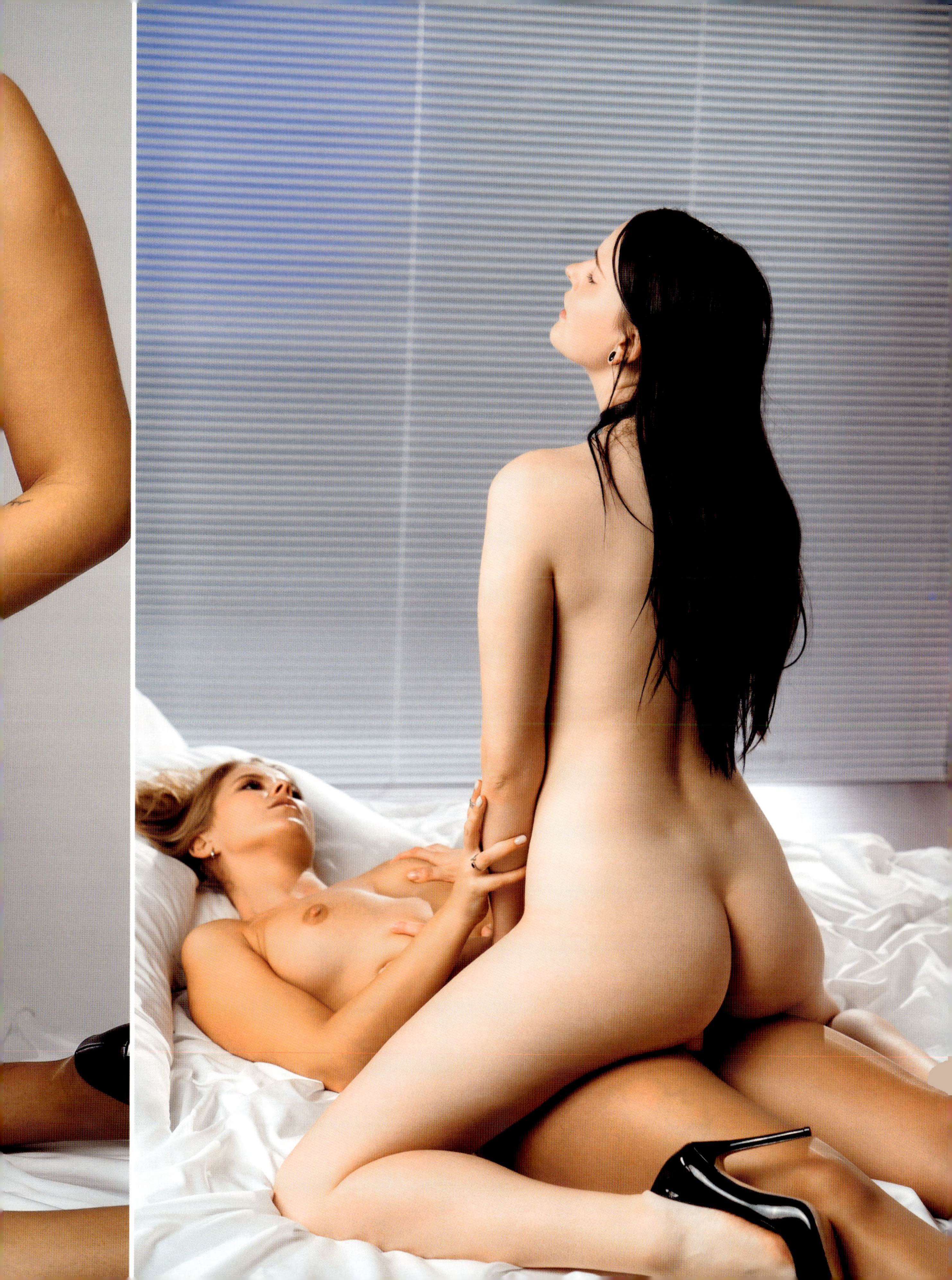

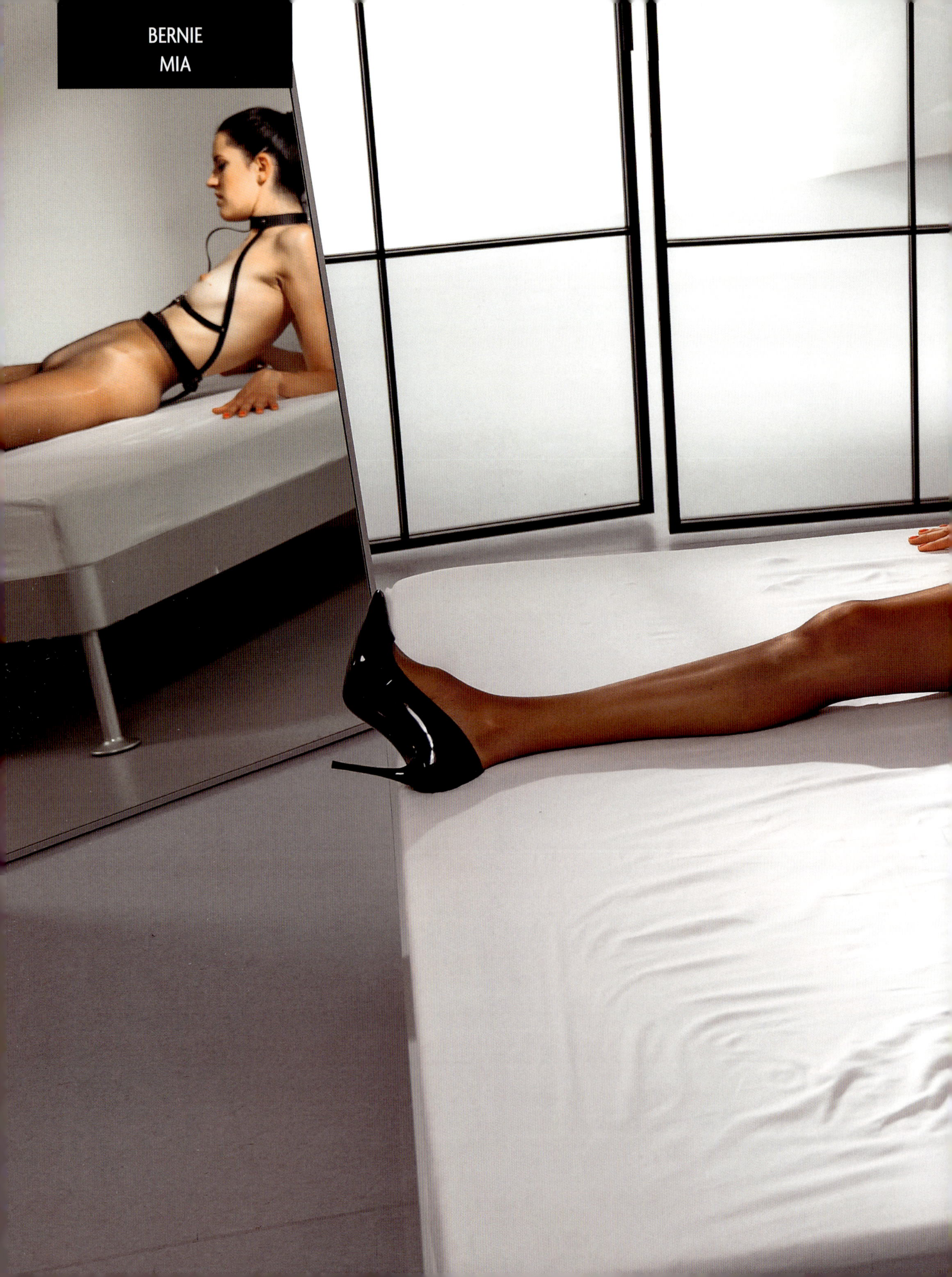
BERNIE
MIA

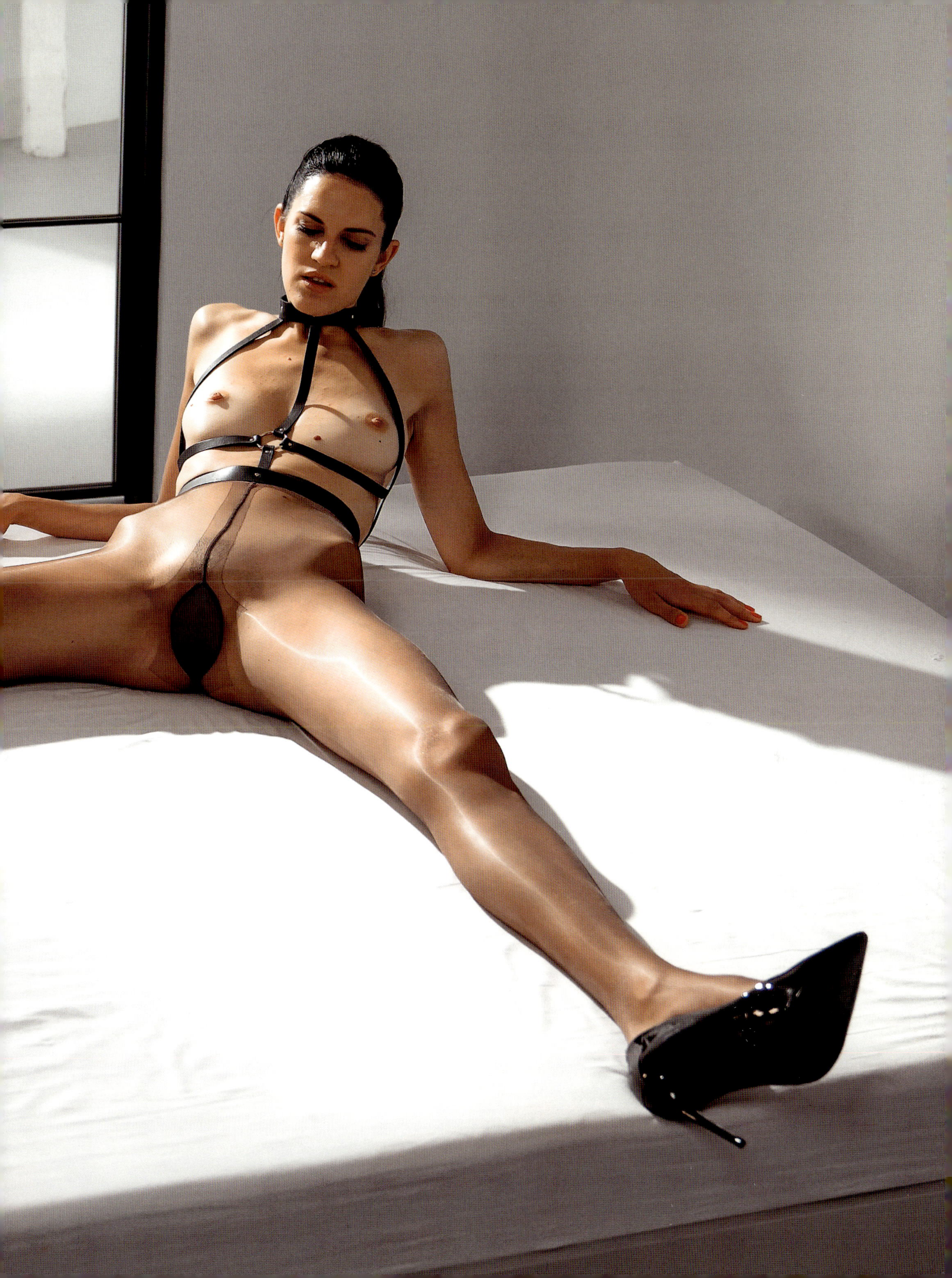

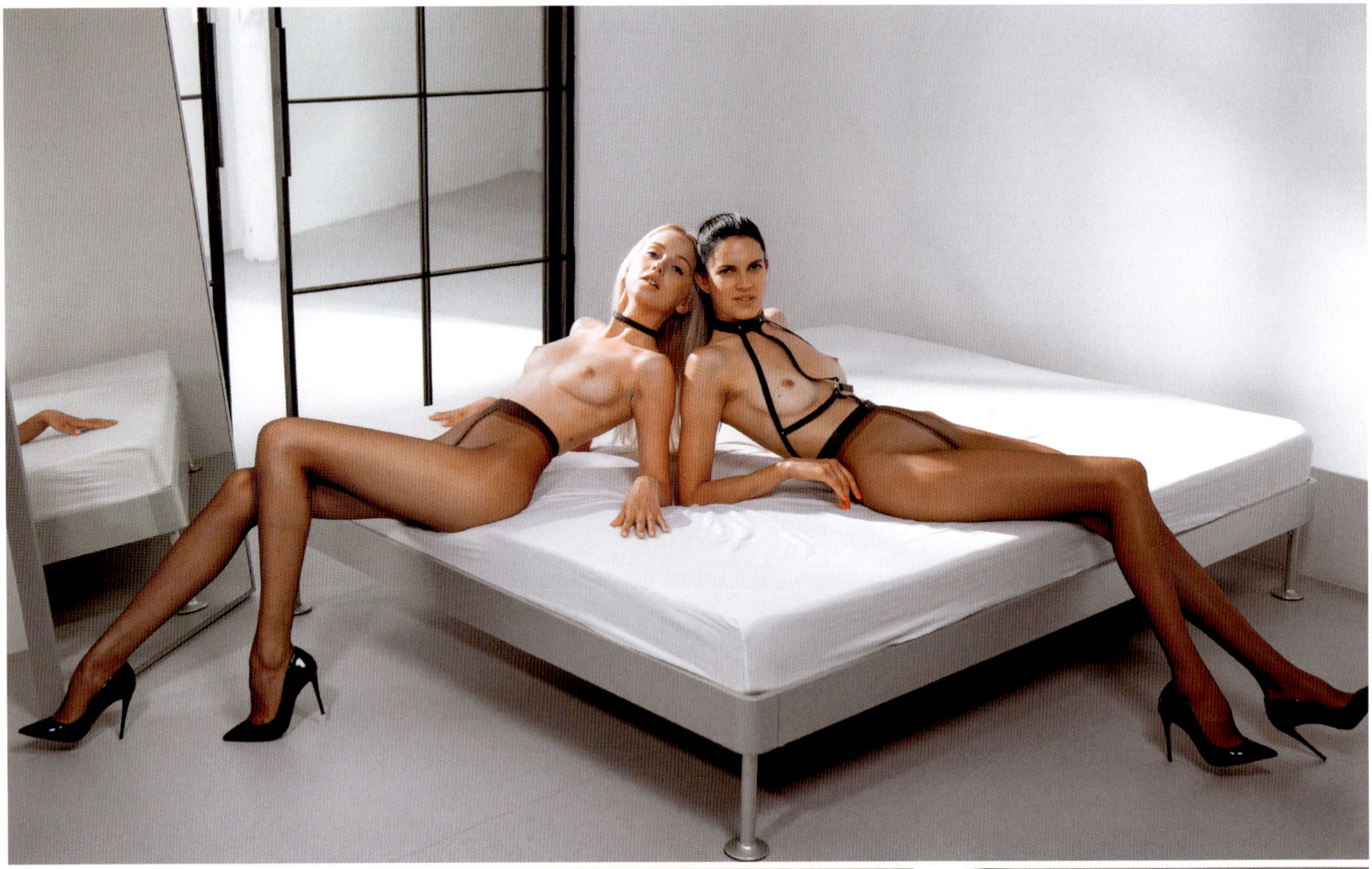

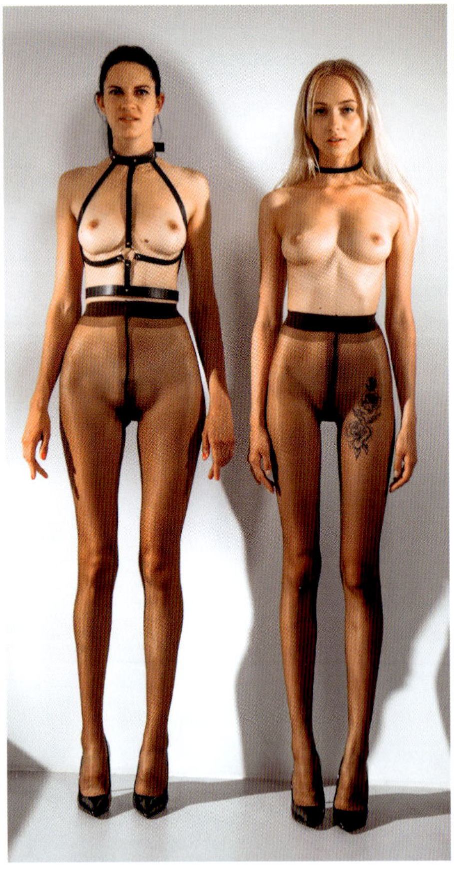

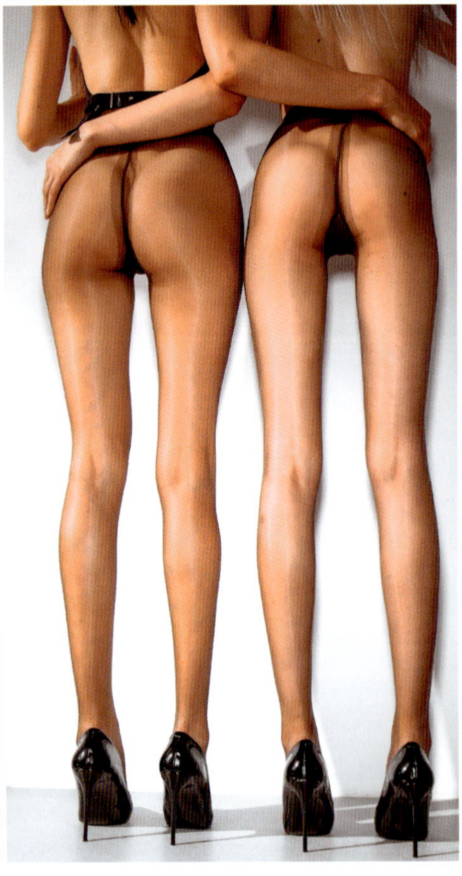

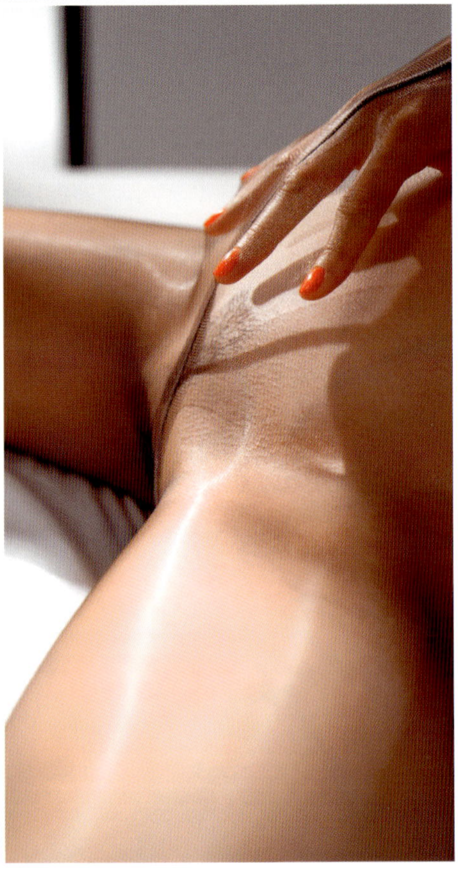

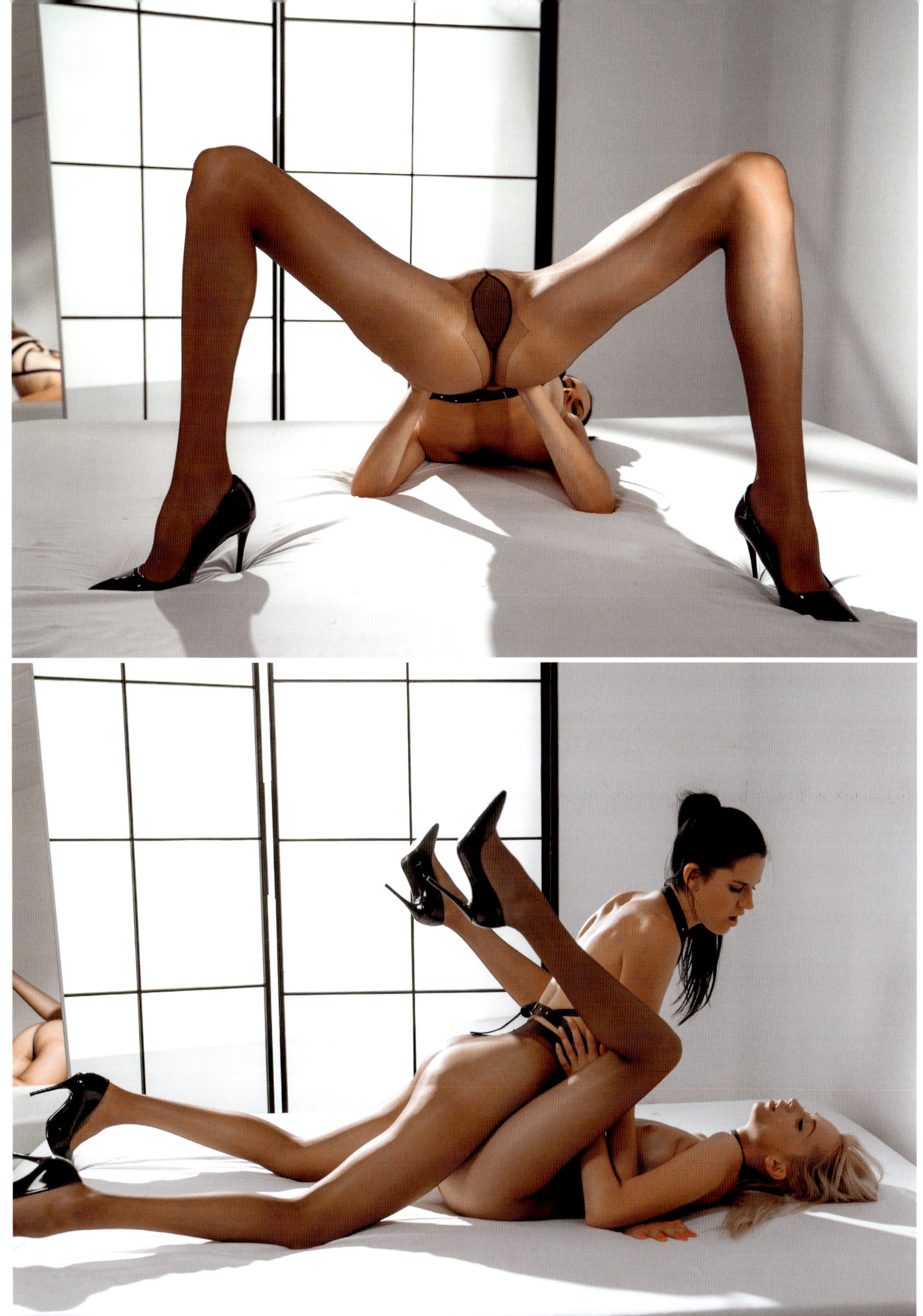

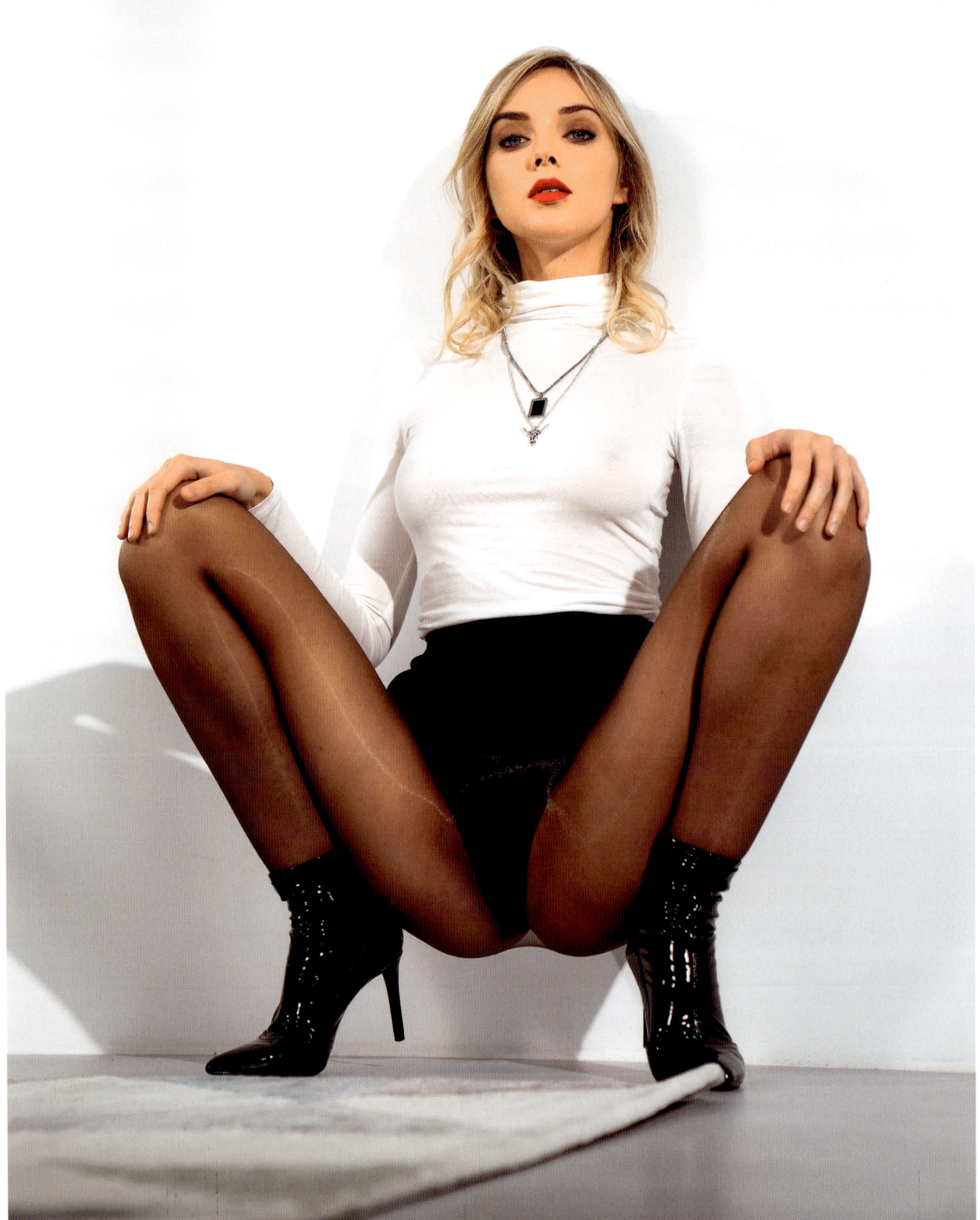

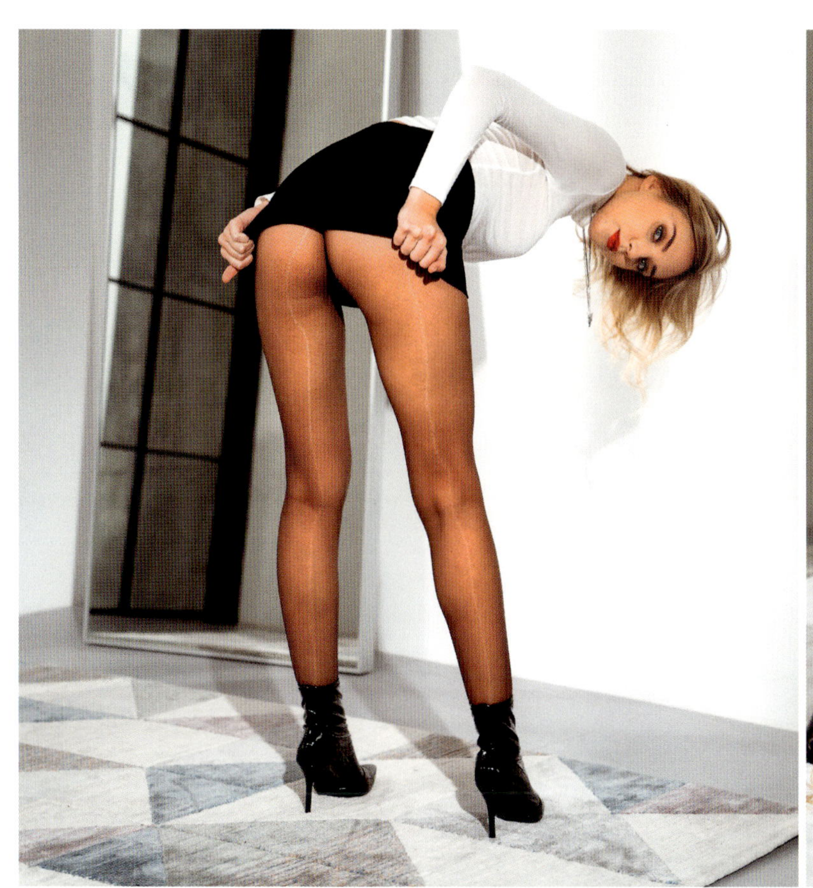
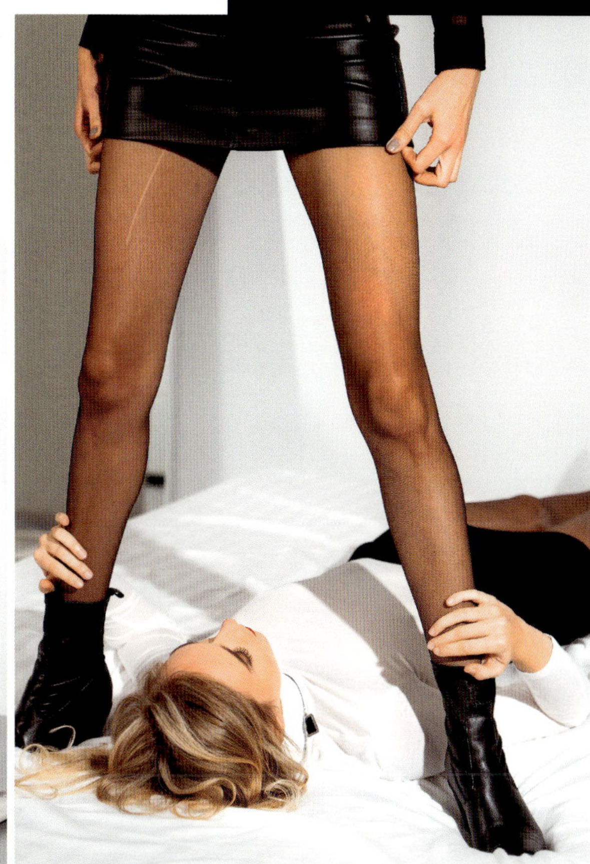
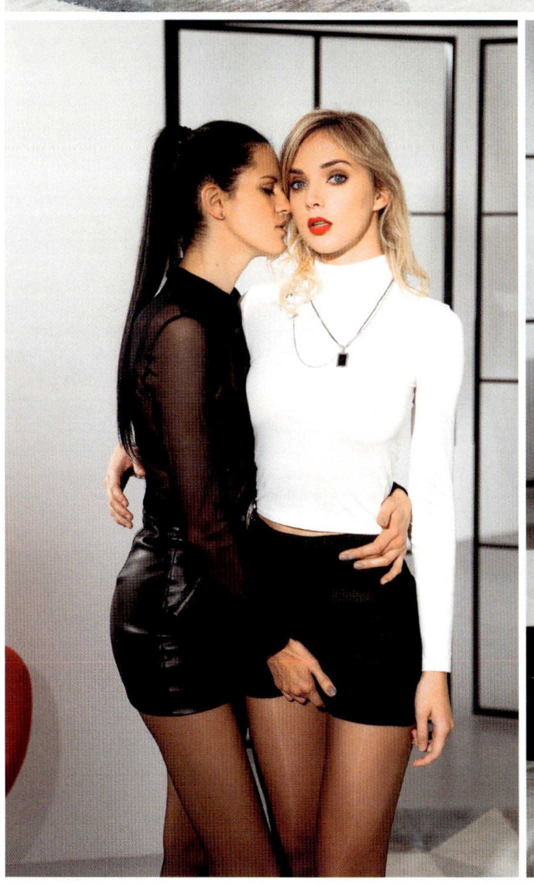
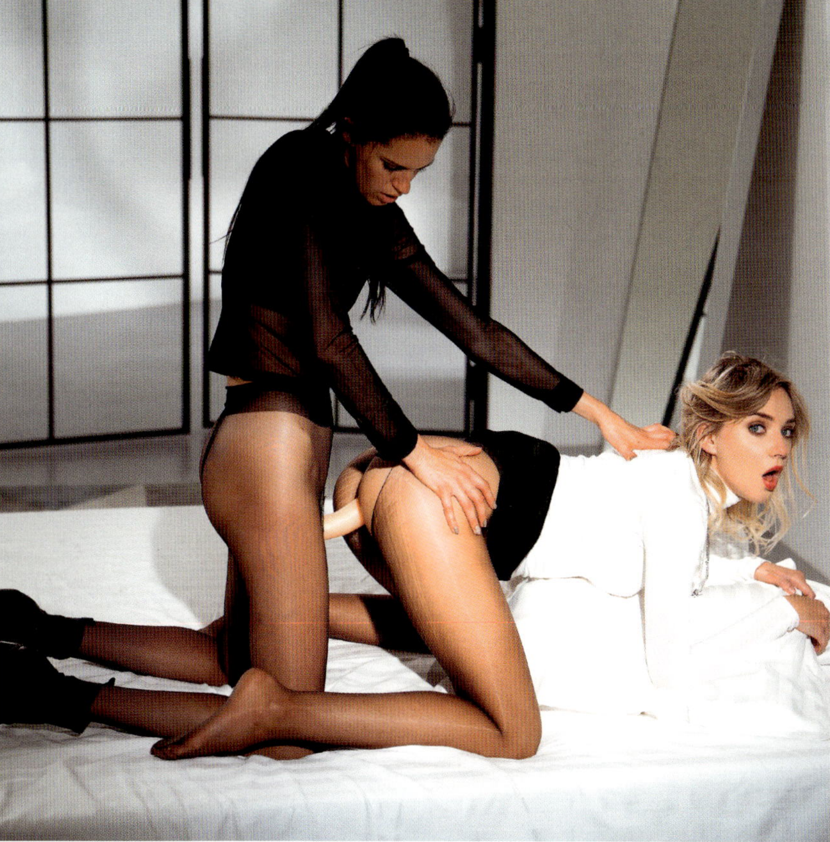

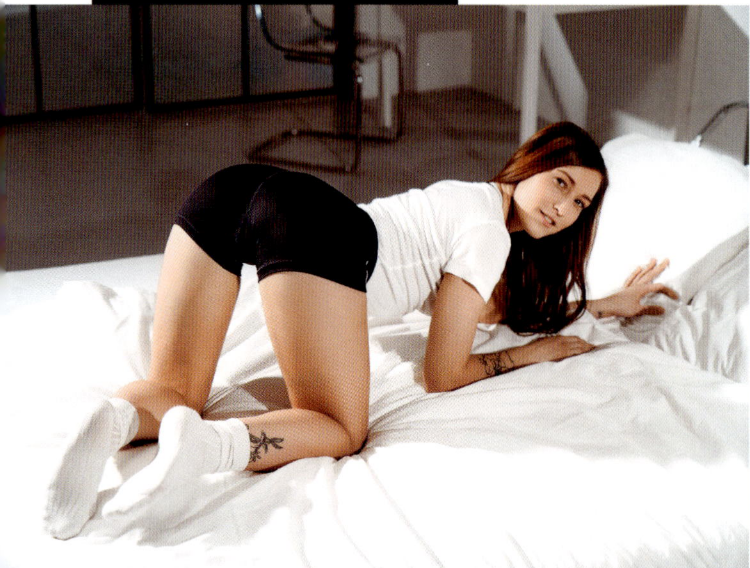

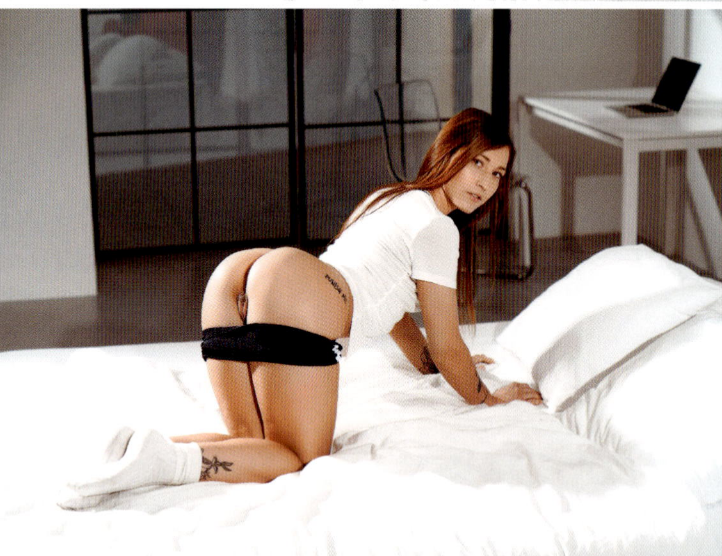

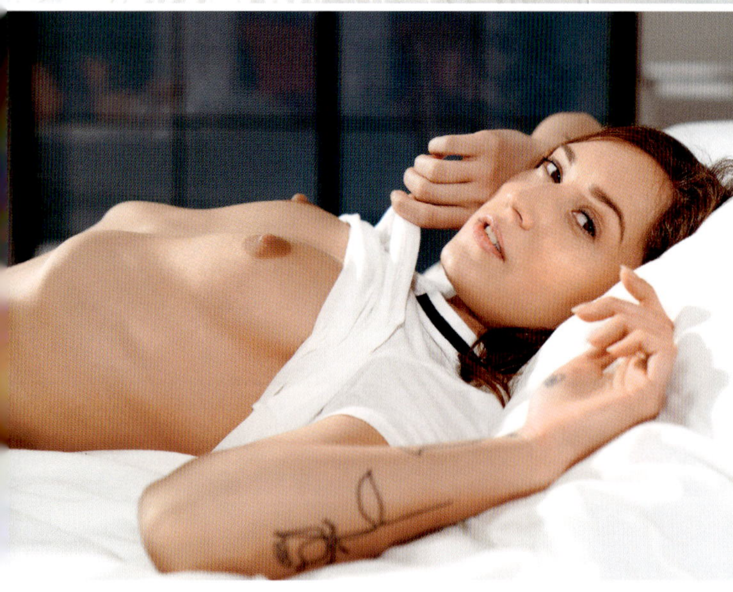

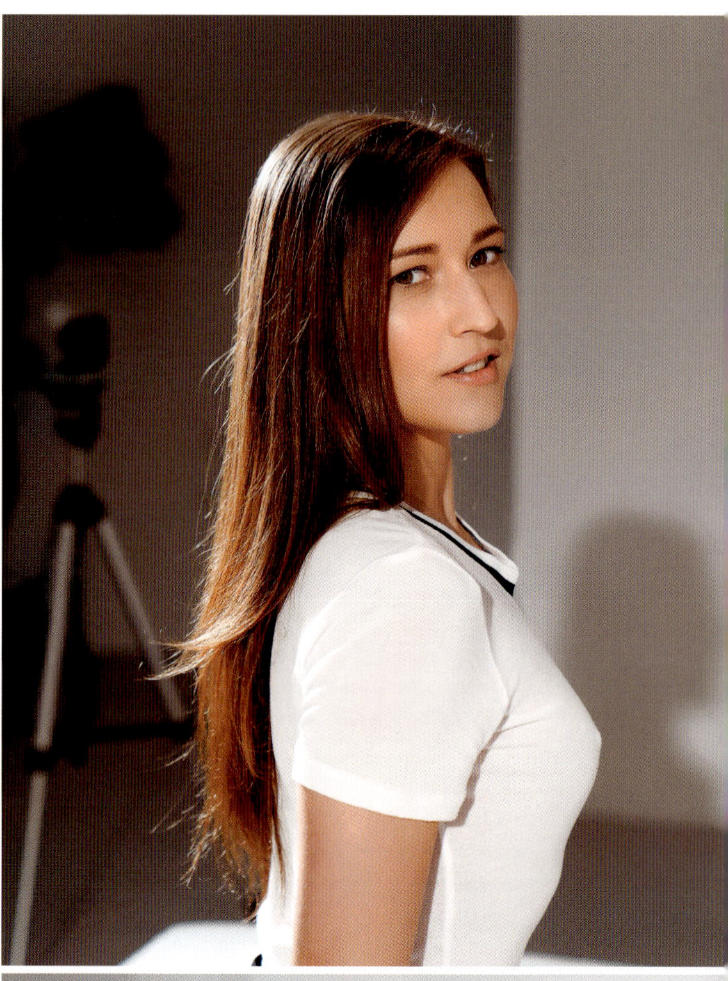

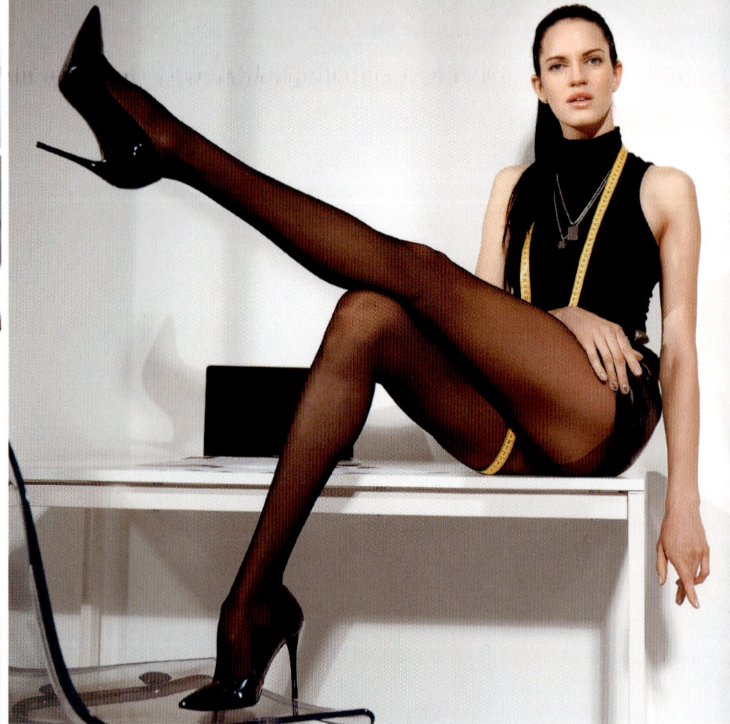

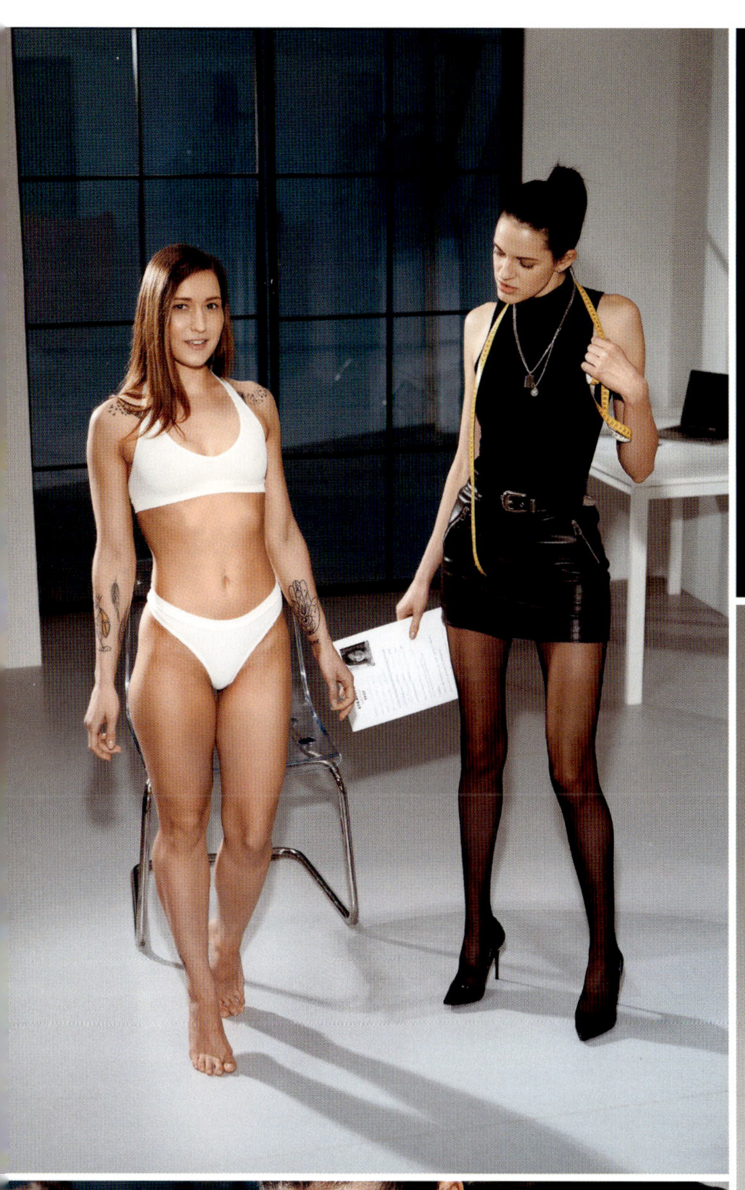

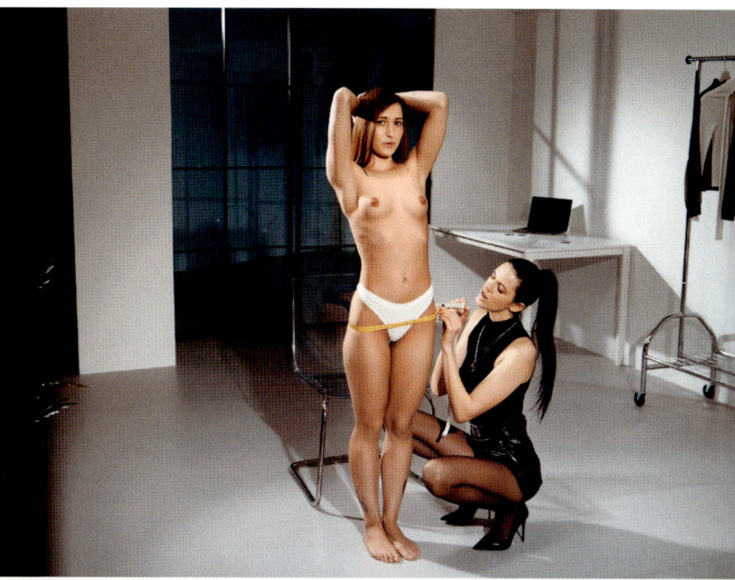

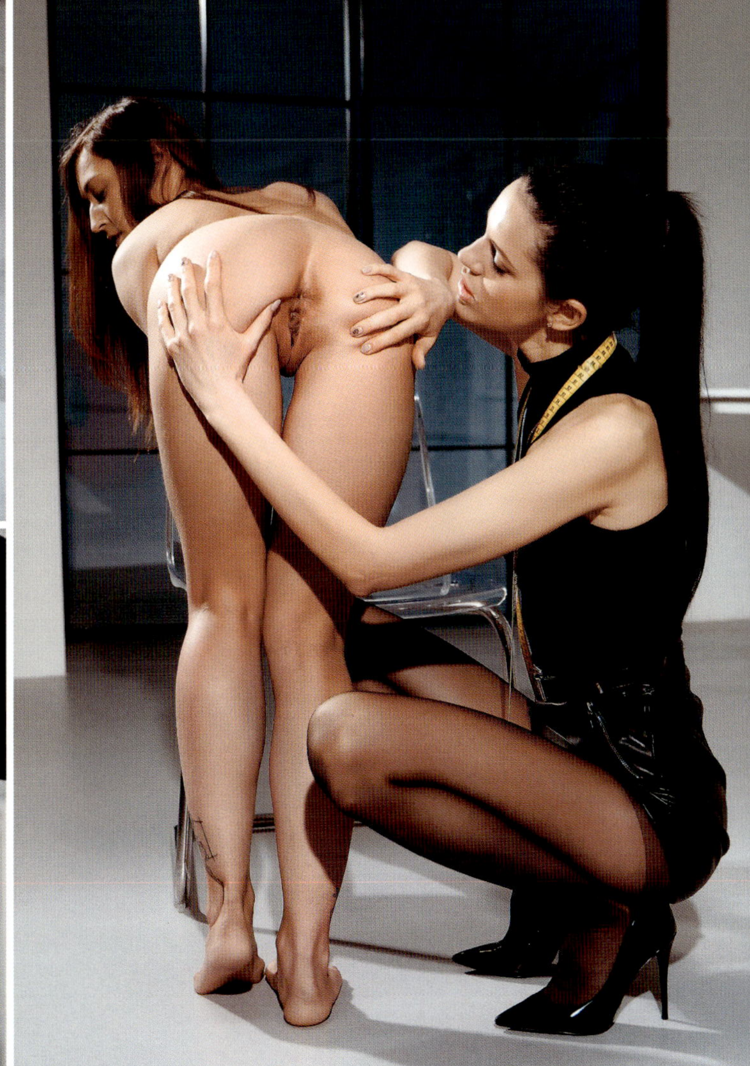

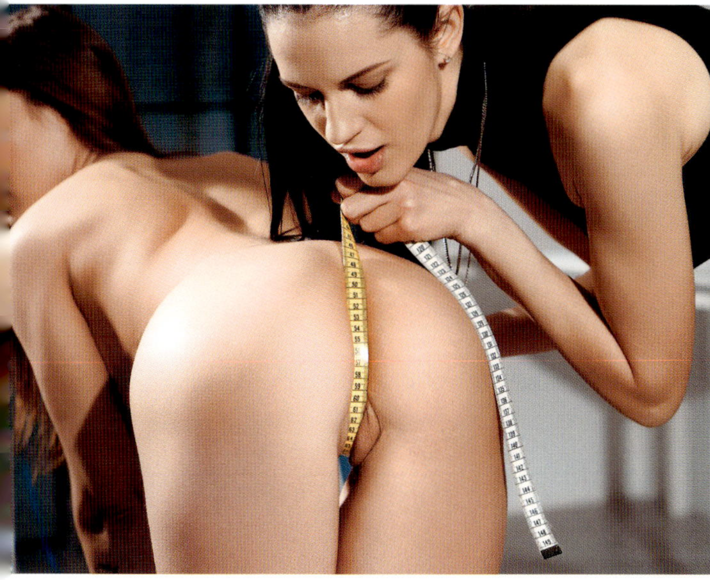

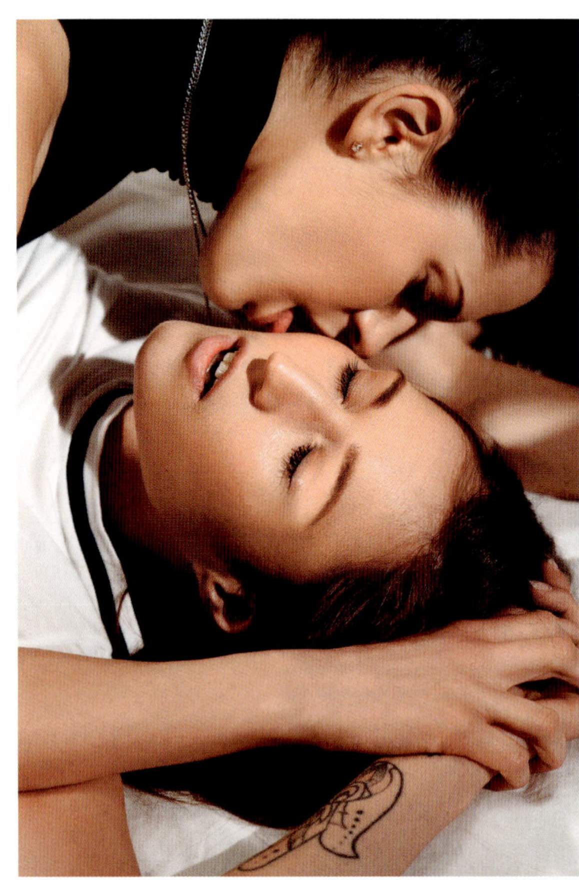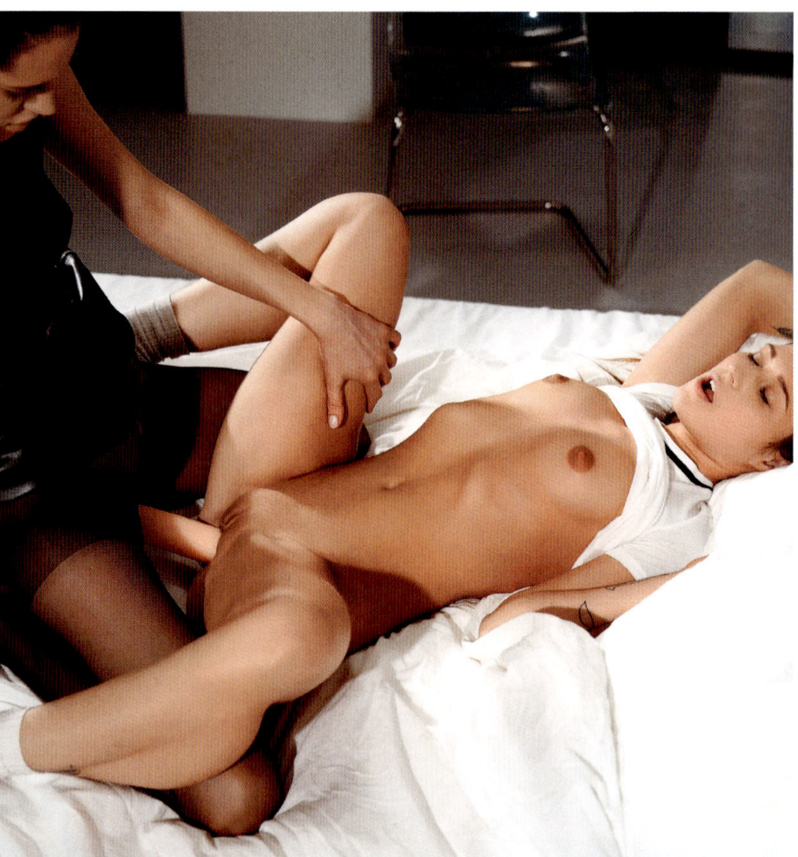

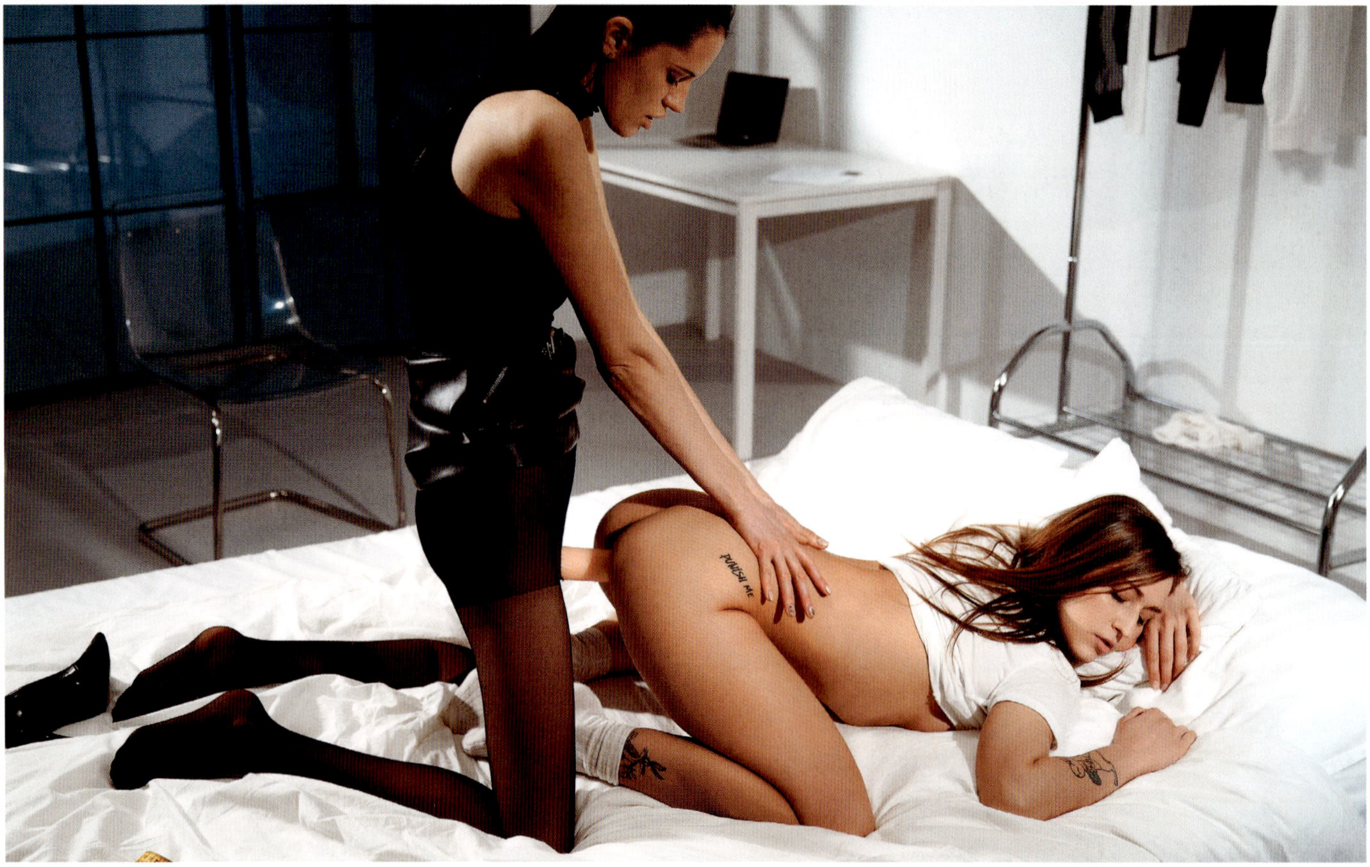

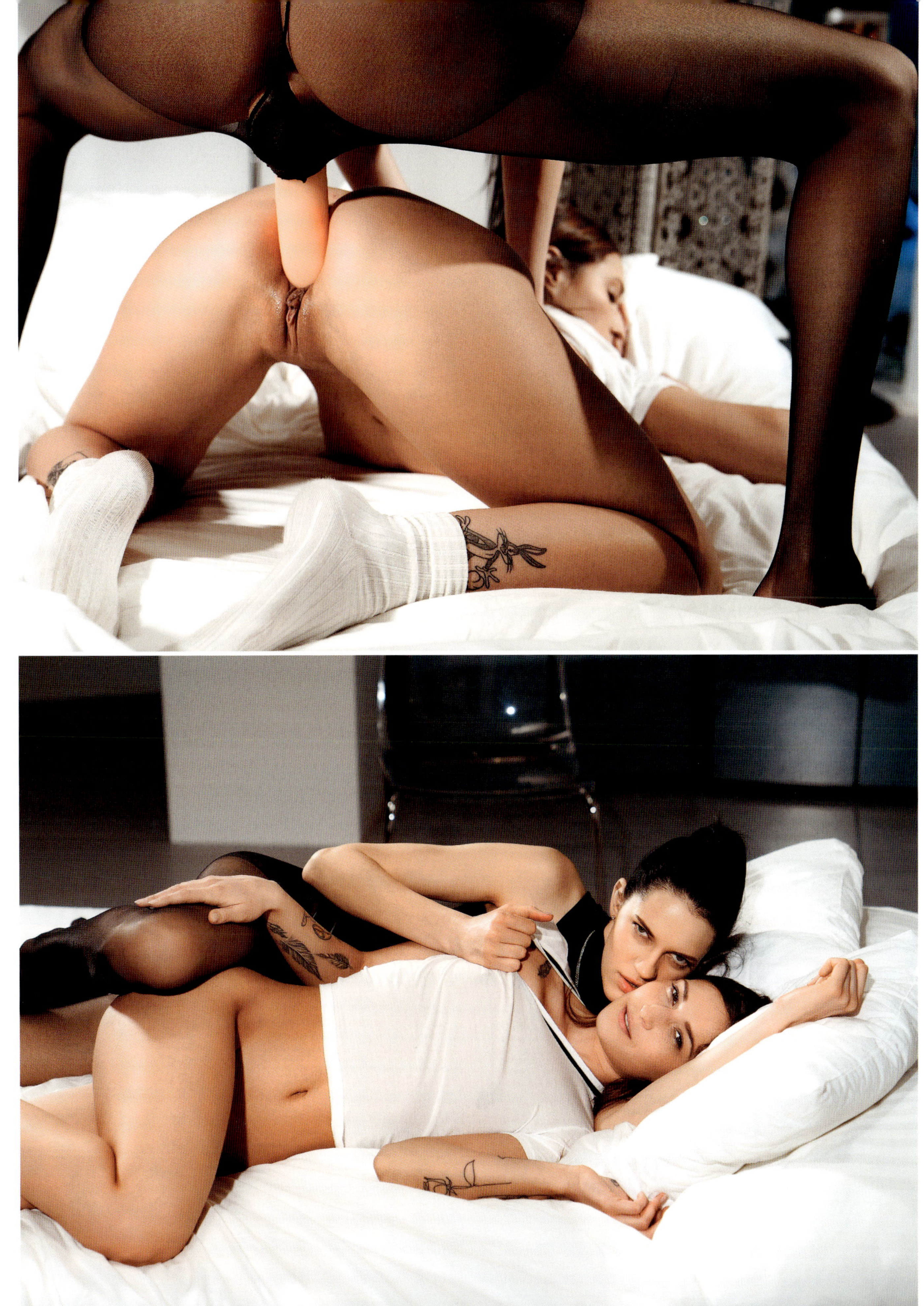

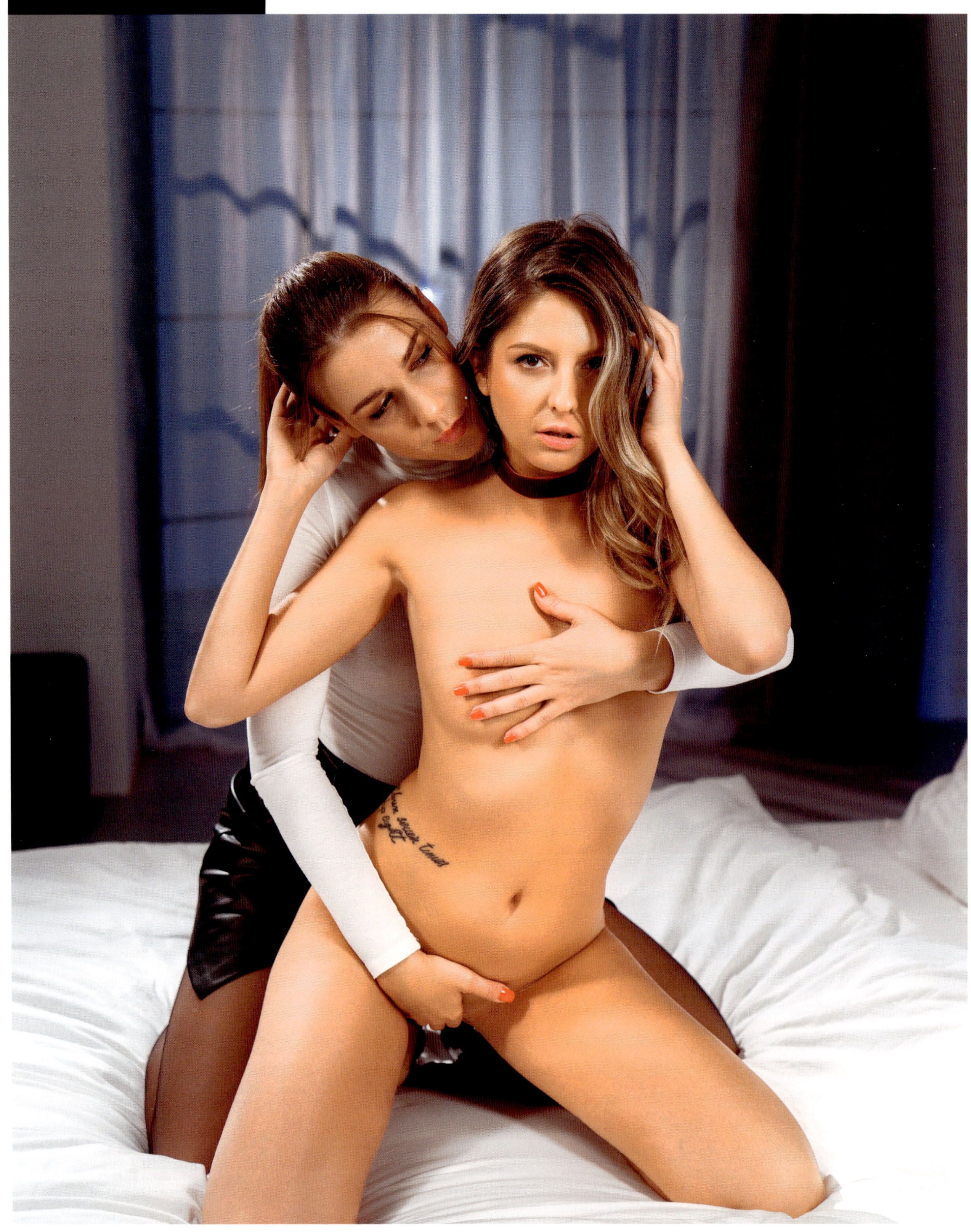

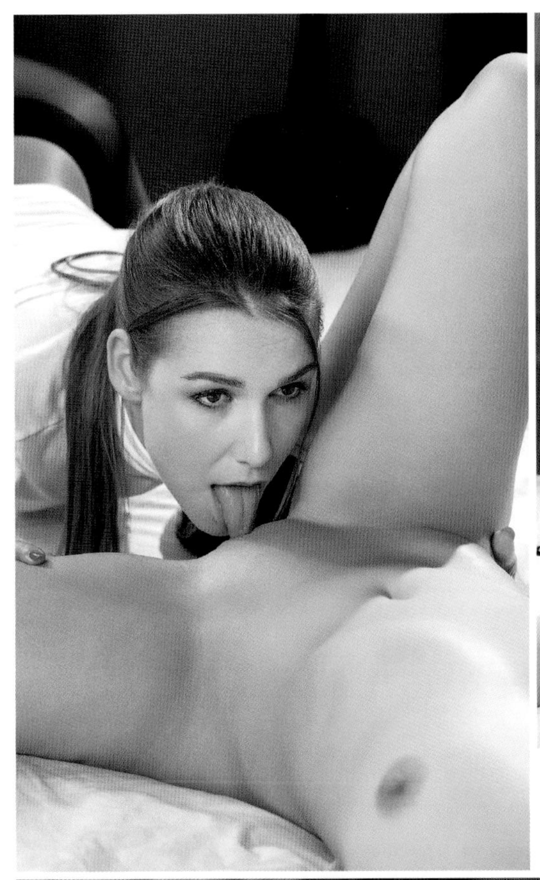
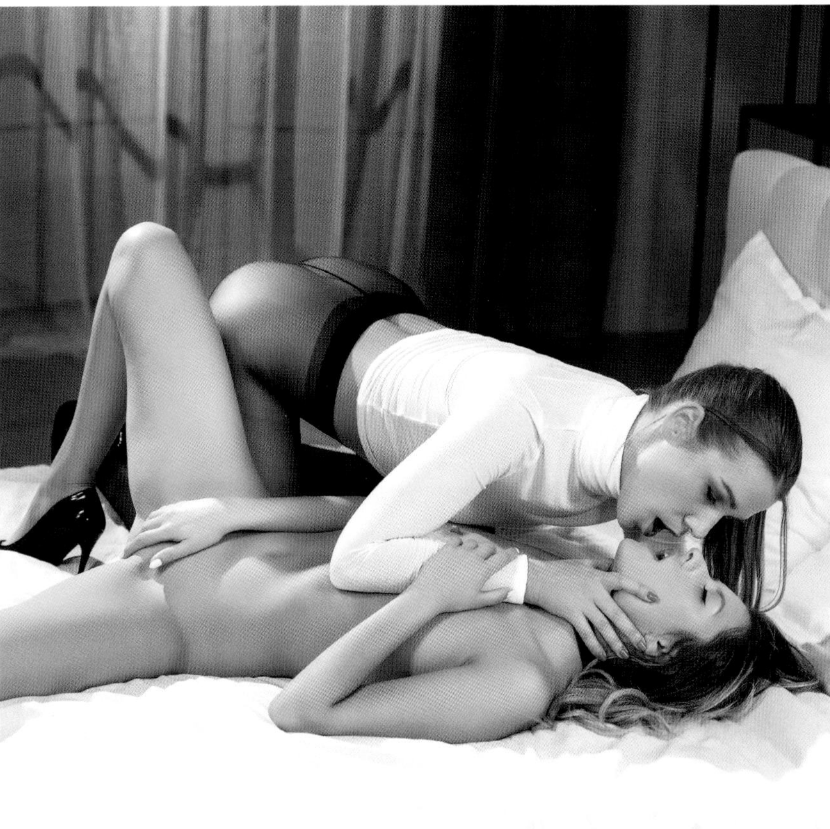

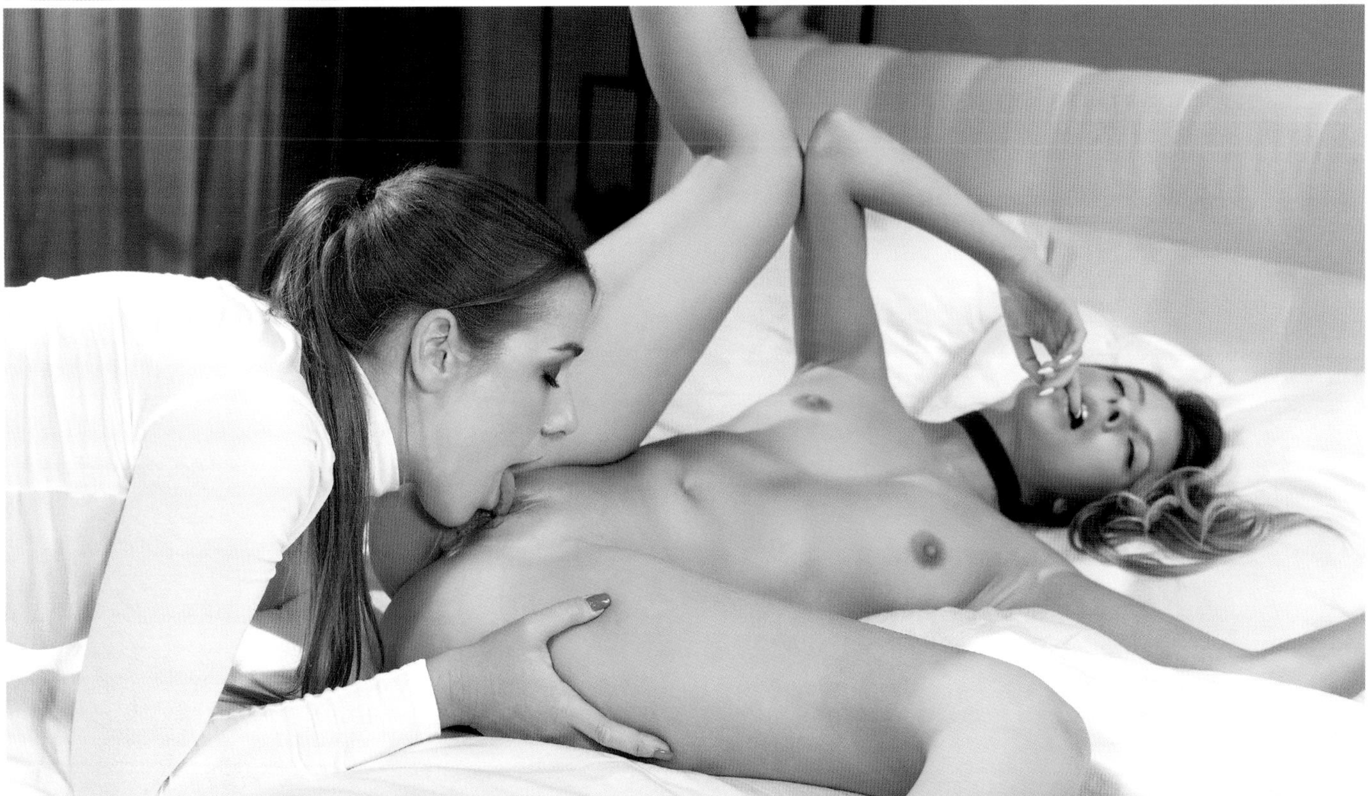

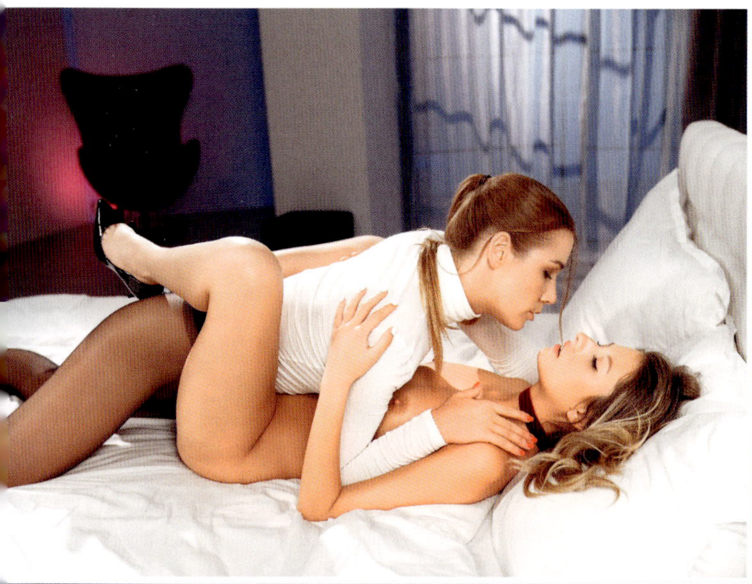

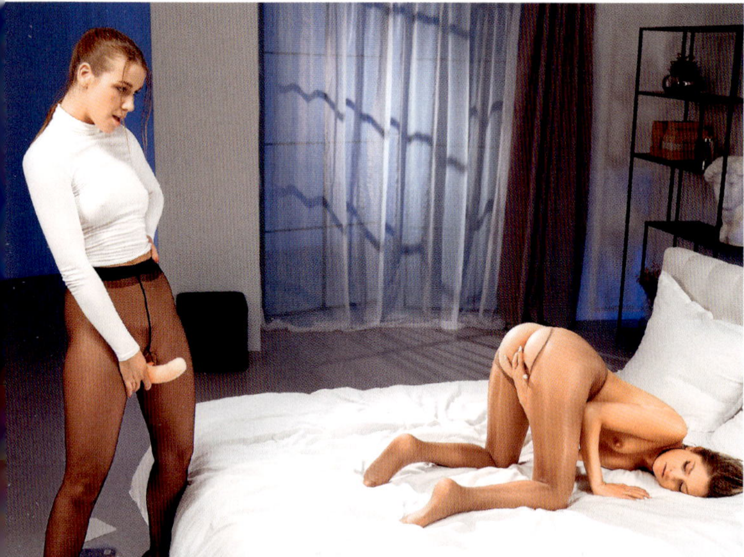

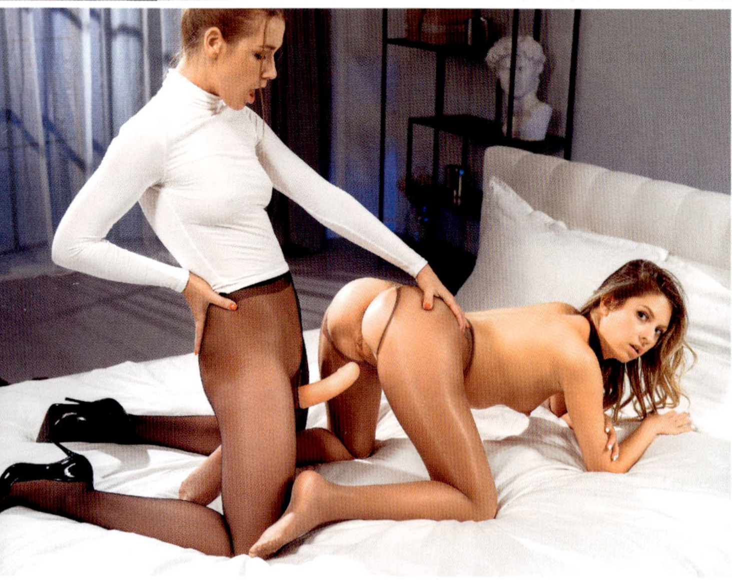

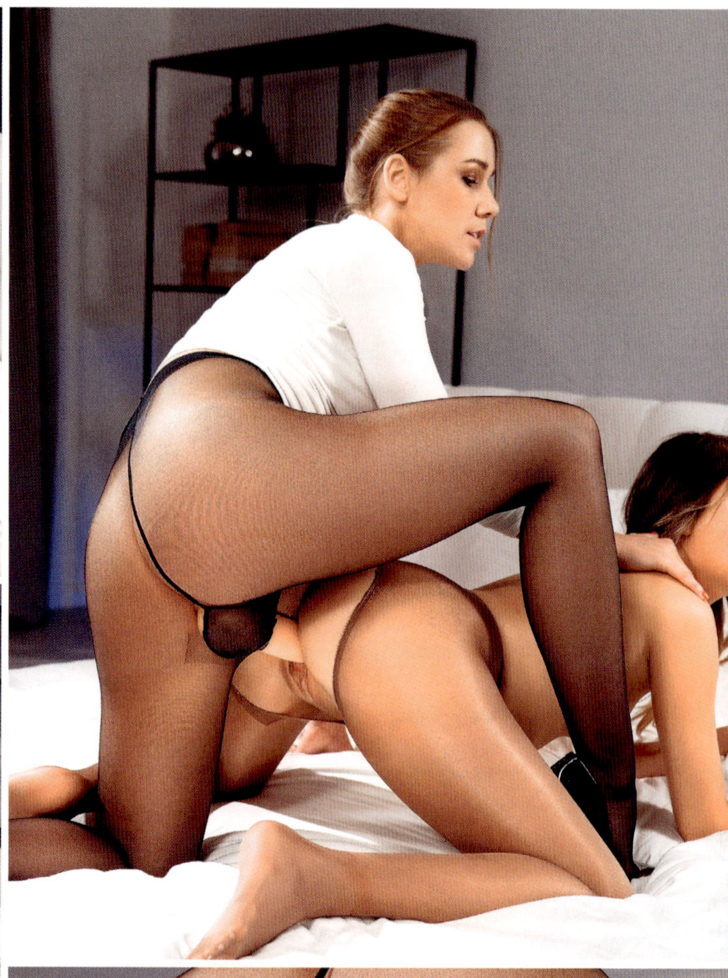

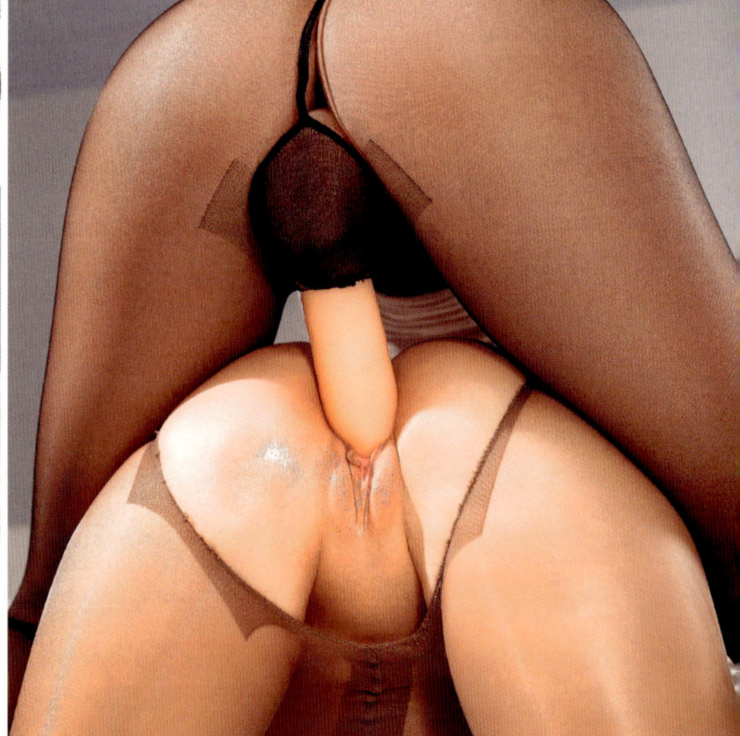

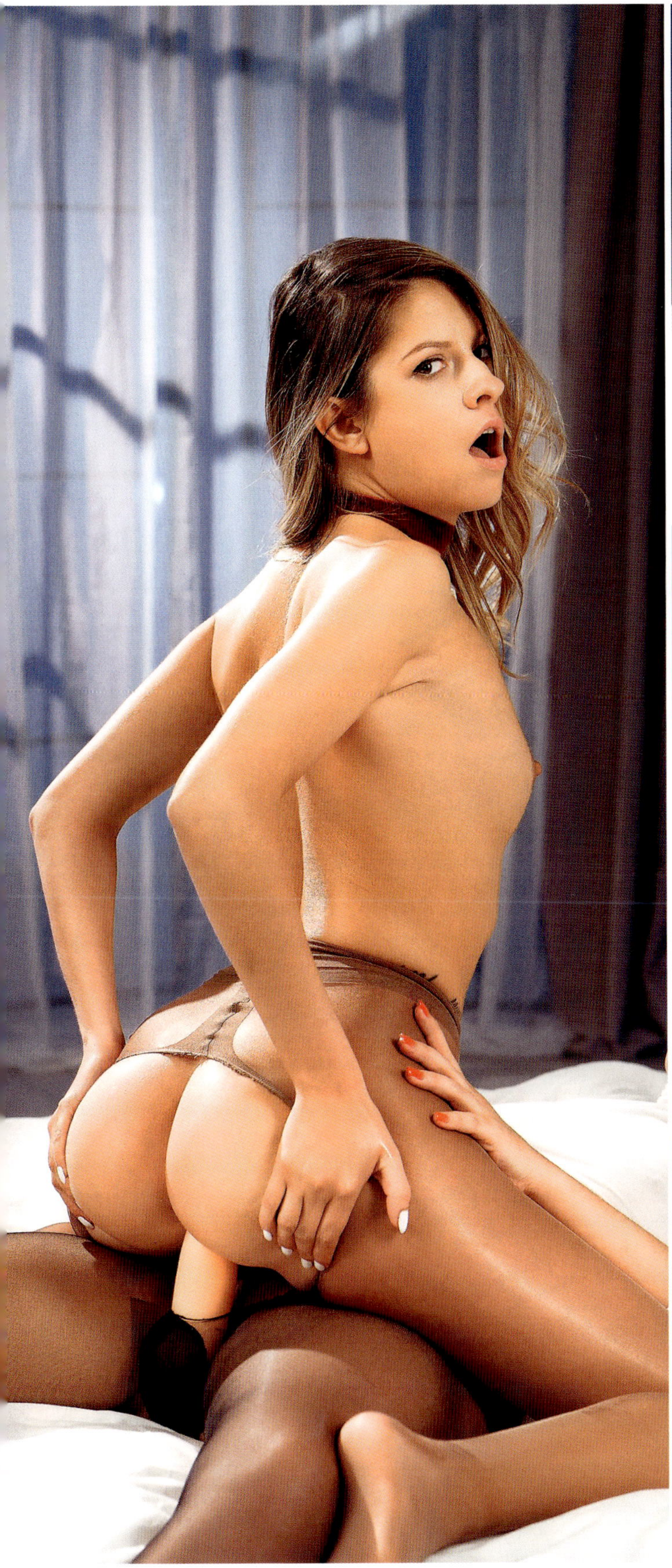

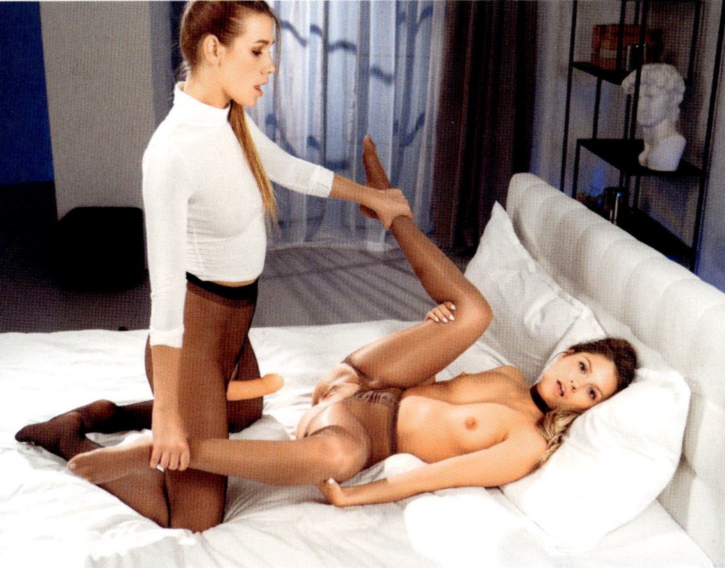

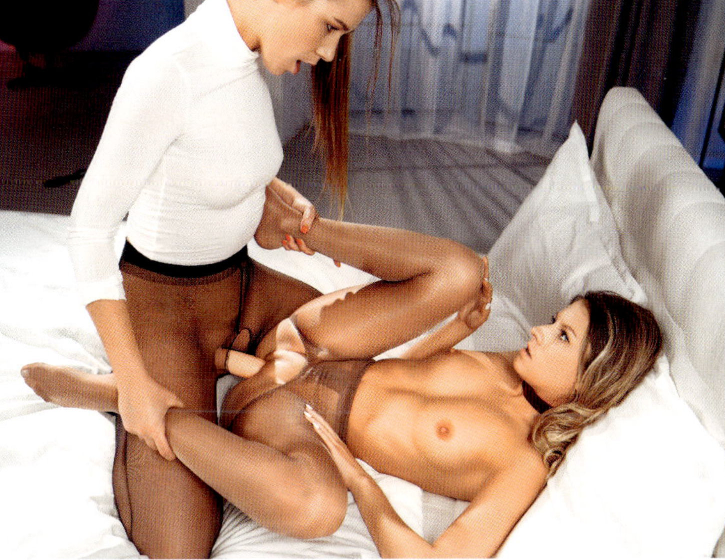

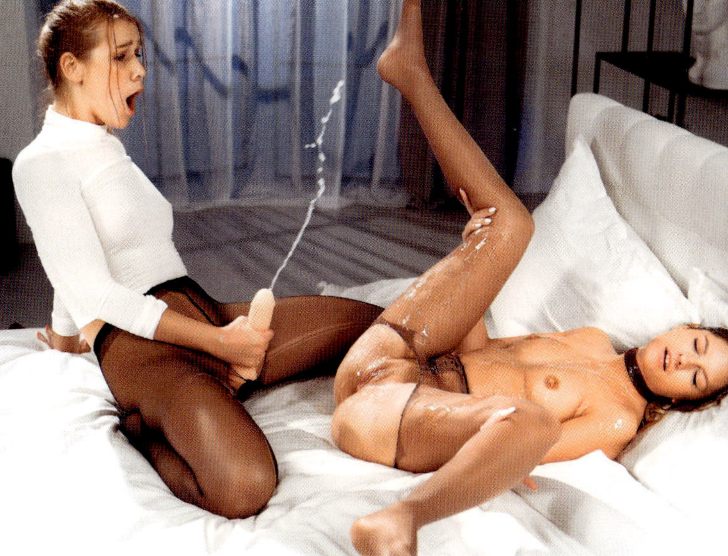

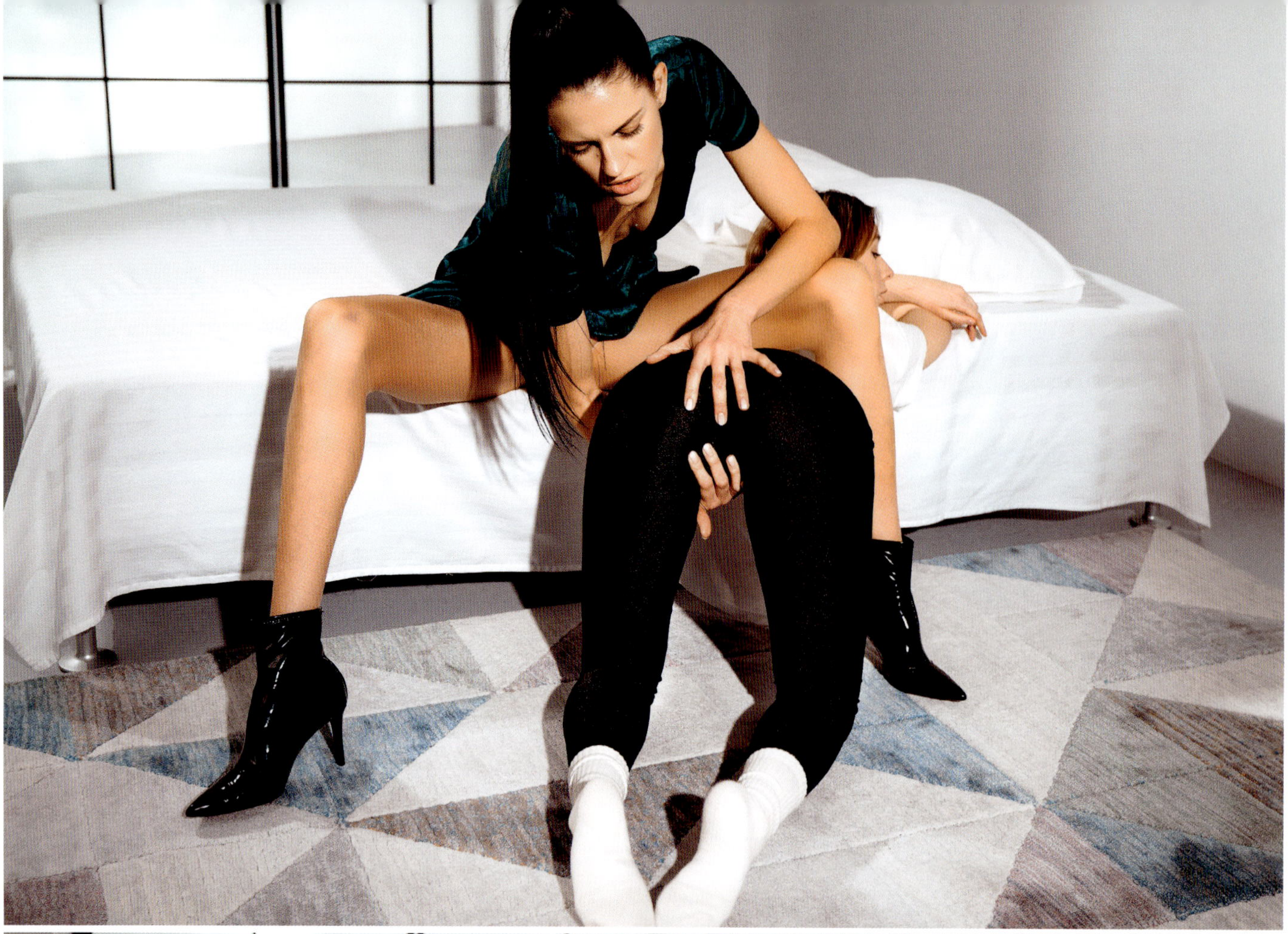

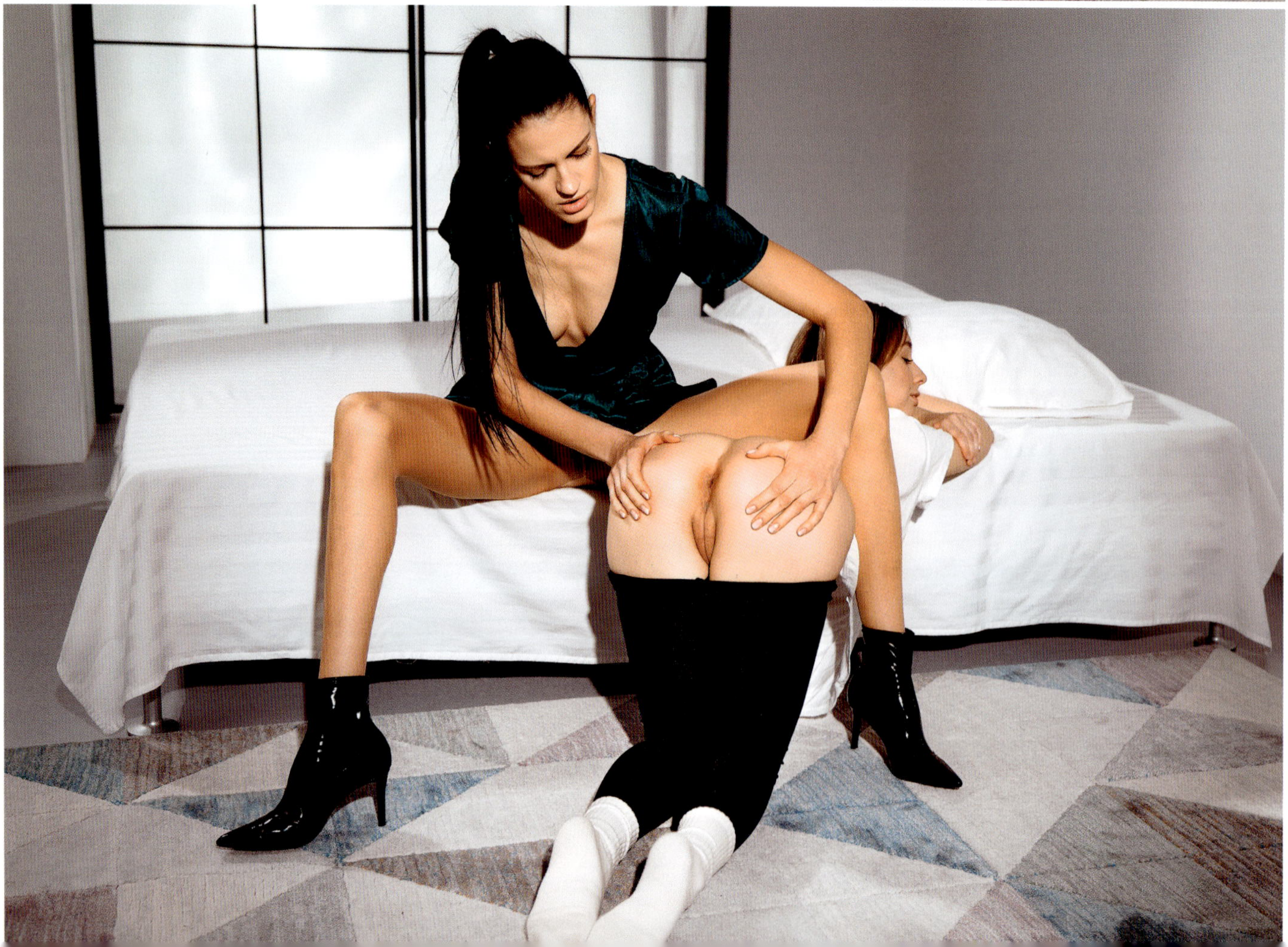

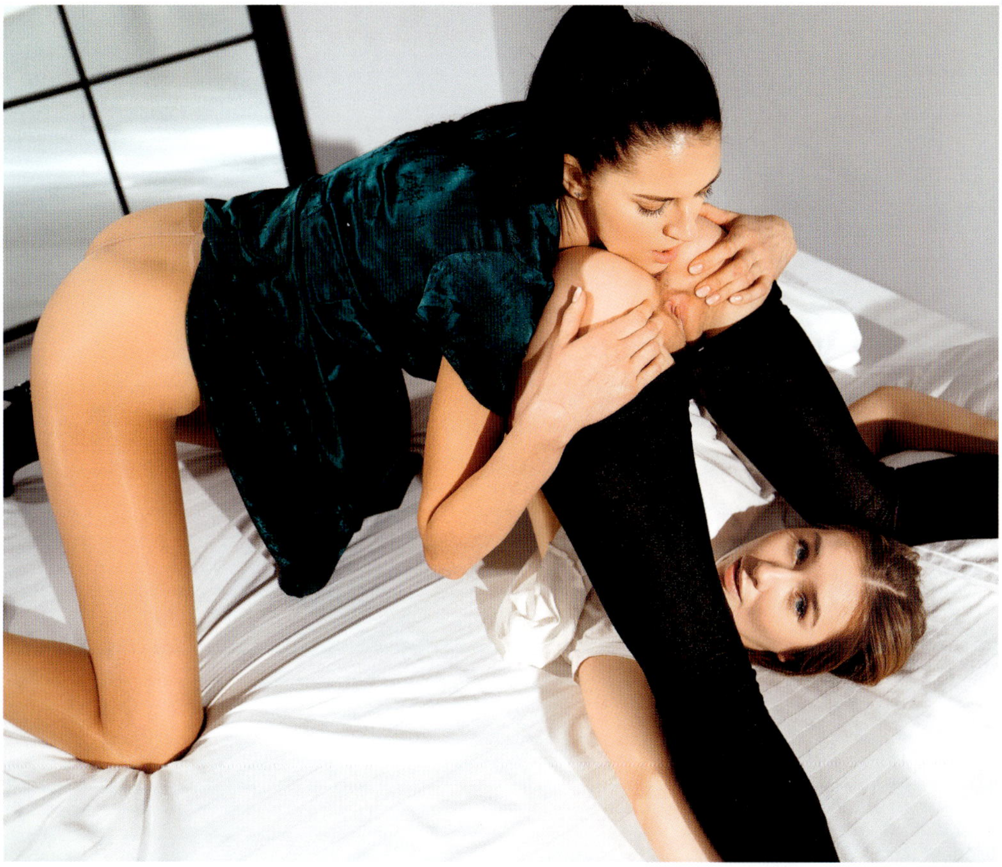

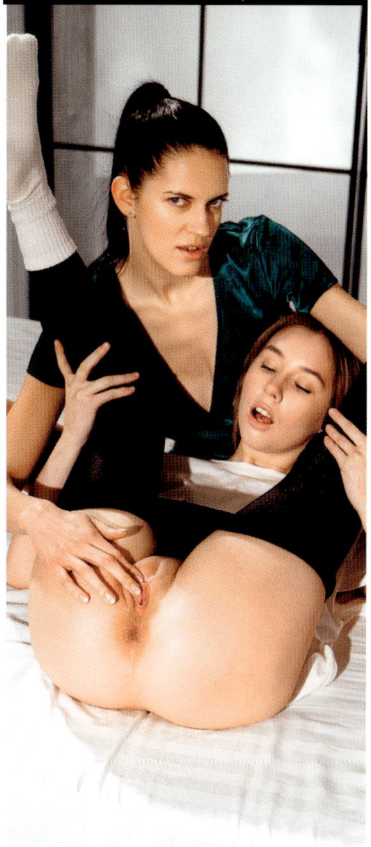

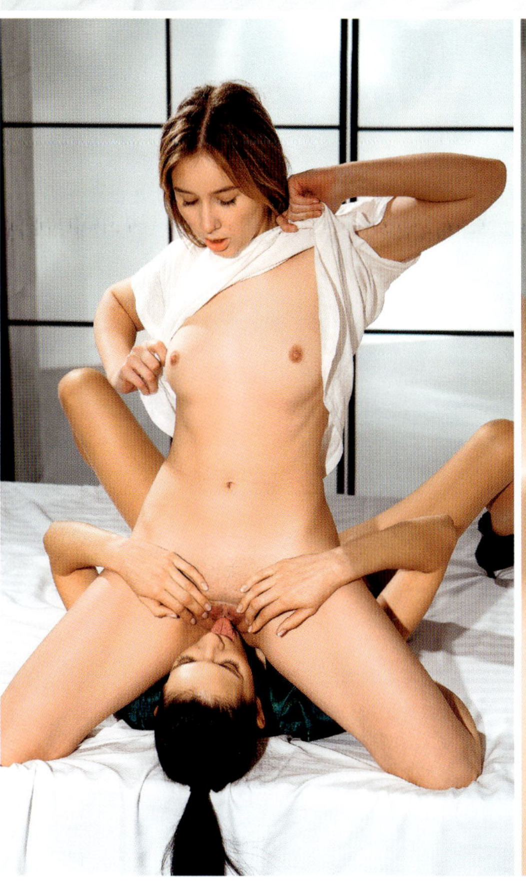

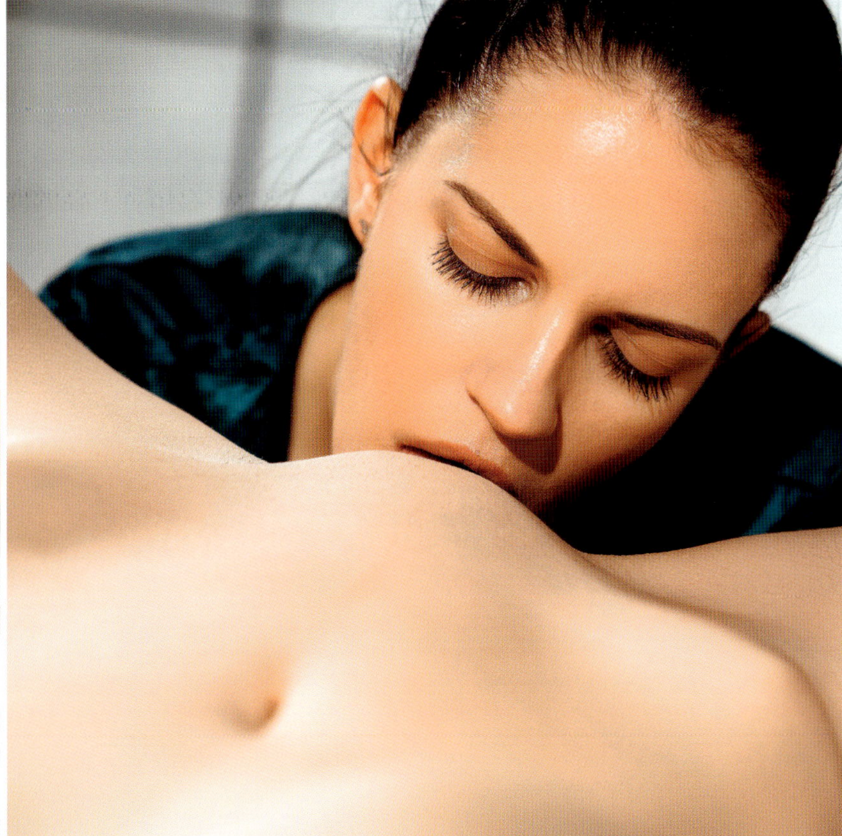

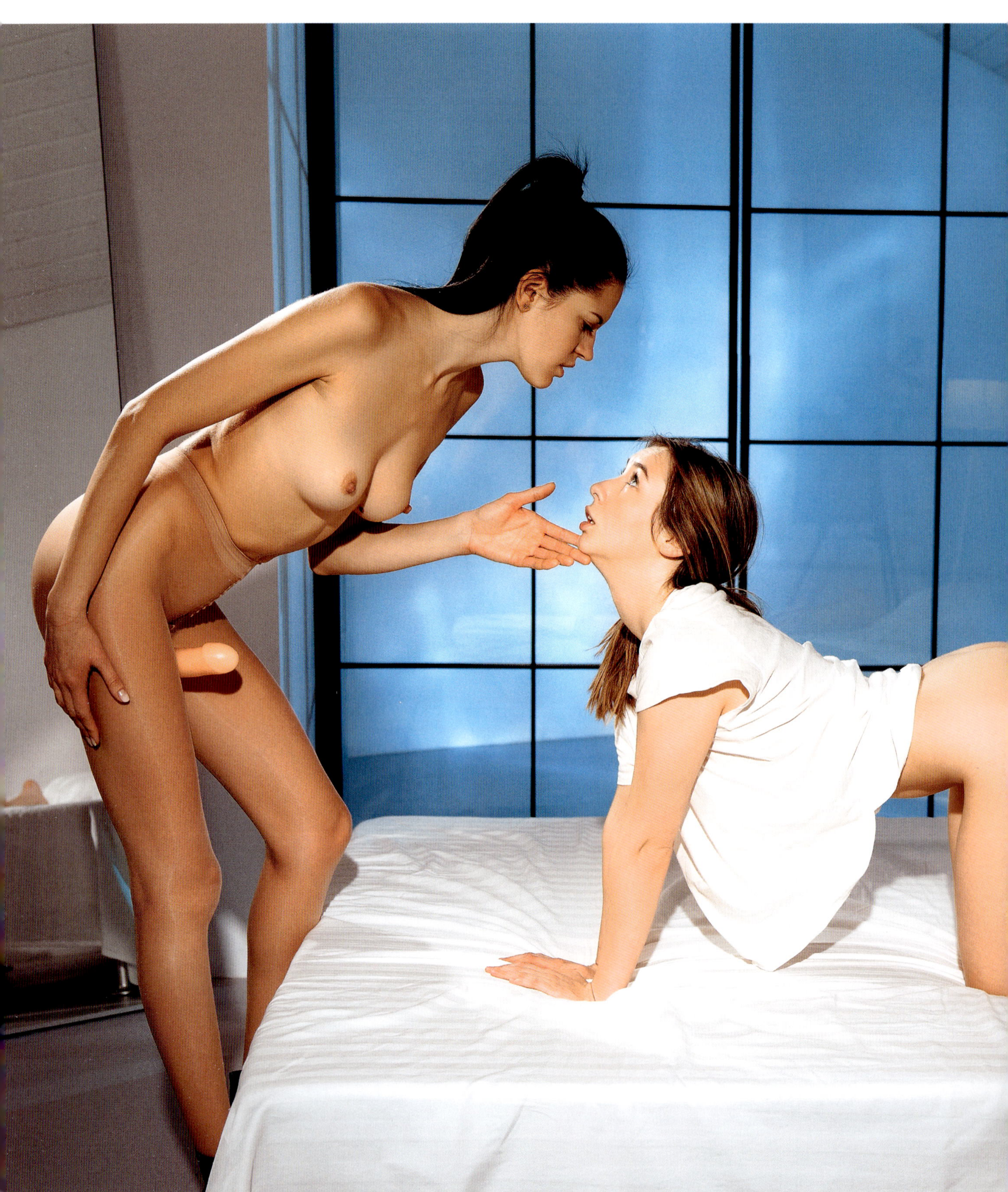

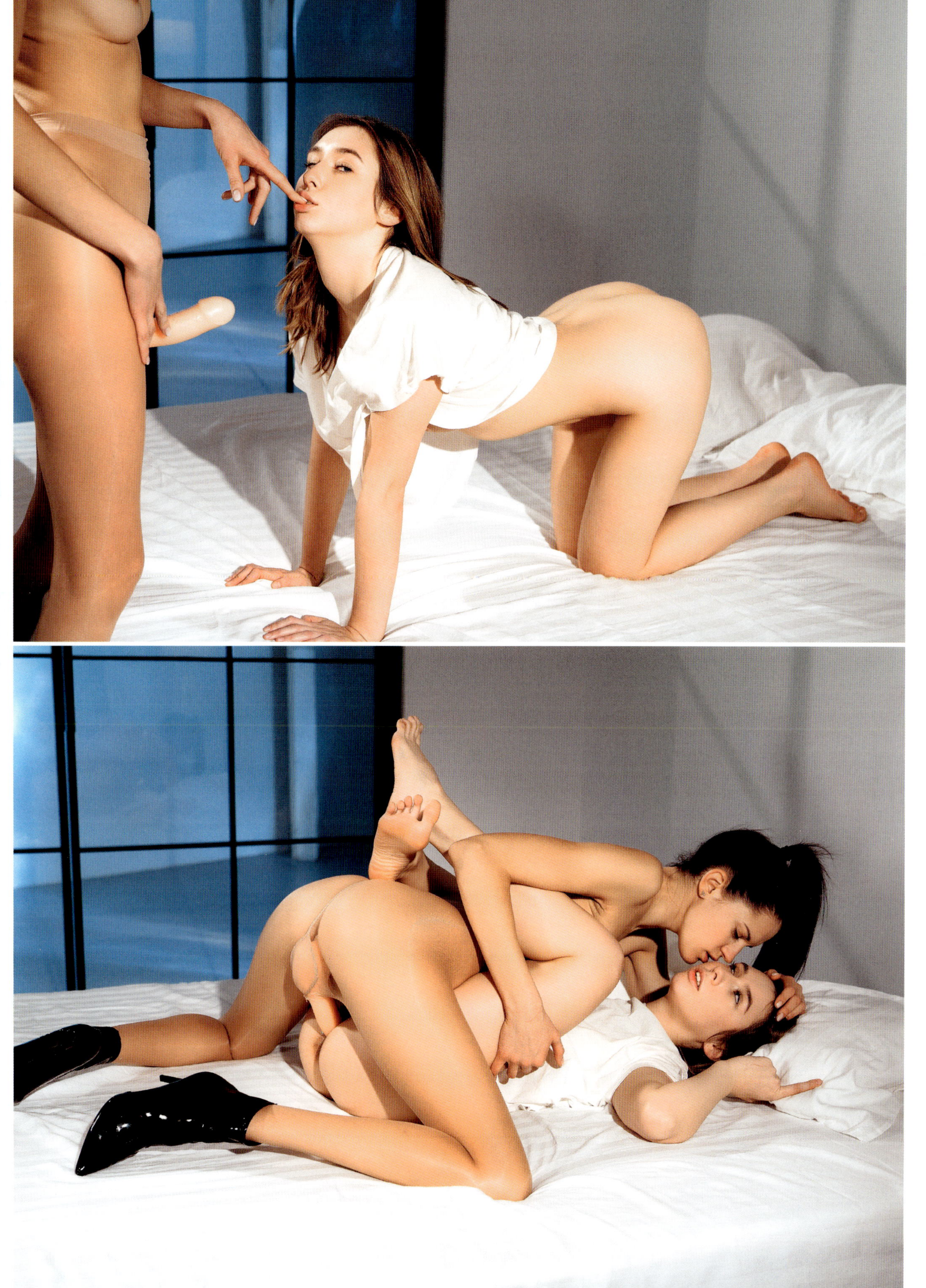

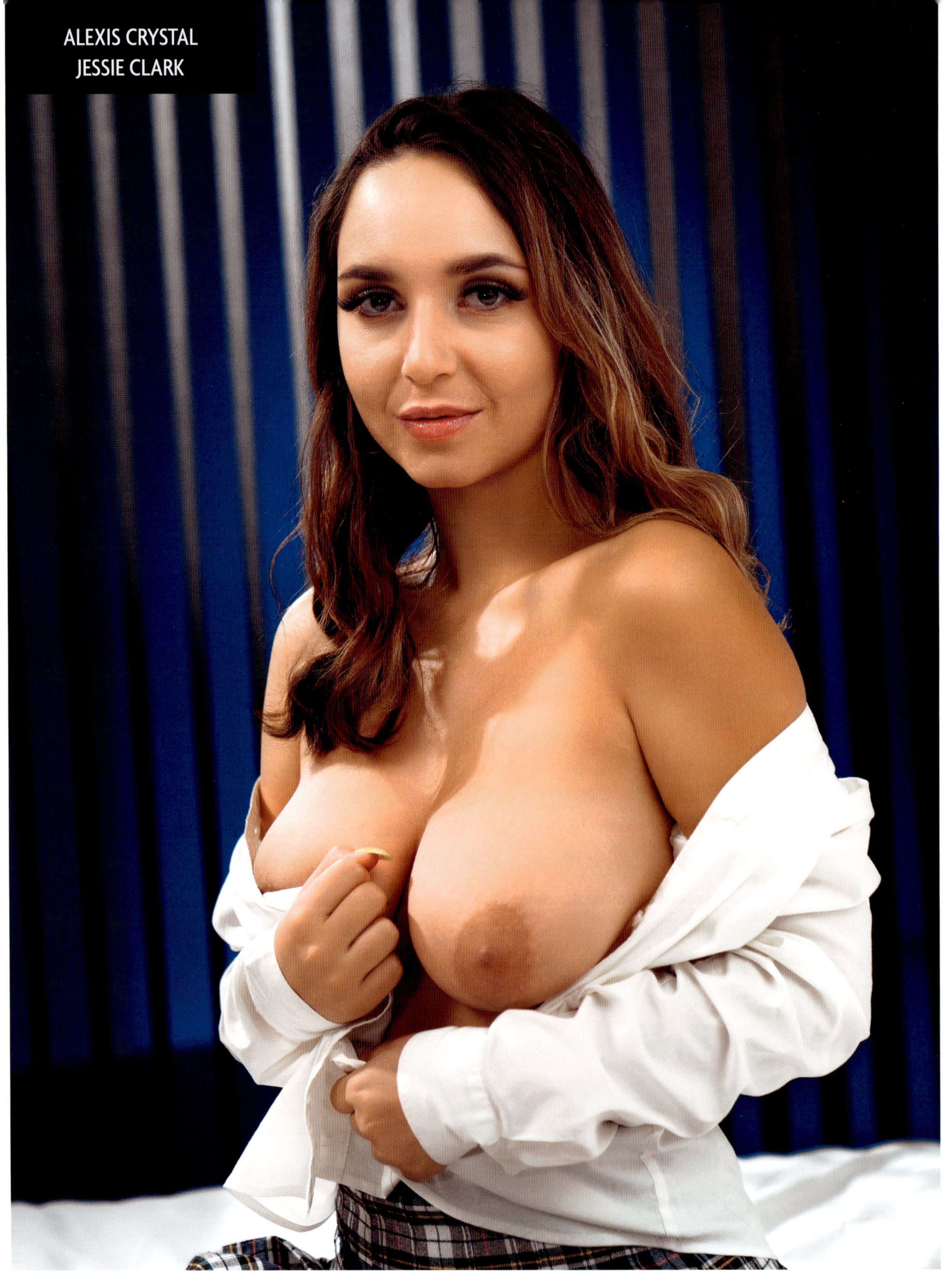

ALEXIS CRYSTAL
JESSIE CLARK

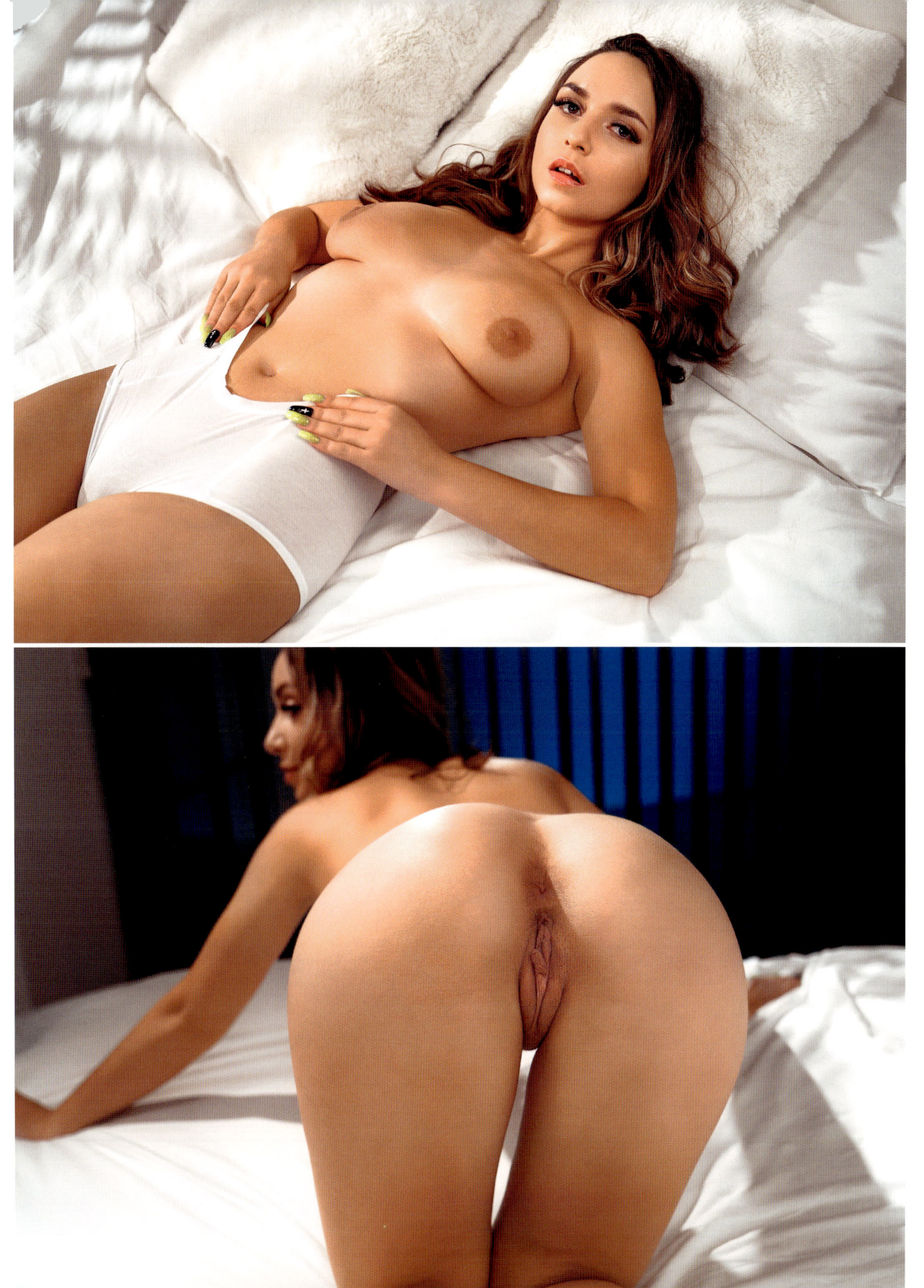

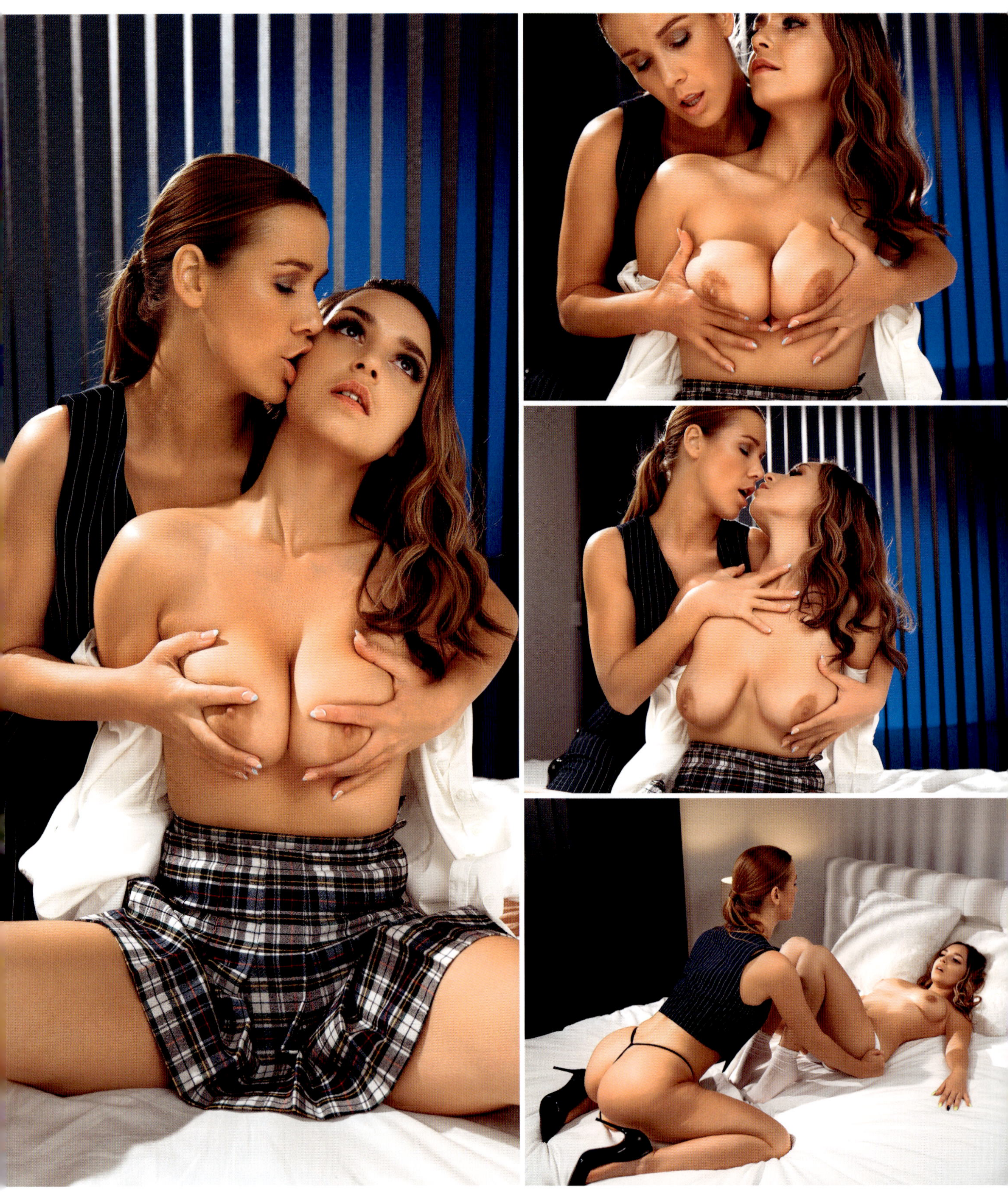

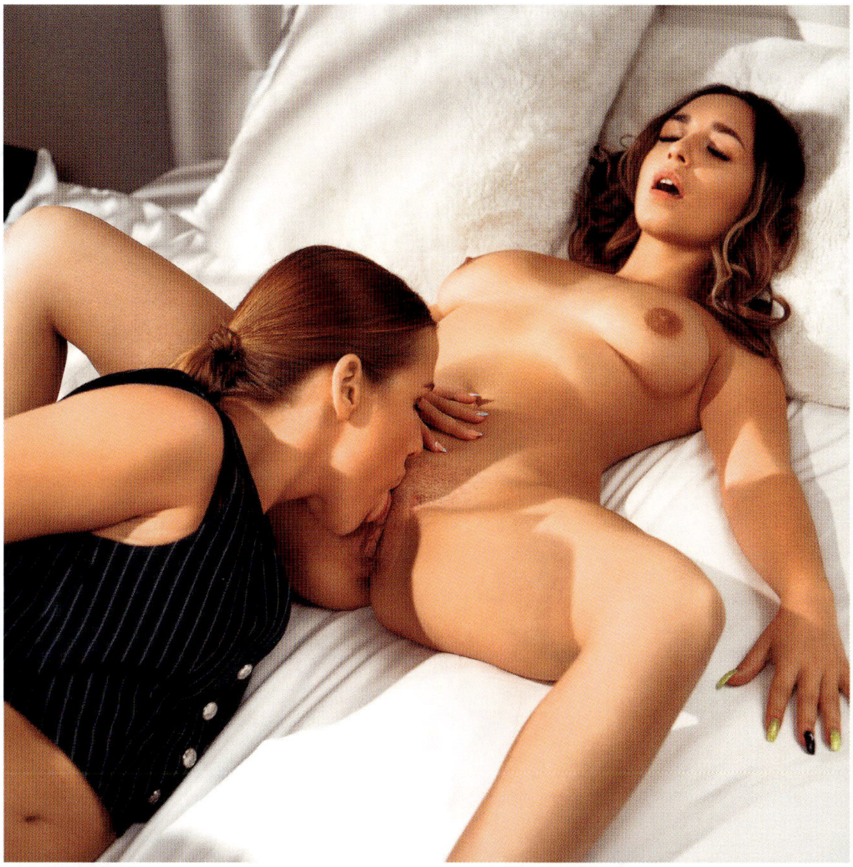

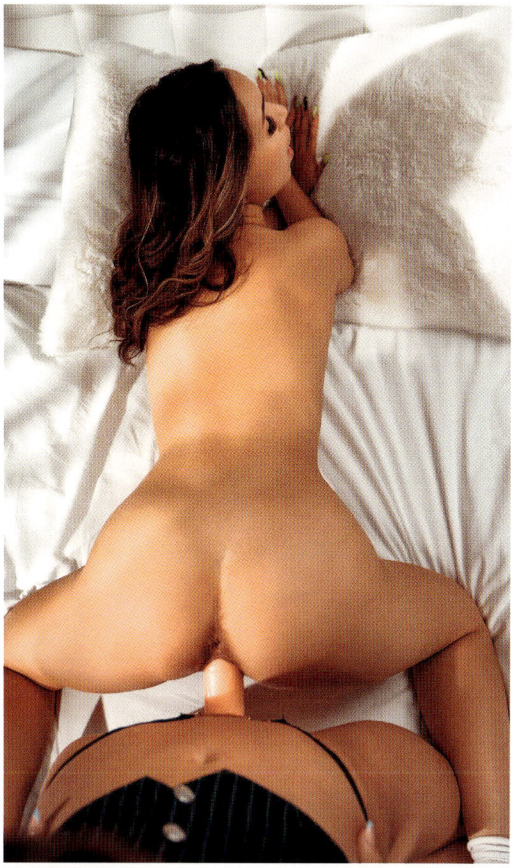

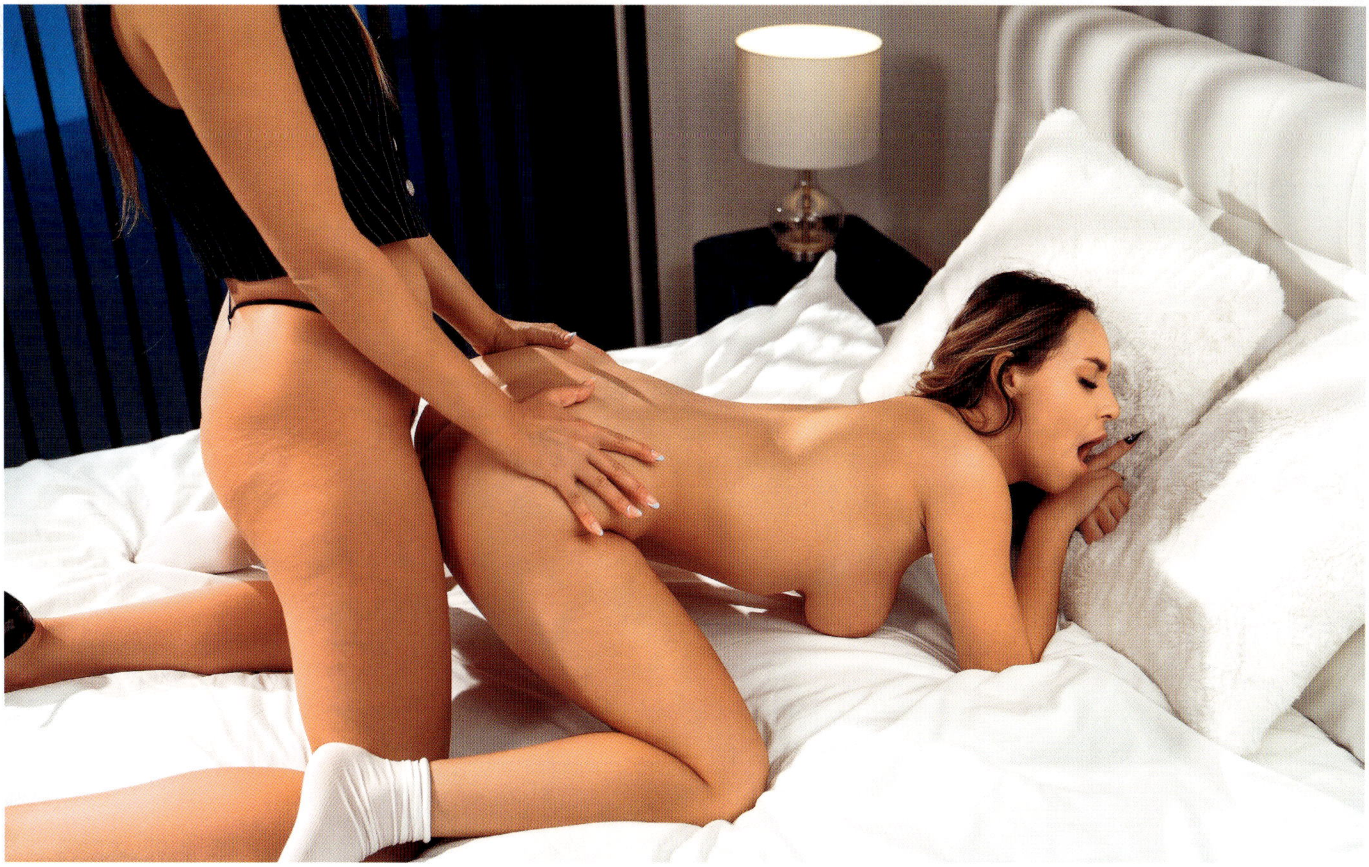

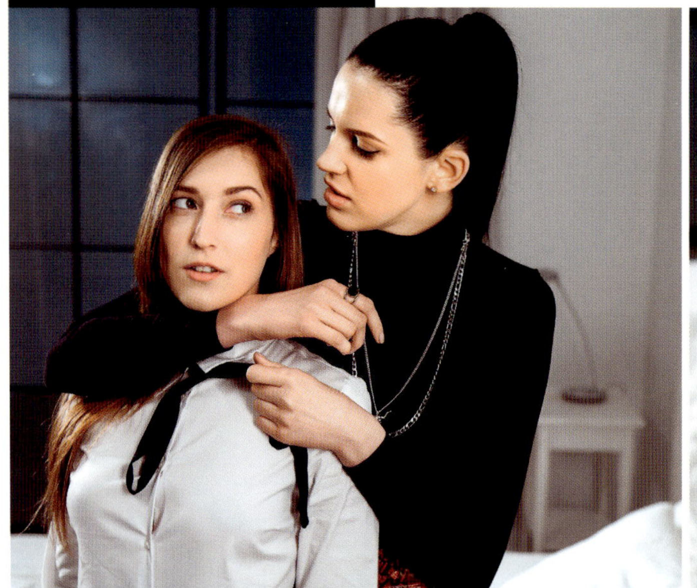

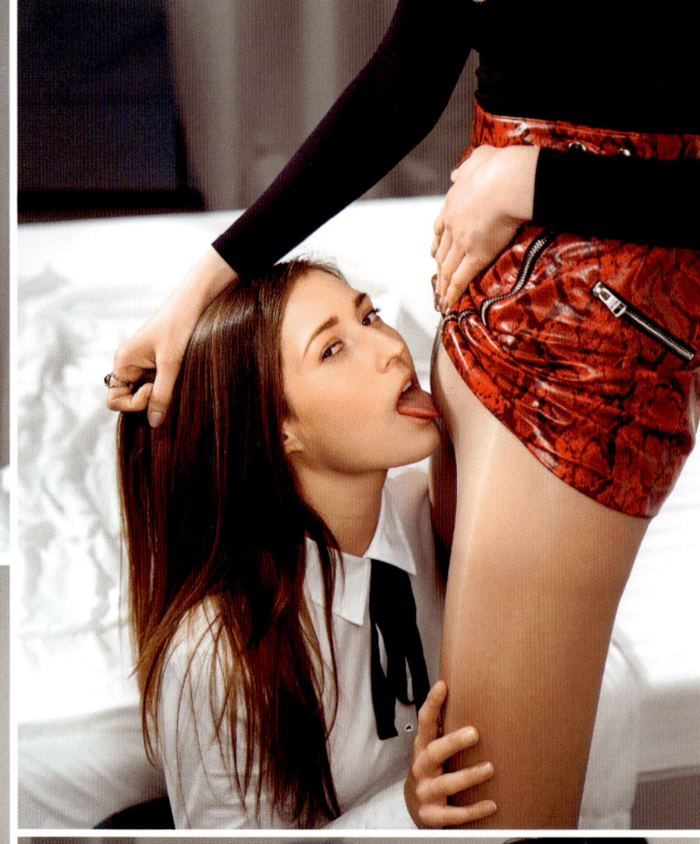

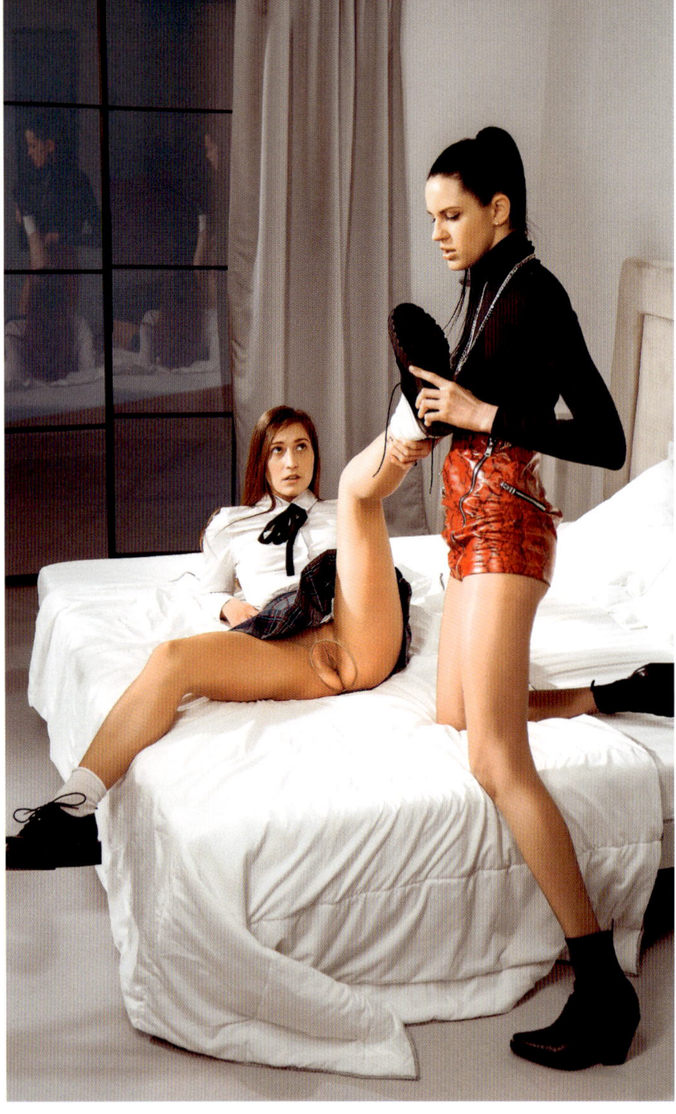

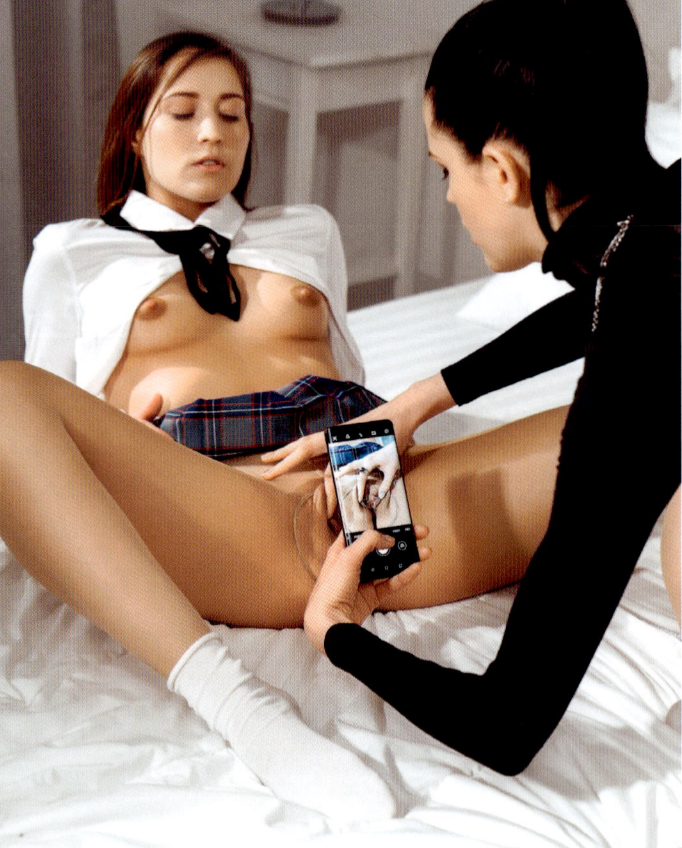

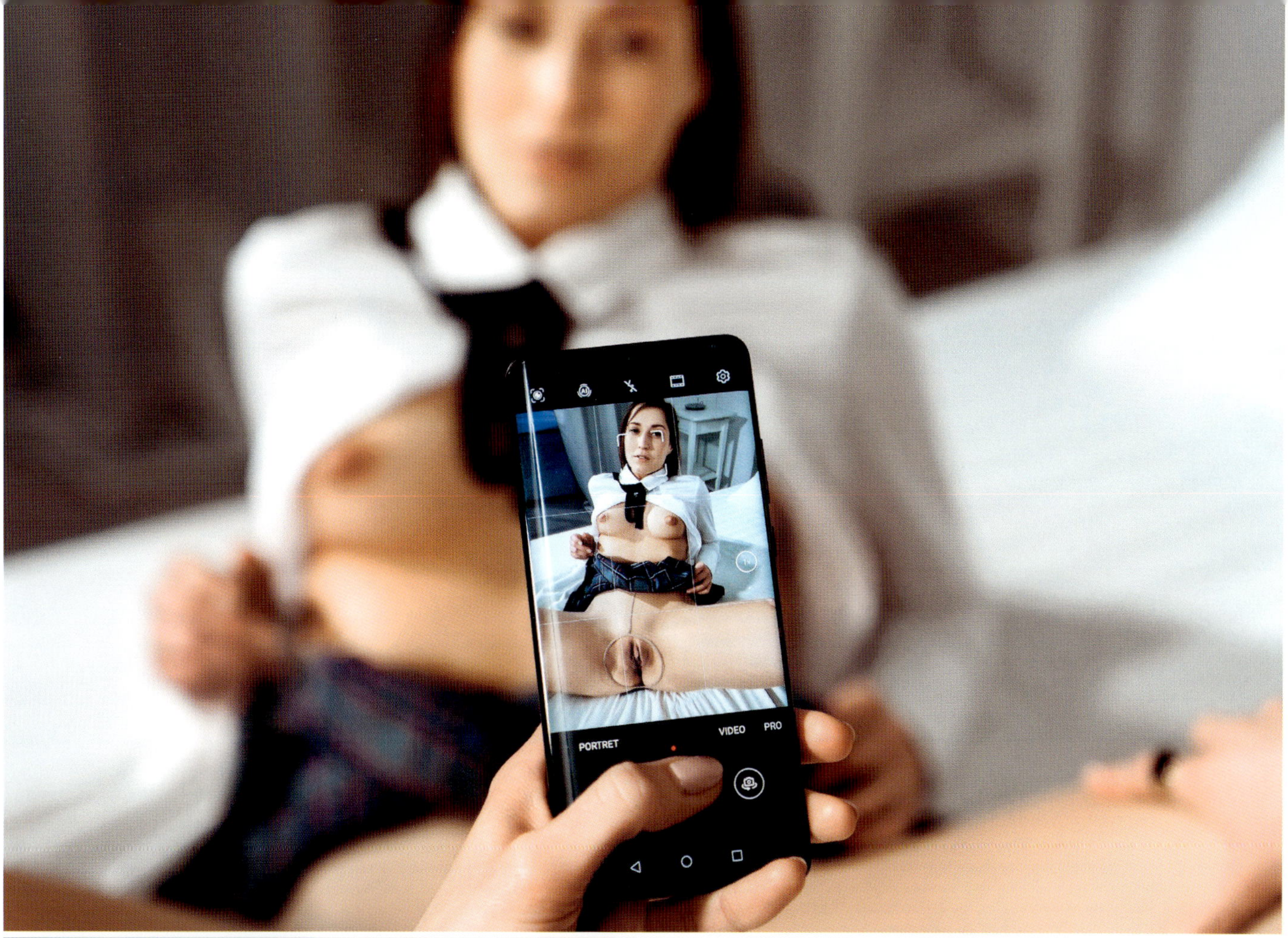

PORTRET
VIDEO
PRO

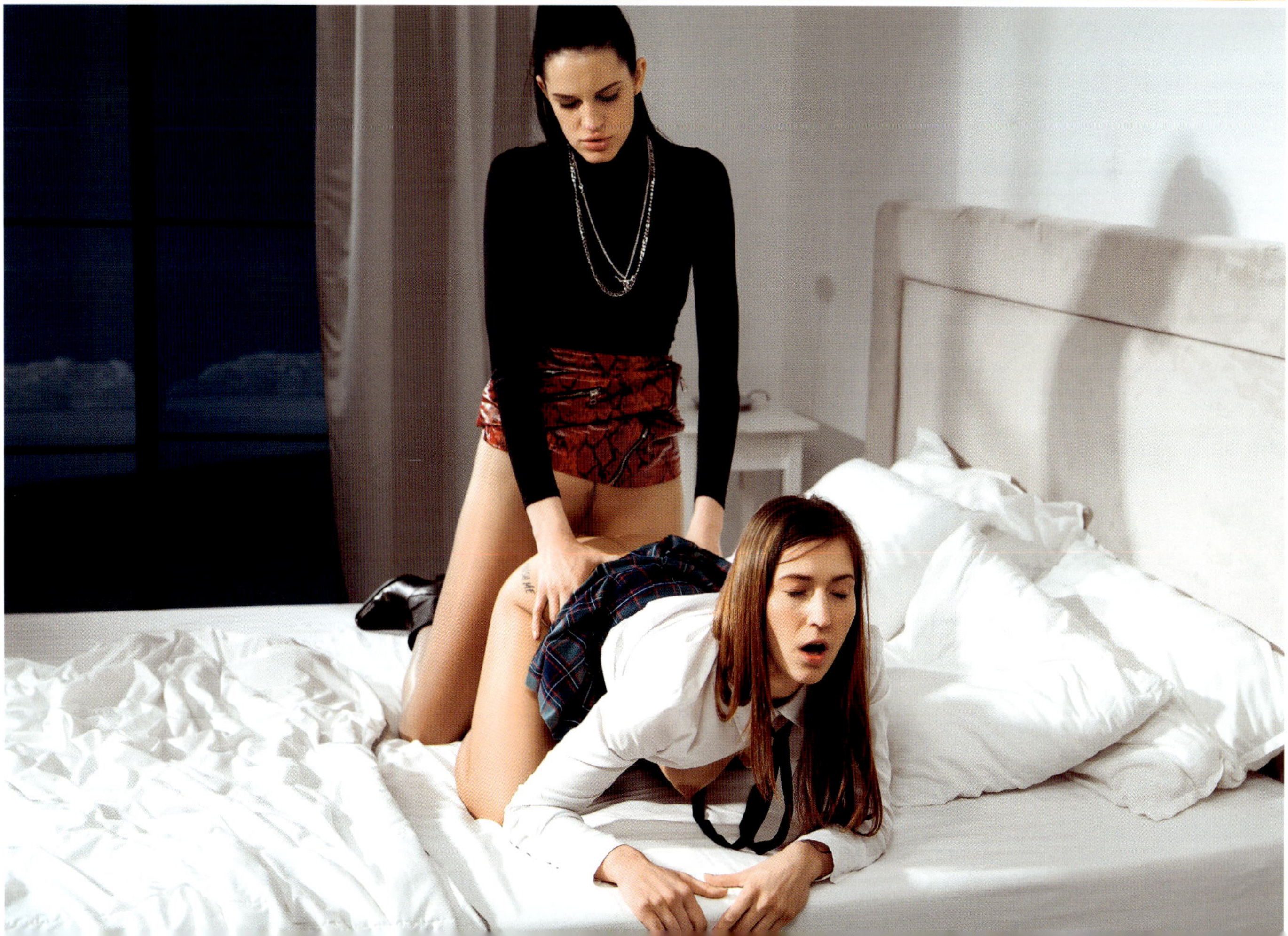

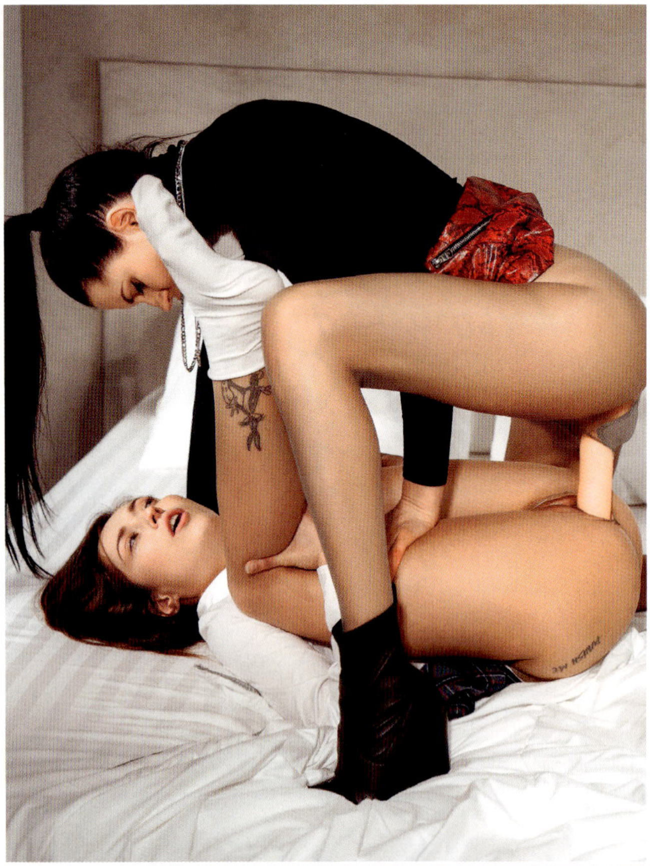

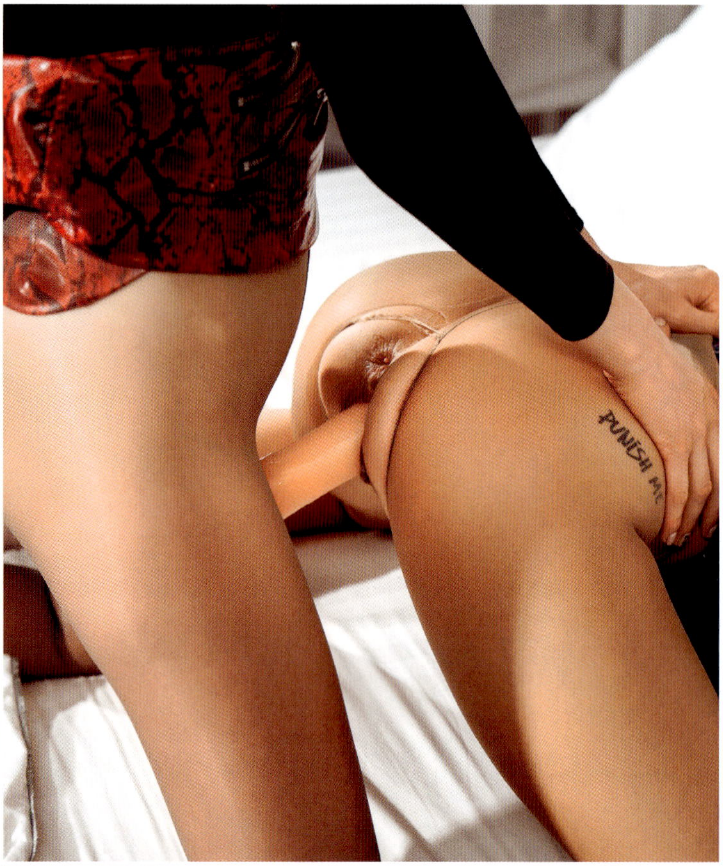

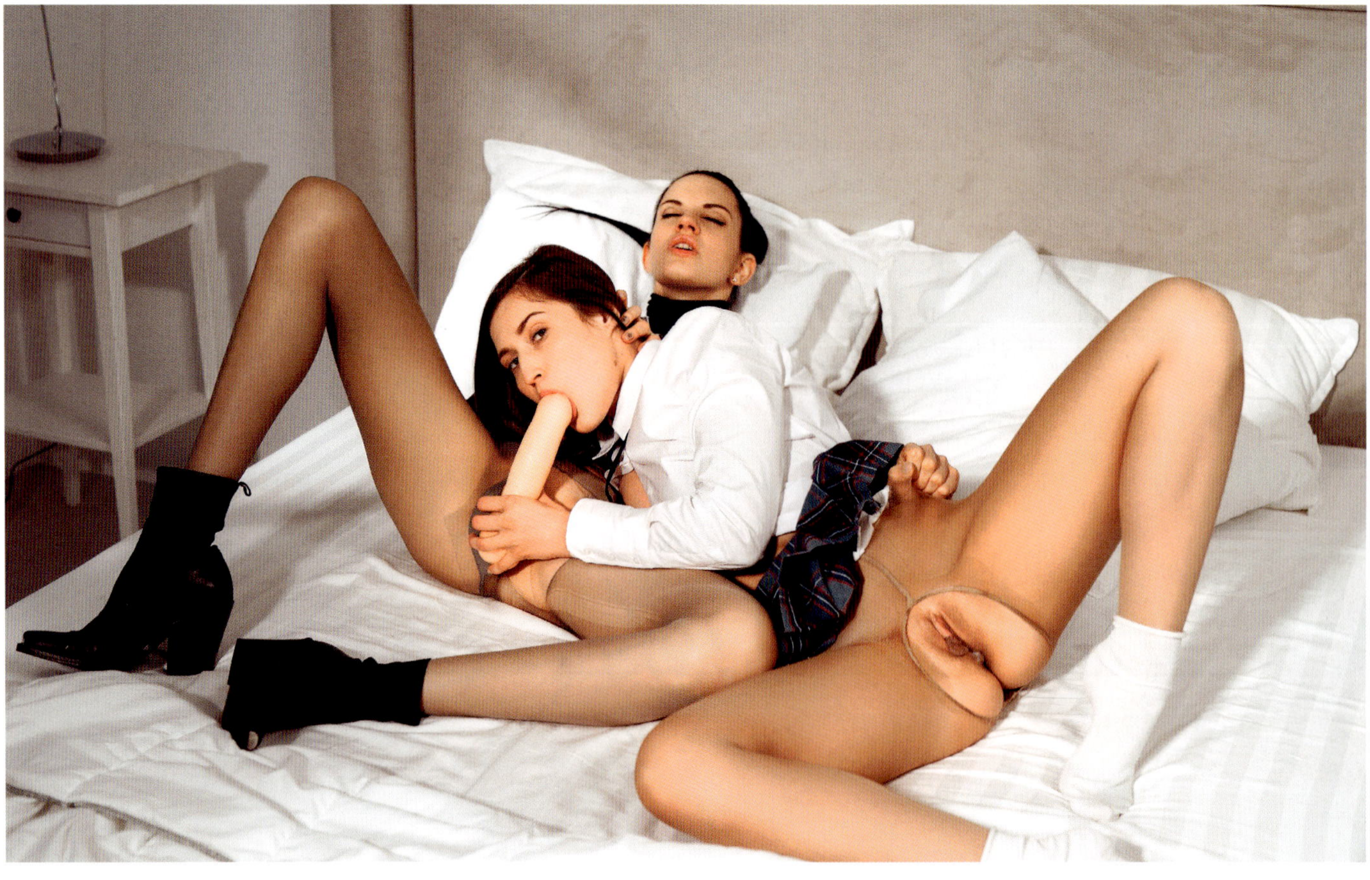

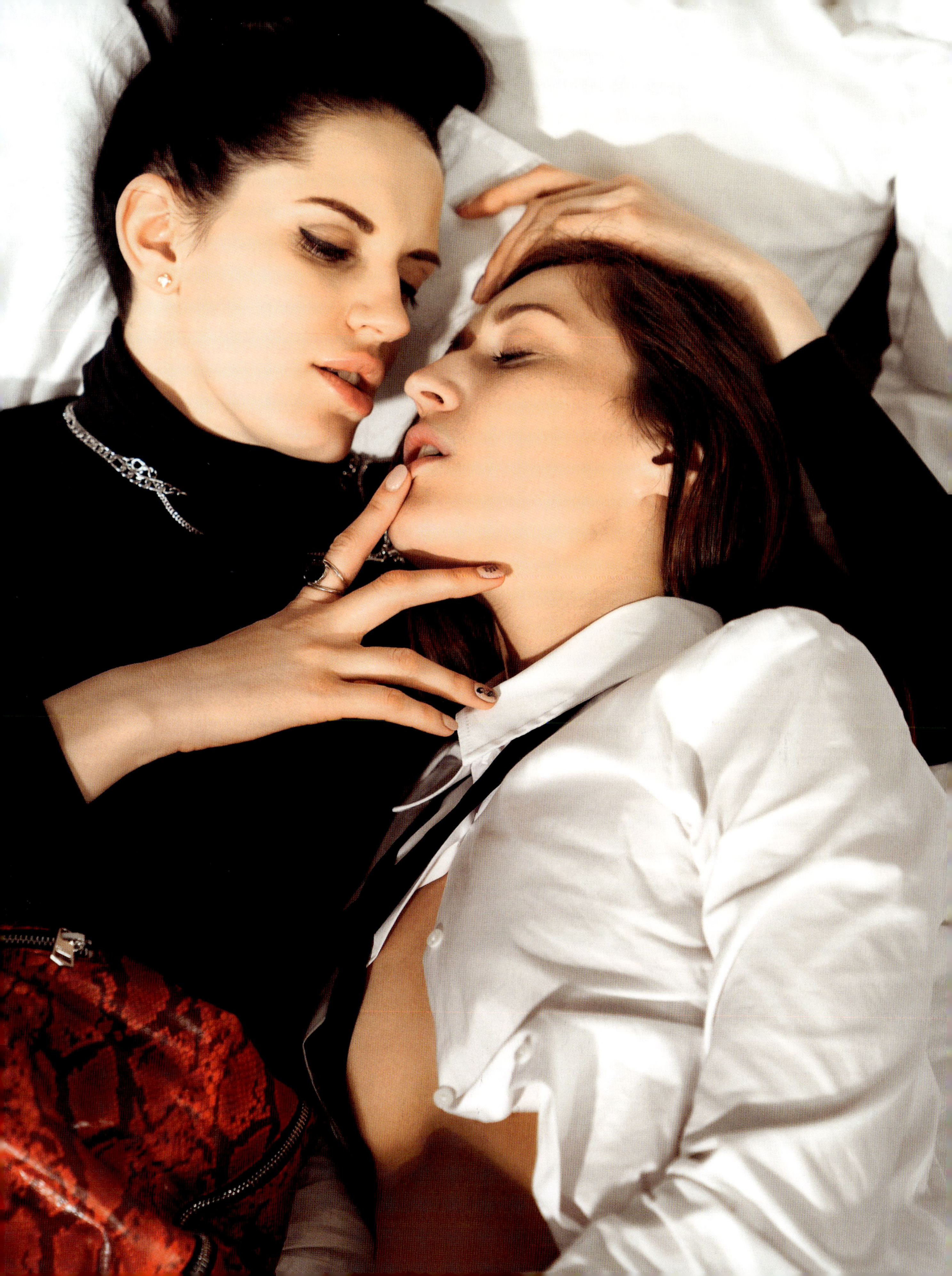

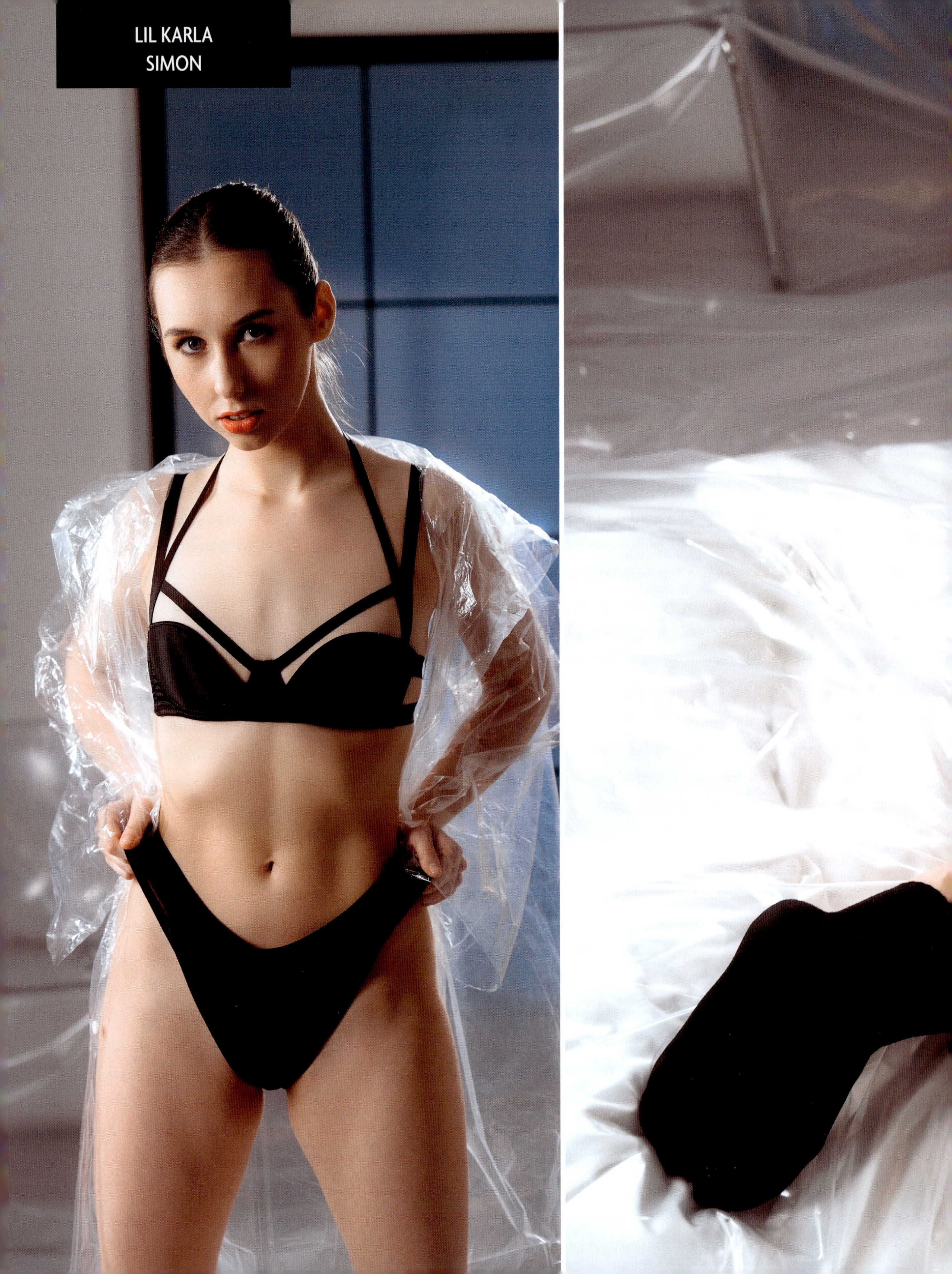
LIL KARLA
SIMON

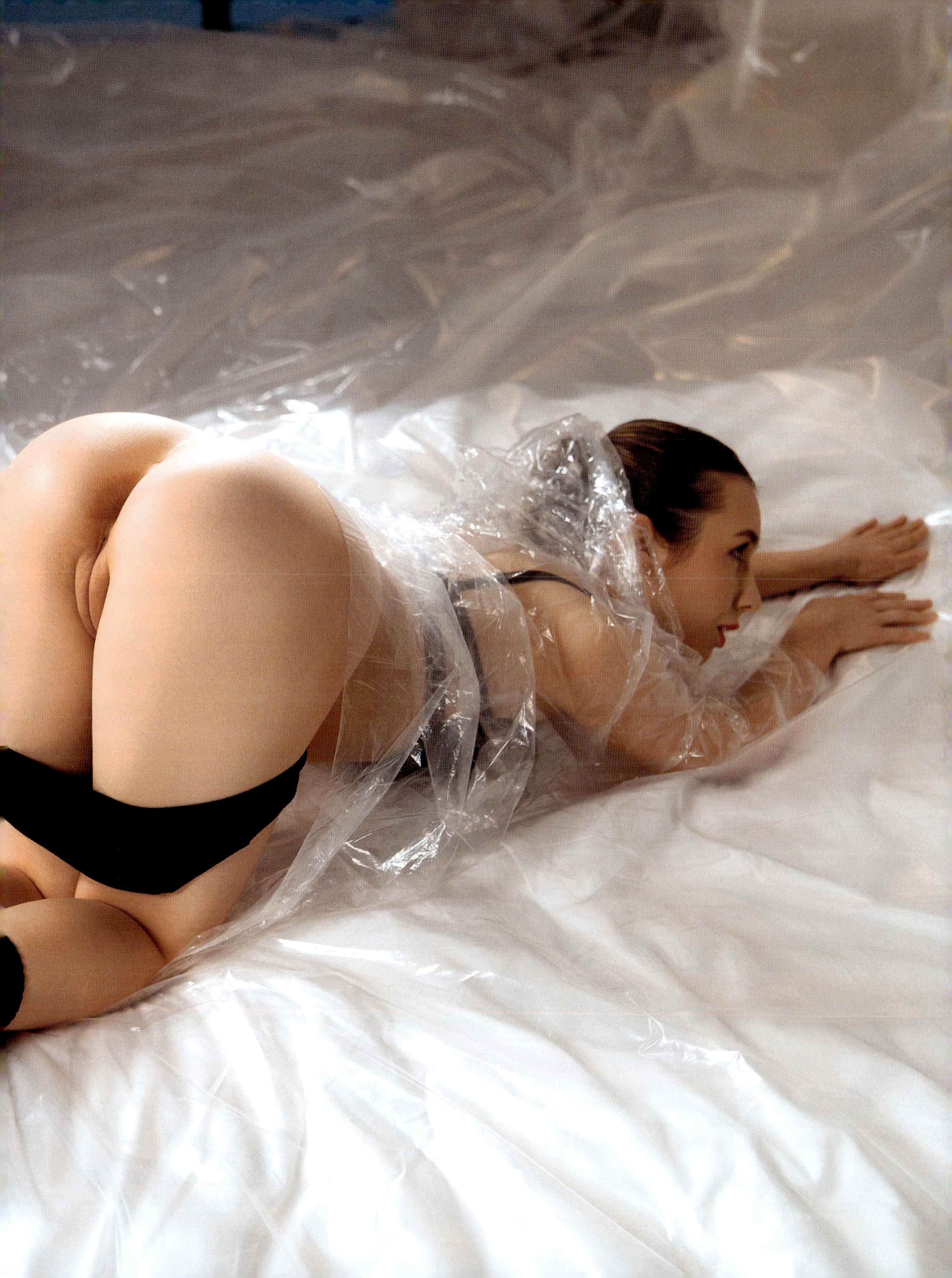

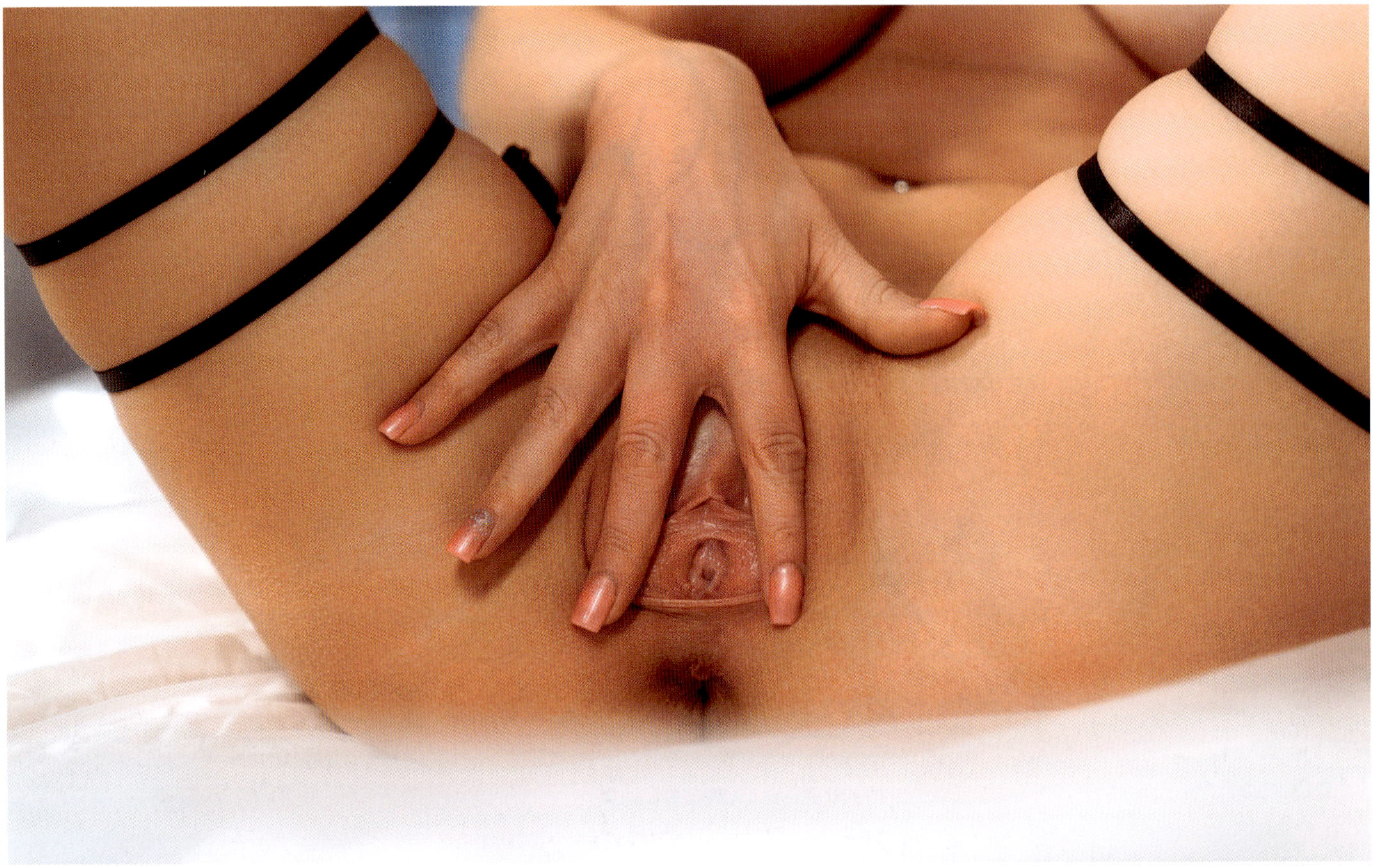

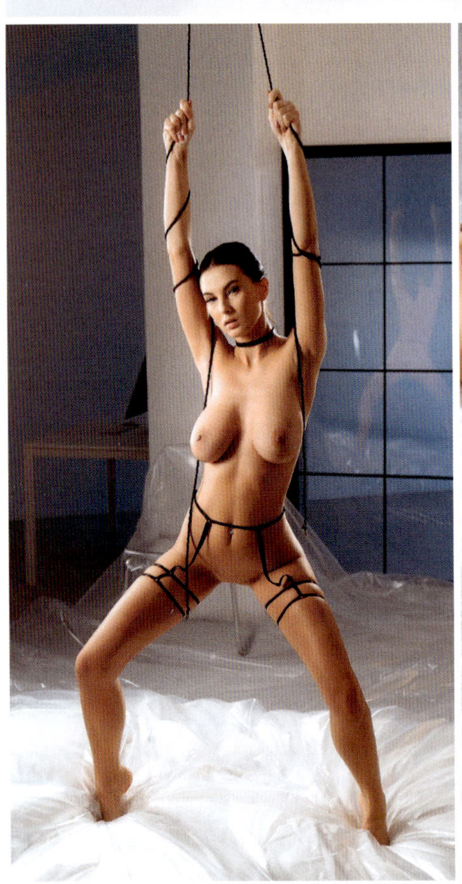
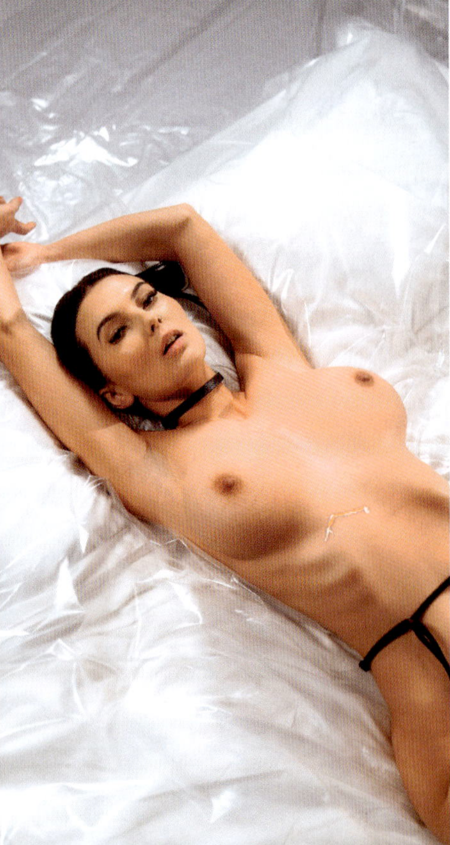
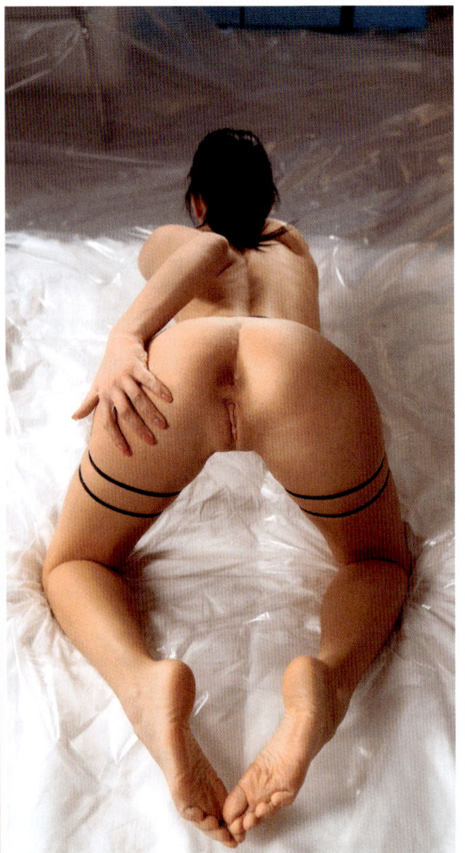

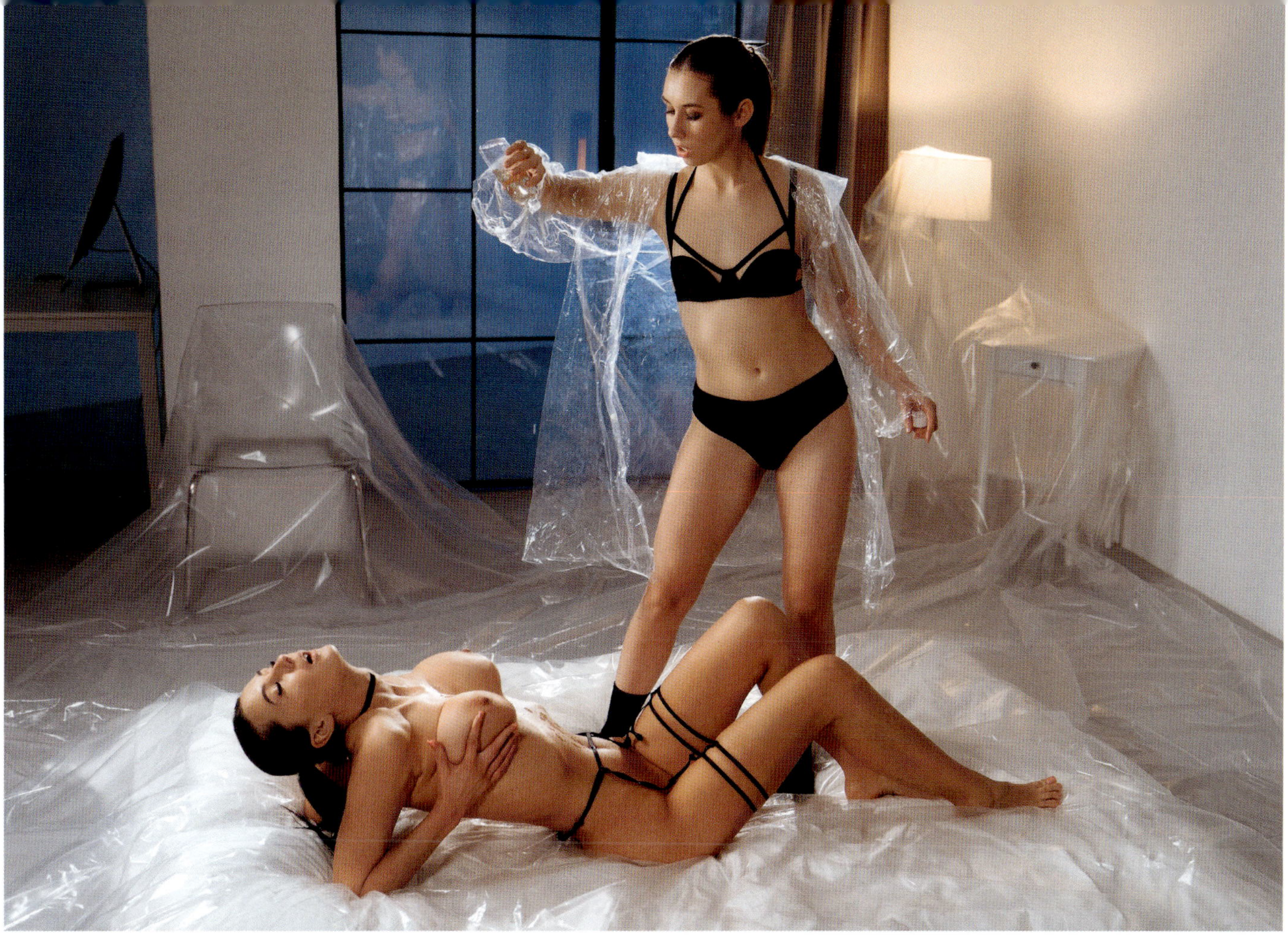

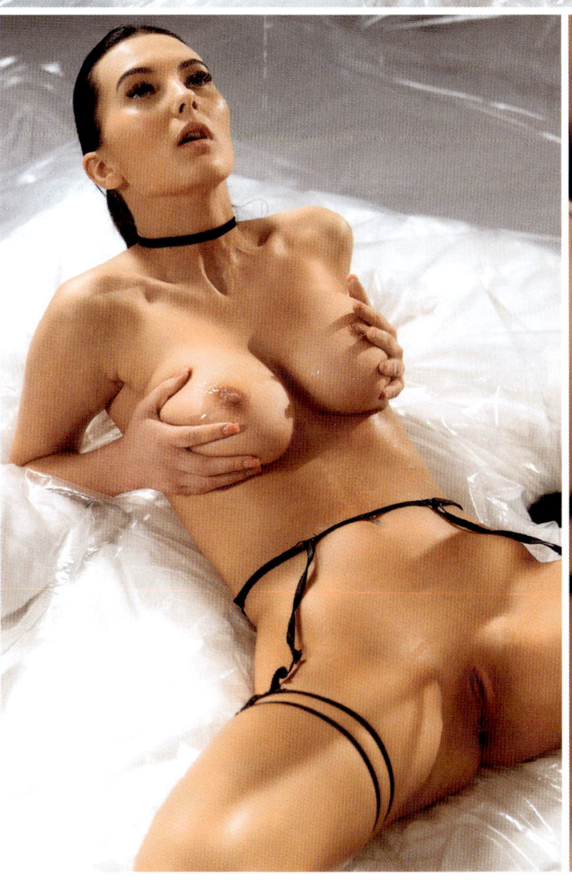
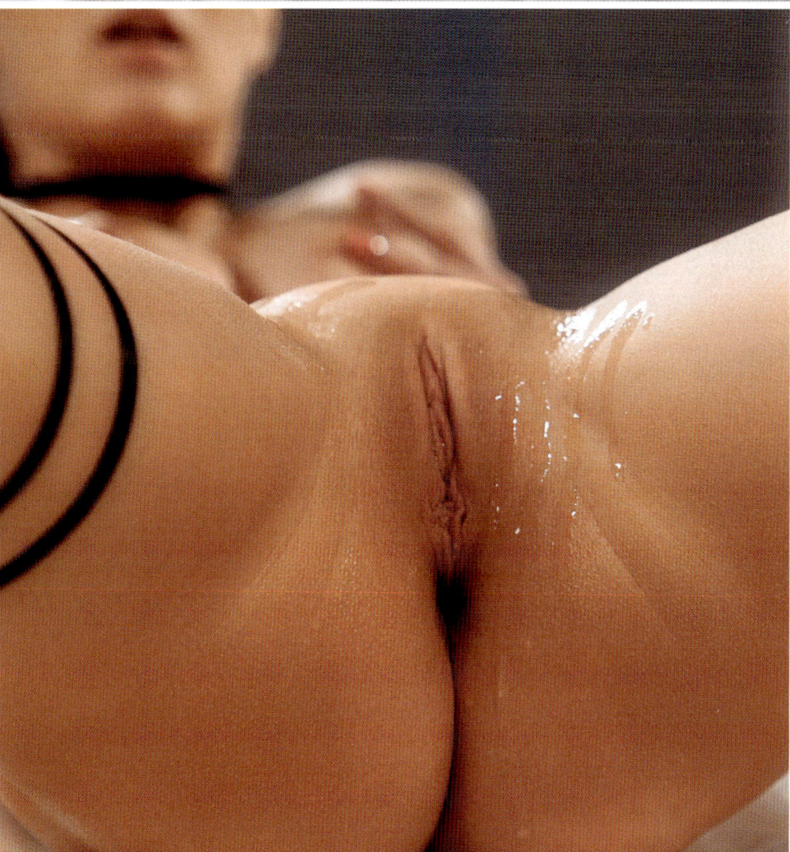

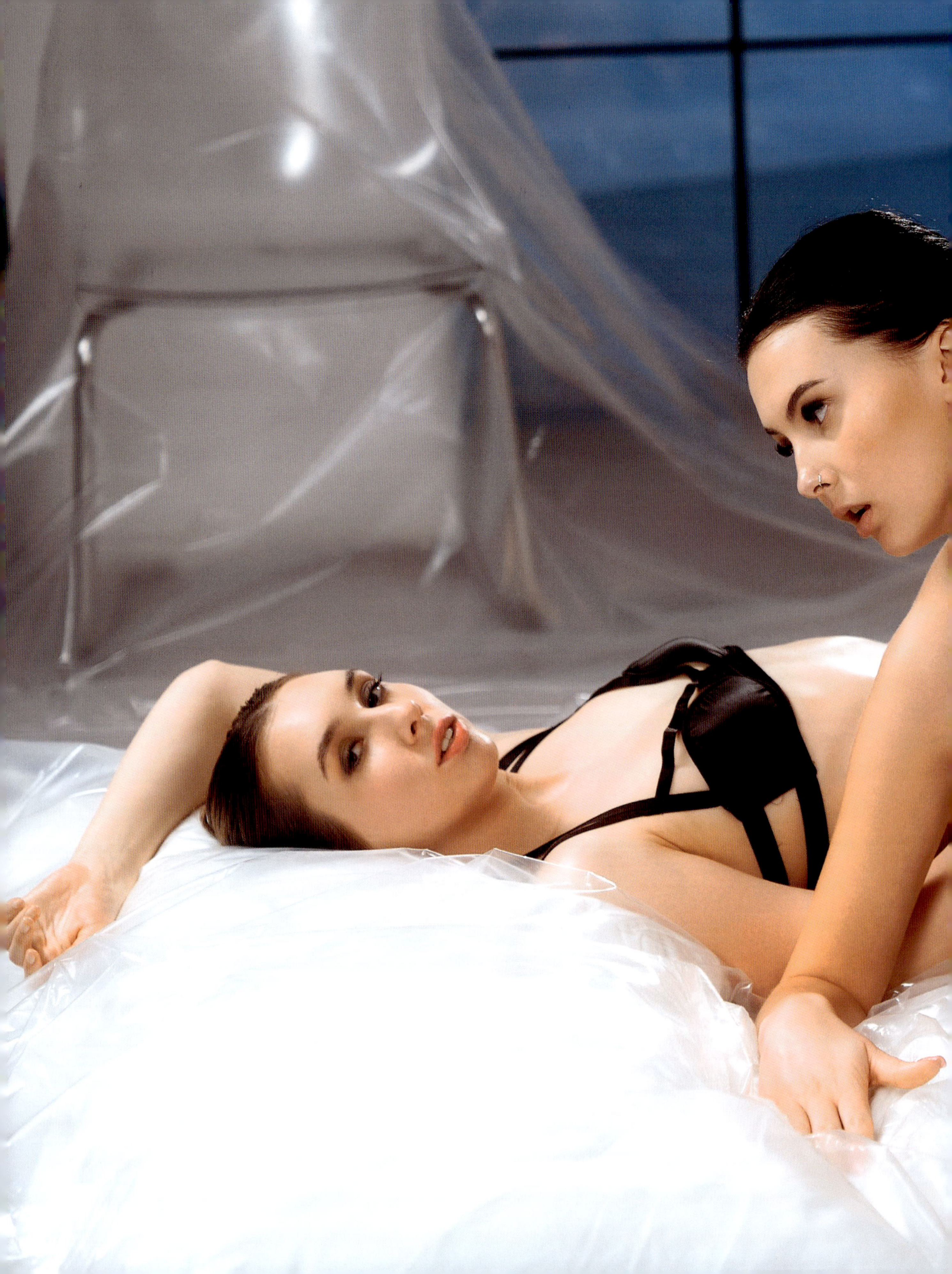

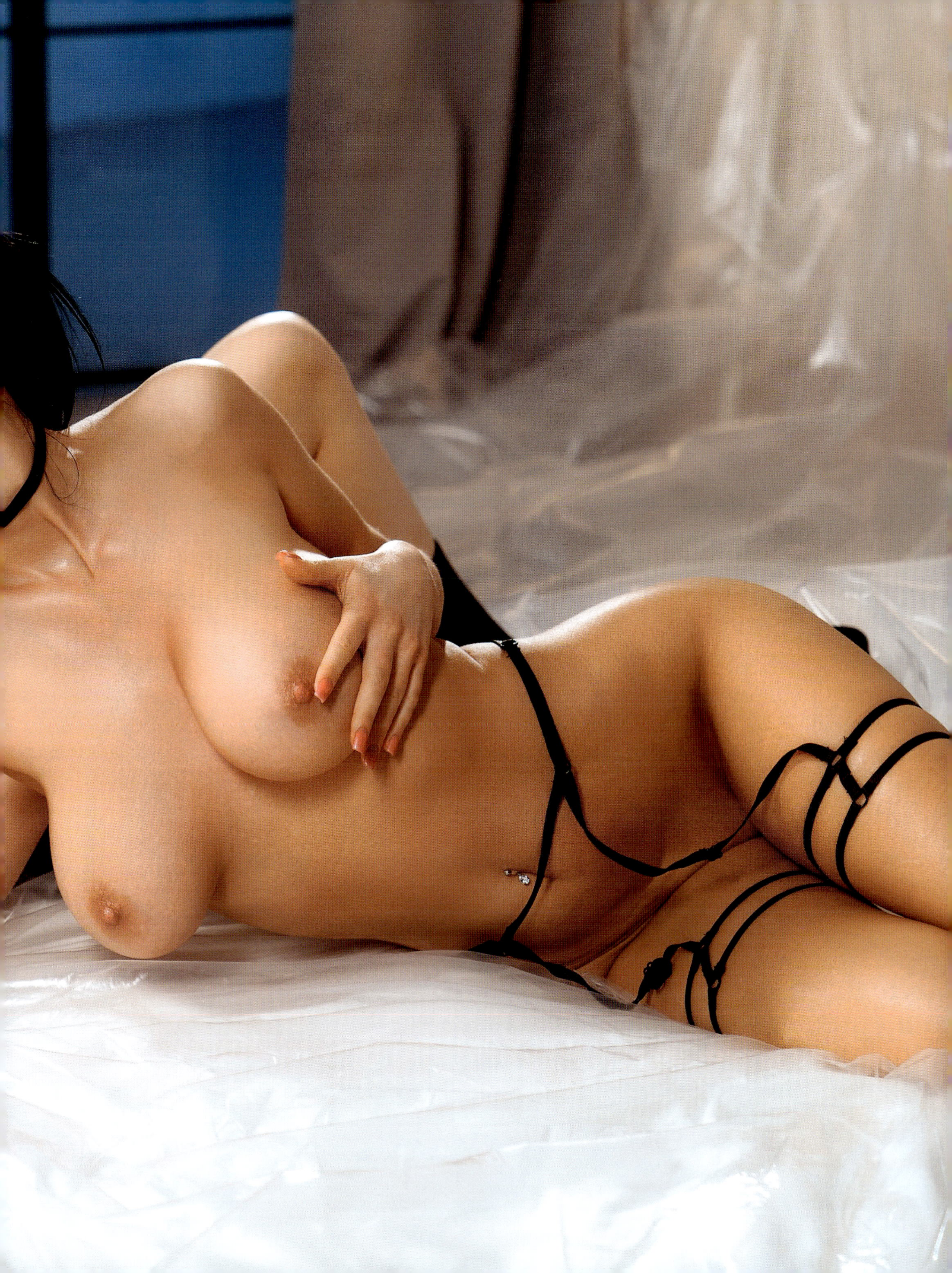

LEE ANNE
STACY CRUZ

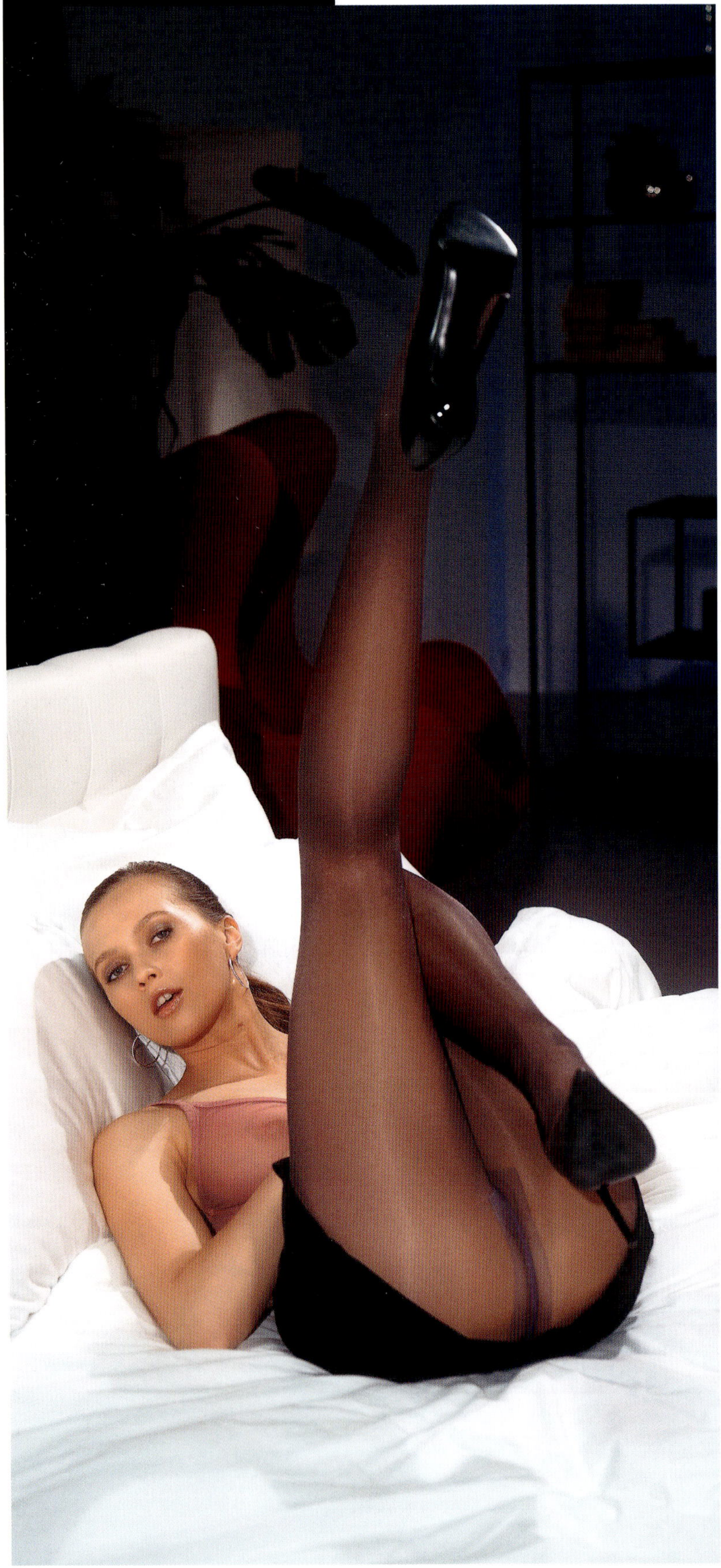

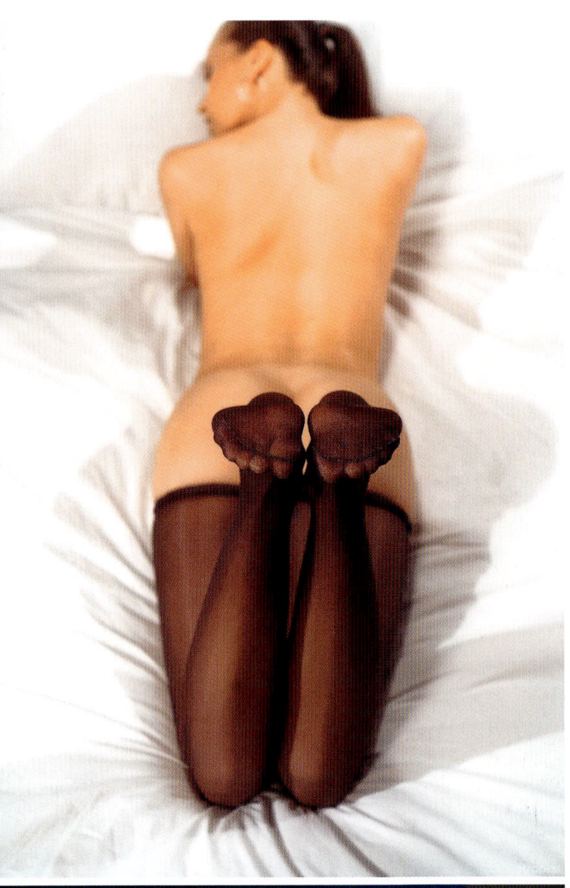

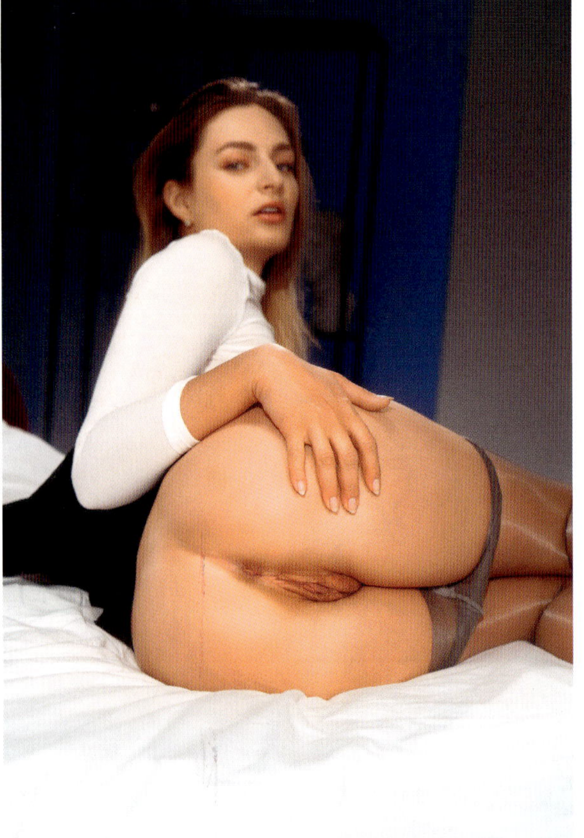

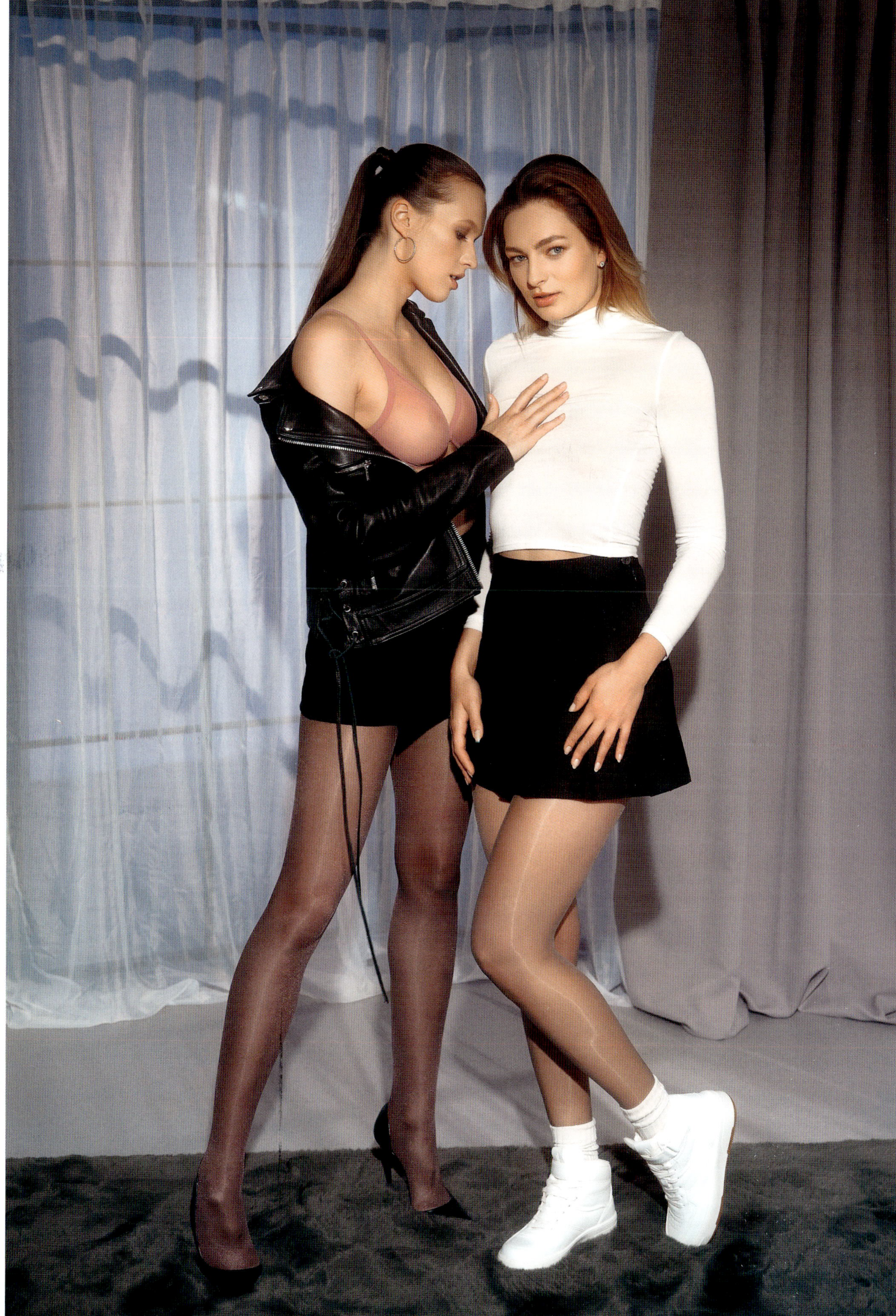

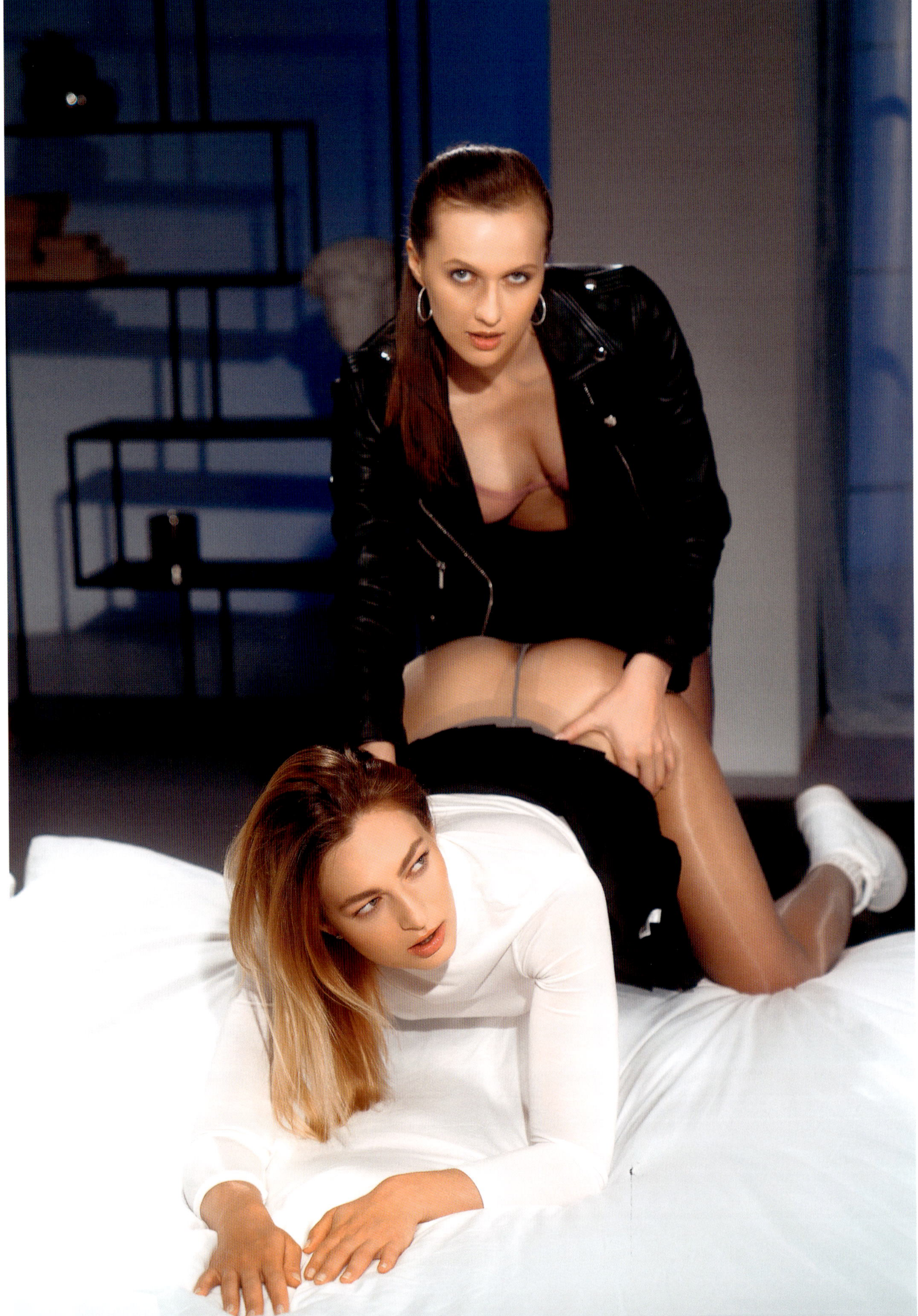

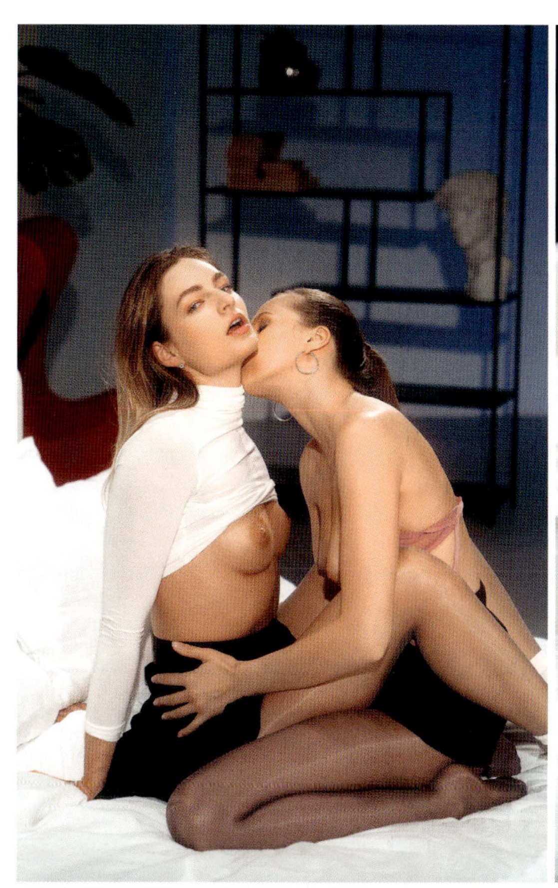
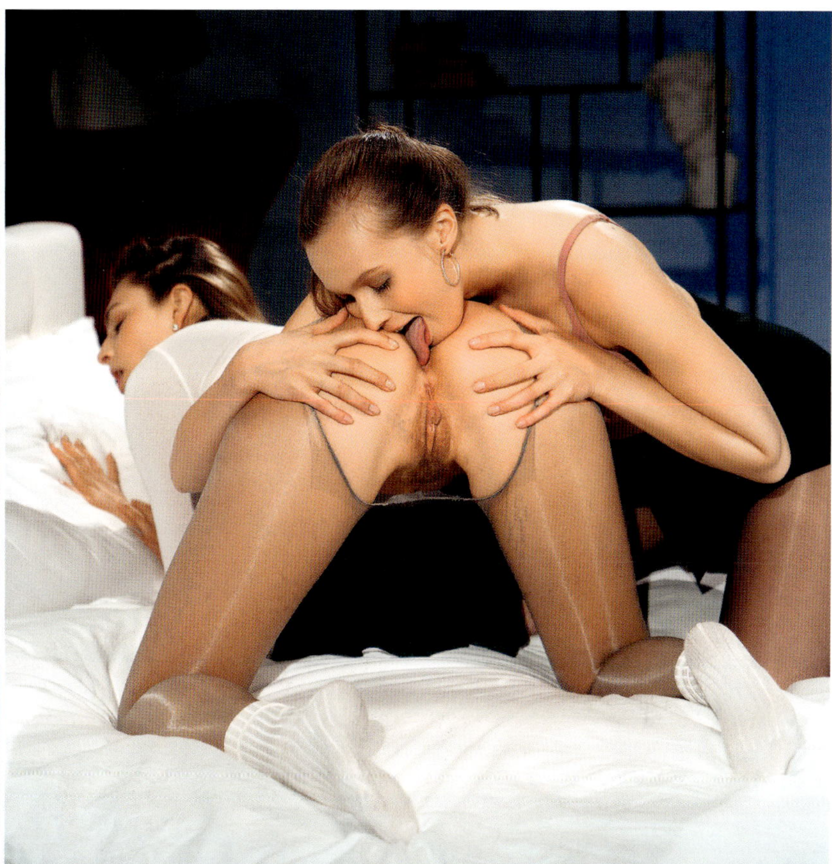
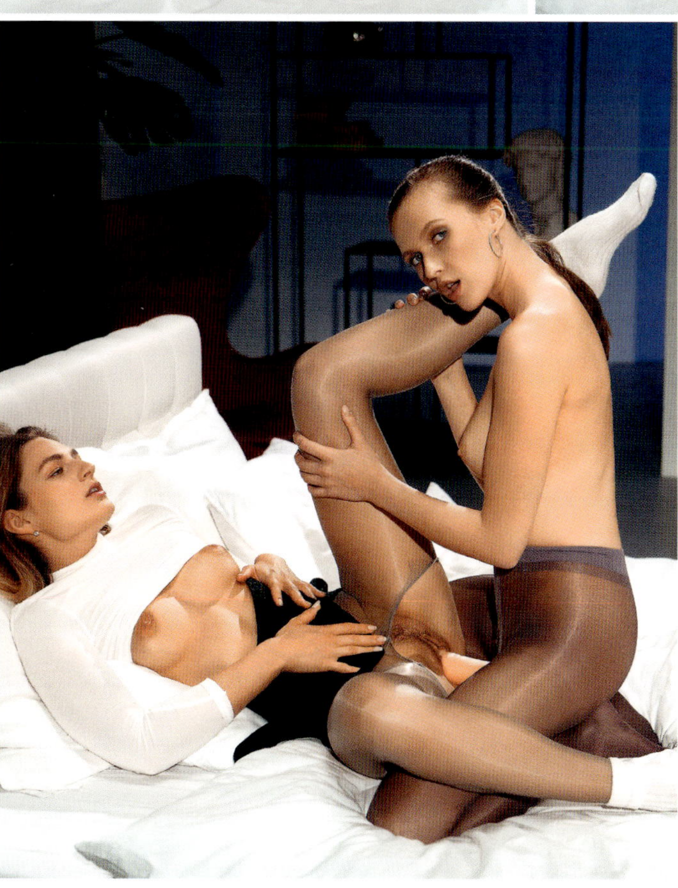
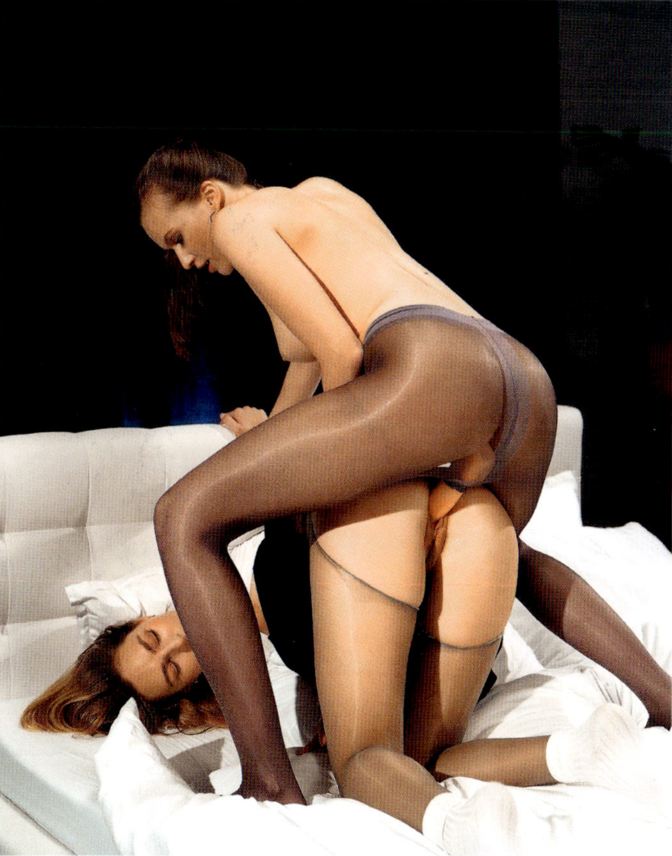

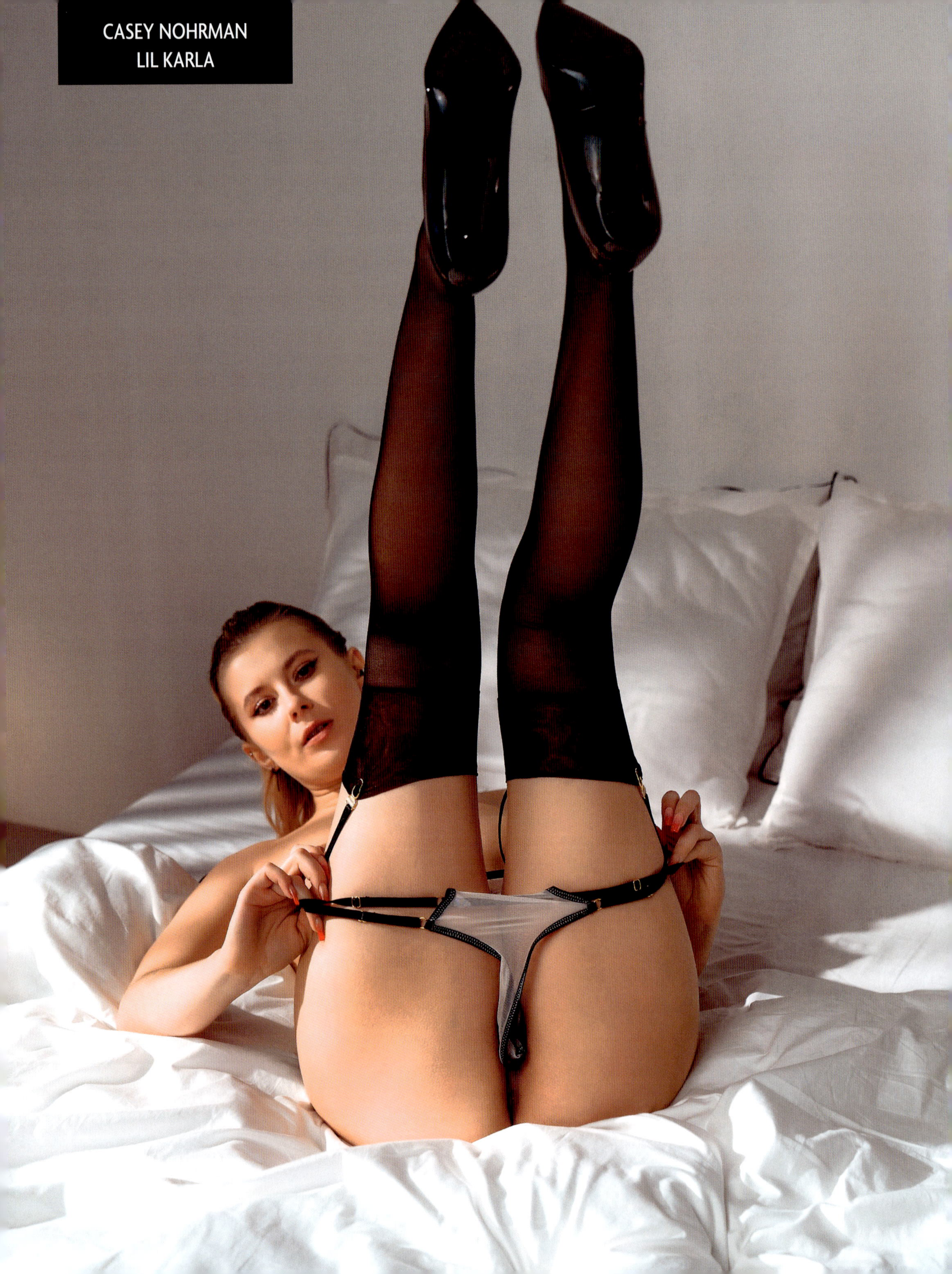

CASEY NOHRMAN
LIL KARLA

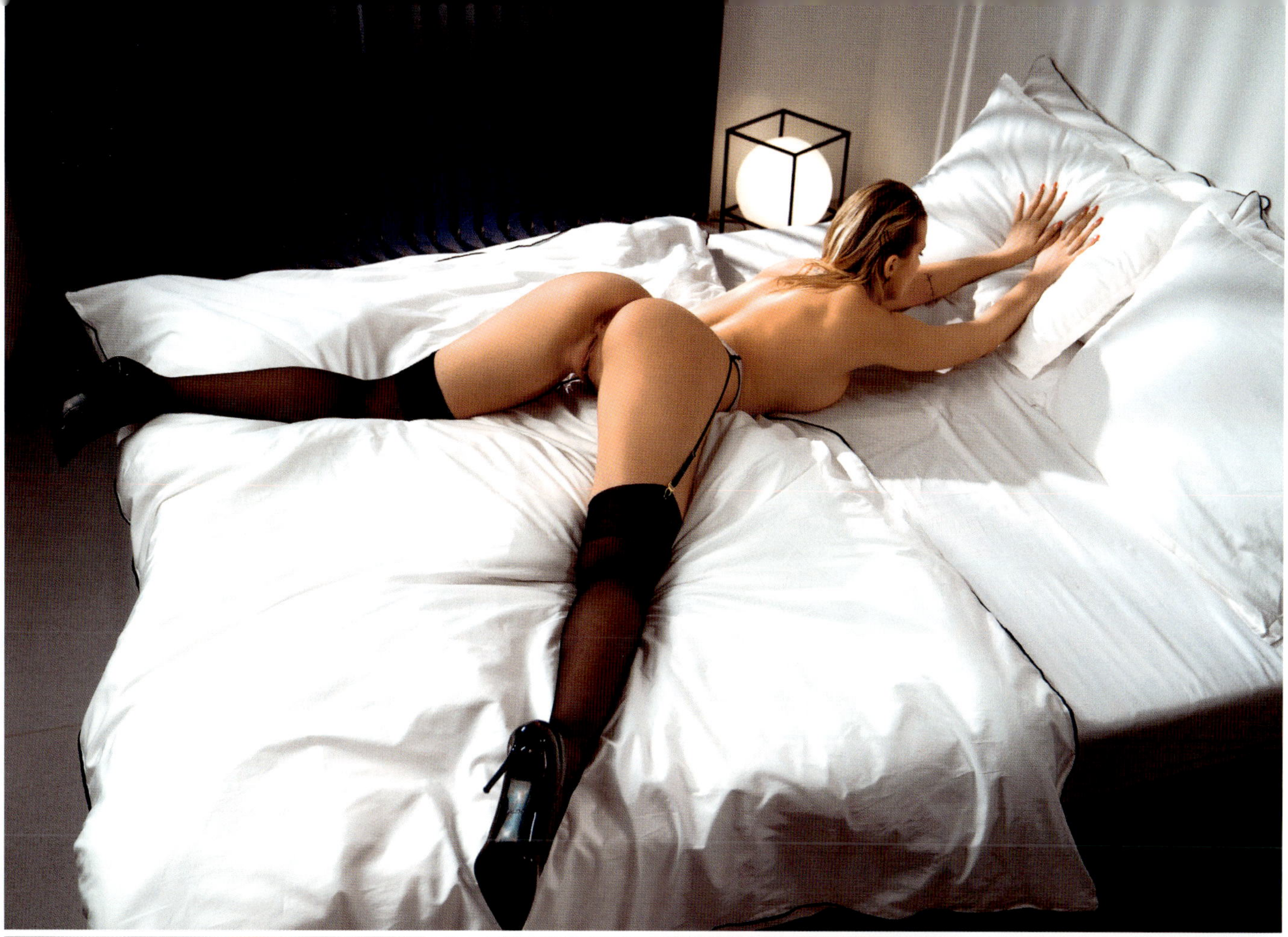

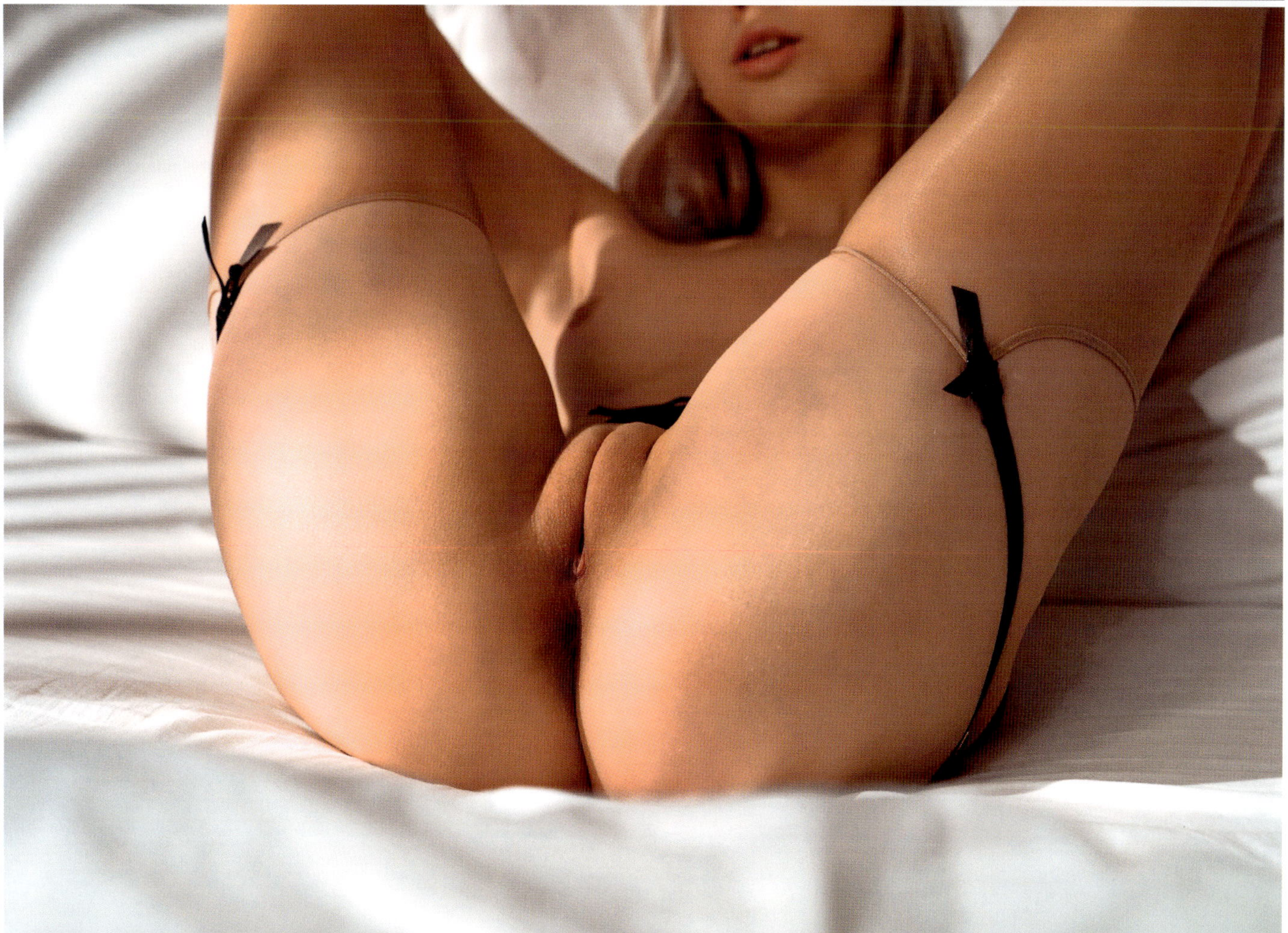

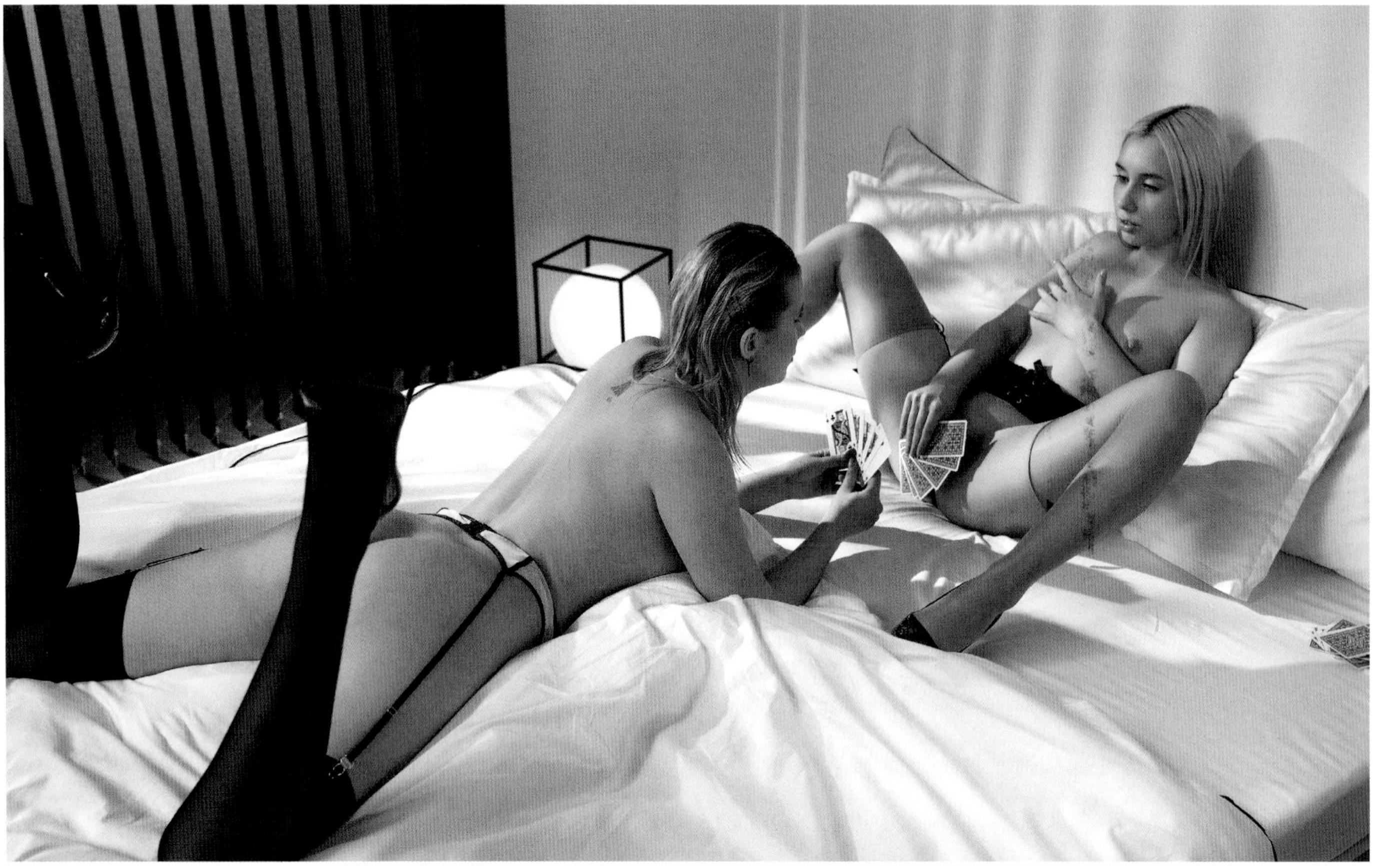

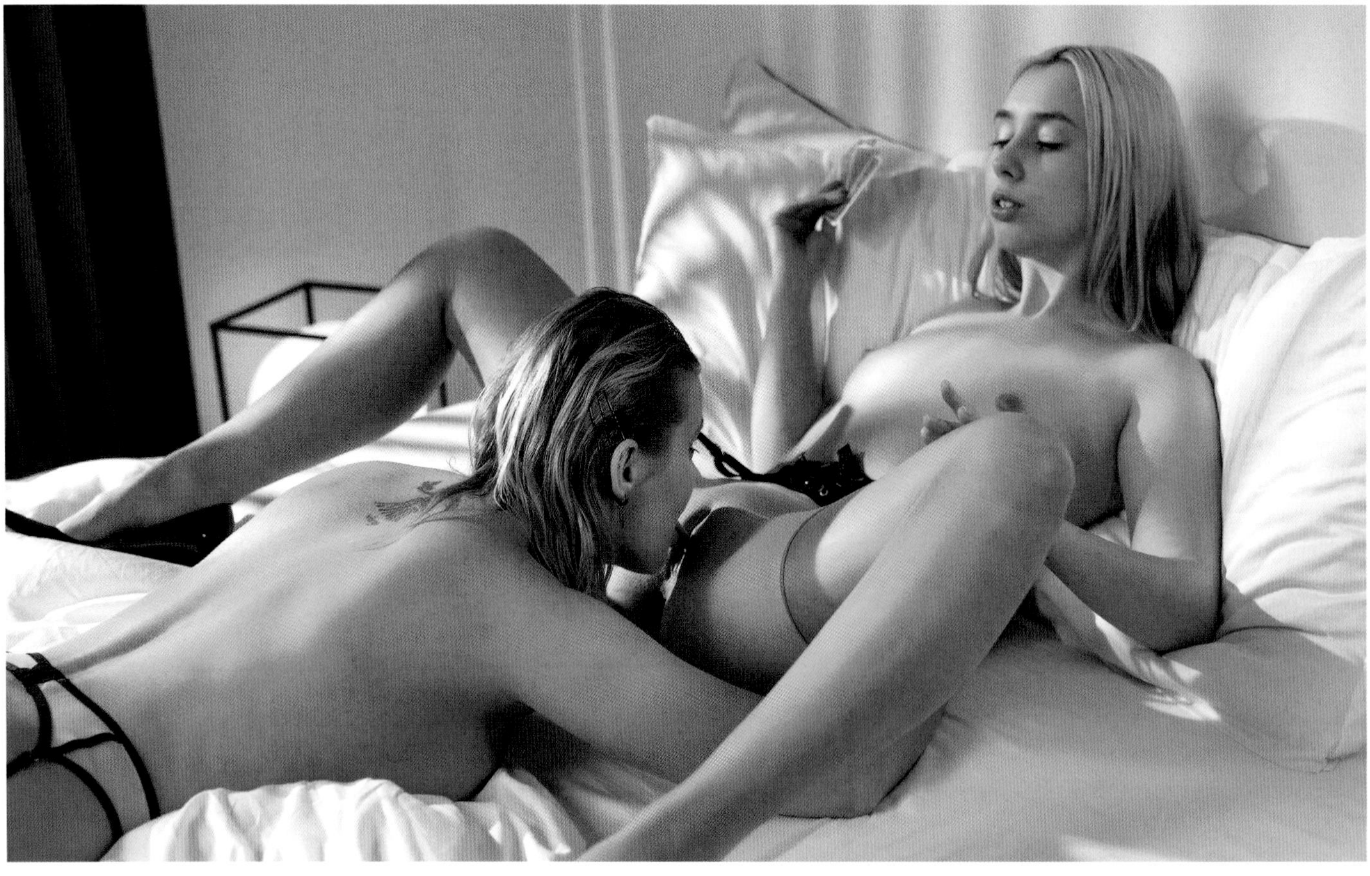

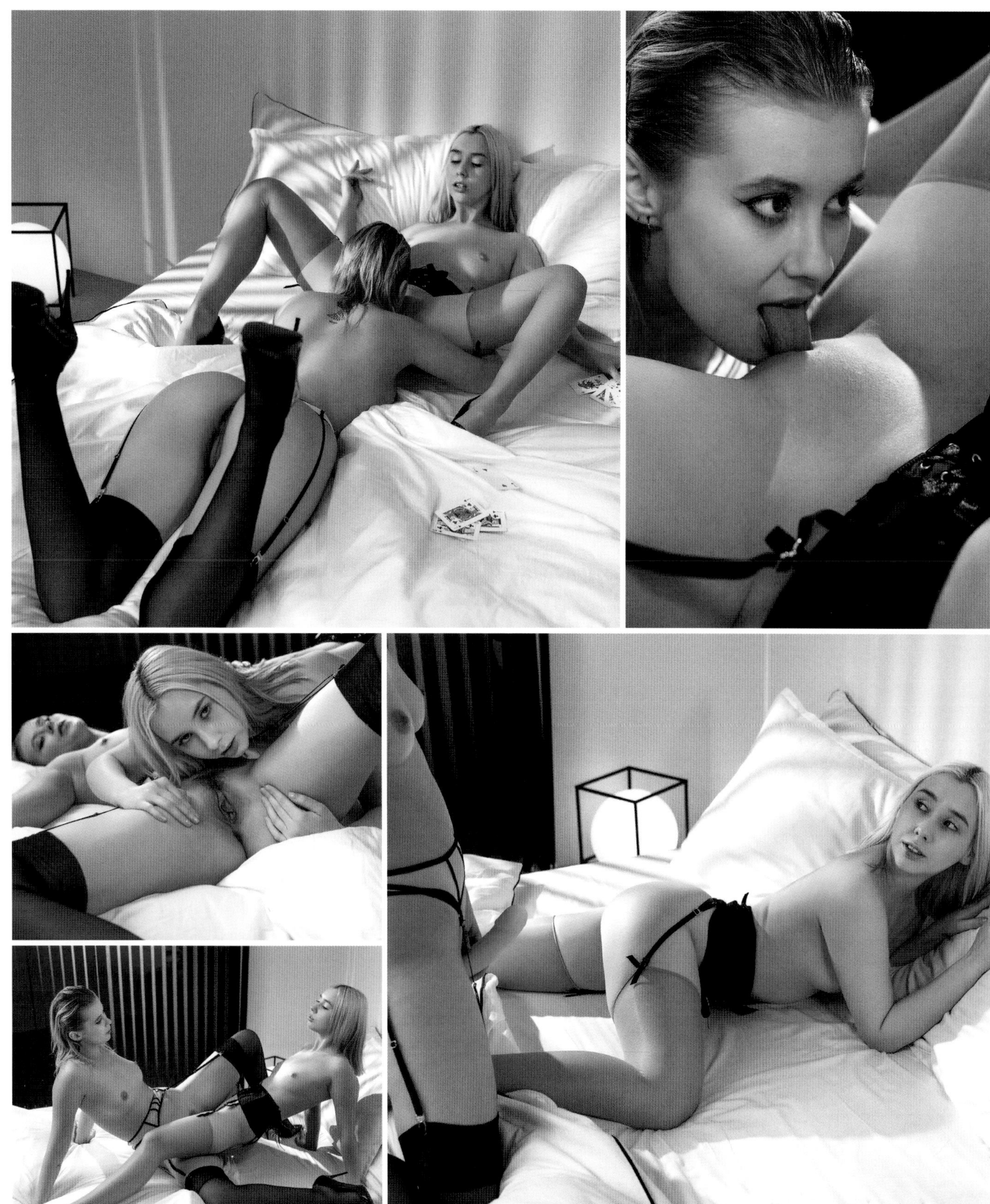

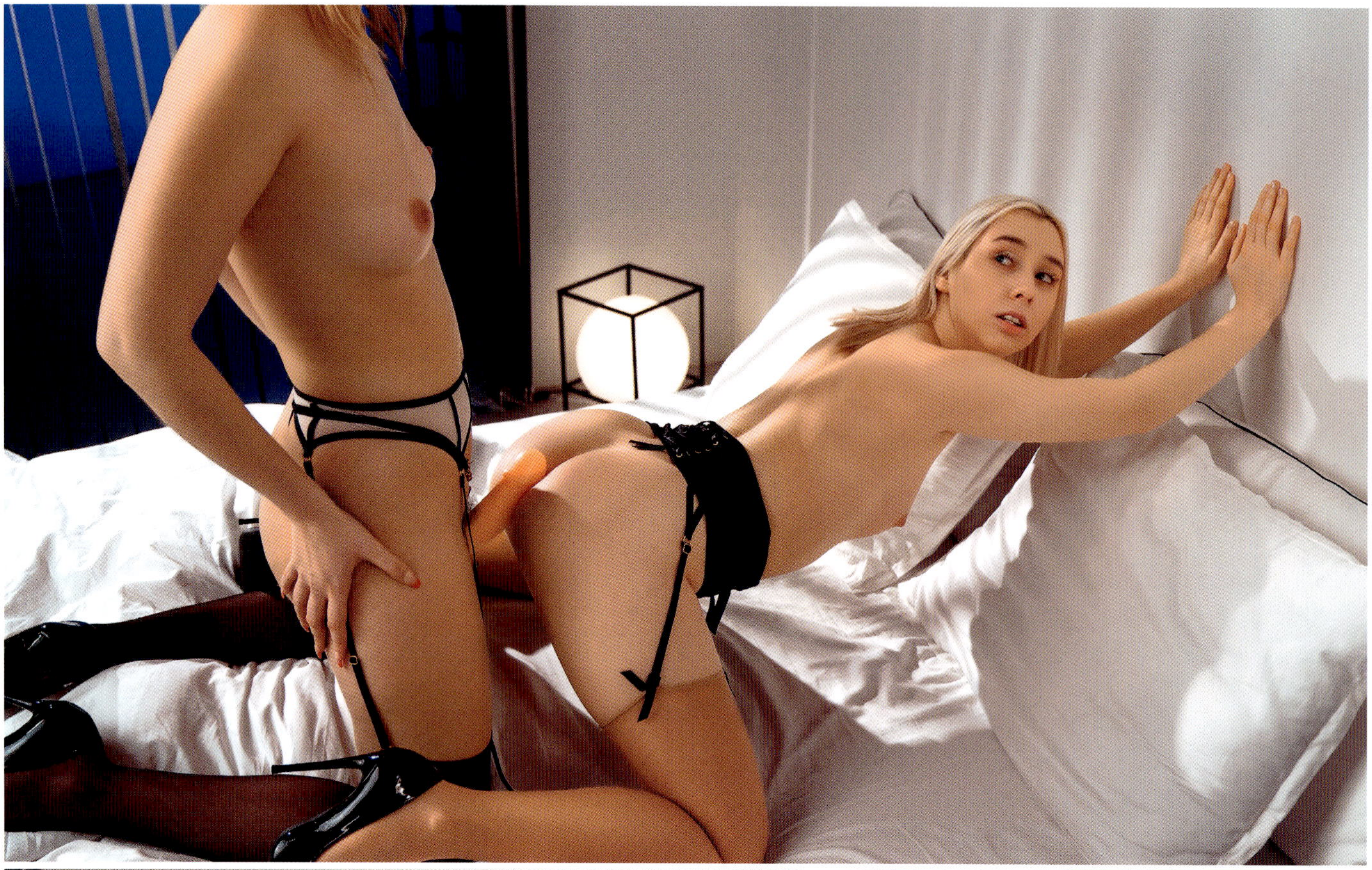

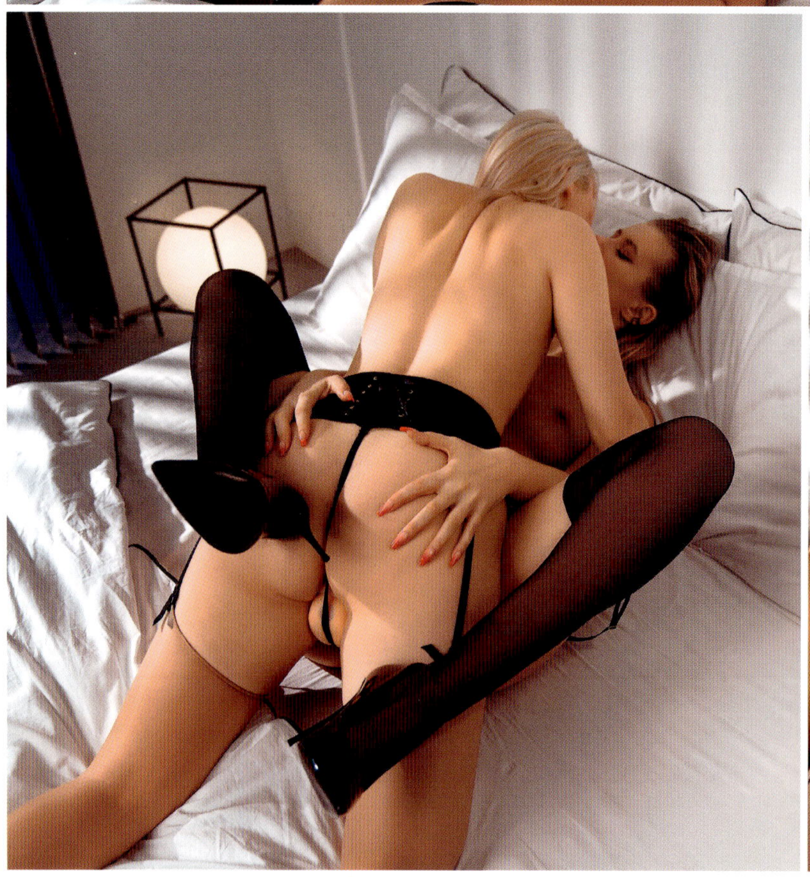
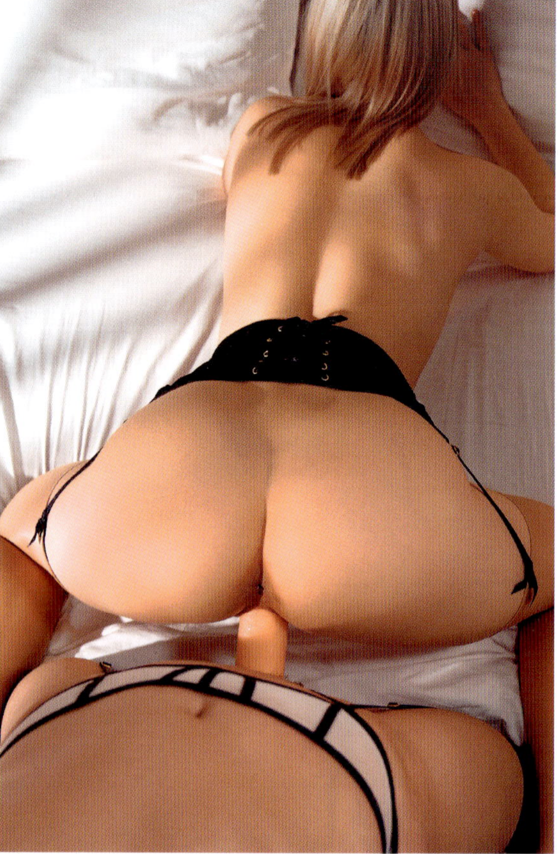

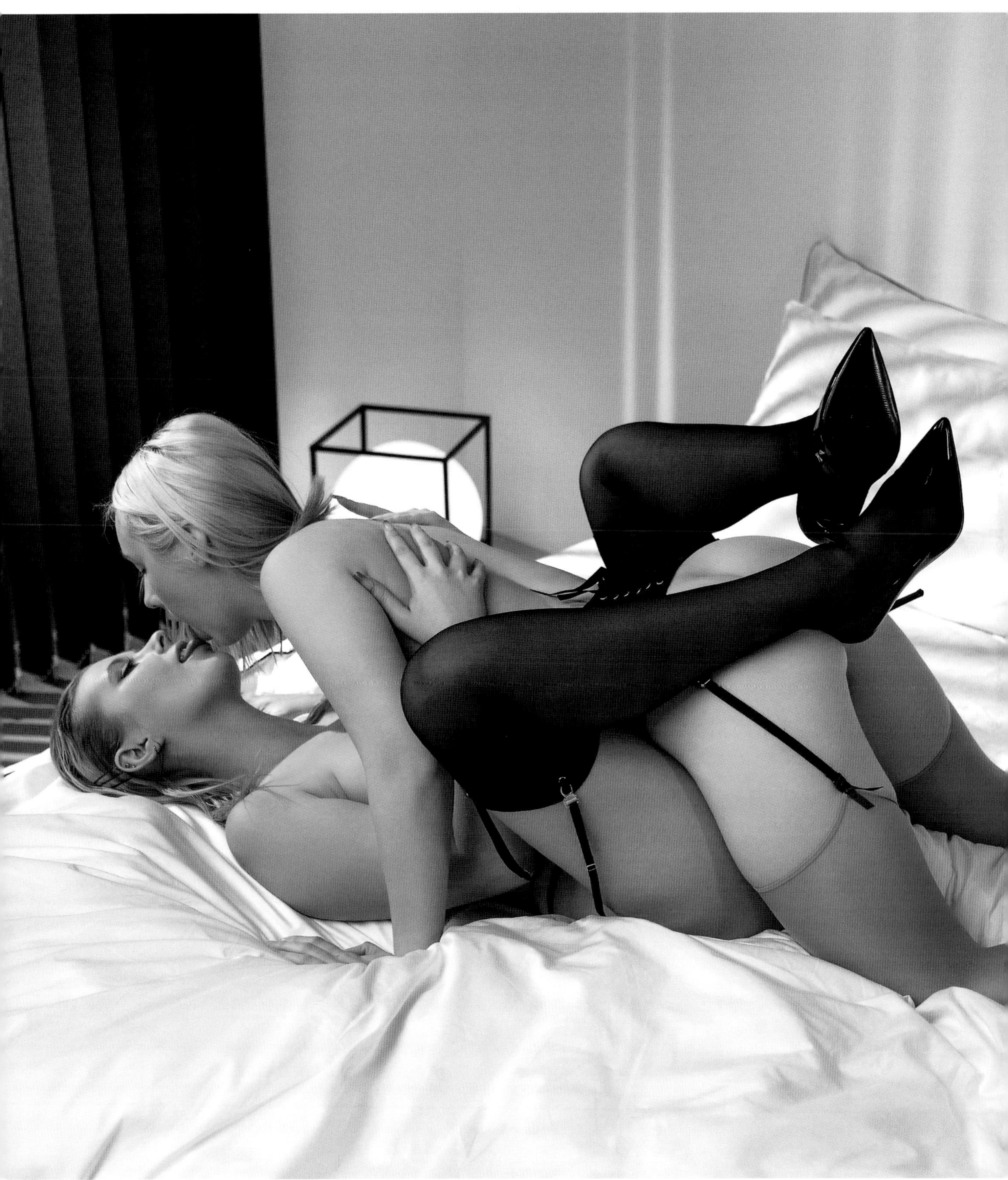

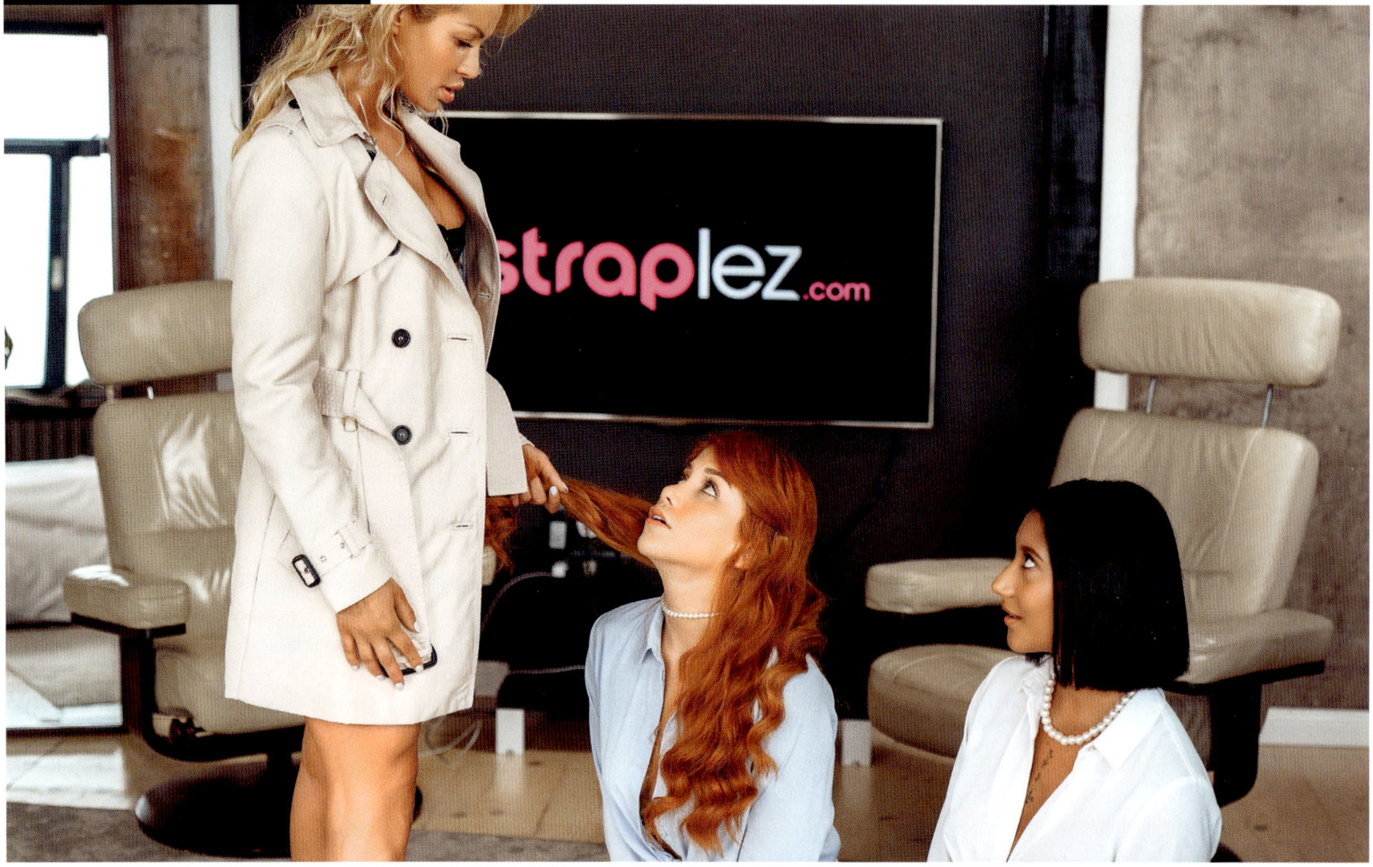

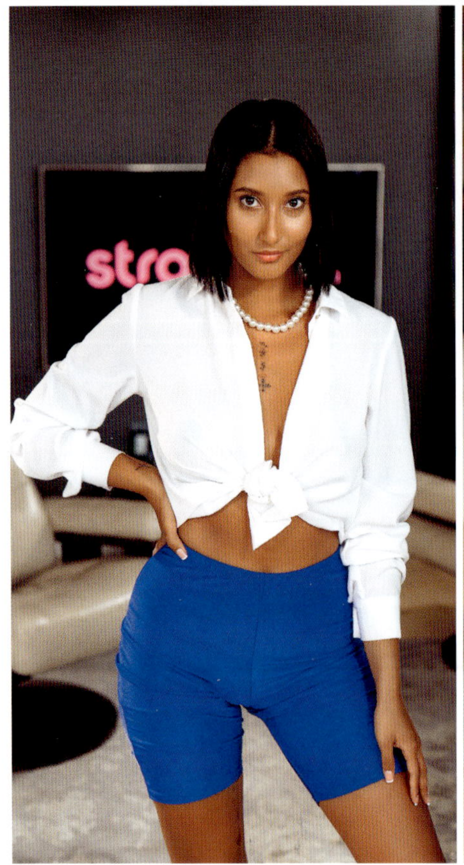
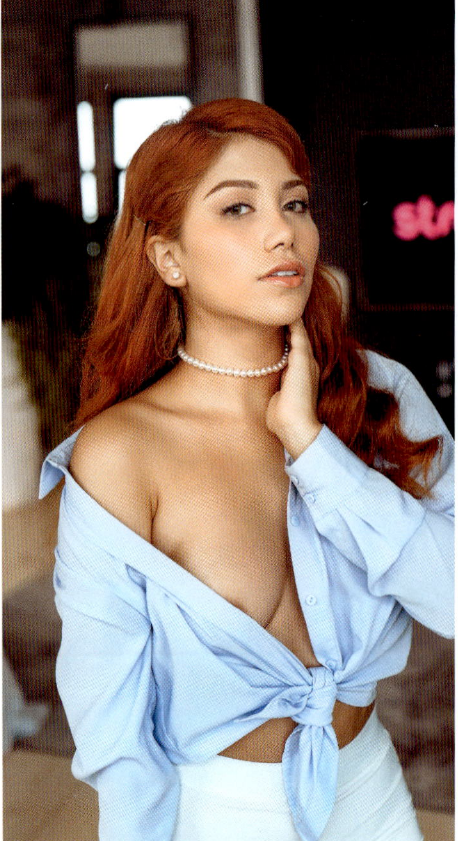
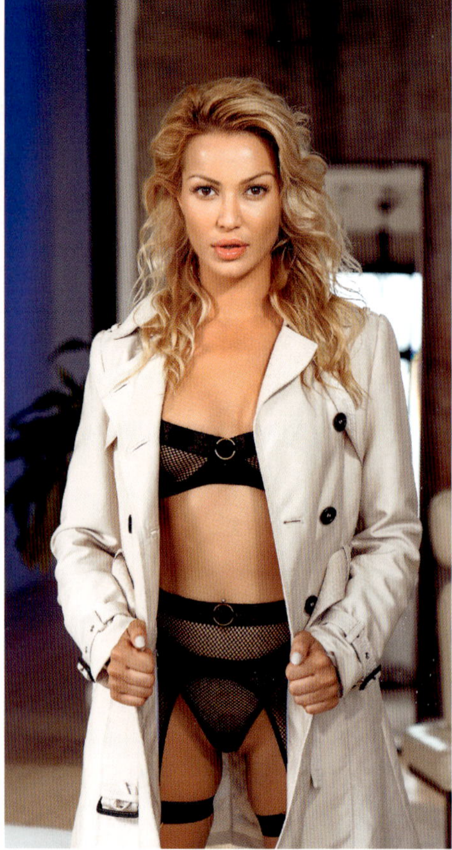

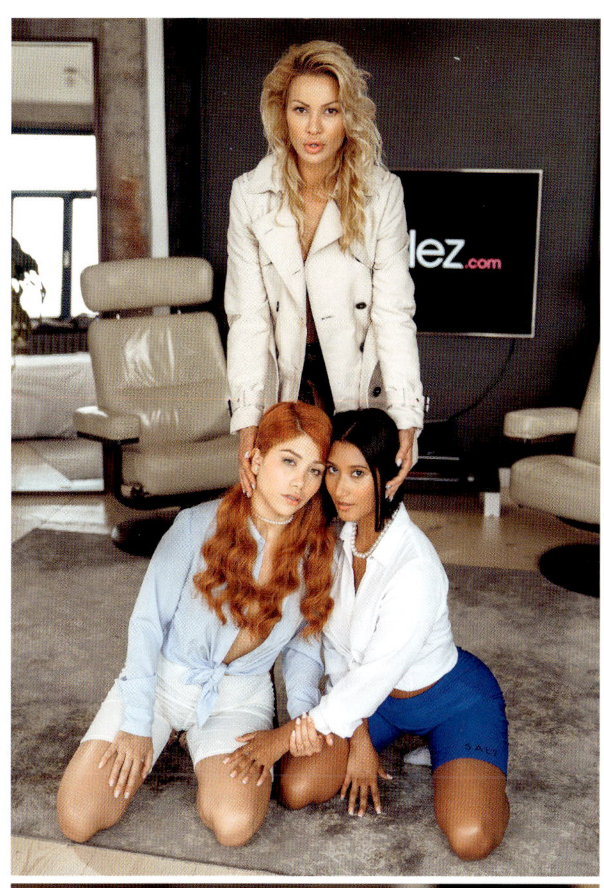

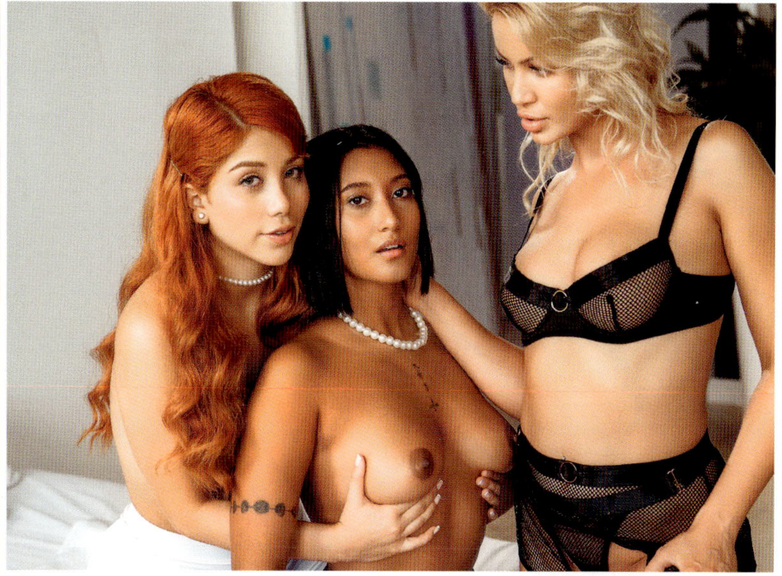

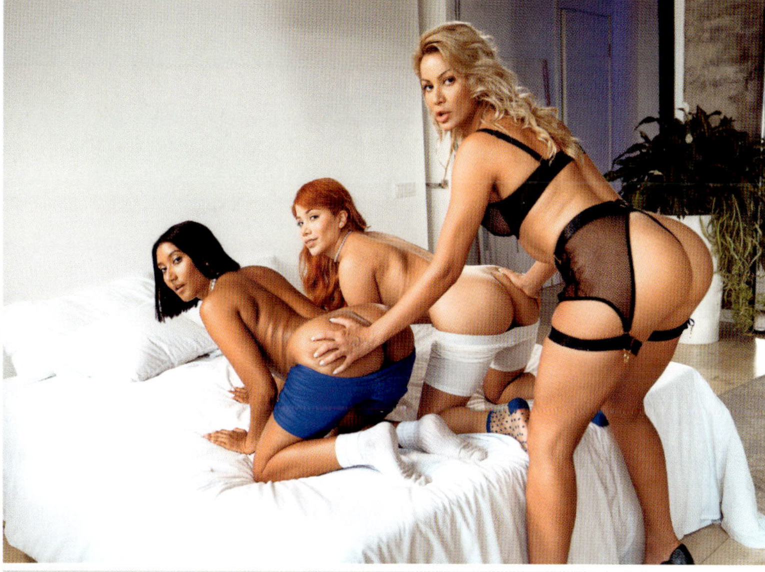

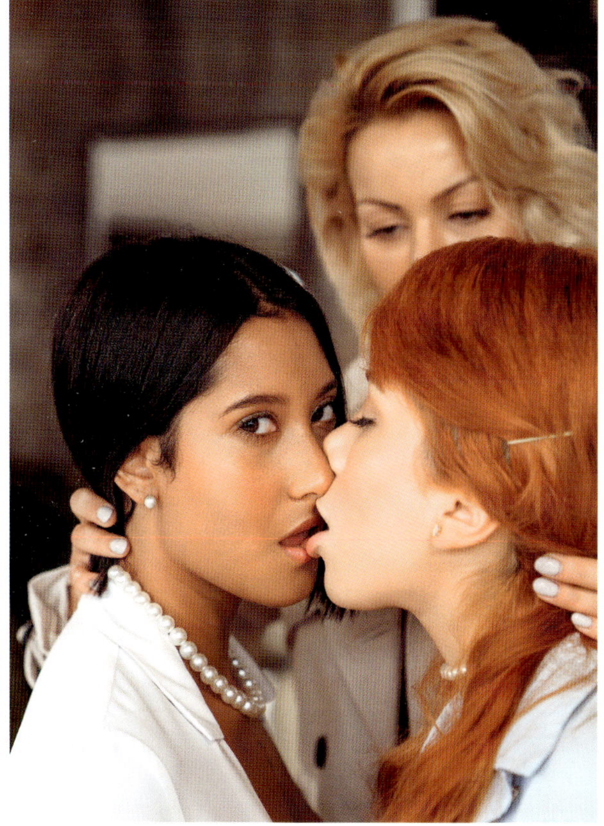

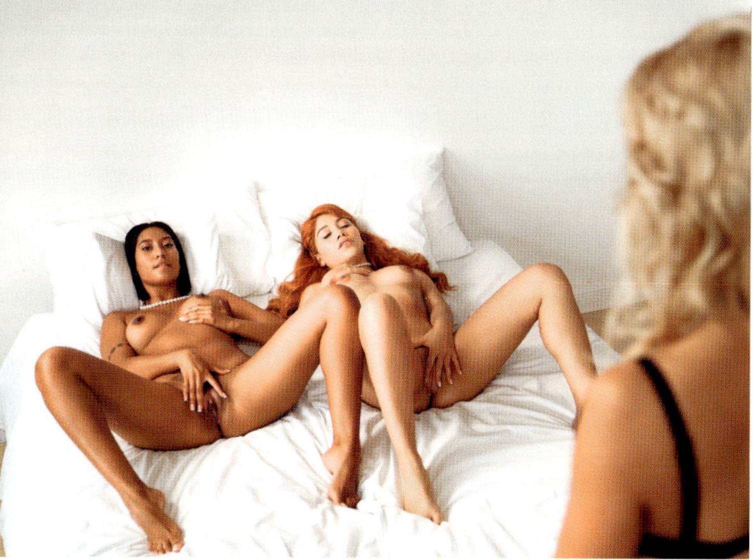

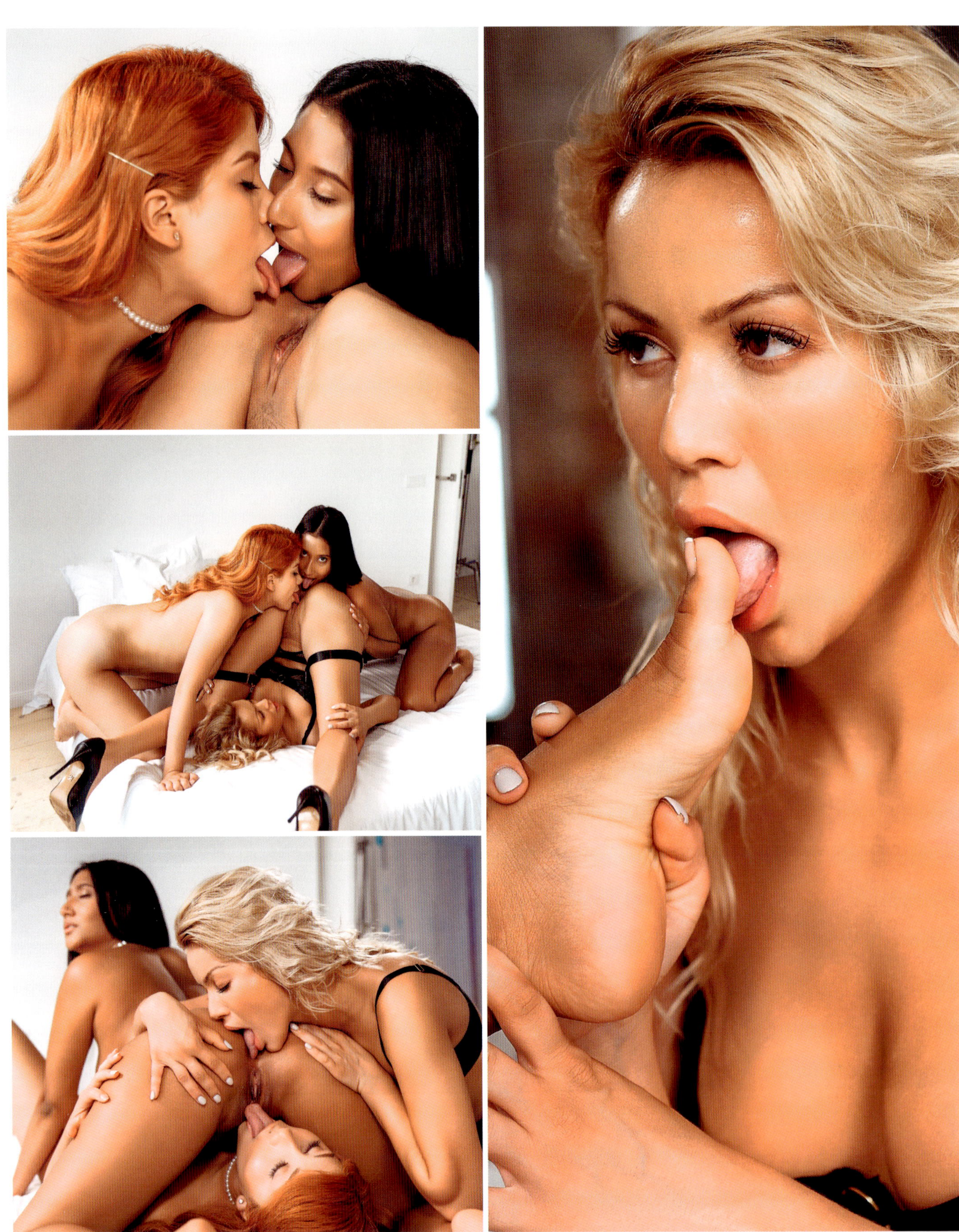

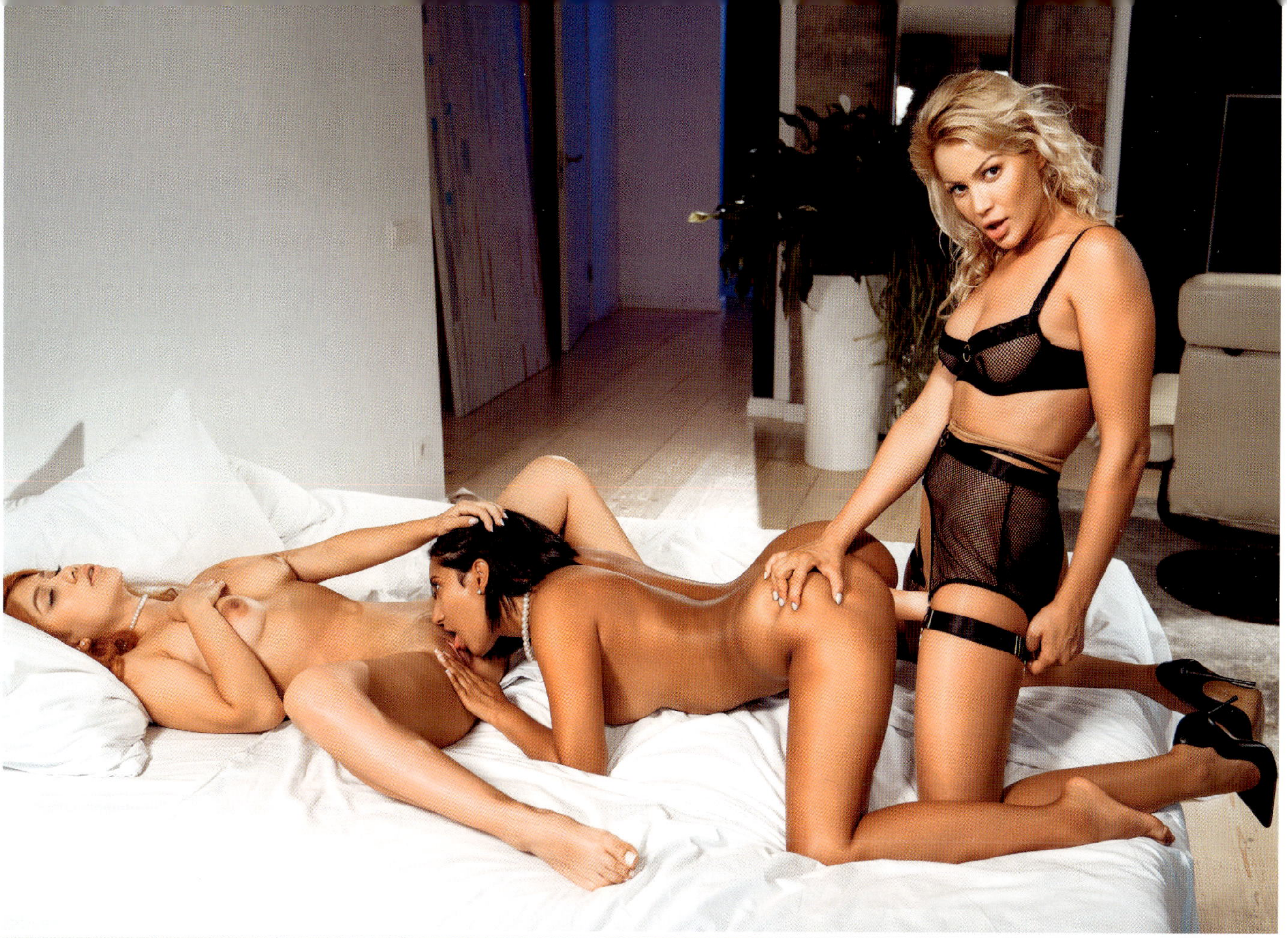

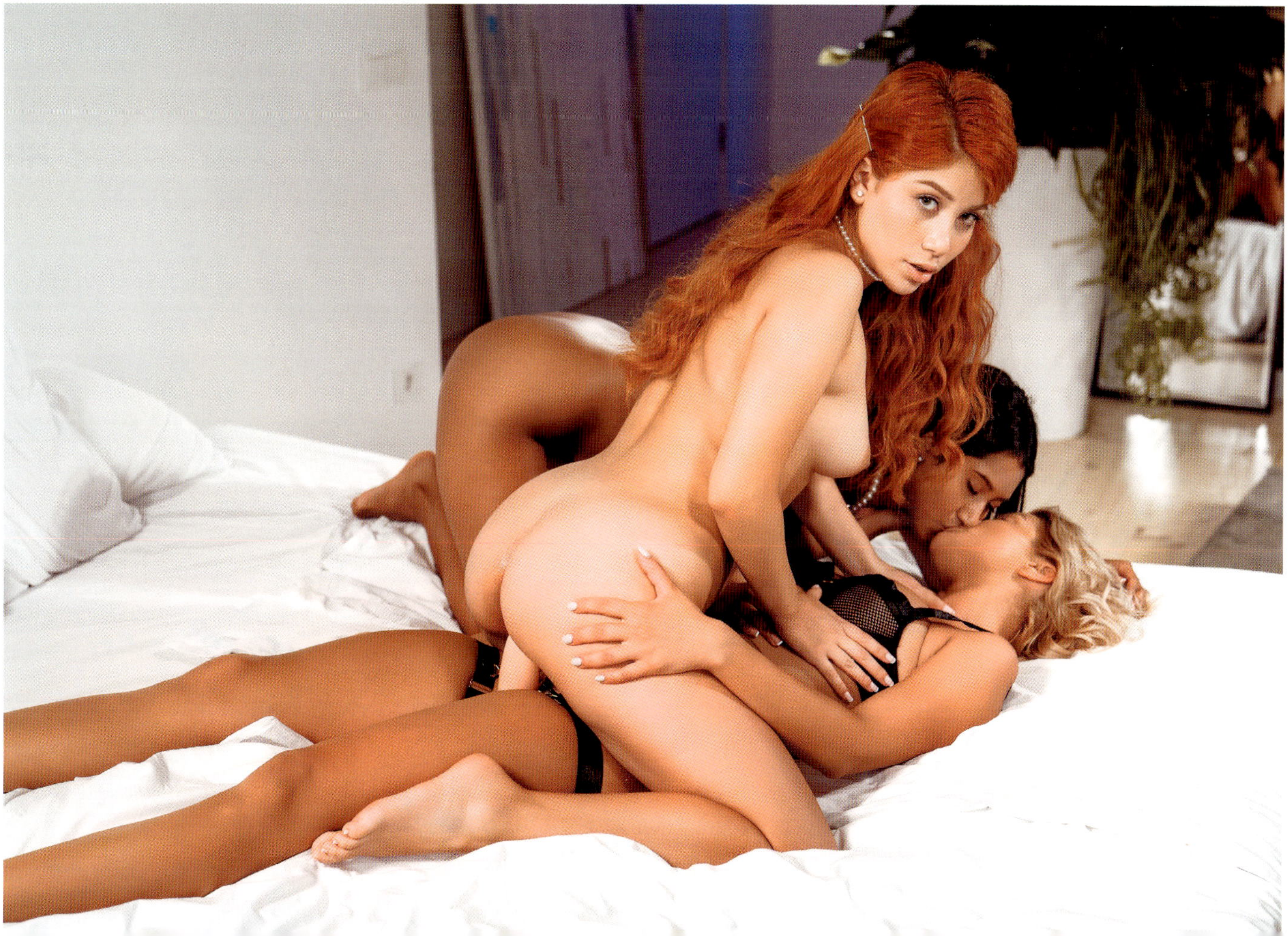

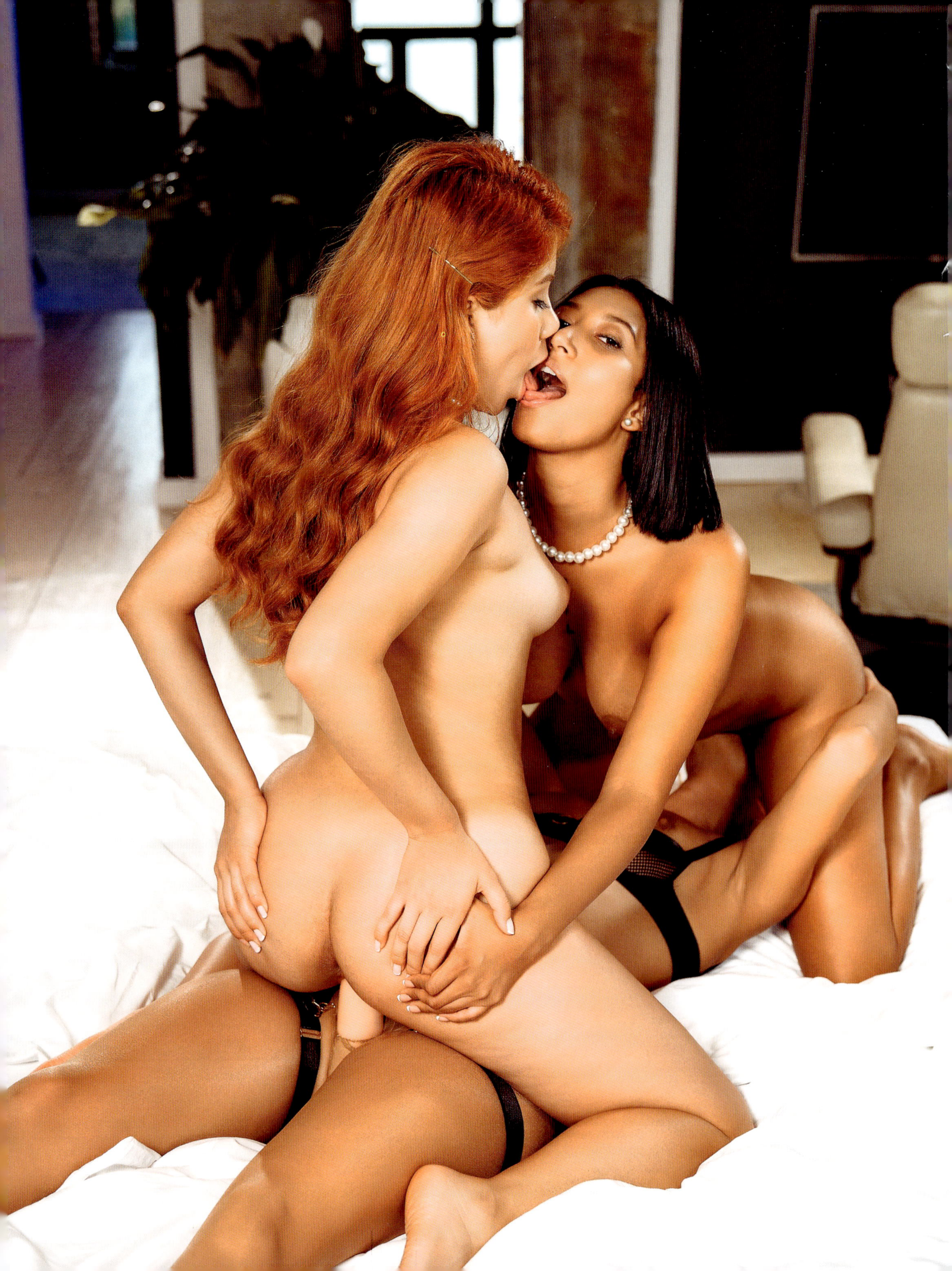

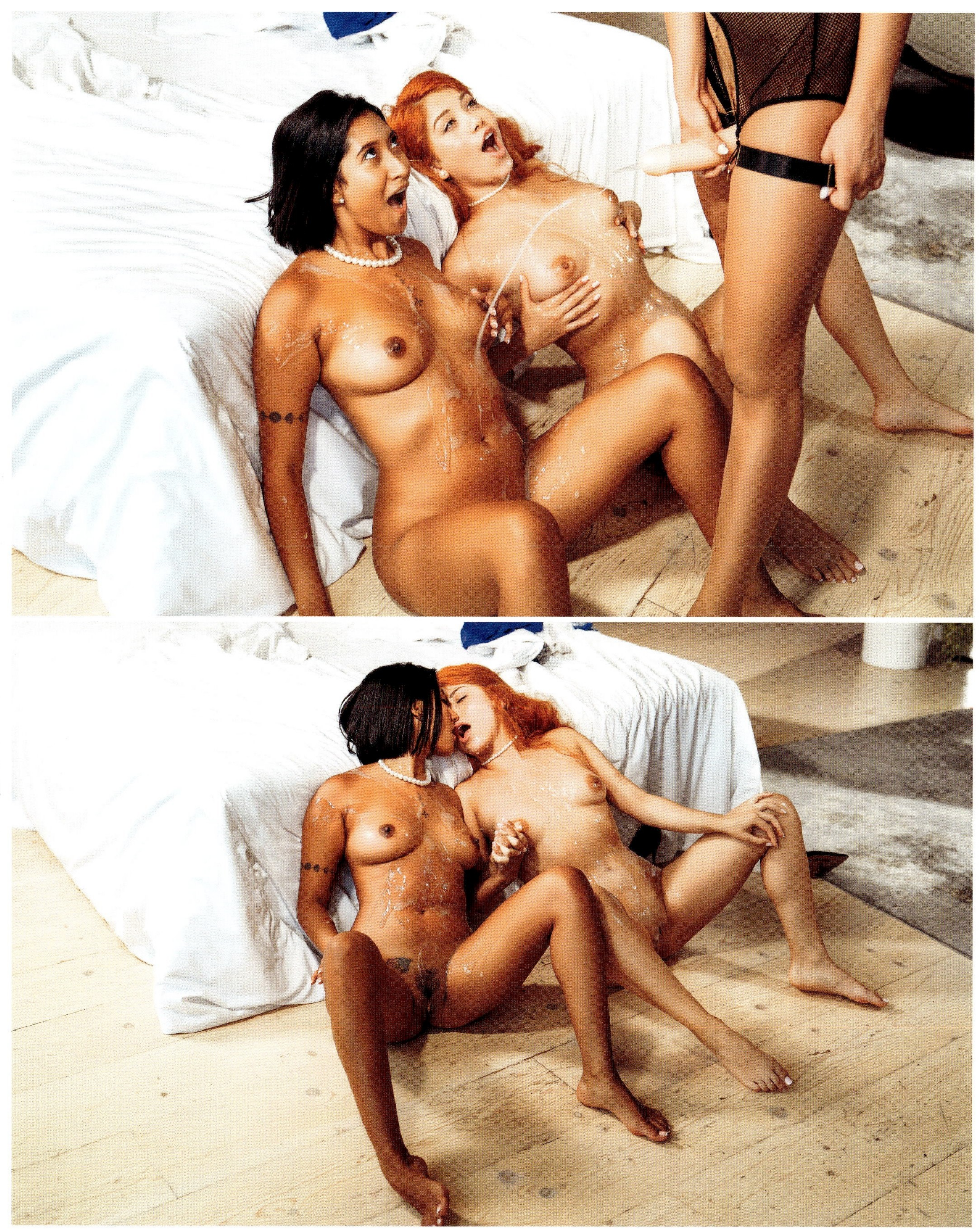

COLLECT THEM ALL: OUR MOST BEAUTIFUL

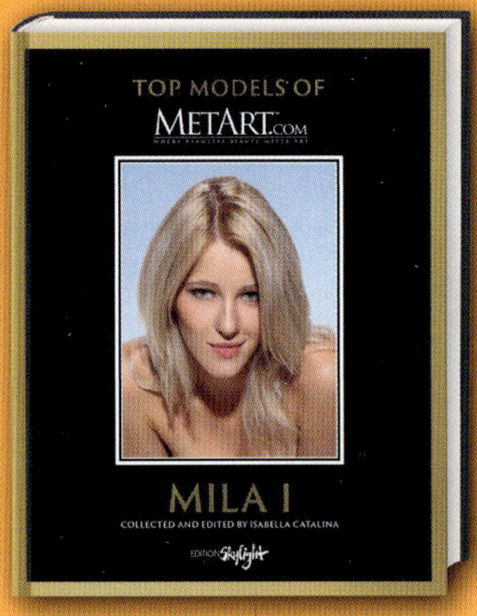

MILA I

ISBN 978-3-03766-703-3

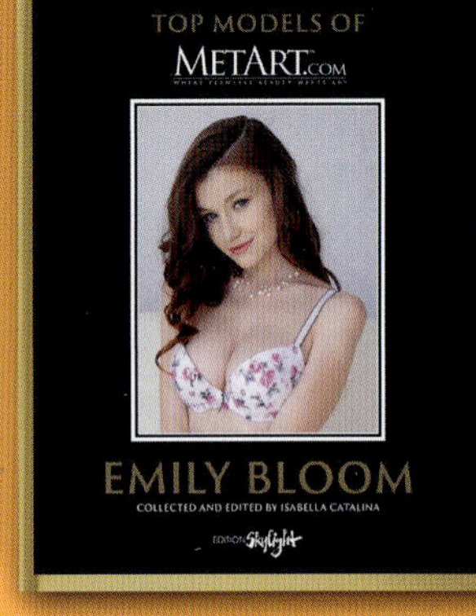

EMILY BLOOM

ISBN 978-3-03766-704-0

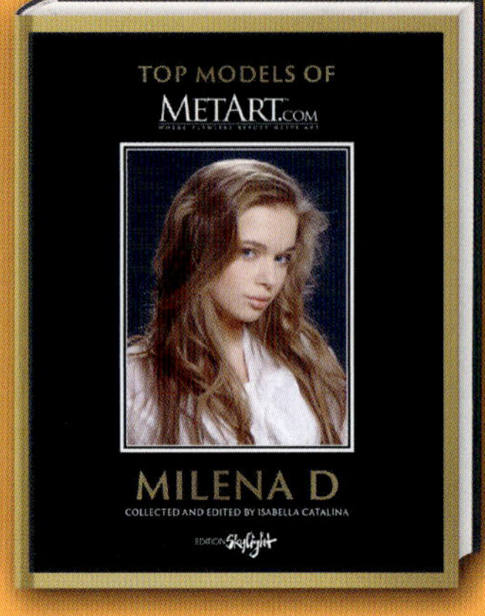

MILENA D

ISBN 978-3-03766-696-8

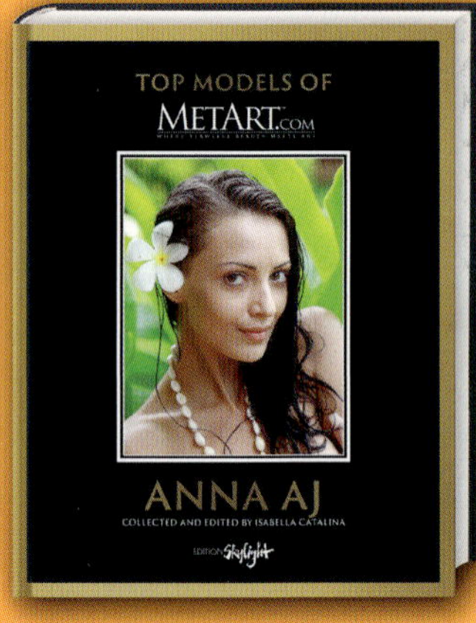

ANNA AJ

ISBN 978-3-03766-695-1

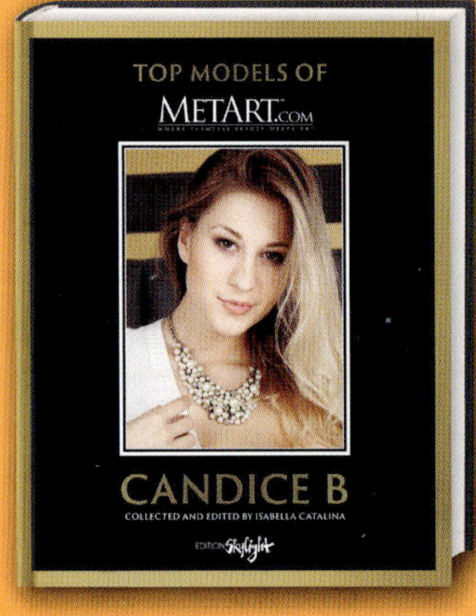

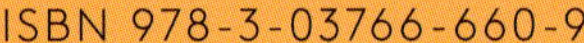

CANDICE B

ISBN 978-3-03766-660-9

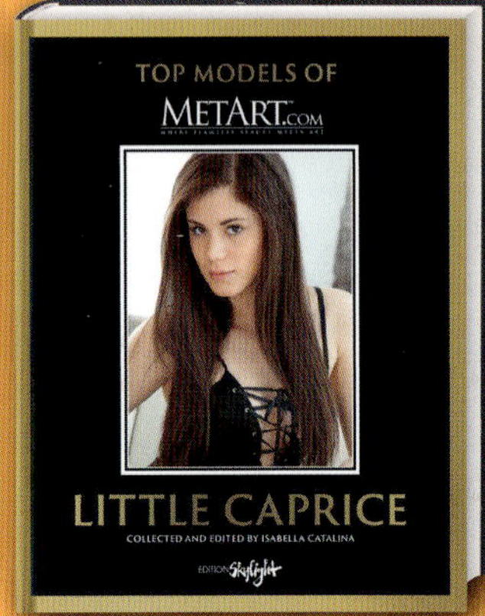

LITTLE CAPRICE

ISBN 978-3-03766-659-3

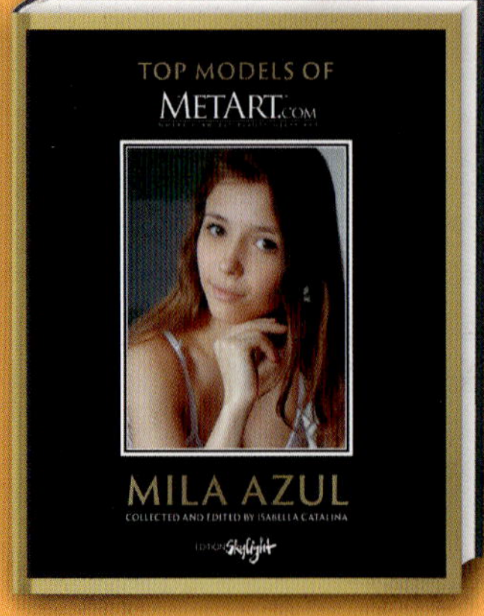

MILA AZUL

ISBN 978-3-03766-680-7

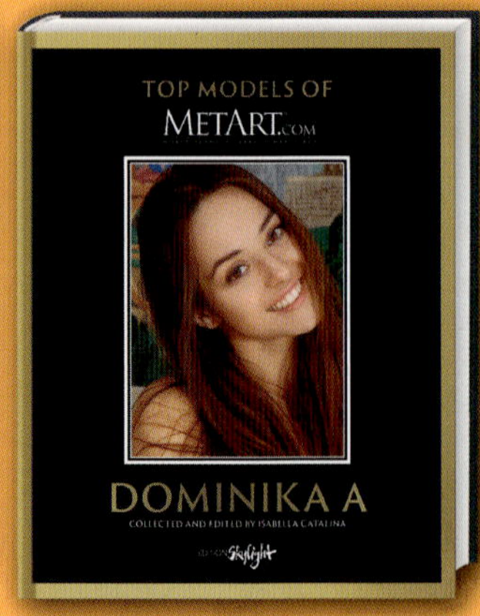

DOMINIKA A

ISBN 978-3-03766-679-1

WWW.EDITION-SKYLIGHT.COM